Economics

Economics

A Core Text
Fourth Edition

JACK NOBBS
Sixth Form Tutor,
Hewett School, Norwich

and

IAN HOPKINS
Head of Economics
Hewett School, Norwich

McGRAW-HILL BOOK COMPANY

London · New York · St Louis · San Francisco · Auckland
Bogotá · Caracas · Lisbon · Madrid · Mexico
Milan · Montreal · New Delhi · Panama · Paris · San Juan
São Paulo · Singapore · Tokyo · Toronto

Published by
McGRAW-HILL Book Company Europe
Shoppenhangers Road, Maidenhead, Berkshire, SL6 2QL, England
Telephone 0628 23432
Fax 0628 770224

British Library Cataloguing in Publication Data
Nobbs, Jack
  Economics: Core Text. – 4 Rev.ed
  I. Title   II. Hopkins, Ian
  330

  ISBN 0-07-707916-7

Library of Congress Cataloging-in-Publication Data
Nobbs, Jack.
  Economics: a core text/Jack Nobbs and Ian Hopkins. – 4th ed.
      p.   cm.
  Includes index.
  ISBN 0-07-707916-7
  1. Economics.   I. Hopkins, I. W. J. (Ian W. J.)   II. Title.
HB171.5.N63   1994   94-34367
330–dc20   CIP

12345 CL 98765

Typeset by TecSet Ltd., Wallington, Surrey
and printed and bound in Great Britain by Clays Ltd, St Ives plc
Printed on permanent paper in compliance with ISO Standard 9706

Contents

Preface to the fourth edition

For many years *Advanced Level Economics* provided an approach to the study of economics at sixth form and college level which gave students an intelligible framework without the intimidating theory that dominates university-level texts. Too many students have been discouraged from continuing studies in the subject as a result of using a textbook which is large and intimidating with complex diagrams and obscure arguments. This book has always aimed to make economics interesting, relevant and understandable.

This edition has been completely rewritten, with a new title and a complete review of the concepts and ideas used. Over the years there have been a number of changes in approach to 'A' level economics and at the time this book is published the whole of 16–19 teaching of the subject is changing. New ways of looking at economic problems are being introduced and those parts of the subject which twenty years ago were considered to be vital are now taught at GCSE level. Ideas and concepts change. We now consider that it is more important whether a market is *contestable* or not rather than whether we can define it as a monopoly, oligopoly or free market. Keynesian answers to economic problems were replaced by monetarism and this in turn is now considered to be inadequate.

Studies of economics in the past have been rooted in the UK and there are few introductory books which give more than a passing reference to any other country. Now the Maastricht Treaty has been signed and 1 January 1994 has seen the birth of the European Union. The economy of the UK is increasingly part of a European and world economy and the authors have tried to introduce the student to this wider economy.

Despite the changes, the objectives of this book remain the same and the new title reflects these. It is intended to introduce economic concepts using language which is comprehensible rather than technical and to deal with the core areas of the subject. A deliberate attempt has been made to see the book as part of the McGraw-Hill 'family' of excellent economics textbooks and the Advanced Study Topics especially are intended to lead students who need to explore an area further to read relevant parts of other major works by the publisher, especially the major general textbook *Economics* by D. Begg, S. Fischer & R. Dornbusch.

It is anticipated that this new edition will be suitable for 'A' level economics students of all abilities, and has also been written with professional courses in mind. Banking, insurance and accounting qualifications usually prescribe some study of economics and the ample treatment of financial markets in this book is intended to make it especially suitable for professional students. Dr Hopkins is a postal tutor for the Chartered Insurance Institute and familiar with the needs of the mature professional student. *Economics: A Core Text* will also provide the economics requirement of Business Studies 'A' level and GNVQ Business modules and should be ideal for AS courses in economics. It will also be useful as an introductory text for university students taking an economics course for the first time.

The third edition of *Advanced Level Economics* approached the general study of the economy (macro-economics) before the study of prices and markets (micro-economics) and there are good arguments in favour in this approach. However, in line with most textbooks, we have reverted to dealing with the micro-economic topics first as this should mean that the order in which we deal with topics is parallel to the syllabus requirements of most examinations. Although theory is tied up with practical application throughout, there are a number of case studies which will give students an opportunity to look at real issues and apply economic concepts and theories to them. Examination questions from 'A' level papers are included and Advanced Study Topics suggest to students where certain themes can be taken further.

For this edition, Jack Nobbs has been joined by Dr Ian Hopkins as co-author. Both authors are on the staff of the largest school-based sixth form in the UK and have wide experience of teaching economics and business studies and to different types of student. We acknowledge help and assistance in reading and commenting on the text from John Eveson of Norwich City College and from two student reviewers, Catherine Akehurst and Karen Hopkins, who ensured that the text was both relevant and understandable. The authors take full responsibility, however, for the text and for any errors or omissions.

We would like to thank the various copyright holders for permission to reproduce material or to use data and acknowledgements are made where such material is used. We would also like to thank examination boards that have given permission to reproduce questions from past papers. Students are recommended to supplement their studies with regular reading of quality newspapers and journals such as *The Economist*, and are recommended to acquire a copy of the Central Statistical Office's brief summary of key figures, *Key Data*, which is published in the autumn each year.

If students of economics at the end of the twentieth century find the subject more understandable and relevant as a result of using our book then we will have achieved our purpose.

Jack Nobbs
Ian Hopkins

In the text, certain abbreviations are made to other textbooks published by McGraw-Hill to which students might wish to refer and full details are given below:

Begg *et al.*:   D. Begg, S. Fischer and R. Dornbusch, *Economics* (4th edn), McGraw-Hill, ISBN 0-07-707831-4

Samuelson and Nordhaus: P. A. Samuelson and W. D. Nordhaus, *Economics* (14th edn), McGraw-Hill, ISBN 0-07-054879-X

Dornbusch and Fischer: R. Dornbusch and S. Fischer, *Macroeconomics* (6th edn), McGraw-Hill, ISBN 0-07-112590-6

Francis: J. C. Francis, *Investments: Analysis and Management* (5th edn), McGraw-Hill, ISBN 0-07-021814-5

Chapter 1

The science of economics

Topic 1.1   What is Economics?

The subject matter of economics is very old and probably dates back to the first cave dwellers haggling over how many flints they wanted in exchange for part of a reindeer carcass. As a science, however, the subject is much younger and regards its founding father as Adam Smith (1723–1790), whose major work *The Wealth of Nations* is seen as the first book on the subject.

Taking the title of Smith's treatise as a cue, some economists have defined the subject as 'The science of wealth'. The nineteenth-century philosopher John Stuart Mill extended the scope of the subject matter when he defined economics as 'the practical science and distribution of wealth'. Today, economics is seen as the study of the allocation of scarce resources among competing ends.

Economics is a very highly regarded subject of study, especially as it deals with some of the most important problems of political life, and on any one day all newspapers will include some economic information or ideas. Indeed, the original name for the subject was 'political economy' and its importance to the nation can be seen by the high profile given to the government's economic advisers.

As we will see later, there are many different views on economic issues, and George Bernard Shaw once cynically remarked that if all economists were laid end to end they would not reach a conclusion! The main schools of thought in economics will be introduced throughout this book as we deal with the issues they seek to solve.

One vital division, though, is into 'classical' economics which evolved during the nineteenth century and early part of the Twentieth century and the Keynesian thinkers who follow the principles of John Maynard Keynes (1883–1946). Keynes has had an enormous influence on post-war governments throughout the world but his ideas are now challenged by the 'neo-classical' economists or Monetarists as they are often known and monetarism has become the dominant economic doctrine for western governments. Then there are those who are attracted to the teachings of Karl Marx although there are fewer of them in the 1990s compared with 30 years ago.

Like most academic disciplines, economics can be divided into smaller areas of study which deal with different questions or use different methods of analysis. There are two major divisions to act as a framework for our studies. One way is to divide economics by topic into:

1. *Micro economics*, which is the study of demand and supply, the prices of goods and of the labour, machinery, etc. which go into producing them. It looks at the decision making of individuals and households as consumers and individual firms as producers and the markets in which the two sets of decisions interact.

2. *Macro-economics*, in contrast, makes a study of the economy as a whole, including national income, investment, inflation, unemployment and the role of governments in the economy. It considers all goods and services together and all individual markets collectively. Macro-economics is the aspect of economics which is most in the news. This can be a problem for the student, who usually starts, as in this book, with the micro-economic issues.

Some areas of the subject do not clearly fall into one category or the other—for example, international economics and development studies. One specific market, that for money and financial services, tends to be investigated as a special case in the macro-economic areas of the subject because of its close relationship with decisions made by governments over the economy as a whole.

The subject can also be divided by approach into *theoretical* and *applied* economics, the first concentrating on developing theories and models of economic behaviour and the latter seeking to study real facts through statistics and observation (Fig. 1.1). Applied economists spend a lot of time testing out the theories and using both official and unofficial statistics as resources for their work.

Then there are special areas of economics which may include some elements of both of the above. For example, there is *development studies*, which looks at economic growth, in particular that of developing countries. *Welfare economics* studies issues of allocating resources using value judgements of what is 'best' and 'fair' as well as purely economic conclusions. *Regional economics* makes a special study of economic regions and location theory, an interest shared with geographers.

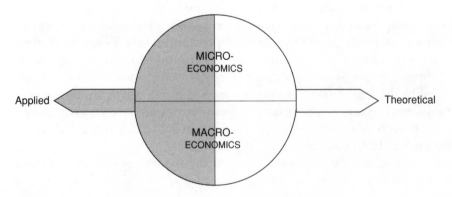

Figure 1.1 Economics divided.

Some aspects of economics consider parts of the subject in more detail such as *fiscal studies*, which takes a special interest in taxation and public spending; *business economics*, which looks in detail at price theory and the theory of the firm usually as part of Business Studies; and *monetary economics* which studies money and the financial institutions. Recently, *environmental economics* has become popular, seeking to examine the economic aspects of environmental pollution and its possible cures.

Finally, there are some specialists who concentrate on a specific approach to the subject rather than on certain areas of study. An example is the mathematical approach which is known as *econometrics* and another is the study of the development of the subject—the *History of Economics*.

Topic 1.2   Positive versus normative economics

In economics we find it is important to distinguish between two types of statement—the *positive* and the *normative*. Economics as an academic subject is concerned with making positive statements but the world at large, including newspapers and the next-door neighbour, will generally make normative comments on economic issues.

Positive statements are those which are objective and free from any pre-set opinions of a political, religious or ethnic nature. They can be verified by reference to facts. Positive economics asks questions which can be answered by objective statements based on facts.

Let's look at an example. We can start by asking 'What is the effect on prices of an increase in VAT?' and perhaps getting the answer 'It will vary but if demand is inelastic prices will rise by the full amount of the tax'. This is an example of positive economics— a question which can be answered by looking at facts and an answer that can be checked against the facts. If you are puzzled, the term 'inelastic' will be explained in Chapter 5 but it is not necessary to look it up now.

In contrast, let us look at another example: 'Is VAT a fair tax?' 'No, because the government should not use this type of tax.' This is a normative conversation. The question poses matters of opinion as no amount of factual evidence can prove or disprove fairness. The answer simply asserts a value judgement. Statements or questions with words like 'should', 'ought', 'fair', or 'wrong' are usually part of normative state-ments ('norm' = moral principle) (see Fig. 1.2).

Economists can sometimes look at whether a course of action is 'right' or 'fair' by prescribed standards but even then they are really using a normative approach. For example, many economists are now saying that it is vital to keep inflation low and any policy act which threatens to increase inflation is judged to be 'wrong'. There may be good arguments in favour of low inflation but economics in itself cannot really decide whether high inflation is right or wrong for a country—economists investigate not the rightness of a policy but the likely effect.

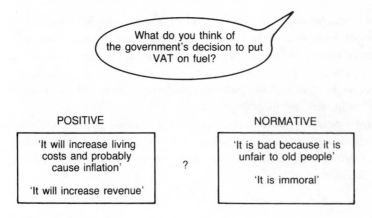

Figure 1.2 Positive and normative economics.

> *Positive economics* is the approach which makes statements that are objective and can only be obtained from unbiased data.

As can be seen from the above discussion, it can actually be very difficult to ensure that we are always positive in our approach to the subject. Many top economists are called on to advise governments or political parties and may well themselves have strong views. There is some move towards making a normative approach more acceptable on the grounds that issues often need moral or political decisions and that economists are as entitled to be involved as anyone else. However, for the sake of taking examinations in the subject or for serious academic study at all levels it is advisable to avoid personal opinions and value judgements.

> *Normative economics* is the approach which makes statements that include value judgements and opinion not necessarily based on objective fact.

Essay questions

1. 'The creation of an internal market in the National Health Service will increase choice, cut waiting times and improve the quality of the service provided' (Rt Hon. Kenneth Clarke MP). Discuss. (*Source*: Oxford and Cambridge Schools Examination Board, June 1991)
2. Should the government subsidize modes of transport that do not damage the environment or tax those that do? (*Source*: Oxford and Cambridge Schools Examination Board, June 1991)

3. Give examples of what is meant by an economic model and explain whether or not it matters if the model is expressed in terms of words, diagrams or equations. Discuss why, if economists can build models of the economy, they can disagree on issues such as the best anti-inflationary policy to be followed by the government. (*Source*: Northern Examinations and Assessment Board, June 1992)

4. In what sense is the pollution of British rivers and beaches an economic problem? Discuss what economic measures might be taken to deal with pollution in general and explain whether or not you regard it as desirable to try to eliminate it. (*Source*: Northern Examinations and Assessment Board, June 1991)

Chapter 2

Basic economic concepts

Introduction—economic terms

As with most scientific disciplines, economics has its technical terms and sometimes it is necessary to use a word in a slightly different way from ordinary speech—otherwise the economist would have to invent new words or adopt rather peculiar terms. A further problem is that writers of economics textbooks have often had different ideas on the meanings of some terms, and definitions have been different in small but sometimes significant ways.

It is the aim of this chapter to clarify some of the basic economic concepts in terms that the majority of economists would accept. At the end of the chapter the reader will be equipped to move into more complex areas of the subject with an understanding of fundamental ideas and tools of analysis.

Topic 2.1   Wealth and income

Earlier we saw that one of the definitions of economics is 'the science of wealth' and so, not surprisingly, wealth is one of the most fundamental concepts we come across. It is very important to distinguish between wealth and income, so the concept of income is also defined and discussed in this section.

What is wealth?

Economics began with a study of wealth by Adam Smith and therefore our first task must be to clarify our ideas about what constitutes economic wealth. In order to be considered as *wealth*, in an economic sense, goods and services must possess three main attributes:

1. They must be desired because of some satisfaction which they offer. A very old programme of a football match may be of no value to most people but it may become valuable if it is desired by a collector.
2. They must be relatively scarce. The stones on the seashore would not normally be regarded as wealth because they are in abundant supply, but certain types of stone would become wealth if they could be utilized as building materials or were sought after as gemstones.

3. They must be capable of being transferred from one person or group of people to another person or group. It is even possible to transfer intangibles such as business goodwill or a milk round, but some things cannot be exchanged. A person's physical or intellectual characteristics may be desirable and scarce and the person may act as a role model to others but the characteristics cannot be transferred to another.

In modern society it would probably be accepted that to be classified as wealth an object needs to have money value. However, this is not an essential feature since in societies where people have exchanged or bartered goods rather than sold them, wealth can still be recognized. In fact many prehistoric burials show evidence of conspicuous wealth in the form of personal trinkets and weapons.

Wealth can take many forms and as economists we are very interested in its distribution within any society. However, the *ownership* of wealth is an important consideration before we look at distribution. There are four broad classes of wealth ownership:

1. *Individual wealth*   In all societies there has been some possession of individual wealth even if it has been restricted. Even in rigid Communist societies some goods like toothbrushes have been individually owned.
2. *Commercial wealth*   Some wealth belongs to business enterprises such as shops, offices or banks. Those businesses which have been established for many years and own freehold city-centre property have considerable 'book' wealth although they may not easily wish to transfer it to a rival.
3. *Industrial wealth*   In an industrial society like the UK, Germany or Japan a lot of wealth is in the form of factories, power stations, railways and other items of infrastructure. Some of this wealth is in the hands of private companies but until the last fifteen years much industrial wealth was in the ownership of the state, i.e. publicly owned.
4. *Social or community wealth*   This is usually owned collectively on the people's behalf by central government or local authorities. Under this heading may be included hospitals, schools, museums, libraries, etc.

The distribution of wealth is an important aspect of economics and is one of the most sensitive in political terms. However, it is very difficult to define wealth in such a way as to make a realistic assessment of total assets of either individuals or corporate bodies. In countries with a wealth tax of some sort there is some mechanism for doing this but it is rarely complete. In the UK it is the existence of inheritance tax and capital gains tax which enables the Inland Revenue to assess wealth, but there are a number of exemptions and loopholes so that even these official figures are unlikely to be complete.

Table 2.1 indicates the type of items that make up personal wealth according to official government figures. We can see that the largest item by far is property, which for the most part consists of household dwellings. Many people forget this when they consider the possibility of inheritance tax since ownership of a house of considerable value may well push a family above the inheritance tax threshold without their being really aware of it.

Table 2.1   Composition of UK wealth (1992)

Assets	% of total
Dwellings (net of mortgage)	33
Other fixed assets	5
Non-marketable tenancy rights	8
Building society shares/deposits	8
National Savings,	
notes and bank deposits	10
Stocks, shares and unit trusts	9
Life assurance and pension funds	31
Other assets net of liabilities	−4

Source: CSO, *Social Trends* (24), HMSO, 1994.

Given the composition of wealth, why is it distributed unequally? Why are some people wealthier than others? To what extent is there inequality? We will attempt to answer these questions briefly in the main part of the text, but for those who wish to pursue the issue further Advanced Study Topic 2.1 will point to some of the tools we can use to analyse inequality of wealth, especially between countries.

Table 2.2 indicates the distribution of wealth in the UK for two years, 1976 and 1990. It can be seen that the wealthiest 1 per cent of the population own a far higher proportion of the nation's wealth (18 per cent in 1990) than we would expect, and if we extend the figures to the wealthiest half of the population we see them owning over 90 per cent of the wealth. We also see a decline in the inequality between 1976 and 1990 but it is small.

Table 2.2   Distribution of wealth: UK

Ownership of wealth Wealthiest proportion of population (%)	Marketable wealth (£ billion)	
	1976	1990
Wealthiest 1	21	18
Wealthiest 5	38	37
Wealthiest 10	50	51
Wealthiest 25	71	72
Wealthiest 50	92	93

Source: *Social Trends* (23), HMSO, 1993.

The causes of the inequality are many and varied. To some extent they are related to inequalities in income (see below) in that the households with the highest incomes can accumulate the largest wealth. There is also, however, in most European societies an important element of inheritance in wealth distribution, especially among those with the largest assets. Wisdom, or lack of it, in choosing investments and luck in one's forebears is important and so are differences in willingness to save.

Income is something we are familiar with as the name for the regular payments also called wages, salaries, rent, interest, etc. To economists 'income' is a term used to describe the *flow* of earnings to people for their work (e.g. wages) or the land (rent) they own or the money they have lent (interest). The term 'flow' is very important because the difference between wealth and income lies largely in the fact that wealth is seen as a *stock* of goods and resources whereas income is seen as a *flow* of value, arising from the stock of wealth. This can be seen in Fig. 2.1.

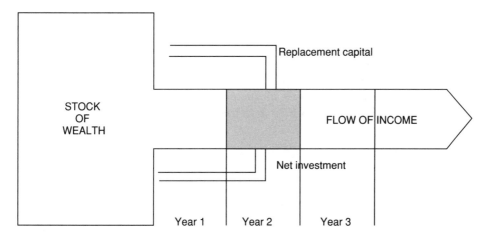

Figure 2.1 Wealth and income. Income is shown as a flow coming out from a stock of capital over three years. Year 2 acts as an example of how income feeds back into stock through the replacement of capital which has gone out of use; the use of some income as fresh capital input; and the rest is used for consumption.

> *Wealth* refers to the stock of assets—goods and resources owned by a nation or household. *Income* refers to the flow of earnings from use of these resources, i.e. to the providers of them (the factors of production).

We can examine wealth and income at a number of levels. In economics the smallest unit we often deal with is not so much the individual, although we can all observe how we act in spending, earning and saving, but the *household*. Most key decisions in the economy are taken at the household level. We also consider decisions at the level of the firm, the industry and by governments at national level.

The terms 'stock' and 'flow' perhaps need a little more explanation here. Stock is seen as an asset assessed or valued at a particular point in time. A house is a stock and so is money in a bank account or 100 television sets in a shop, waiting to be sold. A flow, in contrast, is defined as a stream of value in time—such as income (an inward flow to households) or consumption spending (an outward flow). A flow can be used to increase stocks so in Fig. 2.1 we have the stock of wealth being replenished from income as worn-out machinery and crumbling factories are replaced by new ones.

Later in Chapter 9 we will discuss how the nation's income can be divided into that used for consumption and that used for savings. Savings is a stock of money set aside from income and while to the household it represents a sensible decision to spend in the future rather than today, economists see it as the funds required to obtain additional stocks such as equipment for industry, housing, raw materials, etc.

Just as for wealth, income shows a considerable inequality in distribution as shown in Case Study 2.1. To a large extent this is the result of differences in earnings levels and the reasons for these will be discussed further in Chapters 4 and 8. There are also such considerations as earnings from investments and those who also have the greater share of the nation's wealth will inevitably have the largest share of investment income. Further, for those in retirement, earnings from pensions vary considerably. There are those on a basic state pension which is at a level just adequate to get by and also those with generous executive pensions or who retired with 'golden handshakes'.

Case Study 2.1—Distribution of incomes

Composition of groups of household income by quintile groups (percentages)

Economic status of head of household	Quintile groups of households ranked by equivalized disposable income					
	Bottom Qle	Next Qle	Middle Qle	Next Qle	Top Qle	All households
Employed	9	30	59	74	74	49
Self-employed/employer	5	7	11	10	16	10
Unemployed seeking work	14	5	3	2	1	5
Unemployed sick and injured*	1	1	–	–	–	1
Unemployed sick and injured[†]	6	6	2	1	1	3
Retired	43	41	21	11	7	24
Other economically inactive	23	11	4	2	1	8
Total	100	100	100	100	100	100

Notes: *Unemployed through sickness or injury but seeking work
[†]Unemployed through sickness or injury but not seeking work
Source: CSO, *Key Data 1992/3*, HMSO, p. 41.

The above table is a useful case study for a number of reasons. It is the first such study in this book which looks at actual official statistics 'in the raw'. As such, it is a useful exercise in handling data. Second, it is a useful example of applied economics—in other words, we can take the theory of income distribution and see what is actually happening in reality.

The table divides the income distribution of the UK into five parts, i.e. *quintiles.* For each of the five quintiles the households are further divided into seven categories so that we can compare the distribution of income by category of household, judged by the economic function of the head of the household. As a result, we can see, for example, that a high proportion of the low income receivers are retired. Almost a quarter of the poorest quintile are economically inactive other than retired whereas for the top quintile the figure is much more modest and for the second highest fifth is very small. So much for the idea that a lot of the rich are also 'idle'!! Statistics can demonstrate a few errors in popular thinking.

It would be worth thinking through a few questions:

1.   Why are there a respectable proportion of self-employed in the middle quintile group?
2.   What is the significance of the 9 per cent of lowest quintile who are actually employed?
3.   The figures show *disposable* income, i.e. spending money available after tax, National Insurance, etc. have been deducted. Can you think of ways in which the government could change the distribution of disposable income?

Topic 2.2   What is utility?

In economics *utility* means the satisfaction that a person gains from a good, service or activity. It is not necessary that the good, service or activity be useful, moral or socially acceptable, so it is better to think of utility as describing satisfaction rather than benefit. Drugs such as heroin have utility to the user but we might doubt whether they actually give real benefit.

Utilities cannot be measured but only compared. If a group of people was asked to choose between an orange, an apple and a banana, and only one person selected an apple, the choice would suggest that the person thought that more satisfaction would be gained from the apple on that occasion than from the other fruit. It does not imply that the other fruit gave no satisfaction at all or that on another day the orange or banana might not have been chosen.

In other words, the utility experienced is not uniform to any one product but a matter of comparison and it is very subjective. The choices we are continuously making involve comparing the satisfaction from one course of action with that gained from others.

Although utility cannot really be measured, for the sake of theoretical analysis, economists tend to use the term 'util' when explaining utility. So we might measure an increase in the utility of newspapers to an individual using this theoretical unit, and showing the results in a graph as shown in Fig. 2.2.

In this example you would get a lot of satisfaction or utility from buying one newspaper and a second would give you another point of view and stories not in the first.

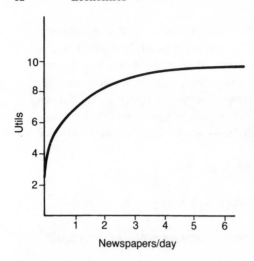

Figure 2.2   Total utility of newspapers.

However, if you continued to buy newspapers the newsagent would be very happy but you would find that increasingly there would be less and less in each additional paper which would be new. So the total amount of satisfaction in 'utils' would increase but at a gradually decreasing rate.

We will explore the way utility changes further by looking at another term, the margin, in the next section. It is, however, useful, first of all to consider the importance of preferences when we are looking at utility.

Each of us has our own scale of preferences and the arrangement of needs which we wish to satisfy will be very flexible and dependent upon changes in income plus the satisfaction obtained from past expenditure. If our income increases, we may decide to buy a car and might then have less to spend on drinks. If the football team which we usually support is losing most of its matches, we may cease to spend money on admission charges and opt for a more satisfying way of spending a Saturday afternoon.

There are two useful concepts of a scale of preferences:

1. The utilities (satisfactions) are arranged so that the most pressing or urgent require-ments are near the top of the scale and those which are just worth satisfying are placed near the bottom.
2. It is also reasonable to compile a scale of preferences so that every £1 spent attracts the same amount of utility. If this were not the case then we would be left with constant feelings of dissatisfaction with our purchases since we would be buying less of some goods than we really want and a surplus of others.

The idea of a scale in order of importance is explored a little further in the next section and both the above ideas are taken up in Chapter 5.

Topic 2.3   What is 'the margin'?

One term that the reader will come across frequently in the study of economics is the word *margin*. It appears in many areas of economic study and is crucial to many basic theories. It is vital that the reader becomes familiar with the meaning and use of the term.

To explore the idea of a margin we can look again at utility. In the previous section we considered whether the reader should go on a newspaper-buying binge, with total utility increasing but at a decreasing rate. As each new paper is bought our total satisfaction or utility is increased but each new paper gives increasingly less satisfaction. The utility from the last newspaper bought is called the *marginal utility*. Take Fig. 2.3 as an illustration. It again measures utility but this time not the total utility but the utility from each newspaper bought. A bar chart is used as it may be easier to understand the concept that way.

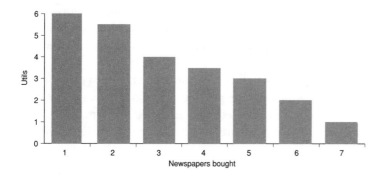

Figure 2.3   Marginal utility.

Marginal utility refers to the satisfaction or utility gained from the last unit consumed.

The first newspaper gives us a lot of satisfaction—which we decide is 6 utils. We are absorbed in the news, sport and cartoons. Government defeat in the House of Commons, German interest rates are down, Real Madrid have beaten Munich in the European Cup . . . The second newspaper gives us $5\frac{1}{2}$ utils of satisfaction—a new version of the government's troubles, details of Arsenal's new signing, a feature on a new species of panda found in China, and a better horoscope than the first paper. The third gives only 4 utils—good cartoons, but little else is new. Gradually as more newspapers are bought the utility of each falls—we have found a 'law' of economics which will be explored in more detail in Chapter 5, the law of *diminishing marginal utility*. As we consume more of a product the utility of each successive unit will fall even though the total utility may rise.

In fact the above illustration is slightly unusual in that there are some perceivable differences between the newspapers. The law of diminishing marginal utility should apply if the units of consumption are absolutely identical—like a succession of vanilla ice creams or chocolate bars.

The marginal unit is the last unit to be added or the first to be taken away and can thus be a positive or a negative concept. As mentioned earlier, the idea is crucial in understanding economics and therefore it would be useful to consider, from the outset, some of the ways in which the term is used:

1. *The marginal unit or product*   This is the last unit produced or not worth producing, depending on the circumstances. It is the last unit bought or sold, or not bought or sold as the case may be. It is important to realize that the marginal unit is not necessarily different in quality from any other unit.
2. *Marginal land*   This lies on the border of change so far as land use is concerned. Often marginal land is thought of as land which it is only just worth cultivating, perhaps only in wartime, but this land might be of considerable use for building purposes. Land can be seen as 'marginal' to any one use, but the margin for one use may not be so for another.
3. *The marginal producer*   This term refers to the trader or firm which just considers it worthwhile to produce a certain commodity or provide a certain service. It does not imply that the producer is inefficient. Indeed, the marginal firm may be very adaptable and quick to change to some more profitable line of business if the opportunity arises.
4. *Marginal revenue*   This is the revenue gained by a producer from the last unit produced. Total revenue would be reduced if sales were curtailed by a single unit. Sometimes it is difficult to find units small enough to use realistically. A producer of ballpoint pens, for example, would probably find it impossible to measure the revenue from one extra pen but would find it easier to measure that from 1000 pens.
5. *Marginal cost*   This is the cost to the producer of an extra unit or the saving in cost of reducing production by one unit. We will see later in Chapters 5 and 6 that the concepts of marginal cost and marginal revenue are crucial in understanding how firms reach an equilibrium level of output.

Other uses of the concept of the margin such as the idea of a *marginal want* and the *marginal rate of substitution* will be found from time to time in our studies of economics.

Topic 2.4   Utility, value and price

Having considered the concept of utility we can use it to good purpose as we look at the use of the word *value* in economics. The term *value* is often used as if it were synonymous with the word *price* but they are by no means identical. If you were to consider that you have gained a bargain it means that either the future exchange value of the article will increase or the use-value to you is worth more than its exchange value. A Wembley ticket tout may have bought a number of tickets a few weeks previously thinking that on the day of the match potential spectators would be willing to pay £100 for a ticket. If each ticket is sold at a profit of £10 then our tout has gained a bargain. The price paid by the tout and the value have not been identical.

However, while value and price are different they can be related. The more value a person attaches to a good or service, the more they are normally willing to pay for it. This is where we bring in utility again, especially the tool of analysis we acquired earlier, marginal utility. Price is determined not by the total value or utility of a product but by the utility at the margin.

Economists have usually used this idea to explain the *paradox of value* which looks at the question of why goods that have a high importance and total utility can be priced much lower than goods with much less real usefulness. The usual example is that of water and diamonds. Water is essential to life and as such has a very high utility and value. Diamonds, on the other hand, while they have an industrial use and a decorative appeal, are quite clearly of lower utility than water. The problem is that in saying this we are considering *total* utilities. We value water a lot lower not because its total utility is low but because of its low *marginal* utility.

If you were travelling across the Australian desert and had no liquid refreshment you might come across the original 'pub with no beer'. Yet you are hot and thirsty and as the bartender offers you a glass of water you are prepared to pay good money for it. You are desperate for a drink and you never knew water could taste so good! Yet back home you regard water as so plentiful that you could easily use not just a glass but a whole 2 gallons on your rose bed. The marginal utility of water is very low with the last glassful practically worthless. Diamonds, on the other hand, may be less vital to life but because they are scarce the marginal utility of the last diamond bought is very high.

The relationship between marginal utility and price will be further explored in Chapter 5.

Topic 2.5   Inputs, outputs and cycles

Much of economics is concerned with using resources to provide for needs and wants (see Chapter 3) and this usually involves some form of production. We often see the process of production as consisting of two stages, *inputs* and then *outputs* (Fig. 2.4).

Consider the manufacture of steel. This takes place in steel mills using plant known as converters. This equipment uses pig iron and often alloy metals to produce steel. We can view this process in terms of inputs and outputs (Fig. 2.5).

The *inputs* into production are usually known as the *factors of production*. These will be looked at in more detail in Chapter 8 when we deal with the 'rewards' which they gain from their productive role. Some older textbooks spent a lot of time in detailed descriptions of these factors.

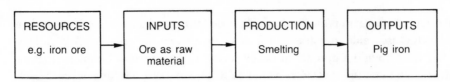

Figure 2.4 Inputs and outputs in production.

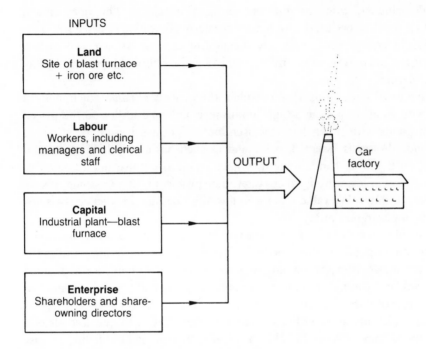

Figure 2.5 Factor inputs and outputs: steel works.

The factors providing the inputs are normally regarded as:

1. *Land*   The land which is used for production, including not just the space occupied by a factory or office but also the resources within the land such as ores and minerals.
2. *Labour*   The men and women making up the workforce which occupies the land. In many respects this is the most important factor since nothing can be produced without some input of human muscle or brain, even if robots or other machines are used to help.
3. *Capital*   This is one of those terms that is used by economists in a slightly different way from that of the average person. It is not primarily money, although in certain contexts it can mean this, but the equipment which is used in production—such as the steel converters mentioned above, tractors, industrial 'plant', etc.
4. *Enterprise* or 'the entrepreneur' as it is sometimes called. This refers to the initiative element in production and is personified by the owner of a business. (See Fig. 2.6.)

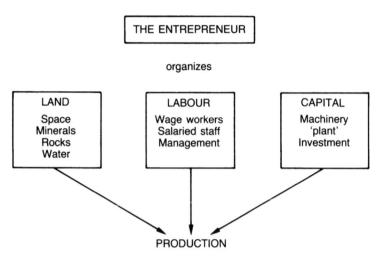

Figure 2.6   Factors of production as inputs.

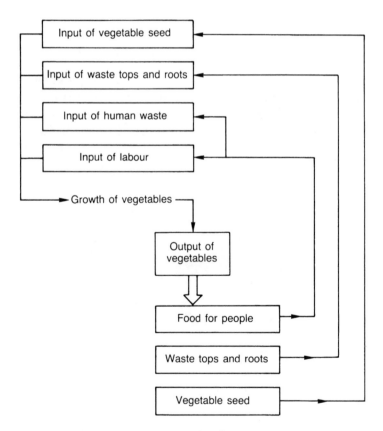

Figure 2.7   An environmentally closed cycle.

If we look at production in relation to resources we can see that it can be studied as part of a cycle of events. Economists sometimes distinguish between *environmentally closed* and *open cycles*. The difference between the two is that in a closed cycle the output of the productive process returns to the environment as a resource again.

Consider Fig. 2.7. We assume a small island which is involved in producing vegetables as food. It does not import anything and what the inhabitants eat they grow themselves. They produce vegetables and these vegetables provide food to sustain them and also renewed nutrients for the soil from the green tops or unused roots or stems. Some vegetables are put aside as a source of seed for the next year. Even human waste can be returned to the soil as nutrient. We could also introduce livestock, consuming the vegetable waste and in turn producing manure as nutrient.

Most economies are in fact environmentally open cycles with some of the output being lost. For example, the burning of stubble which, until recently made illegal, has been characteristic of the arable farms in eastern England, destroys vegetable matter which literally 'goes up in smoke' and is lost. The internal combustion engine burns fossil fuel which is mainly consumed as energy and only a small amount is returned to the environment and that is as destructive waste gases.

Advanced Study Topic 2.1   Wealth and income inequality

Discussion of inequality can be clouded by very subjective and normative language and it is important to be in a position to describe accurately at least the factual situation. To help us do this there are two techniques of measurement called the *Lorenz curve* and the *Gini coefficient*. Figure AST 2.1 shows a typical Lorenz curve based on the figures in Table 2.2.

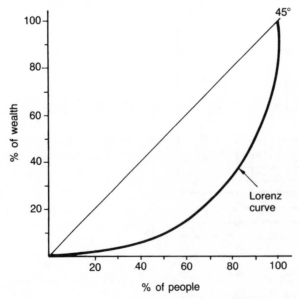

Figure AST 2.1 Lorenz curve for the UK (1990).

Absolute equality would produce a straight line but all countries have a downward-sloping curve. The area between this curve and the 45° line measures the inequality. The ratio between this area and the whole area below the 45° line is the *Gini coefficient*. For further detail see Samuelson and Nordhaus, p. 357.

Essay questions

1. With the aid of both micro-economic and macro-economic examples, explain why the concept of the margin is important in economic theory. (*Source:* The Associated Examining Board, June 1990)
2. (a) Explain why there are inequalities in the present distribution of income *and* wealth in the UK.
   (b) Assess whether the government should introduce policies designed to make the distribution of income more equal. (*Source:* The Associated Examining Board, June 1993)
3. Explain the meaning of 'opportunity cost' and outline its relationship to the market price of a good or service. Discuss how the introduction of commercial criteria into the running of hospitals and schools could affect the supply of and demand for the services they provide. (*Source:* Northern Examinations and Assessment Board, June 1992)
4. Distinguish between consumers' surplus, producers' surplus and economic rent. Discuss the effect on each of these if the government introduces a guaranteed minimum price for wheat above the free market equilibrium price. (*Source:* University of Oxford, June 1990)
5. For each of the following, explain how the economic concept in the first column may help in a discussion of the topic in the second column.
   (a) Production possibilities   Disarmament
   (b) The market mechanism   Rationing
   (c) Opportunity costs   International trade
   (d) Merit goods   Preventative medicine.
   (*Source:* University of Oxford, June 1991)
6. Why do economists classify products? Illustrate your explanation by showing how the following products can be classified: foreign holidays, police services, rented accommodation, jars of jam, TV sets, dwellings, machine tools and NHS hospitals. Explain how, if at all, a change in the rate of interest might affect the market for jars of jam, machine tools and NHS hospitals. (*Source:* Northern Examinations and Assessment Board, June 1993)
7. Define consumer sovereignty and discuss whether or not competition among producers guarantees sovereignty and a wide range of choice of products for consumers. Are recent measures to reduce the BBC monopoly likely to result in greater consumer sovereignty? (*Source:* Northern Examinations and Assessment Board, June 1993)

Chapter 3

Resources and the economic problem

Having defined certain key terms in economics we now come to look at some basic ideas and concepts which repeat themselves throughout the various major branches of the subject. This chapter is basic to further studies of the subject, especially Chapters 5–8.

Topic 3.1 Wants, needs and scarce resources

Fundamental to an understanding of economics are the three ideas of wants, needs and resources. In brief, we can say that people all have wants and needs and economists study the ways in which these are met using the resources available, nearly all of which are to some extent 'scarce'.

First, we need to distinguish between *wants* and *needs*. We all have both of these although some of us are more concerned with the former than with the latter. Wants may be needs also as is the case with much basic food and clothing, but while we may need to be clothed properly we may want a leather jacket or an expensive suit. In fact something a lot cheaper will probably do to supply our need but there may well be social factors which suggest to us that the more expensive clothes will be better for our status, 'street cred', or whatever we call it.

One important difference between needs and wants is in the potential size of the two. Our needs are limited because they are basically concerned with maintaining ourselves as healthy human beings and carrying on our normal occupations. Wants, on the other hand, can be seen as infinite because few people outside religious ascetics can get to the point of being totally satisfied. However, most of us have some wants which we tend to think of as needs and what is considered to be basic and essential can differ between cultures and classes.

Wants and needs are met by use of *resources*. A few resources are in such plentiful supply that we call them *free goods* and they do not normally cause us any expense. Air, the enjoyment of open countryside, and basic water are free. Water is in fact an interesting example because that which is in my water butt is free and if I walk in the high mountains of Europe and drink from a spring it is free. For very good practical and health reasons, however, these free supplies are no longer regarded as adequate and most of us receive our water in a purified state through pipes and taps. It is this processing and supply of water which we pay for as it is not available free and abundantly. (See Fig. 3.1.)

One key characteristic of all resources, except for those which are free, is that they are scarce. This term is used in economics to imply a limitation on supply and does not necessarily mean that they are scarce in the normal use of the term. Thus while both the economist and the non-economist would recognize diamonds as a scarce resource, only the economist would probably consider tap water or grazing land as in this category. Nevertheless, both of these are only free in a basic 'take it as you find it' sense and human energy and skill have to be harnessed to change the free product into the more acceptable version—which, as a result, acquires a relative scarcity.

Most commodities are resources with a relative scarcity including minerals, fuels, food and materials such as wood and metals. We can also regard human labour as a scarce resource, possibly the most important resource, since without it nothing at all will be produced. Even the gathering of berries or digging out building stone from a quarry require human labour.

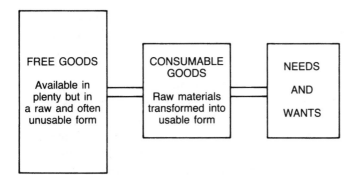

Figure 3.1   Meeting needs and wants.

Topic 3.2   Making choices

As we have our wants and needs and only limited or scarce resources with which to meet them, we have to make a series of *choices* simply because the resources are scarce. We cannot use everything we would ideally wish to. There may be no end to our wants and we may have a long list of needs but the resources to meet them are limited. If we earn only £50 a week and £20 of this goes on rent, then we cannot spend £25 on food and £30 on a new radio. Our financial 'resources', which give us access to real resources, are limited.

In both national and world terms we are often faced in the newspapers with issues concerning resources. Choices have to be made on *what* is produced, *how* it is produced and *for whom* it is produced. The question ultimately is *who* makes these decisions? Usually these questions have a political answer and political and economic systems have evolved to deal with the distribution of resources in accordance with whatever principles seem best to different societies, or at least to their rulers. Some of the systems will be explored in Chapter 4.

Case Study 3.1 is a brief newspaper extract that indicates one issue which at heart is concerned with this problem. It concerns not just a decision on use of a particular building (i.e. answering the question 'from whom?') but also deals with the question 'who should make that decision?' It illustrates further the political implications of economic issues. Here we see a government which is extolling the virtues of the market economy (see Chapter 4) and is giving universities more autonomy and accountability, yet makes a decision which denies the market the chance to operate.

Case Study 3.1—What to do with County Hall?

On 25 September 1992 an announcement was made by the Environment Minister that there would be a lifting of the restrictions on the sale of the old London County Hall. A decision had been made on the use of a very valuable few acres of central London which indicated very clearly that the British economy was firmly a free market one. A choice had been made by the ultimate authority—the Government—that the site was to be open to the highest bidder. An economic choice had been made.

The site had been the administrative centre of the old Greater London Council (GLC) until that authority was abolished, and a quango known as the London Residuary Body was given the task of disposing of it along with the rest of the old GLC property. The prominent bidder to buy the site was a Japanese company, the Shirayama Group, which intended to convert the building into a hotel. However, other parties were interested in the possibilities offered by the building, and many people thought that as it was public property it should remain in public use.

The foremost alternative bidder was the London School of Economics (LSE), a college of the University of London, and perhaps the best-known centre in the world for the study of the social sciences. The LSE was not expecting to get the building free, but was offering £100 million which one might have thought was adequate. It had strong support from many people, including academics, politicians, the press and many educational leaders. The LSE has an extremely cramped site in central London, which is conveniently situated for the law courts, Fleet Street and Whitehall but allows little room for further expansion. However, the Government decided that the County Hall site would effectively be better used as a hotel than as a place of higher learning.

It may be difficult to see all the reasons for this decision. It may not necessarily have been a purely economic one, but it is an example of the sort of economic choice which is constantly being made. A piece of land and a disused building, if not unique at least not the sort of property which frequently comes on the market, was available. The Government, since it was a publicly owned site, could have decided its use by executive decision. It decided to have it sold on the open market and while pressure of public opinion obliged it to commission a report on LSE's proposals, in the end its preference was to see the site as a foreign-owned hotel. Whether this is a correct decision or not, it is representative of decisions made when, on the one hand, market forces are involved, yet on the other there are those who consider that the public good requires some other sort of use.

1.   Could the use of County Hall by the LSE be justified on economic grounds, even if they did not pay the market price for the property?
2.   The Government prevented the LSE bidding against the Japanese company on the grounds that this would involve 'an unacceptable call on public funds'. To what extent might the choice of an option in the use of resources justifiably involve public funds?

One important concept here recognizes that we cannot choose one resource without at the same time doing without another. In everyday language we cannot 'have our cake and eat it'. The prehistoric hunter could spend an extra hour catching another rabbit or sharpening a flint, but not both. We call this the problem of *opportunity cost.*

Consider a series of choices to be made in a decision to satisfy the want of studying for advanced examinations. Note that we have called it a 'want'—whatever politicians, teachers and parents may think, education and training is still really a want and not a need in the strict sense.

The readers of this book will probably have made a decision to follow a course of study. They are certainly unlikely to be casually reading the book on a train because they picked it up on the station bookstall. Figure 3.2 follows the choices you may have had to make to get to this point.

Whether you were aware of it or not, you have probably made a series of decisions which have had consequences in terms of inability to do or obtain other things. In studying economics you may have to turn your back on a full-time job. The loss we sustain as a result of making a decision is known as the *opportunity cost* of that decision. Daily shopping sees us constantly making decisions which involve an opportunity cost. That extra pint of lager means that we have to walk home—either because we have no money for the bus or we are not sober enough to drive! On a different scale, in Case Study 3.1 we see the decision to allow use of former local authority property for commercial purposes rather than for educational purposes.

> The *opportunity cost* of an economic decision is the next-best option which we could have obtained: e.g. if we choose good A instead of good B, then B is the opportunity cost of A.

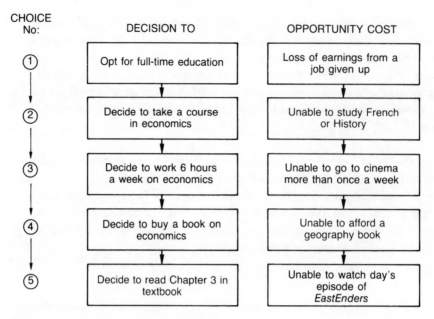

Figure 3.2 Choosing to study economics.

Opportunity cost is a constantly recurring theme in economics as it is crucial to decision making. It is an inevitable consequence of the scarcity of resources. We cannot have all the resources we want and therefore have to choose, and the result of that choice, if we have chosen correctly, is that we receive our best option in terms of the utility we discussed in the previous chapter. The opportunity cost is, in that case, the next-best option. Opportunity cost does not always have a monetary value although it can be given one in most cases.

Choice faces both producers of goods and services, on the one hand, and consuming households, on the other. We use three concepts to help us to understand choice for both producers and consumers.

Production possibility curves help us to understand the nature of decision making of producers. Figure 3.3 is a production possibility curve for a farmer faced with two alternative uses for a farm. The farmer can devote the whole farm to sheep rearing or to growing barley or some point in between. If more sheep are kept, then less barley can be grown so if 10 extra head of sheep are bought and three sacks of barley sacrificed as a result then the barley sacrificed is the opportunity cost of the extra sheep.

The curve is concave to the origin of the graph. This shape reflects the fact that if we substitute sheep for barley when we have not been keeping sheep we can produce a lot of mutton for a small sacrifice in barley, but as we have more and more sheep then the rate of substitution changes and the opportunity cost of mutton increases. In practical terms we probably start by taking barley off the steep or rough ground and giving that over to sheep, but if we persist in keeping sheep we need to use more and more of the good arable ground for pasture.

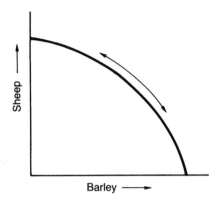

Figure 3.3 Production possibility curve: use of White Oak Farm.

> A *production possibility curve* is a line which links together alternative
> combinations of two goods which can be produced by a firm or a
> country within a specific time period assuming that there is productive
> efficiency.

The production possibility curve, or 'frontier' as it is sometimes called, is often used at
the level of a nation or region more than that of the individual producer. Consider, for
example, the decision faced by the government of the former USSR under Stalin in the
1930s. Figure 3.4 shows a production possibility curve for the decision which had to be
made. The USSR was faced with a decision whether to direct production into consumer
goods or into capital goods such as roads, railways, power stations and factories. In 1939,
like the UK and the USA, it also had to make decisions on producing armaments. Stalin
decided to concentrate on capital goods to build up the economy, especially as under the
Communist system there was little opportunity for people to protest successfully against

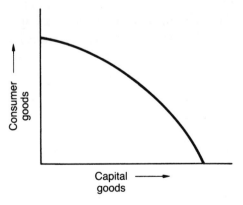

Figure 3.4 Production possibility curve: decisions in the USSR *circa* 1930.

lack of consumer goods. The curve shows the nature of that decision with, again, the opportunity cost of the decision to opt for capital goods expressed as an increasing loss of consumer goods. The repercussions of this decision are still being felt today as Russia and the Ukraine struggle to develop a consumer-orientated economy.

Budget lines are another tool which we can use to look at consumer or producer choices. The budget line expresses the decisions which have to be made by a household or firm given limited financial resources. Figure 3.5 shows a budget line for a student with £5 a week surplus from grant earnings to spend on pleasurable items. The choice facing our student, we will suppose, is between buying extra food items (which, for simplicity, we assume are chocolate bars) or the hiring of videos for entertainment.

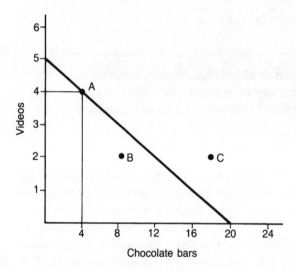

Figure 3.5   A budget line for £5 a week.

It can be seen that the budget line in Fig. 3.5 is a straight line, unlike the production possibility curve. This is because we are looking at a fixed level of output and the gradient of the line is determined by the relative prices of video hire and chocolate bars. If video hire costs £1 and chocolate bars 25p each, then at any point on the line we will be spending £5 a week and so have a balanced budget. Therefore at point A on the line the student is spending:

	Number	Cost (£)
Video hire	4	4
Chocolate bars	4	1
Total cost:		5

The extremes at either end of the line show the position if the student spends all on video hire or all on chocolate bars.

A *budget line* is a line which links points where different combinations of two goods will result in the same total expenditure.

The reader may like to check other points on the line. However, at point B spending is less than £5 and if the student is satisfied with a combination at this point then clearly there is surplus money to be spent elsewhere or saved. At point C, on the other hand, we have a possible combination which is not affordable, however much our student may wish that it is.

What happens if prices change? If the price of chocolate bars increases to 50p, then our student will have to cut the purchases of chocolate and the budget line will change as shown in Fig. 3.6. It can be seen that in increasing the price of chocolate bars we steepen the gradient of the budget line but the principle remains the same. At every point on the new budget line the total spending is the same—£5. It is important to note that it is the ratio between chocolate bars and video hire which is now different, but if the student is not interested in chocolate and spends the full £5 on video hire, the line stays in the same position at the top. The gradient changes but not the whole line. A movement of the whole line, parallel to the old, indicates that with prices the same, the student now has more or less surplus cash to spend.

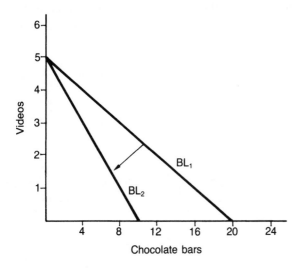

Figure 3.6   Amended budget line (£5 per week).

The budget line represents an operation which economists find useful in many situations, i.e. the *trade-off*. The student will be 'trading-off' video hire for chocolate bars at all points along the budget line, which means that more of one can only be had at the expense of the other.

A *trade-off* is the process by which a firm, person or country will choose one commodity or course of action knowing that there is an opportunity cost to be paid.

The *indifference curve* is the final tool we can use to make an analysis of choices. This will be studied in more detail in Chapter 5 but as a brief introduction we can suppose that our student is thinking of the choice between chocolate bars and video hire in terms of what options would give best or optimum satisfaction. Just as a country may consider what combination of goods to produce, so a consumer may wish to consider what combination of goods to purchase.

An *indifference curve* is a line linking together points where the utility or satisfaction from two goods or services will be constant whatever the combination.

An indifference curve is shown in Fig. 3.7 and it can be seen that, unlike the budget line, it is curved, convex to the origin of the graph. The reason for the shape will be discussed in Chapter 5, but the key point to be understood at this stage is that the line measures equality of utility or satisfaction between the two options. At any point along the curve, satisfaction is equal so that the consumer is 'indifferent' as to which option to choose.

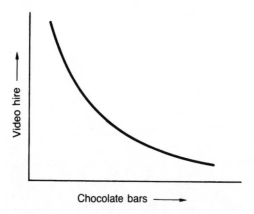

Figure 3.7   Indifference curve: videos/chocolate.

The amount of money available to spend is not considered by the curve, although the more income an individual has, the higher up and further to the right will the indifference curve be.

Topic 3.3   Economic efficiency

Economists assume that in using scarce resources through a range of choices, societies, firms and households seek to operate at a level of maximum utility or profit. As we will have cause to see from time to time in future chapters, this assumption is not necessarily valid in all cases but it is probably the most common motive when human beings operate in economic situations.

This being the case, we see economic systems as leading to a position which is best described by using the word *efficient*. Efficiency is looked on as the objective and ultimate equilibrium of society in its economic activities. What, then, is efficiency to economists and how can we best define the term?

The economist whose name is most often associated with the study of efficiency is Alfredo Pareto. His long life (from 1848 to 1923) was contemporary to that of the British economist Alfred Marshall. An Italian of French birth, he later taught in Switzerland at the University of Lausanne and his major works, the *Cours d'Economie Politique* and the *Manuale d'Economia Politica*, were very influential.

Pareto is usually regarded as the founder of welfare economics and as such will be mentioned again in Chapter 15. He put forward a definition of efficiency suitable to the objective of the total well-being of society, which can be stated as:

Efficiency can be defined as that allocation of resources such that no person, firm or country can become better off without making some other person, firm or country worse off. However, below this level increased output or lower costs can be achieved with increased benefit for all involved.

An improvement in efficiency, in Pareto terms, is a change in which some people are made better off but no-one is worse off. We have already looked at situations where a level of efficiency exists which conforms to Pareto's conditions, and that is the production possibility curve. At any point along the curve (see Fig. 3.8) there can be no improvement in the provision of goods and services for one person or section of society without a diminishing of the provision for another person or section. This is often called *Pareto efficiency*.

So in Fig. 3.8 we assume a fixed level of resources to be divided between children and the elderly. We cannot increase benefits to children (such as moving from position B to A) without reducing those for the elderly as long as we are operating along the curve. However, if we are in position C, then we can enjoy a 'Pareto improvement' in that both sections of society can see increased benefits.

Economic efficiency is a term sometimes used rather vaguely, but is best used as the equivalent of *allocative efficiency*. This describes the optimum allocation of scarce resources between competing demands. There are, however, other types of efficiency which can be useful concepts in economics.

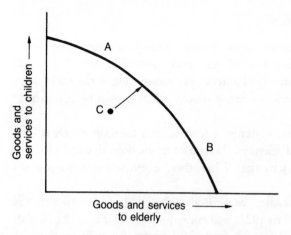

Figure 3.8   Production possibility curve and efficiency.

X-efficiency is the nearest we get to the sort of definition which the ordinary person would see as meaning 'efficiency'. It is an unfortunately meaningless term but has gained some currency in the subject. X-efficiency refers to the way in which firms may enjoy lowest possible costs and smoothest operation by eliminating waste and unnecessary spending at management level. Excessive costs and inadequate budgetary control leading to *X-in*efficiency is a common feature of monopolies, state and private. One of the motives behind the privatization of state-owned corporations across Europe has been to eliminate X-inefficiency by reducing state monopoly.

Productive efficiency takes the idea of efficiency and extends it into the productive processes. It simply describes the position of a firm, or perhaps a country as a whole, when output is achieved with the lowest possible costs.

Technical efficiency goes even further and refers to the situation when the minimum number of inputs into the productive process are used for a specific level of output. So if one farmer produces 1000 gallons of milk a week with 100 cows and his or her neighbour the same amount with 90 cows, the neighbour will be more technically efficient.

Finally, we can mention *dynamic efficiency*, which differs from the others in that it looks at output over a period of time and really measures ability to adapt and increase output. It is a feature of fast-growing economies such as Japan or Taiwan. (See Fig. 3.9.)

Topic 3.4   Market failure: externalities

In the previous section we considered the issue of efficiency and saw that while there are many different types of efficiency they are all basically concerned with the best distribution of scarce resources. The objective is an equilibrium in which resources used in production are allocated in the optimum way. But optimum for whom?

An individual firm may consider that it is functioning at optimum efficiency and yet from the point of view of society as a whole or of the industry of which it is a part, the

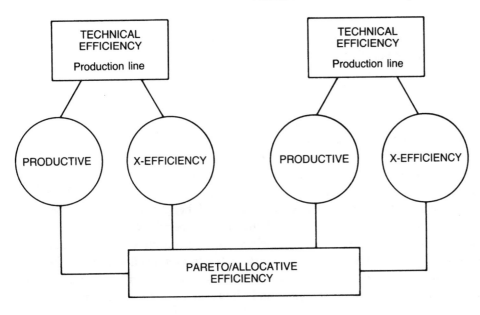

Figure 3.9 Efficiency in operation.

efficiency may be limited. The market mechanisms do not always lead inevitably to Pareto efficiency as might be expected, and where this happens we have a condition described as *market failure*.

There are three main types of market failure which we will consider in this book: externalities, discussed in this section; the problem of public and merit goods in the next section; and failure through imperfect competition which is dealt with in Chapters 6 and 7.

> *Market failure* refers to the situation when the operation of a free market fails to produce the expected benefits from an efficient allocation of resources.

An *externality* is found when there are costs and benefits attached to production or consumption which are received 'outside the market', i.e. by those who are not buying or selling the goods or services concerned. If this occurs then the price paid for the goods/ services may not fully reflect the total costs involved or benefits received.

There are a number of examples of production which create unpaid-for costs to society as a whole, especially in the form of pollution. If creation of electricity for the UK produces emissions into the atmosphere which produces acid rain in Scandinavia then there is a cost of production which is not being paid by the electricity generating company or even by UK consumers. The cost is paid for by the citizens of Norway and Sweden! This type of problem is called a *negative externality*.

> An *externality* is a situation when the production of goods or services gives costs or benefits which are received outside the market and not usually reflected in the price paid.

To help in an analysis of externalities we can distinguish between *private costs* and *social costs*. The former are costs to the individual firms and people involved in the market transaction, e.g. the costs of production and distribution. Social costs include private costs and also all other costs to society as a result of the process.

Some externalities give free benefits and are known as *positive externalities*. Examples include the emission of warm water from a factory which benefits fish stocks lower down a river or the amenities provided by the building of a reservoir for water supply. In many cases there are both types of externality, as when a new road is built. The noise and dust created when the road is built is a negative externality to local residents, but if the road reduces traffic congestion on existing roads they will subsequently receive positive externalities in the form of peace, quiet and ability to cross the high street without heavy traffic.

Cost-benefit analysis

In the practical world of business the likely costs and benefits of a project are analysed using a technique called cost-benefit analysis (CBA). Those readers who are using this book as part of a Business Studies course may well come across these techniques as applied to private firms.

In economics it is traditional to use CBA in relation to public projects such as road building, although there is no reason why it cannot also be used in connection with firms or industries. With CBA we attempt to include *all* costs and benefits, which means trying to assess the social costs and benefits and not just the private ones. This is not always very easy for two main reasons:

1. Putting a cost or benefit value on non-private costs can be difficult. The benefit of building a college or school is in an educated workforce, but how do we measure the value of this? Are likely higher earnings for individuals adequate? We need also to consider the benefits for society as a whole, including benefits of a cultural and aesthetic nature and not just occupational. If a road is built through an area of distinctive scenery, how do we measure the loss of amenity?
2. Most projects, private or public, take some time to get from the planning stage to completion and then have many years of 'life' during which benefits hopefully will accrue and perhaps some additional costs may be incurred. Yet if we add up the costs and benefits in today's money values we are ignoring the loss of value through the passing of time.

The second problem is easier to get round than the first as techniques are available to deal with it. The problem of placing a money value on future benefits and costs can be seen if we consider a simple example.

Suppose that you take out a savings plan to mature in 5 years' time and an insurance company promises to pay you a lump sum of £1000 on that date. Since the company is not Father Christmas plc it expects you to pay for this but it has the job of working out how much you should pay. Now £1000 in 5 years' time is not really worth £1000 to you *now* because you have to wait for it. If you were desperate for the money you might have to borrow from a bank on the understanding that you would later be getting this lump sum. So there is a cost of waiting—the holiday you have promised yourself, for example, cannot be enjoyed yet unless you go to the expense of borrowing.

The value of that £1000 in today's terms is called its *net present value* (NPV). In order to arrive at the NPV for a future benefit (or cost) we apply a rate of interest called a *discount rate* and the whole process is known as *discounting*. You will notice that no mention has been made of inflation. This is because while we may wish to include an inflation element in the discount rate this is not necessary since there is a cost of waiting, even if inflation is nil.

The reader is advised to refer to Case Study 3.2 for a worked example of this principle. Discounting is one of those concepts which is best learned by doing and the case study should not be regarded as optional—it really will help to clarify the meaning of the terms just introduced. For those whose mathematics is uncertain, there are tables available for easy calculation of NPV given an assumed discount rate.

Case Study 3.2—Cost-benefit analysis: flood prevention

THE floods, which saw parts of Surlingham and Brundall thigh-deep in water, have reinforced riverside residents' calls for a Yare barrier.

But a barrier for the River Bure is emerging as the frontrunner of two schemes now being assessed.

The £37 million barrier across the River Bure would block sea surges into the Broads network, channelling flood water into a washland in Haddiscoe island. Residents will have to be moved.

A barrier in the Haven at Yarmouth would cost £9 million more.

The schemes were due to be discussed by county councillors today but the debate has been given new urgency by the events of the weekend and fears of further floods.

The flooding left tempers running high at Brundall. James Cole, managing director of Norfolk Yachts Agency, said it should show the authorities that the Yare barrier scheme had to be backed.

"The River Bure has not really suffered, it has always been the Yare because it surges. A Bure barrier would not do us any good," he said.

And John Brown, secretary of the Broads Hire Boat Federation, said: "We are being sacrificed to prevent salt incursion on the northern Broads.

"If they think a washland the size of Haddiscoe is going to stop it doing this, then they're one short of a six-pack."

Landlord of Coldham Hall Tavern Michael Roberts suffered extensive flooding at his pub on the edge of Surlingham Broad.

"It is going to get worse if they put a barrier across the Bure. If they do that we might as well write our business off," he said.

Neighbour Jimmy Upton and his wife Mary were busy helping elderly neighbours clear up as the water began to shrink from their homes.

"You just want to bury your head in your hands — but you've got to get on with clearing up the mess," Mrs Upton said.

The couple are very philosophical about the damage — they have seen it all before — although they both echo Mr Roberts' fears about the Bure barrier.

The final decision on the scheme will be made on March 5 by the NRA Norfolk and Suffolk Flood Defence Committee.

Source: Eastern Evening News, 22 February 1993

The press extract in the Case Study is a report of the aftermath of serious flooding in coastal areas of Norfolk in 1993. It discusses some ideas which were already under consideration for flood prevention and mentions the cost of one of these, the Bure Barrier, as £37 million.

Although further figures are not given we can use this as the basis of an exercise in cost-benefit analysis by making a few assumptions. One difficulty is that floods are not an annual occurrence but on this coast, at least, occur periodically. We will assume that benefits include:

1. Saving loss of £3 million a year on average in agricultural output.
2. Saving loss of damage to property—assume £5 million a year on average.
3. Saving loss of damage to Norfolk Broads—we will assume £1 million a year on average.

Benefit 3 above is interesting in that it is a social benefit rather than a private one and difficult to cost. We can estimate possible loss of tourist income or fees for fishing but in many ways an amenity like this is difficult to cost.

To undertake CBA we need to calculate the net present value as explained above. NPV is needed for both future benefits and future costs to account for the time delay involved and possibly inflation. The formula used is:

$$NPV = A \frac{1}{(1 + i)^n}$$

where A is the future benefit/cost, i is the discount rate applied (which may include an inflation element) and n is the number of years or other units of time involved.

Let's assume that our benefits as listed above total £9 million a year and the costs are all incurred on building of the system. What we need to do is to reduce the future benefits to present value to compare with £37 million. If a discount rate of 8 per cent is used this might represent a reasonable rate of return from alternative uses for our investment. The NPV can be calculated in a simple manner as follows:

End of year (n)	Discounted value (£)
1	8.33
2	7.72
3	7.15
4	6.62
5	6.13
6	5.67
Total NPV:	41.62

We can see that soon after 5 years has gone by the benefits of the Bure Barrage, when reduced to present-day values, will equal the initial costs. Notice how the net value falls as each year goes by, reflecting the cost of time so that benefits in the sixth year, although nominally the same as in the first year, are less when reduced in this way because of the waiting element. There are simpler ways of making the calculations and tables are available.

The student would find it a useful exercise to undertake a similar example from a newspaper report of some public or major private project. There are two areas where assumptions have to be made which can be difficult to prove. One is the discount rate to apply, which can be the current bank base rate but, of course, this may not be relevant in 4 years' time! The other major problem is estimating money values of social costs such as pollution, noise or loss of amenity.

Environmental economics

Consideration of externalities and cost-benefit analysis brings us to a new area of economics which is growing in importance—the study of the economic aspects of the environment. The problems of environmental pollution, including the thinning of the ozone layer, are now newsworthy items and a lot of research is being undertaken by natural scientists in analysing the causes and cures. We are being urged to use unleaded petrol, refrain from using aerosol cans and limit industrial and private water and air pollution.

Economists are beginning to apply themselves also to this problem as the nations of the world attempt to wrestle with the practicalities of reversing the pollution trend. Case Study 3.3 looks at this whole issue. We recognize pollution as a negative externality and see the need to cost both the pollution and the remedies which are suggested. If the world's governments and major firms are to take strong action to halt environmental disasters we need to be able to calculate the price which we are all paying for the pollution and the cost of taking action.

There are two levels at which environmental problems are considered by economists:

1. At the *local level* individual firms may produce externalities, usually of a negative kind, received by neighbours. This includes not only the more obvious ones of atmospheric pollution from factory chimneys or discharge into rivers or the sea but also the many examples of externalities from the supposedly healthy country-side. Farmers use fertilizers and insecticides which wash into rivers. In fact one of the concerns of the EU regulations on water purity is with the level of nitrates in drinking water, excess of nitrates being usually the by-product of arable farming.

2. At the *global* or at least *regional* level, the Chernobyl disaster a few years ago reminded Europeans that some deadly pollution can travel a long way. We also have considerable concern over acid rain and the hole in the ozone layer. As a result, there has been much activity on an international level including the World Environmental Summit in 1992 and in the European Union there has been activity both by the Council of Ministers and the Commission on pollution.

The major question is what can be done about negative externalities of an environmental nature. Several suggestions have been made, including:

1. Legislation to prevent dumping and pollution with heavy fines for offending firms. This is especially applicable within nations but is less easy on an international scale, except within the EU. The UK and most other developed nations have laws on pollution but many doubt their effectiveness. In many cases the fines are too low to be effective and proof is not always easy.
2. Taxation can be used as a means of restricting the use of products which either create pollution themselves, like cigarettes or petrol, or whose production involves the creation of pollution. Again, it is difficult to be sure that the level of taxation is adequate enough to have an effect. Taxation can also distort the market, although in many respects it seems a fair way of dealing with the problem since the state usually has the cost of remedying any environmental defects.
3. Voluntary action is encouraged in many quarters and the Confederation of British Industry is among the organizations urging firms to see public interest as identical to self-interest. Many firms are proud of their environmental record and use it as a feature in their publicity.

Environmental economics is a new branch of the subject but one which gives considerable scope for those who wish to contribute to one of the world's major problems, and newer examination syllabuses will be requiring an understanding of the issues involved.

Case Study 3.3—Cleaning up Europe

A visit to the seaside is a traditional opportunity for the inland city dweller to get fresh air, clean bathing and feel refreshed away from the exhaust fumes, smoke and stuffy office. However, we are being made increasingly aware that the beaches, water and air which we have for so long taken for granted are as polluted as the inner cities.

In recent years there has been much controversy over the EC regulations on water quality. The UK, almost alone in the world, has had a public water supply which is completely 'potable'—i.e. it can be drunk by human beings from the tap without further treatment. Yet we have been under fierce criticism from many European countries as well as from inside the UK for allowing water to become contaminated. In many seemingly clean rural areas of the country, agricultural chemicals such as nitrates and pesticides have infiltrated the water system and as a result drinking water is less pure than we imagine. In 1980 the EC issued a directive that in public water supplies all traces of certain chemicals should be removed, yet the cost of doing this would seem to be far in excess of likely benefits.

The same happened with the sea water and the beaches. A directive as far back as 1975 dealt with the cleanliness of bathing water and beaches are now classified according to a rather vague measure of purity. It might be thought that a clean beach is an asset to a seaside resort and many do make a lot of any accolades for environmental purity, but the typical family on holiday is less concerned.

There is as always a cost to all the attempts to deal with impure water, beaches and air. In recent years accountants have been busy attempting to devise systems of environmental accounting which will ensure that polluting firms pay the social costs in full and some have warned firms that such costs could be high. Yet throughout Europe, the member states of the EU show a very wide range of commitment to environmental purity—especially if commitment is judged by the amount of finance committed to the cause. Germany is the most generous, with over 16 million ECU spent on environmental programmes, but Portugal and Ireland have been spending less than 500 000 ECU a year on measures to improve the environment. The UK dishes out between 8 and 9 million ECU a year and so does France.

1. Why should the state foot the bill for environmental pollution instead of the culprits?
2. For an economist, what is included in the social cost of allowing sewage to be released into the sea a few miles from a seaside resort?

Topic 3.5   Market failure: types of goods

Market failure can also occur with certain types of goods which cannot be provided, in part or total, through the market system. We can distinguish three types of good which are not provided properly by the market mechanism.

Free goods have already been mentioned and for the most part a 'mention' is all they do get in economics because, by definition, they are not only not dealt with in a market system, they are also not scarce resources and so not the matter of our subject. We are concerned with *economic goods* instead. However, free goods can become economic goods if a local scarcity exists or if they are required in a processed form. While water may be free, few of us wish these days to use a water butt or local river as the source of our morning tea. Sand is free in the Sahara but a builder in Sicily would expect to pay at a builders' merchant for a truckload. (See above.)

Public goods are another form of market failure. These are goods which are available to all and consumption by one person does not reduce the amount available to another. They are not necessarily free in the sense of a free good as there is a cost of producing them, but it is difficult, if not impossible, to charge for their use. Classic examples of public goods are lighthouses and the defence forces. We may object to a war in which the UK is involved but if the country is successfully defended then we benefit from this whether we like it or not. We may refuse to pay any special tax imposed for the defence of the realm or be unable to pay—but we still benefit from the service. We are a 'free rider' on defence benefits.

As a result of their nature, public goods are usually provided by the state. Private armies are not unknown but usually only exist when there is a strong private benefit for some individual or group which impels them to take the expense on board.

Merit goods are a third type of good in which market failure can be seen. They are more complex than public goods and it is important not to confuse them. Merit goods can be provided by the market but not in a large enough volume to satisfy the needs of society. Individuals may not see the wider benefits and may be prepared to pay a share towards them or it may be difficult to enforce payment. Some examples will clarify the meaning.

Educational institutions such as schools, colleges and universities are examples of merit goods. They can be and are provided privately. In the UK there are many private schools, some of high academic reputation; there are private colleges, mainly teaching specialist professional subjects; and there is one private university (Buckingham) not funded by the state. In the USA private colleges and universities are more widespread and most European countries have private educational institutions.

However, if we left education to the marketplace the benefits of education would be received only by the rich or by those combining ability and fortune in gaining access to schools and universities with scholarships and bursaries. Most of the population would be left outside and not only would they suffer as individuals but the nation as a whole would be worse off. There is increasing evidence that a high level of educational attainment in a nation is linked with economic performance. So the state provides a basic educational framework, which is 'free' up to age 18 in the UK, to ensure at least a level of minimum provision.

Health services are similarly placed. In most European countries there is a state health service supplemented by private hospitals and medical consultants. In the USA the private sector is more important and all but the most basic health care has been privately funded, although changes are now taking place. Basically, the market will provide health care but at a high price and at the exclusion not only of those who cannot afford that price but of the long-term sick and those with incurable ailments.

A road network is a third example of a merit good. In past centuries many roads were privately owned with turnpikes to ensure payment for use. Today only a few bridges and scenic routes are privately owned and paid for by tolls, although there has been discussion about the viability of private motorways. In fact it may well be that we see an increase in tolls or some other form of payment for motorways in the future. However, in general, roads are held to be of too great an importance to be left purely to the market, and the traffic jams which result from some of the toll points which do exist are not an encouragement to make private payment more widespread.

Merit goods provide an active current issue in economics in view of the government's privatization of public corporations in the 1980s. Twenty years ago it was generally held that many key aspects of the infrastructure and many basic industries had the nature of merit goods and needed state involvement. Many politicians are now in favour of allowing the market a greater role in these areas and, as a result, the telephone system and provision of electricity, gas and water are provided by public limited companies with vague public oversight by *quangos* (see Chapter 15).

One current debate is over the railways. The privatization of the railway services is in process but this has been hotly resisted by many. One of the centres of the debate is over the continued existence of certain lines which are not really economic in themselves but which provide a valuable service to local communities or provide feeder services to main lines. Market forces would insist that most of these lines be closed yet there are strong social reasons for keeping them open. Some services are subsidized by local authorities on behalf of their citizens and this may be a more prominent feature in the future. As with most merit goods, the market will not provide enough to satisfy the total needs of society, and the debate centres around the issue of whether social, political or moral needs should be considered as valid in such a context.

An *economic good* is a commodity or service which has a scarcity value, is the object of demand and so acquires value.

A *public good* is a commodity or service which cannot be restricted in supply and so free riding cannot be prevented.

A *merit good* is a commodity or service which is inadequately provided by the market to the level which society considers is desirable.

Essay questions

1. If bus services are inferior goods, what effects will the following changes have on consumers' total expenditure on bus journeys?
   (a) A rise in incomes;
   (b) A rise in bus drivers' wages;
   (c) An increase in the annual licence fee payable on private cars. (*Source*: University of Oxford, June 1990)
2. What is meant by 'the use of the market mechanism'? Outline the arguments for and against the use of the market mechanism in *two* of the following cases:
   (a) Wage determination;
   (b) The provision of education;
   (c) Floating exchange rates;
   (d) Dealing with regional problems. (*Source*: University of Oxford, June 1993)
3. Explain what is meant by equity and efficiency and why they are important in evaluating economic systems. Is it possible for an economic system to be both equitable and efficient or must the increase in one automatically decrease the other? Illustrate your answer from recent experience. (*Source*: Northern Examinations and Assessment Board, June 1993)

4. Why are many theories of economic decisions, such as to buy, to produce and to save, expressed in marginal rather than total or average values? Explain whether or not you think that this is realistic and whether realism is important in formulating economic theories. (*Source*: Northern Examinations and Assessment Board, June 1993)

Chapter 4

Economic systems

Topic 4.1   What are economic systems?

We have already seen that economics is concerned with the key problem of how to use scarce resources to satisfy human needs and wants. In particular, the subject attempts to answer the questions 'What is to be produced? How is it to be produced? For whom is it to be produced?'

In answering these questions we have to consider what sort of economic system any society can have in order to best provide for the distribution of the resources—'best' being usually interpreted as the system that is most likely to lead to Pareto efficiency. If we look at economic history from the time when the first cave man exchanged a bear skin for a coupled of flint axe heads, there have been many ways of dealing with the issue.

Before looking at the three main types of economy we need to consider the two ways in which we can approach the subject—the question of ownership or the question of mechanics. In other words, are we concerned about the *who* or about the *how*?

Ownership of the means of production and distribution is a major economic and political issue. Karl Marx founded his Communist economics on the question of ownership and the recent programmes of privatization in Western Europe and *perestroika* in the former USSR are also largely about who actually owns or should own firms. We can depict the options on ownership as in Fig. 4.1.

It is difficult to find genuine examples of the two extremes but some countries such as the USA or Hong Kong have a large preponderance of privately owned firms and companies in the People's Republic of China and Albania are still largely state owned, although with distinct moves towards the market in China (see Case Study 4.1 below). The situation is changing in many areas and Western Europe has moved a long way from a 'mixed' position towards capitalism, while Russia, the Czech and Slovak Republics and Poland have been moving from state ownership into a mixed ownership situation.

A couple of points are worth making here. Capitalism does not necessarily infer that there are a lot of owners. A capitalist system can exist with just a few prominent individuals or firms dominating markets, and it is almost possible to see much of the non-Communist world as an economy dominated by a few large multinational companies such as Ford, Union Carbide and IBM. We should also note that state ownership does not necessarily imply Communism, although every example in the experience of the

CAPITALISM	MIXED OWNERSHIP	STATE OWNERSHIP
Property, firms and wealth owned by individuals or private groups	Mixture of state and private ownership	Property, firms, wealth owned by the state
USA	FRANCE	USSR *circa* 1980

Figure 4.1 Types of economy by ownership.

present generation has involved Communist ideology. Historically there have been economic systems with resources owned by kings or small oligarchies. It is worth remembering that medieval Europe had a system of private ownership of land but this was held under strict feudal conditions rather than modern freehold, and ownership was by a few wealthy aristocratic families.

Case Study 4.1—China moves to the market

The Chinese economic reforms initiated in 1979 constitute a pioneering example of an abrupt switch from a command economy based on administrative directives towards a market economy founded on contractual relations between independent economic agents. In terms of economic growth, the Chinese reforms would seem to have been an outstanding success. In the period of the reforms, real national income grew by over 9 per cent per annum (1978–90).

Even with a population growth rate of 1.2 per cent per annum there was an annual growth rate per capita of over 8 per cent. Such a rate of economic growth would not look out of place among the growth records of the 'high performance' East Asian economies. As compared to what is happening in the present-day East European and Soviet economies, the Chinese economic reforms did not bring economic hardship to a significant segment of the population. On the contrary, they brought in their wake a record rise in personal incomes, albeit at different rates for different groups.

Only a few years ago the Chinese economic reforms appeared radical when compared to the then still cautious reforms in the Soviet Union and Eastern Europe of the 1980s. But it now seems the reverse. Whilst the East European and the Soviet economy seem to have opted for a 'great leap' into a market economy, the Chinese economy is still following a two-track policy of selective reform while maintaining elements of the old command economy. This two-track approach does not seem to have hindered economic growth. Nor has it retarded the expansion of foreign trade or the inflow of foreign investment. The expansion of China's exports in the 1980s would compare very favourably with those of other developing economies.

The main reforms of the last 10 years comprise: a shift from collective farming to household farming; financial and operational autonomy for state-owned enterprises; the de-centralization of government, delegating control from higher to lower government tiers; encouraging private and foreign enterprises; and an open-door policy towards foreign trade and investment.

Extract from an article by N. Stern and A. Hussain in *LSE Magazine*, Winter 1991/2, pp. 16–17

The gradual move of China towards a freer economy is summarized in the above extract. The following questions would be worth considering:

1. What have been the advantages of the Chinese approach to moving away from a planned economy as opposed to that of Russia?
2. How important is foreign trade and investment to the growth of the Chinese economy?

Capitalism is the type of economic and political system which is characterized by private ownership of property and enterprise.

The *mechanics* of economic systems involves consideration not so much of who owns resources and the means of distributing them but how this is done. Most of the rest of this chapter will divide systems on this basis as it is the most useful. We usually recognize three main types of system as seen in Fig. 4.2.

MARKET ECONOMY	MIXED ECONOMY	PLANNED ECONOMY
Resources distributed by means of markets of buyers and sellers	Resources distributed by both markets and state	Resources distributed by state decision and state planning
HONG KONG	EUROPEAN UNION (EU)	CHINA (PR) *circa* 1985

Figure 4.2 Types of economy—mechanics of the market.

It can be seen that for the most part private ownership goes hand in hand with a market economy and state ownership with state planning. In times of war, however, the state may take absolute control even though private ownership still exists—as in both the UK and Germany during the Second World War. You can also have a measure of state ownership with markets in which state-owned firms compete with each other as is happening in some areas of Eastern Europe at present.

Topic 4.2   Market economies

Although there are few (if any) societies which have no government intervention in the economy it is useful to consider the ideal situation of a pure or 'free' market economy at least as a standard against which actual economies can be judged. As noted in the previous section, this type of economy is usually associated with a capitalist system involving private ownership of resources, firms and distribution networks, but not necessarily so. A market system does not depend on private ownership so much as individual decision making. At its heart is a concept we call *free enterprise*—the freedom of firms to sell and households to buy the goods and services which they wish to without state intervention.

A *market economy* is an economic system in which firms and households buy and sell without state interference and in a free enterprise legal framework.

The market is the meeting of buyers and sellers, although this need not be a physical 'market' in the traditional sense. It is any system which enables buyers and sellers to arrange transactions or deals. Two main assumptions are made about those involved in markets—that firms are motivated by profit and that households or individuals aim at getting maximum value for money when they spend.

'Profit' in this sense can include surplus earnings for a cooperative enterprise or a state-owned firm operating in a competitive market, on the assumption that higher earnings produce larger wages or bonuses. In the case of households it is also assumed that quality is sought as well as, or perhaps in preference to, the lowest price.

The key to the free market system is in the price mechanism. The answers to our questions 'What, How and for Whom?' lie in prices. Recently some economists have used the term 'signal' for the way in which prices produce reactions in both firms and households. (See Fig. 4.3.)

Suppose that we consider the market for compact discs. If the price of CDs is high then this will 'signal' to households that the product is rather expensive and they might do better to buy their album in cassette tape or good old-fashioned vinyl. On the other hand, it will 'signal' to manufacturers that here is a product which could give them higher profit than the existing tapes and records. So high prices will keep demand low but encourage output. As we will see in Chapter 5, eventually an *equilibrium* price and output level will emerge because if there is too much output firms will have to reduce prices to get rid of stock. The interplay of supply and demand ensures a long-term stability to the markets.

The market also allocates products to households by the price mechanism. If CDs are expensive then only comparatively better-off households will be able to afford them. Goods are not distributed on the basis of need or moral entitlement or a 'fair shares for

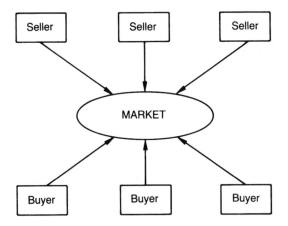

Figure 4.3   The mechanics of a market economy.

all' principle but on what households can afford. Ownership of wealth or income determines distribution. So the question 'Who?' is answered by 'Whoever can afford'.

The question of 'how' goods or services will be produced is also determined in the market. Firms are also buyers and they have to buy land, machinery, raw materials and labour at a price. In order to maximize profits they will try to use a method of production which will keep costs as low as possible.

A market economy will include innumerable individual markets which relate to each other. So the market for computers, for example, will interface with the market for labour as firms seek to employ skilled workers; with the market for plastics as they seek to obtain raw materials for production; and with the market for capital as they seek a bank loan to buy new equipment. These markets are connected in various ways and some of them will experience *derived demand*, i.e. demand for the product or service is the result of demand for some other product. For example, the demand for computer-literate labour is dependent ultimately on the demand for computers.

One further important feature of market economies is the importance of freedom of choice, especially for households. As a result, in market systems economists often say that there is *consumer sovereignty*, indicating that it is the wishes of consumers which ulti-mately determine *what* is produced, *when* it is produced and at *what price*. If consumers as a whole want to buy more bread, for example, demand will rise and create a shortage. Prices will then rise, encouraging bakers to produce more, so the demand will be satisfied.

Consumer sovereignty exists in market economies and describes the situation when the demand of the consumers ultimately determines the level of output and producers do not have control over prices.

So the price mechanism operating through a network of markets will, in theory at least, produce an economy which experiences Pareto efficiency without government interference. It is assumed that the state provides a legal framework (free markets do not assume anarchy!) but little else. Unfortunately, the perfect free market can rarely have existed in practice if only because of the other objectives of society and the need to cope with externalities, public goods and other market failures (Chapter 3).

Topic 4.3   Planned economies

Although, as noted above, it is possible to have a planned (or command) economy with private ownership of resources, for the most part we associate such systems with totalitarian regimes of a Communist nature. It might therefore be a useful start to this topic to consider a few of the aims and intentions of Communism.

Communism as a political and economic system was derived from the writings of Karl Marx, Friedrich Engels and other nineteenth-century writers and was then modified in a Russian context by Lenin and Stalin and in China by Mao-tse Tung. In origin it was not intended to produce a totalitarian political system but considered that private property is 'theft' and that resources, firms and distribution systems should be owned by 'the people'—effectively, by the state or as cooperatives. After Stalin's decision to develop Communism in the USSR as a priority, as opposed to Leon Trotsky's aim of world revolution, the theory began to develop a harsh and repressive political reality with a rapid state-led drive to industrialization.

Planned economies in the Communist world were centred around state-made (or perhaps, to be more accurate, we should say, 'party-made') decisions in response to our questions on 'What, How and for Whom?' In theory, 'For Whom?' was intended to be the people as a whole, but in practice central government objectives became important. Thus during the 'cold war' and before this the real war with Germany, priority was usually given to military supplies. Also important were heavy industry, including power production, steel and engineering. Consumer goods were not considered very important and in many cases only Communist Party members could afford or obtain many such goods.

> A *planned economy* is an economic system in which the major decisions are made by the state and markets play only a very minor role. They have tended to be associated in the last hundred years with Communism.

In a planned economy the price mechanism is reduced to a humble task—that of providing a token system by which food and other goods can be bought with the earnings from labour which, for the most part, would be in state-owned enterprises or cooperatives. Prices do not influence production decisions and changes in demand only affect the length of queues and not prices or levels of output. Basically, goods and services are mostly rationed. Even if there is no formal rationing system, they are rationed by limited availability and the necessity to queue.

It might be argued, of course, that this system is beneficial. People may not have much choice and may not like the long queues, but when they do get to the counter, assuming that the goods are still there, they know that they can afford them. Although in practice Communist Party élites emerged, had the system worked properly as intended by Marx it might have provided for an economy which reduced inequalities in consumption.

The problem for planned economies is ensuring that the inputs and outputs of individual enterprises add up. In the former USSR, planning was in 5-year cycles and within each 5-year plan there were set targets for each industry and then for each factory. Ideally, the system should ensure that a known level of output resulted but, as most factories depended for inputs on others, any variation from target had repercussions throughout the system. Shortages were common and quality was often poor, as there were few incentives to improve quality or produce in excess of target.

Since the Gorbachev era the USSR has not only ceased to exist but all the countries of Europe which were formerly under Communist rule are now moving into market-led systems. Many farms and factories are still state-owned or cooperatives as privatization takes time, but there is more competition between factories and farm collectives.

The People's Republic of China, Albania and Cuba have still not formally changed governments but there are signs of a move towards a more market-friendly society and increasingly some elements of private enterprise are being encouraged or at least tolerated. Again, we come back to the fact that, like the market economy, the planned economy in its ideal state is a concept rather than ever having been an actuality. Perhaps both exist mainly in the minds of economists and political scientists!

Topic 4.4   Mixed economies

The conclusion we can reach, then, is that whatever the virtues of market and planned economies, the reality has been that human societies have opted for the most part for a mixture of both approaches. It is, of course, possible to identify economies which are predominantly market-led such as the USA, Canada and, increasingly, the UK. It is also possible to identify a few economies which are still predominantly planned.

Mixed economies combine market operations and government activity in varying proportions. One significant feature which can be seen at present is the dynamic nature of the mixed economy in the world. We have already noted that most of the former Communist nations are moving towards a market system and so are currently at the 'planned end' of a spectrum representing the mixed economy whereas the UK, France, Italy, Spain and many other Western countries are moving towards the 'market end' of the spectrum (see Fig. 4.4). The USA, in contrast, is moving a little towards more government direction as a way of dealing with the problems caused by recession.

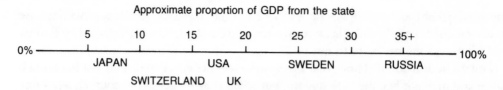

Figure 4.4   Mixed economies 1991. (*Source*: OECD surveys.)

There are two types of mixed economy identified by economists, although they are really as much poles at either end of a spectrum. We call these *market socialism* and the *social market*.

'Market socialism' refers to an economy which contains a mix strongly dominated by state activity. Among Western economies Sweden has a mixed economy with strong tendencies to market socialism, but the best examples currently are some of the former Communist states—especially the former USSR territories where it is proving difficult to extract the state from the productive part of the economy. Cuba is also in a similar position and the UK during the Attlee administration (1945–51) was moving into this category as a result of the introduction of the welfare state, public ownership of assets and remaining problems following the end of the Second World War.

At the other extreme is the social market which perhaps best describes the UK in the post-Thatcher era and is the position towards which most of the West European countries are moving. In this situation the market dominates but there is significant state involvement.

How, then, is the state involved in mixed economies? In any country the state is a major player in that taxes are raised and money borrowed for essential expenditure on justice, defence and other public goods and general administration. In a capitalist society property rights are important and need the protection of law while the competition between firms which is characteristic of markets has to be within a legal framework. Apart from this essential framework, as far as economic life is concerned the state is involved actively in three main areas:

1.   State ownership of productive or distributive enterprises. Since the Post Office was set up the UK government has been involved in business enterprises but after the election of a Labour government in 1945 it moved strongly towards state ownership or control of the 'commanding heights of the economy'. Chapter 15 deals with the issue of nationalization in more detail. Most countries of Western Europe also developed state ownership of key industries, railways, power supplies, etc. It is this area of state control and ownership which has been much reduced over the last decade in Europe.

2.   Regulation of trade and industry. In the Middle Ages governments enforced laws on quality control, weights and measures and entitlement to trade but in the *laissez-faire* era from the seventeenth century onwards controls became outdated and inadequate.

In the last half-century there has been a considerable amount of consumer protection legislation in Europe including, in the UK, laws such as the Trades Descriptions Act, the Data Protection Act and the Financial Services Act. The European Union is very active in this area—some would say too active—in standardizing names and descriptions of products, sizes, shapes and other characteristics of goods, and setting qualification standards for workers.

In many respects the reduction of direct state involvement in production has increased the amount of legislation and, in the UK at least, the number of *quangos* (see below for definition) set up to police specific industries—for example, OFGAS for the gas industry or the Securities & Investment Board for financial services. This aspect of government activity will be examined in more detail in Chapter 15.

A *quango* is the abbreviation for a body known as a Quasi-Autonomous National Government Organization. They are not elected but members are appointed, usually by government ministers, to oversee some area of government administration.

---

3. All governments try to ensure that the economy as a whole is moving in the direction of prosperity and growth and all have various objectives such as reducing inflation or unemployment or dealing with inequalities. Using taxation and government spending, known as *fiscal policy*, or controlling the money supply (*monetary policy*), governments seek to create an economic setting suitable for business development. The importance of this can be seen in the early 1990s with the struggle to get Western countries out of recession, and governments trying to bolster business confidence and oppositions blaming governments for the crisis. See Chapter 15 for a detailed discussion.

    Many governments attempt more specific interference in the 'free' market by using subsidies to support key industries which are in difficulties, import duties to protect employment levels, or schemes of supported training or employment such as the British Youth Training Scheme. The specific financial support of industries is often given the label *supply side policies* and as such will be discussed later in Chapter 15.

    One of the best ways to study the mixed economy is to look at the changes taking place in many countries and the decisions which are having to be made. The experience of *perestroika* in the former USSR is a case in point. Another useful example is to consider the European Union as an economic unit—the European *Economic* Community. In many ways West European customers and firms are part of a large mixed economy stretching from Greece to Eire and expecting in time to embrace many of the former Communist countries of Eastern Europe.

    The EU is acknowledged to have a large bureaucratic structure representing the state input into the economy and the Common Agricultural Policy especially can hardly claim to represent a free market approach to foodstuffs (see Chapters 5 and 10) as it attempts to deal with some of the problems which farmers face in an open market. On the other hand, the concept of a single market with removal of trading barriers is part of the ideal of establishing a large market where firms can compete equally across national borders and consumers have a wide choice of goods and suppliers. (See Table 4.1.)

Table 4.1 The European Union as a mixed economy

EU Commission and Parliament	National government activity	Free market
Standard sizes, weights, descriptions and names	Additional requirements for trades description and labelling	Freedom to sell across borders
Price fixing through Common Agricultural Policy	Subsidies for regions in difficulty	Freedom to hire workers from any EU country
Regional subsidies and grants	Control of trade and business—standards	
Exchange rate mechanism to facilitate trade	Ownership of key industries by state	Economies of scale from a larger market.

Essay questions

1. (a) Explain the functions of the price mechanism in a market economy.
    (b) How might these functions be affected by:
        (i)   The organizers of the Wimbledon lawn tennis final fixing the price of tickets below the market–clearing price.
        (ii) The government fixing a minimum legal wage above the market–clearing wage. (*Source*: The Associated Examining Board, June 1991.)
2. (a) How are resources allocated in a mixed economy?
    (b) In the light of the economic changes that have occurred within the UK in recent years, discuss whether it is still correct to describe the UK economy as a mixed one. (*Source*: The Associated Examining Board, June 1990.)
3. Is the notion of a pure market economy merely a theorist's pipe dream (*Source*: Oxford and Cambridge Schools Examination Board, June 1991.)
4. 'The existence of a wide variety of theories of oligopoly suggests that this is the most realistic market model.' Discuss. (*Source*: Oxford and Cambridge Schools Examination Board, June 1991.)
5. Explain what is meant by an 'economic system' and discuss the main criteria for distinguishing between types of economic system. Explain whether or not in your view recent events in Eastern Europe confirm that the market mechanism provides the best approach to the problems of running national economies. (*Source*: Northern Examinations and Assessment Board, June 1992.)

6. Outline the essential differences between free market and centrally planned economies. Discuss the economic problems which may arise in the transition of the East European economies to the market system. (*Source*: Northern Examinations and Assessment Board, June 1991.)

7. What are the functions of profit in a market economy? If the directors and managers of companies are given the incentives of profit-sharing schemes will it prove beneficial to the whole economy. (*Source*: University of Oxford, June 1993.)

Chapter 5

Micro-economics: how prices are determined

Topic 5.1 Supply, demand and price

Underlying all our economic analysis will be the fundamental fact that economics is concerned mainly with *prices*. Economics is also the study of scarcity, and this means that individuals, as we have already seen, must exercise *choice*. The selection and allocation of scarce goods, services and resources is conducted largely through the *price mechanism*, at least in a market or mixed economy.

From the beginning of economic studies people have been preoccupied with the forces that determine price. In the Middle Ages the prime question was 'What is the *just* price?' but as we have already seen (Chapter 1), economics as a modern science is not concerned with ethics but with an objective study of how scarce resources are distributed.

In looking at how prices are determined and their importance in economics we make three key assumptions:

1. We are looking at a *market economy* rather than a planned economy (see Chapter 4). In other words, a situation where prices are determined by the interplay of the desires and objectives of consumers and producers and not those of political leaders.
2. Both consumers and producers have a reasonable level of free *choice* in making key decisions. Even more fundamental, of course, is the assumption that these choices are rational ones and in line with logical objectives of profit maximization on the part of producers and consumers.
3. Finally there is a *price mechanism*—in other words, goods and services are allocated by means of prices and not rationing or some form of arbitrary allocation. In Western societies, apart from time of war, this is normally the case, but in the planned economies which until recently were dominant in so many countries this was not always the situation.

Case Study 5.1 below looks at some of these assumptions around a very practical feature—an advertisement.

Although we have assumed the existence of a market economy we do not make any assumptions about the type of market. For the most part we usually start our study of price theory in the context of a *perfect market*, but as we will see in the reality of the typical market situation this is rare, or even non-existent, and various degrees of market *imperfection* need to be considered. This will be explored further in Chapter 6.

In a free enterprise or market economy, differences in prices can only be explained by reference to supply and demand as the governing economic forces. Case Study 5.1 indicates a point at which supply in the form of available goods meets the consumer as a reader of the newspaper. As a result of reading the advertisement, customers in the area make decisions on whether or not to visit Tony's Discount Warehouse.

Case Study 5.1—What's in an ad?

Source: *Norwich Mercury*, 27 November 1993

Here we have a fairly ordinary local advertisement in which a firm marketing low-price foods and other household items advertises itself and in doing so makes certain assumptions which are at the core of price theory. In the market for household foods, an advertisement like this is the retailer's way of reaching potential customers and the message has to be clear. The reader might like to consider the following questions:

1. What basic assumptions are being made by the advertiser about the consumer and the consumer's buying habits?
2. Has the advertiser freedom to change prices at will?

According to the classical economists, the cost of labour was the main determinant of price and Adam Smith argued that the price of an article depended upon the labour expended in its production. In fact David Ricardo, John Stuart Mill and, later, Karl Marx argued that labour cost was the determinant of value. Later economists, especially William Jevons, Karl von Menger and Léon Walras, in the latter half of the nineteenth century, emphasized the demand side and the role of marginal utility.

Both supply and demand play a part in determining prices and it was Alfred Marshall who brought the two approaches together to develop modern price theory. He saw cost of production and demand as two sides of the picture like the two blades of a pair of scissors. In the long run, costs of production tend to be most significant, but in the shorter term demand plays a greater role.

Topic 5.2   The theories of demand and supply

At the heart of the study of price theory lies a key theme which is one of the best-known and most fundamental ideas in economics—the theories or 'laws' of demand and supply.

The theory of demand

The theory or 'law' of demand states that there is an inverse relationship between the price charged for a commodity or service and the quantity demanded, or in simpler terms, if the price rises, less will be bought and if the price falls, more will be consumed. The words 'bought' and 'consumed' have been used here purposely rather than the word 'demanded' because in economics we are concerned only with *effective demand*, which means that the person requiring the article must not only be willing to buy but must also have the money or other means to make that demand effective.

> The *theory of demand* states that effective demand for a good or service varies in an inverse relationship to price.

To explore the way demand operates it will be worth looking at a hypothetical example. Below is the demand schedule for chocolate bars showing prices and the amount likely to be purchased per week from a local sweetshop.

Price (p)	5	10	15	20	25	30	35	40
Bars/week:	400	350	300	250	200	150	100	50

For the most part we express a demand schedule like this in the form of a graph—known (even if it is a straight line) as a *demand curve*. The figures above are expressed as such a curve in Fig. 5.1. For the moment we will keep the demand curve as a straight line although later we will see that usually it is in fact curved.

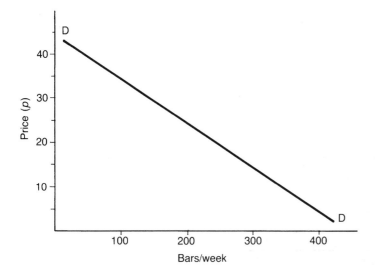

Figure 5.1   Demand curve—chocolate bars.

The characteristic shape of the demand curve is that it normally falls to the right, assuming the standard practice among economists of using the vertical axis for price and the horizontal axis for quantity demanded. This shape expresses the idea that price influences demand in that the lower the price, the more will be purchased. This fits in with everyday experience for most people, and is in fact the basis behind the traditional shopkeepers' device to increase turnover—hold a sale!

It is vital that we understand what we are showing in the demand curve—that the quantity required by the customer varies according to price, i.e. that the movement along the horizontal axis reacts to movement on the vertical axis and not the other way round. In fact the curve shows a relationship only between those two variables—*price* and *quantity demanded.*

What is meant when people talk about 'an increase in demand'? Sometimes this phrase is used rather glibly and we need to take care in interpreting such statements. If demand is changing as a result of a change in price then we are moving *along* the demand curve and we say that there is a change in quantity demanded. On the other hand, if there is a general increase in demand for some other reason such as a rise in incomes or a change in desire following an advertising campaign, then there is a move of the whole curve. The *curve shifts* to the right for an increase in demand and to the left for a decrease in demand. Movements of the curve simply express the idea that the whole schedule of price/quantity relationship has been moved. This can be seen in Fig. 5.2.

The example we have used would involve a small number of customers and one retail outlet. In fact when we speak of 'demand' we can mean a whole range of things, from an individual's personal demand schedule, to one firm's demand, or even to the whole industry or *market demand.* The market demand is very important and consists quite simply of all the individual demand schedules combined together.

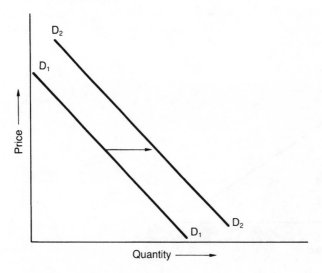

Figure 5.2 Shift of demand curve.

We can examine how this might influence the shape of a demand curve by looking at Fig. 5.3. Here we see how in the left-hand graph, we have different-shaped curves for different individuals. If we transform that into a market demand, assuming that the individuals form the total market, then we get a combined or composite *market demand*.

Exceptions to the theory of demand

The type of good with a demand such as we have been looking at and which produces a demand curve which slopes down to the right is known as a *normal good*. However, some goods and services have upward-sloping curves for all or part of the price range. Of particular importance are *inferior goods* and the type of inferior good known as a *Giffen good*.

> An *inferior good* is a basic commodity consumed more by those on low incomes and the demand for it tends to fall as income levels rise.

There are four main types of society which might produce exceptions to the normal operation of demand:

1. *An affluent society* In an affluent society the demand for inferior goods, such as potatoes or bread, may decline even though prices fall. People on higher incomes tend to spend a smaller proportion of their income on foodstuffs, an observed feature

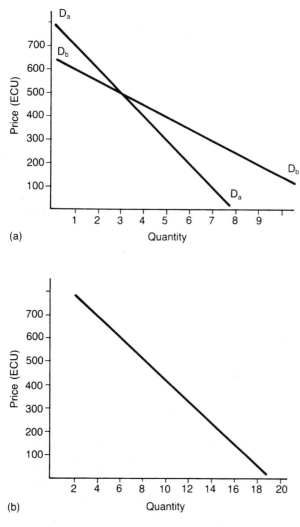

Figure 5.3   From firm to market demand. (a) Demand curves for firms (a) and (b). (b) Industry demand curve: firms (a) and (b).

known as *Engel's law*. In particular, for this to happen the increase in income needs to be of *real* income, i.e. the additional money less any reduction in its value due to inflation. The topic of inflation will be dealt with in some detail in Chapter 13.

2. *A subsistence society*   In this type of society there is little trade and people mainly consume what they produce themselves. Sir Robert Giffen put forward, in the nineteenth century, the idea that in very poor societies there are goods which would enjoy an increased demand if their price rose. People will increase consumption of some types of inferior good because the rise in price makes them less well off and they will concentrate on basic items of food rather than other goods. There are

now doubts among economists as to whether Giffen goods, as they are called, really exist in the world outside the economist's study!

> A *Giffen good* is a commodity of such basic importance that in a very poor society, an increase in price may produce an increase in demand, and demand for other goods will be reduced.

3. *A 'status symbol' society*   Some goods carry status because they are perceived to be expensive and convey on the owner an aura of respectability, status or what is sometimes called 'street credibility'. If the price is lowered then the article is seen to be 'cheap' and status is lost. Expensive trainers with known quality brand names are a good example—cheaper versions may be as good but they do not give the same status to the wearer. Case Study 5.2 will be of interest in exploring this notion. A similar feature is the suspicion which can attach itself to cheap prices. Some people, on principle, avoid the cheapest goods because they suspect that they may be faulty. Many goods in the traditional British town market are of excellent quality but goods bought 'in the market' carry lower status than those bought in shops. It is often thought that they are cheap because they are of low quality when in fact they may simply be bankrupt stock or surplus from an export consignment.

4. *A speculative society*   If it is believed that there will be further increases in price then consumers may buy larger quantities even if the price is rising. The commodity, currency and share markets are good examples of this type of feature. If there is a 'bull market', i.e. a market of rising share prices, demand would increase while the price was rising because speculators are likely to think that the price would rise even higher. On the other hand, some economists consider that the apparent irregularity with speculators is in fact a shift of the demand curve rather than a move along it, since the speculators have changed their attitude to prices and now operate on a new schedule.

The theory of supply

The theory or law of supply states that there is a direct, not an inverse, relationship between the price of a good or service and the quantity which is supplied. Some students have difficulties in understanding the supply position because it concerns the motivation and actions of firms rather than of individuals.

If you are facing a market for your goods and competitors are raising their prices, will you not follow suit? Of course you will, because unless your costs have risen by the same amount you will make more profit for each unit you sell. Even if your costs have risen, lower costs per unit resulting from producing more (economies of scale) may begin to operate and offer you more profit per unit. In the case of retailing and some service activities like insurance broking and estate agency, a rise in prices means more money in the form of higher mark-up or commission.

> *The theory of supply* states that the quantity of a good or service which is supplied to the market will change in direct relationship with prices.

It is important to remember that producers and retailers usually have a choice of which goods they can make or sell or which services they can provide. The range of choice varies. At one extreme is a very specialist firm such as a steel producer with expensive equipment designed for a limited range of processes. A steel producer can vary a product range but can produce only metal products. A blast furnace cannot produce toffee!

At the other extreme is a supermarket which can sell a very large number of products as can be seen if we look at the increasing product range of most supermarkets. If the price of one commodity rises and others do not then our supermarket management will want to expand shelf space for that product at the expense of others. This concept is known as *substitution* and is an important idea in economics.

An industry where substitution is important is farming. A farmer, as we will see later in this chapter, cannot change plans in the short term but if in one year prices of wheat are low (and presumably therefore also profits) a change can be made in the autumn and rapeseed or barley sown instead. Many farmers have moved out of dairying as a result of low milk prices and quotas.

The supplier of goods acts in the same way as the consumer, and exercises a degree of choice. The real cost of producing 50 loaves lies in the opportunity to produce 200 rolls instead (opportunity cost) and the profit that might have been made by supplying rolls to customers.

Let's see how increasing prices might produce an increase in output. We will take chocolate bars and look at a hypothetical supply schedule for the manufacturer.

Supply schedule for chocolate bars

Price per bar (*p*)	5	10	15	20	25	30	35	40	45	50
Supply (hundreds per week)	10	20	30	40	50	60	70	80	90	100

We have assumed so far that supply changes by firms substituting in or out of producing a particular good. However, even firms like steel producers or fishing companies will look at profitability before deciding on the level of output desired. Here we can look at the reaction to price changes from another angle.

A firm may wish to increase output, perhaps in pursuit of economies of scale (see p. 92) or market share, but is hesitant about doing so because of increased costs. If extra workers are employed this means not only a larger wage bill but if this involves overtime a higher per unit wage cost. If lorries, boats or other commercial vehicles are used more or they carry larger loads there may be higher maintenance costs or increased breakdowns. So if a firm has an adequate profit situation it may hesitate to expand, unless a sufficient motive can be provided for it.

Price increases provide this motive. If prices rise then a firm will be more likely to receive extra profit or at least have its current level of profit guaranteed even if some diminishing returns occur. In other words, some firms may regard price increases simply as the green light to expand output rather than as an opportunity for fast profit.

We can plot supply schedules as graphs just as we did for demand. Figure 5.4 indicates a typical normal supply curve, showing that output increases as price increases, although not necessarily at the same rate. We sometimes describe the supply curve as falling to the *left* as opposed to the demand curve which falls to the right. Alternatively, it can be described as 'upward-sloping' assuming a movement from left to right.

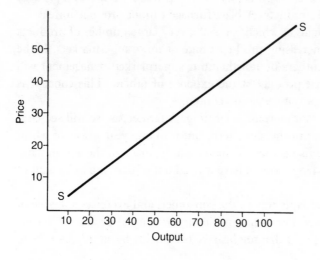

Figure 5.4 Supply curve for chocolate bars.

As in the case of the demand curve, there is an important distinction to be made between a move *along* the curve and a move *of* the curve. The supply curve measures the reaction of the market (or of an individual firm) to price changes. The horizontal axis movement varies in reaction to a change on the vertical axis. So a move *along* the curve expresses a reaction to price.

What about a movement of the whole curve (Fig. 5.5)? We saw with the demand curve that the move of the curve tended to be a result of non-price changes such as income levels or taste. In the case of the supply curve we are looking at non-price changes which will induce a firm to alter its output or the retail stock of goods. These include changes in taxation, which will change the price at which a firm will be willing to sell a given quantity of goods, or a change in costs. These will be examined later in this chapter.

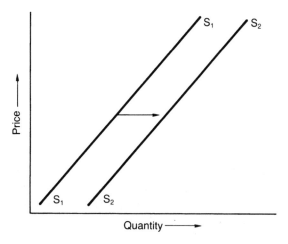

Figure 5.5 Shift of supply curve.

Exceptions to the upward-sloping supply curve

The typical supply curve, as we have seen, slopes upwards as we move to the right or downwards if we move to the left. There are, however, a few exceptions to this shape.

One type of exception arises because a higher price, apart from giving opportunity for more profit, also gives an opportunity to keep profit the same and achieve other objectives. In the 1970s an increase in oil prices encouraged some oil-producing countries to restrict output in order to maintain reserves and, at the same time, to maintain the high price levels. It is also a feature of the labour market that increasing wages (seen as the price of labour) may result in workers taking more leisure and working fewer hours, thus restricting supply of labour rather than increasing it. There are also firms which cannot adjust to changes in price easily in the short term and so have supply curves which are vertical. This introduces us to a feature known as *elasticity*, which is the subject of the next section.

Topic 5.3   Elasticity

So far we have looked at demand and supply and have seen that they can be represented by sets of figures (schedules) or more normally by curves. While we have examined the general shapes of the curves we have not looked at the *slopes* which those curves possess. In fact the slope is a very important aspect of a curve as it is a measure of the degree of change in quantity for a given move in price. This concept is known as *elasticity*.

There are three main concepts of elasticity used in economics:

1. *Price elasticity*   This is a measure of the responsiveness of demand and supply to changes in price.

2. *Income elasticity*   This is a measure of the responsiveness of the demand for goods or services to changes in the real incomes of the consumers of those goods and services.
3. *Cross-elasticity*   This is the ratio of the change in demand for good A with the change in price of good B. The price change for B is the cause of the change in demand for A.

It may be easiest to start with a look at *price* elasticity as this is perhaps the most fundamental. To illustrate this idea we can suppose that a chocolate bar is increased in price from 25p to 30p. In percentage terms this is an increase of 20 per cent (5p is 20 per cent of 25p). Now if demand falls from 100 000 a week to 80 000 a week the quantity demanded has fallen by 20 per cent—the same proportion.

> *Price elasticity* is a measure of the degree of responsiveness of demand or supply to a change in the price of a commodity or service.

However, in real life demand rarely changes as consistently as this. Economists use special names for the different types of changes found. Demand is said to be *elastic* if a 1 per cent rise in price brings about a reduction in demand for the product of more than 1 per cent; demand is *inelastic* if a 1 per cent change in price brings about less than a 1 per cent change in demand; *unit elasticity* takes place when demand and price changes are in equal proportions.

Luxury goods tend to be in relatively elastic demand while goods considered by consumers to be necessities, such as salt, follow a pattern of inelastic demand. There are many reasons for elasticity, however, and it must not be assumed that all luxuries are elastic and all necessities inelastic. More detailed reasons for the differences will be discussed shortly.

Elasticity and the curves

In general, inelastic schedules tend to produce relatively steep curves for both demand and supply, with total inelasticity ($E = 0$) producing a vertical line. This is what we would expect since a steep curve denotes a small move in quantity for a large change in price. Conversely, a relatively elastic demand or supply will have a comparatively flat curve with complete elasticity ($E = \infty$) producing a horizontal line. It might be thought therefore that unitary elasticity should be at 45° to the axes (Fig. 5.6).

However, the student needs to beware of assuming that elasticity will be the same for all range of prices. In many cases elasticity will change from comparatively inelastic supply and demand at higher prices through unitary to elastic movement. In the case of demand, a straight-line 'curve' will always have variable elasticity unless it is one of the extremes of completely elastic or inelastic demand. This feature will be explored below.

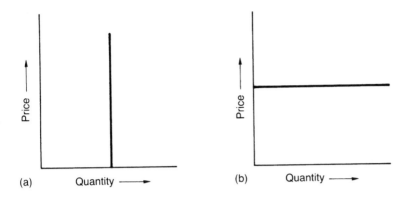

(a)   Quantity ⟶   (b)   Quantity ⟶

Figure 5.6   Elasticity of demand. (a) Inelastic. (b) Elastic.

Elasticity and numbers

It is also usual to express elasticity in a numerical form as well as in the form of graphs. The formula for doing this is simple and can be written, in the case of demand as:

$$E(D) = \frac{\%\ \text{change in quantity demanded}}{\%\ \text{change in price}}$$

where $E(D)$ is known as the *coefficient of elasticity*.

It can easily be seen that if the changes of price and quantity are the same (i.e. we have unitary elasticity) then the figure which is used to express elasticity is 1, e.g.:

$$E(D) = \frac{\text{change in quantity demanded}}{\text{change in price}} = \frac{25\%}{25\%} = 1$$

Clearly if the change in quantity consumed is greater than the percentage change in price then $E(D)$ will be > 1. If, on the other hand, the percentage change in quantity is less than that in price, E/D will be < 1. We can therefore conclude that:

If $E > 1$ elasticity is *elastic*
    $E = 1$ elasticity is *unitary*
    $E < 1$ elasticity is *inelastic*

As has already been mentioned, a demand curve is not always relatively elastic or inelastic along the whole of its length and we can demonstrate this using numerical analysis. In Fig. 5.7 we have a demand curve which is a straight line and we will look at elasticity at three points.

If price moves from 50p to 40p this represents a change in price of 10p out of an initial 50p and this represents a 20 per cent change in price. On doing this, demand increases

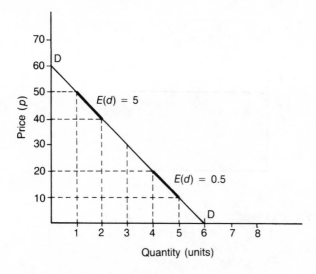

Figure 5.7   Straight-line elasticity.

from 1 unit to 2 units, an increase of 100 per cent. So elasticity of demand for the price change can be expressed as:

$$E(D) = \frac{100}{20} = 5$$

We would clearly describe this as 'elastic'. However, if we then look at the change from 20p to 10p we have a price change of 50 per cent and a demand change from 4 to 5, i.e. 25 per cent. The elasticity in this case is

$$E(D) = \frac{25}{50} = 0.5$$

This is a relatively inelastic case. It is worth noting that in both cases the *amounts* involved were the same—10p changes in price and 10 units change in demand, but the percentage changes and therefore the elasticities were totally different. In general, we can conclude that a straight-line demand curve exhibits relative elasticity above the mid-way point and relative inelasticity below this point. At the mid-way point elasticity is unitary. Figure 5.8 shows this in graphic form. There are, however, problems in measuring elasticity. (The student who wishes to explore this further is advised to refer to Advanced Study Topic 5.1.)

What determines the elasticity?

Elasticity varies from product to product for reasons which have been well documented and it might be useful for the student to read through Case Study 5.2.

Case Study 5.2—Cover Girl cosmetics

Cover Girl is the brand name for a series of cosmetics marketed in a number of countries including the UK. It is made by an American company called the Noxell Corporation. The original pricing policy of Noxell has been deliberate. They have successfully tapped into the market for budget priced cosmetics including teenagers. In many cases prices have been a quarter or less than more expensive brands. The result has been a very successful company and marketing strategy whereas the competitors lost custom in the 'bottom end' of the market and have had to rely on customers linking higher prices with high quality and prestige.

Noxell have recognized, however, that while customers will buy more products at a lower price and that the increased sales will more than compensate for the reduced income per item, there has been scope for moving a little 'up market'. Currently their prices are much more in the middle of the range, perhaps hoping to gain some increased quality credibility without losing too many sales. Customers appreciate the lower price but Noxell know that should they increase prices to a level similar to the competitors with a larger range of colours and products they might easily lose custom. The demand for a product like this is elastic. It is not a necessity (although some socialites may disagree), it is subject to change of fashion and taste and there are a large number of competitors.

In the 1990s Cover Girl has been advertised extensively in the UK; including television, with an appeal to the younger female who wishes to feel attractive without going to a lot of expense.

In Cover Girl we have a product which is being sold on price. The producers have therefore made some decisions based on what they perceive to be the price elasticity of the product.

1. What assumptions have Noxell made about the demand elasticity of Cover Girl?
2. To what extent is the existence of substitutes a key factor in determining demand elasticity for a brand of cosmetics like Cover Girl?

A useful 'field' exercise would be to undertake a price survey of brands of cosmetics in your locality—choose an item which can be readily standardized, e.g. a particular size of lipstick. Many chemist chains have a section devoted to the display stands of brands like Cover Girl and it is not too difficult to undertake a comparison.

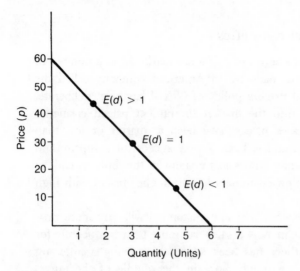

Figure 5.8 Elasticity at a point.

Elasticity is most frequently influenced by the following:

1. The availability of *substitutes*. The role of substitutes as an element in demand will be explored in the next section but it can be seen here as a matter of common observation that if there are few alternatives to the product, then the price can be increased without much movement to reduce purchases. For example, the cost of electricity can rise but, on the whole, people are 'stuck' for at least the short term with electric cookers and heating and few people have any alternative to electric lighting. Firms find that if they are geared to using electric-powered machinery, to maintain output they cannot do much about reducing consumption. Demand for electricity will thus be inelastic. Figure 5.9 illustrates the concept of substitutes.

    In contrast, however, a particular brand of chocolate bar, while it will no doubt have its share of 'addicts', will have a lot of competition from other bars—there will be many substitutes, so demand will be relatively elastic. In Case Study 5.2 we can see that a specific brand of cosmetics successfully competed with other brands on the basis of price. One of the determinants of the elasticity of demand for Cover Girl cosmetics was the degree of competition. This can be reduced by brand loyalty, which is discussed below.

2. The degree of *importance*. Even if there are few substitutes, if a product is not vital to life but is in the luxury category it may well have an elastic demand for at least part of the price range. At higher price levels, the remaining customers may well be the very rich in any case and they will tolerate a price rise if the product conveys prestige like some of Cover Girl's more 'up-market' competitors.

3. The question of *time scale*. Many products are comparatively inelastic in the short term, for both demand and supply. In the case of demand, many firms manage to produce strong brand loyalty among customers and even convince them that their

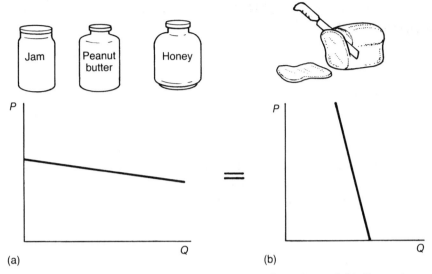

Figure 5.9 Substitutes and elasticity. Demand curves for (a) jam and (b) all spreads.

brand of soap powder, make of car or brand of beer are so superior to others that it takes a considerable increase in price to get them to look at substitutes. In the long run, however, the customer will begin to look around. At the time of writing, this is actually beginning to happen in the insurance industry, where people tend to be fairly conservative and remain with one company for motor and house insurance, quietly renewing each year. However, in the early 1990s there have been a number of large 'hikes' in premium levels for personal insurances as a result of bad claims experiences and after a few years of paying more, people begin to ask brokers for alternative quotes.

Other types of elasticity

We have so far largely looked at elasticity in terms of variations in demand as a result of changes in price. However, changes in demand can also be the result of alterations in income or in the prices of other goods. This leads us to examine not just price elasticity but also income and cross-elasticities.

Income elasticity measures changes in quantity demanded as a result of changes in the incomes of consumers and is calculated using the formula below, where Ey is the symbol for income elasticity:

$$Ey = \frac{\%\text{ change in demand}}{\%\text{ change in income}}$$

In the case of a normal good we would expect the quantity demanded to increase with income on the grounds that the higher the income of people, the more they will spend.

Thus the change would be positive and the elasticity positive in contrast to price elasticity which is really negative in nature.

Income elasticity measures the degree of change in demand as a result of a change in income.

This relationship can be expressed in the form of a graph as shown in Fig. 5.10. This type of graph is known as an *Engel curve* and measures change in demand alongside change in income. One basic assumption which is made here is that while incomes are changing, prices stay the same. The curve, in other words, measures just two variables—income and demand.

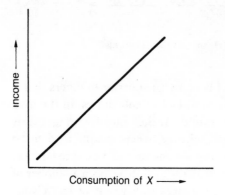

Figure 5.10   Engel curve for good *X*.

Now if we measure quantity on the horizontal axis as above, a relatively small gradient to the curve will indicate a comparatively elastic income demand, although we must remember the comments already made in connection with price elasticity, that the slope of a curve can be deceptive. The reader should refer to the following section on supply elasticity for comments on positive line graphs.

An *Engel curve* is a graph measuring change in demand against change in income.

We have already considered Giffen goods and while there is now some doubt about whether or not Giffen goods really exist, it is a useful theoretical idea. For a Giffen good, an increase in income could result in a fall in demand and a negative-sloping Engel curve.

Cross-elasticity is another version of the same idea but here we are looking at the change in demand which results from changes in the prices of other goods. For example, if we take goods which are normally consumed together or complementary goods such as cars and petrol we can see that an increase in the price of one may well produce a change in the demand for the other.

> *Cross-elasticity* describes the proportional change in the demand for a good following a change in the price of another good.

A recent example can be seen in the housing market. The demand for domestic houses has generally been regarded as relatively inelastic for small changes in price at least. However, the rise in mortgage rates in the early 1990s contributed to a dramatic slump in the demand for housing at most levels. In other words, a change in the price of one product (interest as the price of a mortgage) led to a relatively elastic response in the demand for a linked product, the domestic house. Cross-elasticity is expressed as:

$$E(x) = \frac{\% \text{ change in quantity demanded of good B}}{\% \text{ change in price of good A}}$$

Elasticity of supply

So far we have used demand elasticity to show what the concept is and how it works. We can, however, also look at elasticity for the supply of goods and services. There are a number of similarities between the two as the principles are much the same. A crucial element as far as the degree of elasticity of supply is concerned is, as with demand, the question of substitutes. If a firm has highly specialized equipment and cannot readily change to different products then the supply is likely to be inelastic. On the other hand, if a firm can easily switch from one product to another the supply will be comparatively elastic.

For example, farm products tend to have an inelastic supply, largely because it is not easy for a farmer to switch products, especially in the short term. This especially applies to changes from arable farming to livestock or vice versa. In both cases specialist equipment and skills are required and to change the type of farm system, even assuming that the land and climate are suitable, requires considerable expense and retraining. On the other hand, a firm making plastic buckets could easily switch to many other products made from plastic.

Farming is a good example of the importance of timescale in elasticity of supply. Few firms can make any changes in the immediate short term while most can make significant changes in the long term. It has taken many years of pressure and the introduction of milk quotas to move many farmers from dairying to other land uses, but some specialist heavy industry has also been reluctant to change. Inelasticity is very common in the short term but supply becomes much more elastic in the long term.

> *Elasticity of supply* describes the degree to which the supply of a good changes in response to a change in price.

As far as supply curves are concerned, the student has to take care. Total inelasticity of supply and total inelasticity of demand give curves of identical shape—vertical—while total elasticity of both supply and demand are again identical—in this case a completely horizontal line. This feature, shown in Fig. 5.11, arises because the axes are the same for both types of curve and total insensitivity to price would, for example, produce a totally vertical line.

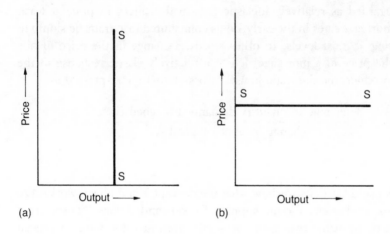

Figure 5.11   Elasticity of supply. (a) Inelastic supply. (b) Elastic supply.

On the other hand, if we look at supply curves which lie between these two extremes we find some important differences. A supply curve which is a straight line will, unlike a straight-line demand curve, show more consistent elasticity. Figure 5.12 looks at three options which illustrate this:

1. The first option is shown by supply line S_1, which commences part-way up the vertical axis, i.e. there is a minimum price below which there will be no output at all. If the price moves from A to B then there is an elasticity of:

$$E(S) = \frac{\% \text{ change in output}}{\% \text{ change in price}}$$

i.e.

$$E(S) = \frac{100}{20} = 5$$

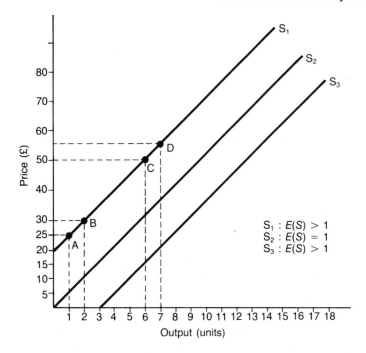

Figure 5.12   Types of supply elasticity.

If we move up the curve and look at a price move from C to D then we can calculate elasticity of:

$$E(S) = \frac{16.5}{10} = 1.65$$

Clearly as we progress up supply curve S_1, elasticity changes but it is still elastic, i.e. greater than 1.

2. S_2 is a supply curve with a slope parallel to S_1, but it begins at the origin of the graph. Any change in price must, inevitably lead to an identical percentage change in quantity. In other words, elasticity is unitary throughout the length of the 'curve'.

3. S_3 begins with a certain minimum amount of output even at a price of nil. If the elasticity is examined closely by measurement it will be seen that there are changes but $E(S)$ will always remain less than 1, i.e. elasticity will always be comparatively inelastic.

We can conclude from this that supply curves which are not totally elastic or inelastic but are straight lines will exhibit the following characteristics:

● A line which begins at the origin will exhibit unitary elasticity.
● A line which begins above the origin will always be elastic although of varying degree.

- A line which begins to the right of the origin will always be comparatively inelastic although of varying degree.

Economic rent

The term 'economic rent' is associated with inelastic supply of land, labour, capital or enterprise—i.e. the factors of production. A study of the markets for these factors will follow in Chapter 8 but for the moment it would be useful to consider the elasticity aspects.

David Ricardo stressed that 'rent' was a surplus. He confined his arguments merely to the supply of land which he regarded as being in fixed supply; but although land was in inelastic supply it could be put to alternative uses. Inferior land was at the margin of cultivation, i.e. only just worth using, and any land that was superior to this gained for the landowner a rent from the user of the land, which was the reward, not of sacrifice or service, but of ownership—merely a fortuitous income arising from the possession of something that was in inelastic supply.

Later economists realized that other factors of production or economic goods could gain a surplus or economic rent. Capital, especially in the form of new machinery, could gain temporary 'rent', termed *quasi-rent* by Alfred Marshall. Quasi-rent is produced by a sudden increase in demand that cannot be met by a sudden increase in supply and is likely to be only temporary because the passage of time will remove the special advantages.

Economic rent is now regarded as the amount which is paid to any factor of production over and above the sum that is required to keep the factor in that particular line of production in which it is engaged. Before suppliers can obtain the use of any factor of production, they must pay at least as much as the factor could earn in any suitable alternative employment. This is known as *transfer cost*.

These two concepts are illustrated in Fig. 5.13, using labour as the sample factor used. Let us suppose that two people have a hobby of making pottery. They make some vessels in their spare time for pleasure and do not expect any payment. In time, however, a demand for their products is apparent and they look around for someone to help them. However, in a business it is normal for workers to want to be paid, so they have to pay a small wage to employ another potter. This wage is the transfer cost—that which is just enough to persuade another person to join the pottery.

> *Economic rent* is the amount paid to a factor of production over and above that which is required to keep the factor in that line of production.

As success follows success, other potters are invited to join but as more potters are needed an increasingly high wage is required to persuade the latest potter to join the

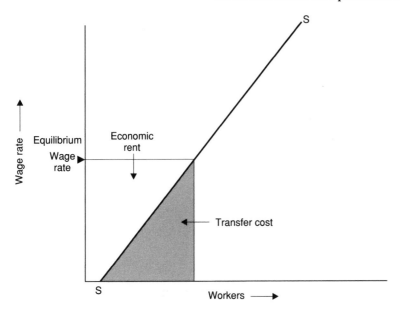

Figure 5.13 Economic rent and transfer costs.

firm. This is because we are now having to recruit from increasingly less enthusiastic potters. If each person will work for their transfer cost then the supply curve will follow S–S in Fig. 5.13.

The area underneath the supply curve and below the wage of the last person employed represents the transfer cost of the operation. If this last person is employed at the wage which is equal to the average revenue gained for their work, then we have an equilibrium situation (see Chapter 6). However, it will be necessary in all probability to pay all workers the same as the last person, and so all except that last person will have earnings over and above the transfer costs—i.e. economic rent.

> *Transfer cost* is the payment necessary to persuade any factor of production to move to a particular use. It is normally equivalent to the best earnings which could be obtained elsewhere.

The degree to which any payment to a factor is economic rent or transfer earnings is largely determined by the slope of the supply curve and its point of commencement, which will reflect a level of elasticity. If the supply curve for a type of land, for example, is represented by the supply curve S(A) in Fig. 5.14, which is relatively inelastic and has a steep slope, we can see that transfer earnings are relatively small and most of the price is represented by economic rent. A relatively elastic supply curve S(B) commencing part of the way up the vertical axis would have a much larger area representing transfer earnings.

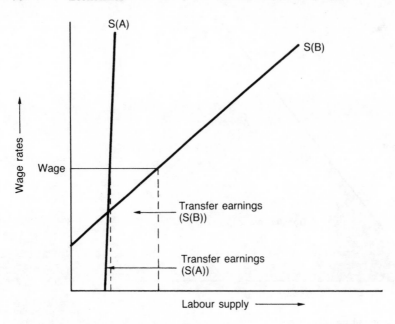

Figure 5.14 Elasticity and transfer earnings.

This introduction to elasticity is by no means exhaustive but it will soon become clear that it is of fundamental importance to the subject of economics. In later chapters we will be exploring its role in influencing taxation, how it is the crucial factor in deciding whether or not a supply or demand shift influences revenue, and how it influences wages and other factor rewards.

Topic 5.4   Behind the demand curve

So far we have examined briefly the way consumers behave in adjusting the level of their purchases to changes in price and have seen how the degree of reaction can vary from product to product according to their elasticity of demand. In this section we delve a little deeper into the ideas behind the downward-sloping demand curve and the forces which determine both individual and market demand.

Income and substitution effects

We have seen that if the price of a commodity falls then, with a few exceptions, demand will increase. Conversely, if the price rises then demand will normally fall. Consumers react to price changes by making a choice or a series of choices based on how the price changes influence them. Economists see two main effects on the consumer—the *income effect* and the *substitution effect*.

The term *income effect* is used to describe the way in which a price change for a commodity or service, especially if it is an important part of a household's regular purchases, has an effect on the net income available to spend on other things. So if the price of petrol rises we have less income to spend on chocolates, drinks, clothes, etc. because we are having to spend more on petrol which is needed to get us to work each day, take us to the theatre, etc. Being a little poorer as a result of the price rise we might seek to alter our spending by reducing our consumption either of the petrol which caused the problem or of other commodities.

What has happened is that our *real* income has fallen. Our nominal or money income is unchanged by price fluctuations but the selection of goods which the money can buy has become more restricted.

The *substitution effect* looks at our ability to react to the rise in price of one commodity by substituting others. So if petrol prices rise could we not buy a bicycle and travel by that means some of the time? If the price of beef decreases we might decide to buy more of that and less ham or chicken. The budget line, discussed in Chapter 3, is a useful tool to help analyse substitution, at least where only two products are concerned.

When the demand curve falls to the right we are looking at the result of two influences—a change in net income resulting in consumers changing the amounts purchased (including the commodity which has been altered in price) and a decision by consumers to substitute other goods which might do the job almost as well. Clearly the degree to which either effect influences the shape of the demand curve for a product will depend on how essential it is for consumers and what substitutes are available. This is largely expressed through elasticity as explored in the previous section—the more essential a commodity and the fewer the substitutes, the less influence both income and substitution effects will have on the demand for that product, and demand will be described as relatively inelastic.

The *income effect* describes the reduction or increase in net income as a result of a rise or fall in the price of a good.
The *substitution effect* describes the way in which consumers substitute one good for another in reaction to a price change.

More on utility

In Chapter 2 we introduced the concept of utility including the idea that we can speak of the *total* utility available in the consumption of a commodity and the *marginal* utility from the consumption of the last unit.

The idea of marginal utility is very important in our exploration of what lies behind the demand curve and how it is formed. We can recall that if an individual consumes increasing amounts of a good or service then while the total utility from the consumption will increase, the utility of each additional unit will decrease as more is consumed. It may even become negative.

Consider the graphs in Figs. 5.15 and 5.16. In Fig. 5.15, a consumer purchases (during one evening session) successive pints of bitter. It is a hot night just after summer exams. The student is thirsty so the first pint gives a lot of utility. In Fig. 5.15 we measure the total amount of utility gained from the whole evening's drinking, pint by pint. Utility is not really a measurable concept but economists use the term 'utils' as a means of producing some precision for tables and graphs.

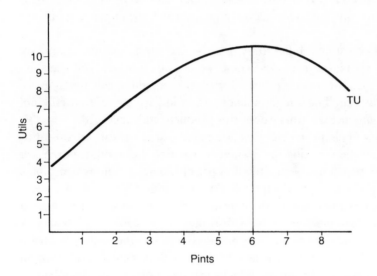

Figure 5.15   Total utility of beer consumption.

Observe that the total utility graph rises steeply and then, after a while, flattens off and even begins to fall. In other words, as a drinker buys more pints the total satisfaction obtained from the drinking session will increase but at a rate which is slowing down, and there will come a point when our student drinker feels that he has gone 'a pint too far'. (His friends may have felt that he reached the limit earlier, but we are measuring utility to the individual consumer here.)

The marginal utility curve looks at this on a pint-by-pint basis and measures the utility of each pint in turn. So the first pint gives a high degree of satisfaction (our drinker is dying of thirst, remember), the second one a little less but still a high amount of pleasure and yet each successive pint yields less and less satisfaction or utility. In the end the 'pint too many' is bought and utility is so low it is now zero. Continued consumption will lead to negative utility, probably indicated by loss of friends, being thrown out of the bar and a hangover the next day!

Notice that the point where the marginal utility curve cuts the horizontal axis of Fig. 5.16 is the same level of consumption as the point where the total utility curve begins to fall. In other words, once satisfaction from the consumption of a commodity reaches the

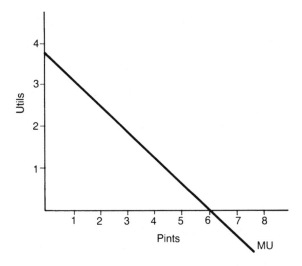

Figure 5.16 Marginal utility of beer consumption.

point where marginal utility is zero or negative then total utility, while it may still be positive, is in fact falling.

We can now look again at the trade-off game which all consumers play. Not only are we juggling with limited funds with which to buy the goods and services we need, we are also involved in balancing up the satisfaction or utility to be gained from them. In general, we can say that the law of diminishing marginal utility will operate so that we arrange our purchases to produce an equilibrium or balance. This equilibrium point will be reached when the marginal utility of the goods and services we buy is equal; in shorthand, when:

Marginal utility   = Marginal utility = Marginal utility = Marginal utility
of good A   of good B   of good C   of good D

Assuming that we have £1 left to spend from our weekly income, we will have reached equilibrium if in spending it we receive equal satisfaction from all purchases. If our choice is between a video hire and a four-pack of chocolate and we have eaten well but are short of entertainment for the night we will probably opt for the video hire, as spending the £1 on this will yield more satisfaction than spending it on chocolate.

If we look at any individual product we will find that we will consume units of it to the point where the amount of satisfaction per £1 spent on that good is the same as the satisfaction per £1 on other goods. In other words we can re-express our shorthand equilibrium statement as:

$$\frac{\text{MU of good A}}{\text{Price of A}} = \frac{\text{MU of good B}}{\text{Price of B}} = \frac{\text{MU of good C}}{\text{Price of C}}$$

So we can state that at the equilibrium point, the marginal utility of each commodity/ service which is consumed, as a ratio of its price, is equal to each other commodity/ service. Each £1 or even each 1p spent will yield the same utility whatever item from our range of possible purchases we choose to buy.

Clearly if there is a price change in any good it will alter the balance and produce a change in purchasing behaviour. So if the price of A falls we will purchase more of A until its marginal utility falls to the old ratio. Looked at another way, if we are to consume more of a product, its price has to fall.

Indifference curves and the law of substitution

We are now going to look at the question of utility from a different viewpoint. It must be stated at the outset that the material presented in this section is not required in all syllabuses of 'A' level or equivalent. Nevertheless, it is a useful piece of analysis and a simple and basic treatment is worth including even in an introductory textbook such as this. Readers who are using this book as part of an examination course should check whether indifference curves are required and, if so, the next few pages will be relevant. If your syllabus does not require this material you are advised to pass on to the next section.

One important difference between indifference curves and marginal utility theory outlined above is that the latter has a *cardinal* approach while indifference curves approach utility from an *ordinal* viewpoint. 'Cardinal' numbers carry no implications of order (1,2,3, etc.) whereas 'ordinal' numbers indicate order or priority (1st, 2nd, etc.). In using the idea of the 'util' we are, as we have seen, attempting to ascribe a measure of objective value to utility using cardinal numbers. In turning to indifference curves we begin to see utility in terms of order and comparison between the satisfaction to be gained from different products or services.

In Chapter 3 the *indifference curve* was introduced as a graph showing combinations of two goods which yield the same total utility to the consumer. This is not to be confused with the budget line which also looks at two goods. The budget line examines combinations which can be obtained for the same outlay and so looks at prices while indifference curves consider utility and each curve represents a possible combination of the two goods which will yield the same level of satisfaction or utility.

Consider Fig. 5.17 (see p.79). As we move along the indifference curve the total utility is the same but the combination of videos and chocolate bars varies. At position A we are spending many hours at the video hire shop but not much time at the sweetshop. At B the position is reversed but the total satisfaction obtained is identical.

Normally we plot indifference curves in groups representing ever higher levels of utility. These are known as indifference 'maps'. Figure 5.18 (p. 80) adds further possible curves to Fig. 5.17.

Assuming that consumers react rationally (i.e. they try to choose combinations of goods/services which yield the greatest satisfaction) then indifference curves have certain important characteristics:

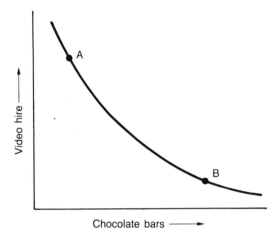

Figure 5.17   Indifference curve.

1. The curve *slopes downwards* because if the level of utility is constant then the only way we can increase consumption of, say, chocolate bars is to reduce the number of hirings of videos.

2. The curve is *convex to the origin* of the graph––in other words, it flattens out as we move right or steepens as we move left. This is based on the *law of diminishing marginal rate of substitution*. This takes point 1 above a stage further and says that to keep utility constant, if a consumer wishes to obtain successive amounts of one good then this can only occur by sacrificing diminishing amounts of the other. At point A in Fig. 5.18 we are keen to get more chocolate and will give up a number of video hirings to buy some extra chocolate; but at point B we have ample chocolate and to obtain more we will not be too keen to surrender much video hire at all.

3. In an indifference map, *the curves never cross*. This rests on simple logic once we make the assumption that successive curves, moving to the right, offer increasing levels of utility. If in Fig. 5.18 there were a curve linking A and C then both point A and point C would give us equal satisfaction; yet at the same time A and B would also give equal satisfaction. Yet point B offers more of both video hire and chocolate than C. Hence crossing indifference curves are illogical.

For the reader who is interested in following up the analysis on this subject the Advanced Study Topic 5.2 points to the combination of indifference curves and budget lines and how price changes alter the indifference curve on which the consumer operates.

Consumer surplus

We have been looking at the concept of utility or satisfaction and seeing how consumers attempt to obtain some equilibrium or state of balance in their consumption patterns as far as utility is concerned. We have also seen that an equilibrium of utility for the consumer revolves around a ratio between utility and price.

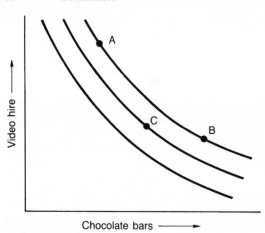

Figure 5.18   Indifference curve map.

However, the market price of a product or a service may be a lot less than that which would reflect the utility of most of the units bought. In fact according to the law of diminishing marginal utility the more of a commodity is purchased, the lower the utility. The price which the consumer will be prepared to pay is a reflection of the utility of the last unit bought. If the price is lower then the consumer will buy more units and, if it is higher, fewer. Therefore it must follow that the price paid reflects the satisfaction from the final unit bought.

Now if we assume that the consumer buys more than one unit, all but the last unit are bought at a price less than that which reflects the amount of utility gained. This can be illustrated in Fig. 5.19.

The equilibrium price in the graph is at P and at this price the amount purchased is Q. However, all units bought before Q gave a utility higher than Q and the area shaded below the demand curve above P represents this *consumer surplus*.

> *Consumer surplus* is the utility gained by consumers as a result of the equilibrium price of a product being below that which they would be prepared to pay.

Topic 5.5   Changes in demand

Case Study 5.3 illustrates a feature of demand which was touched on early in this chapter—the difference between movement *along* a curve and movement *of* the curve. The demand curve measures relationships between the amount of any good or service which consumers wish to consume and the price they are being asked to pay. Reduce the price and, for a normal good, the quantity demanded will increase.

Case Study 5.3—Interest rates and mortgages

THE latest reduction in interest rates is not a source of unambiguous pleasure for the building societies and their customers.

Cheaper mortgages are certainly welcome – the battered housing market needs all the encouragement it can get – but the accompanying cut in investment rates is another blow for savers whose incomes have fallen by two-thirds over the past two years.

However, the dire state of the housing market continues to dominate the news, with new figures from the Council of Mortgage Lenders confirming the severity of the slump.

According to the CML, 68,540 homes were repossessed by mortgage lenders last year. But this dreadful figure was an improvement on 1991's record 75,540, and was achieved in the teeth of rising unemployment and falling house prices.

The mortgage lenders have learned some bitter lessons from this housing crisis and are now committing huge resources to the management of arrears. This is keeping more people in their homes, but it is also increasing the number of borrowers who are making reduced repayments which do not cover the cost of their mortgage. Such individuals are slipping ever further into long-term debt, prompting housing charity Shelter to argue that 'the crisis has been postponed, not solved'.

The latest cut in interest rates has given a noticeably competitive edge to the centralised lenders' mortgages, with the Household Mortgage Corporation undercutting the building societies for the first time since 1988. HMC's standard mortgage rate will be 7.69 per cent from 1 April. The building societies' new standard rate is 7.99 per cent, although they offer a range of discounts to first-time buyers and larger borrowers.

Any more interest rate reductions will tilt the balance of advantage further away from the building societies, according to Jeff Wagland, HMC's spokesman. 'The feeling is that the building societies have basically hit rock bottom. They cannot afford to go much lower, while we are in a position of being able to chase rates down.'

Source: *Observer*, 31 January 1993

This newspaper extract deals with the reduction in interest rates by the government in order to stimulate the economy. Interest rates and the mechanisms used to bring about such a change are explored in Chapters 11 and 12. In the context of this section the reader might like to consider the following:

1. What types of business are likely to benefit from the reduction in interest rates?
2. How will individuals benefit?
3. What would be the effect of the interest rate reduction on demand for the following:
   (a) New houses
   (b) New cars
   (c) Offices
   (d) Machinery?

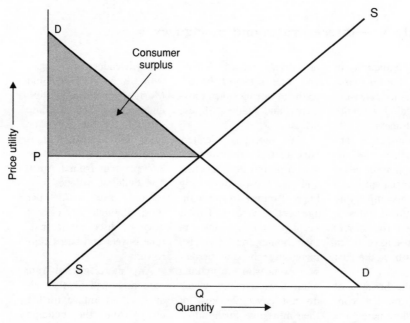

Figure 5.19 Consumer surplus.

However, many other things can affect demand even if prices stay the same. A factor other than price causes the demand curve to shift in its entirety, usually keeping the same slope and elasticity characteristics. An increase in the demand (at the existing price) will cause the curve to move to the right and a reduction in demand will result in a shift to the left.

What factors produce these shifts? There is a large number but to simplify matters we will highlight the most important ones:

1. *Interest rates*   Reference again to Case Study 5.3 suggests that a reduction in rates makes a lot of people very happy. The reason? Whether one likes it on moral grounds or not, many of the more expensive goods ('high-ticket items' as sales people like to call them) are not bought by cash, cheque or cash card but by some form of loan. This might be on-the-spot hire-purchase arranged by the shop, lease (most business equipment is obtained this way) or by a personal loan from a bank or building society. For house purchase or an expensive extension it is normal for most people to use a loan which is 'secured' on the property, and this is known as a mortgage. Sometimes mortgage money is also used for other expensive items. Clearly, this being the case, a reduction in interest rates is going to cause a shift of the demand curves to the right for many expensive items (Fig. 5.20). An increase in interest rates, as happened in the UK in 1990–91, will make borrowing more expensive and reduce general demand (Fig. 5.21). In many respects changes in interest rates can be regarded as a special case of the influence of complementary

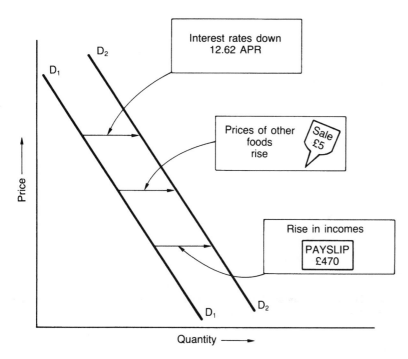

Figure 5.20   What moves the demand curve to the right?

goods since the availability of loan money is a complementary product to the high-ticket goods being bought.

2. *Prices of other goods*   A loan is a 'product' which has a price (called 'interest') and as many goods are bought with the use of a loan the level of interest rates, i.e. the price of the loan, influences the demand for larger goods from washing machines to houses. We have already seen how elasticity of demand can be influenced by other goods in cross-elasticity, and so it is easy to see how the effect of a price change for one product has an effect on the demand for another.

Substitutes influence demand on each other, so that if tea is regarded as a substitute for coffee, then an increase in the price of coffee, perhaps as a result of a poor harvest, would be expected to increase the demand for tea, shown by a rightward shift in the demand curve (see Fig. 5.22). Of course, not all coffee drinkers will be prepared to take to tea, and this is where demand elasticity plays a part in influencing the degree to which the price of one good affects the demand for another.

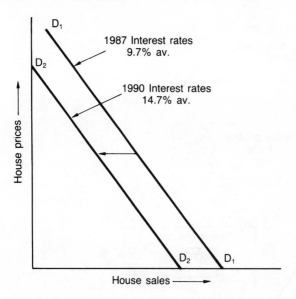

Figure 5.21   Interest rates and demand for houses. Interest rates quoted are average money market rates for year. (*Source: Barclays Bank Economic Review* (3rd Quarter 1993.)

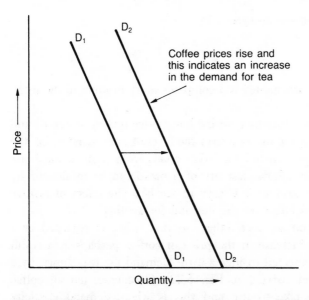

Figure 5.22   Demand changes for tea in response to coffee price changes.

Figure 5.22 shows how, assuming that there is a degree of substitution between tea and coffee, the demand curve for tea would shift if there were a significant and prolonged increase in the price of coffee. Later in this chapter we will see how this shift would in turn influence the price of tea.

Complementary products would influence each other in the same direction. A reduction in petrol prices is likely to produce not only an increase in the quantity of petrol in demand (by a move *along* the demand curve) but will also shift the demand curve for cars, especially those with high fuel consumptions, to the right.

3. *Changes in income levels*   If there is a change in incomes in real terms then there will be more or less money available to spend. A person may consider that his or her money income is of great importance, but what is vitally important in economics is the income in *real* terms, i.e. what that money income will buy in terms of goods and services. If wages lag behind prices, then demand for various goods will decline.

   Demand is very dependent on marginal utility, as we have seen, and it can be dangerous to make generalized statements about the effect of income changes on certain types of goods. However, it is generally accepted that a change in real income will have the greatest effect on goods and services which are considered to be in the luxury category. Demand for essential foods such as potatoes, bread or salt remains relatively static, but for expensive furniture or cars it is subject to the general level of income. It is these items that have suffered most in the recent recession.

4. *Changes in income distribution*   Apart from changes in income levels in general there can be changes in the distribution of income and wealth. Although we live in a society described as 'democratic', it is not egalitarian—in other words, there are wide variations in wealth and income. Modern governments, as a matter of political or ethical principles, tend to favour redistribution of income and, in some cases, wealth. Any redistribution of the means of turning wants and needs into effective demand is likely to produce shifts in demand for goods. In some cases, such as luxury items, demand will increase, i.e. the demand curve will move to the right. However, in the case of basic food products which may be 'inferior' goods, the curve may move leftward as more people feel that they can change to more expensive commodities.

5. *Taste and fashion*   One common factor which can produce changes in the position of a demand curve is the public's perception of the product concerned. Tastes, fashions and interest change over time. The clothing trade is especially subject to this, which explains why clothes' shops feature so highly in the 'sales'—there are usually a number of items of stock which have gone out of fashion—and, in effect, the demand curve for last year's trend has shifted significantly to the left and prices need to be reduced. Advertising plays a large part in influencing demand and a vigorous advertising and publicity campaign can have a major effect on the desire for a product.

6. *Other factors* which may produce a demand curve shift include social changes such as the current interest in keep-fit equipment and sports centres, transport links to sources of a product such as a ski resort, and the weather, which especially influences the attendance figures at summer sporting fixtures and demand for weather-related goods such as umbrellas and foreign holidays. Changes in the distribution and structure of the population of a country will influence demand, so that the ageing of most European populations currently being witnessed is increasing demand for retirement homes and mobility products that are currently growth industries.

Religious beliefs have also influenced demand. The relaxation of the Roman Catholic ban on meat eating on Fridays is an often-quoted example of this in its effect on fish and meat consumption in predominantly Catholic countries. The growth of vegetarianism and concern over environmental issues are currently moving the demand curves for a number of products.

Finally, demand may be temporarily shifted as a result of speculation (see p. 58). This may be associated with the financial markets which will be explored in Chapter 12 but can also occur with raw materials and 'commodities' such as coffee, tin or grain. Some of the major increases in prices have been blamed on speculators, although they have not always been the sole culprits.

Topic 5.6   Behind the supply curve

We have seen that the typical supply curve rises as price increases, and we have explained this in terms of producers expecting higher profits as prices rise. Rising prices do indeed encourage manufacturers to produce more and retailers and the service industries to seek more sales. It is, however, not as simple as that!

In Chapter 7 we will look at the growth of firms and consider what is their optimum size. Here we need to examine why firms seek to increase output and sales as prices rise. In other words, why do we get a supply curve which is positive, rising to the right rather than falling like the negative demand curve? It is worth recalling that the supply curve represents the change in output relating to changes in price. So the questions we need to answer relate to this reaction.

Before we consider some of these questions it is important to define the timescales with which we are concerned. Economists usually refer to the *short run* (or short term) and *long run* (or long term) as very different time considerations. The short run is defined as the time period in which at least one of the factors of production is fixed; the long run is the period when all factors are variable. Sometimes we also refer to the very short term or *immediate* term in which all factors are fixed. At the other end of the scale the long run can get into the realm when not only can all factors be changed but technology can also alter. We have to leave to theologians consideration of the implications of the infinite term, but Keynes once commented that in the ultimate long run we are all dead!

What happens when output increases?

It may seem obvious that if a firm manufacturing, say, motorcycles is making a fair profit that it will be in its interests to increase output. After all, if we produce more then the rent and other overheads can be spread over more units of output. This may be true for a time, but economists recognize an important effect of short-term growth—the principle of *diminishing marginal returns*, sometimes known as diminishing marginal product. Let us assume that our motorcycle firm has a fixed amount of space and equipment in the short term and can increase output only by increasing the number of workers. What will happen?

Output will certainly increase unless they all take the opportunity to discuss football rather than spark plug performance, and if there is unused capacity in the equipment and space then the average output per worker may well increase. There will, in any case, be advantages in teamwork and specialization of labour. However, in due course as the number of workers increases so the extra output per worker will fall. Table 5.1 and Fig. 5.23 illustrate this. It should be remembered that the word 'marginal' refers to the last unit of a factor which is used. In this case the term 'marginal returns' refers to the extra output achieved as a result of employing the last worker taken on.

Table 5.1 Total, average and marginal product

Workers employed	Output: total (units)	Average	Marginal
		Units/worker	
0	0	0	0
1	4	4	4
2	10	5	6
3	15	5	5
4	19	4.75	4
5	22	4.4	3
6	24	4	2
7	25	3.4	1
8	24	3.0	−0.4

In Table 5.1 we can see how with a one-at-a-time increase in workers three things happen to output:

1. Total output increases but from the third worker onwards the increase begins to level out. It may even begin to decline eventually if the number of workers interferes with output. Figure 5.24 illustrates the changes in total output.
2. At the same time, the average output per worker increases at first and then declines.
3. Marginal output, i.e. the output from the last worker taken on, rises steeply at first and then enters into a long decline. The marginal output of each successive worker changes the average. For example, if the marginal is below the average so far then the new average will be lower. Successive workers contribute less and less and the last one may do little more than make the tea or fetch the lunches from the chip shop.

Notice in Fig. 5.24 that the curve which represents diminishing marginal returns cuts the average returns curve at its maximum value. In other words, as long as marginal returns (or marginal product) is at a higher level than average returns per worker it will pull up the average returns, but as soon as marginal returns falls below the average returns level the latter begins to fall. In other words, in the short term taking on

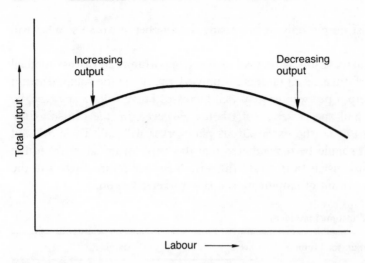

Figure 5.23   Short-term total output changes.

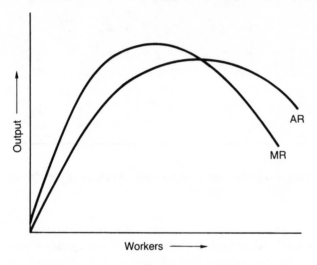

Figure 5.24   Short-term returns on labour inputs.

additional workers will lead to greater output but after a while the output per worker will begin to fall.

Now suppose that this firm decides, as Honda did some years ago, to enter the car market also. Some workers are now absorbed into the car production unit. How does the firm decide on output levels for both cars and motorcycles? To consider this we need to refer to the production possibility curve, first discussed in Chapter 3 (see Fig. 5.25).

The firm has a choice of product but if it is at maximum efficiency the firm holds a position on the curve and it can only increase the output of, say, cars by taking workers off the motorcycle line. The shape of the curve is an indication of the operation of diminishing marginal returns.

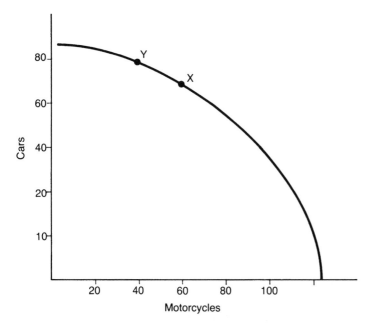

Figure 5.25   Production possibility curve: output of vehicles/week.

To demonstrate this we can look at position X. At this point the firm is producing 70 cars and 60 motorcycles. If the management decide to increase the output of cars it moves to position Y. However, while this increases car output by 10 it is at the expense of 20 motorcycles. As we move further up the curve, the increase in car production becomes successively smaller and the number of motorcycles 'traded off' to enable us to do this becomes larger. In terms of sacrifice of motorcycles, there is diminishing returns.

> *Diminishing marginal returns* refers to the observed feature that increasing the units of any factor of production while other factors stay unchanged will eventually produce a decrease in the output of the marginal unit.

So far, we have looked at output but we can translate this into costs and see what happens to costs if output is increased. Figure 5.26 shows the short-term cost situation which is a mirror image of the diminishing returns situation in Fig. 5.24. The marginal costs, i.e. costs of producing the additional unit, while below-average costs, will bring those average costs down, but once they rise above the AC line will induce an increase in average costs.

This is a vital part of the explanation of costs, output and pricing and rests on a very simple feature. Suppose that a firm of car manufacturers finds that its current output

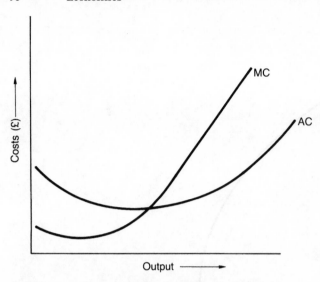

Figure 5.26 Short-term costs. Average and marginal costs.

level gives average costs of £4000 per vehicle and marginal costs of £3500. Will it want to increase output? Almost certainly, since an extra car will cost about £500 less than average to produce. As a result of the addition of this extra car, average costs will fall because the latest addition to stock costs less than average. Let us use the figures to show this assuming that with average costs at £4000 the number of cars produced is 1000:

$$\text{Average costs} = \frac{\text{Total costs}}{\text{Number of vehicles}}$$

$$AC = \frac{TC}{N} = \frac{4\,000\,000}{1000} = £4000$$

Now if we produce an extra car with a marginal cost of £3500 the figures are:

$$AC = \frac{400\,000 + 3500}{1001} = \frac{4\,003\,500}{1001} = £3999$$

As long as MC < AC then average costs will fall and it will be worth the firm's while to increase output. Once MC > AC then average costs will begin to rise. As AC represents total costs per unit, a rise in AC means a lower profit if prices stay unchanged.

> *Marginal costs* are those costs involved in employing the last, or marginal, unit of a factor of production.

To see why these curves reflect the earlier analysis of changes in output per worker we need to consider what will happen in real life. An insurance broker employs sales people who contact clients to sell investments and other products. They are paid by salary.

One or two sales people get on well together and productivity increases but a third sometimes puts a 'spanner in the works' by contacting another sales person's clients and a fourth is a good talker, resulting in a lot of chatting in the office over coffee. In other words, there is diminishing returns as increasing sales reps compete for a finite client bank, a limited office space and two computers!

In terms of costs, if they are all paid a salary and the rent and other overheads stay the same, then costs will increase per sale. The last (marginal) sales person will make few sales and may well prevent others making sales, yet will still claim the same salary as the others.

The conclusion we can come to is that as output increases in the short term both average and marginal costs may well initially fall, but at some point marginal costs will rise and eventually induce a rise in average costs. This means that if a firm is to increase output it will need to have a higher price available in order to make such expansion viable. This will especially be the case in the perfect market when the firm has no influence on prices. It will have to adjust output to price without the chance to increase prices on its own initiative in order to cover extra costs.

In the very short term, which can be just a few days in some cases or a month if staff are on that length of notice, there is likely to be a chance to increase output and increase profits only if there is spare capacity in the firm. If workers, for example, are working to full capacity on a 40-hour week the only way output can be increased for, say, a special order, is by working overtime and this is traditionally paid at 'time and a half'. Thus unit costs increase.

However, there may be some cost savings even in a situation like this. In the short term it may well be that there is a fixed amount of equipment and 'plant', including the factory or office. Commercial property is usually rented and equipment leased, so there may well be outgoings which will be the same whatever the level of output. These, together with administrative staff salaries and certain other items, are known as *fixed costs*.

The costs which increase as output increases, such as raw material and energy costs, are known as *variable costs*. Whenever output increases variable costs will rise but fixed costs, while the same in total, will fall when measured as a cost per unit.

Fixed costs are those costs which do not change with the level of output.
Variable costs are those costs which do vary with level of output.

Now if a firm finds that fixed costs are a major proportion of costs, as in most service industries, increasing output may well produce initial cost savings until the factory space is fully occupied and the equipment used to maximum capacity. A firm in this position may well seek to increase output if prices rise because it will see the chance to increase profit as average costs fall (Fig. 5.27).

So far, we have looked at the short term, the period in which at least one factor of production is fixed. However, firms will also consider the longer-term implications of price and cost changes. In the long term the average cost (AC) curve is made up of a series of short-term AC curves. Each of these shorter-term curves represents a different stage of growth as different factors of production are changed to enable the firm to increase output.

One important feature of long-term growth is that as factor inputs are increased and the scale of operation also increased, so long-term costs begin initially to fall before rising again. The fall in average costs is known as *economies of scale* and the subsequent increase as *diseconomies of scale*. To increase scale means to increase all factor inputs to some extent at least and so these economies cannot be present in the short term.

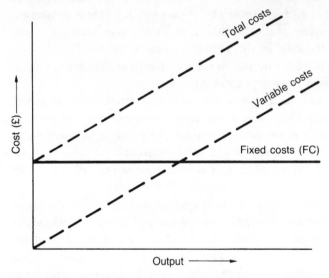

Figure 5.27 Types of cost.

> *Economies of scale* are those reductions in cost which occur in the long term as a result of increasing the level of all inputs.

Economies of scale are associated with the appearance of *increasing returns to scale*. The latter refers to the observation that as the scale of output increases so output may increase by a greater proportion than the increase in inputs. For example, suppose a farmer drains some adjacent fenland, buys some cows and employs a worker to look after them. The total increase in costs is 6 per cent of the farm's costs. Now if the output in milk and butter is 10 per cent of revenue, the farmer will be enjoying *increasing returns to scale*. If the milk and other dairy products increase only by 2 per cent, on the other hand, the farmer will experience *decreasing returns to scale* (Fig. 5.28).

> *Returns to scale* are the changes in physical output resulting in the long term from an increase in the input of all factors.

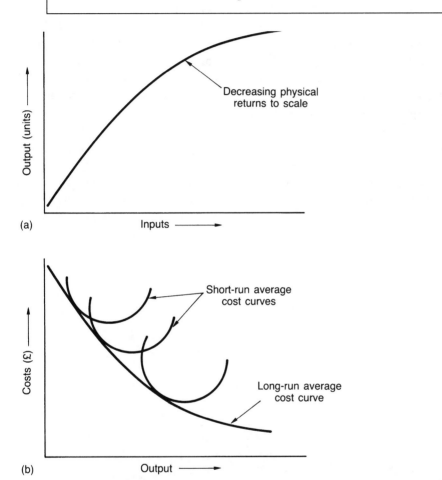

Figure 5.28   Returns to scale and costs. (a) Output—units. (b) Costs (£).

Costs and the supply curve

We have seen that if prices increase firms will be encouraged to increase output either as a result of an opportunity to increase profit or because only a price rise will enable them to cover the increased costs of the extra output. The supply curve demonstrates the levels of output at which the firm will be prepared to operate for a specific range of prices. How is this supply curve derived?

Suppose we have a baker's shop which has a special line in currant buns. These prove popular and sell for 20p each. If they cost 15p to produce the baker makes 5p or 25 per cent profit out of the selling price. The buns, we will suppose, are baked in trays which hold 30—so 30 is effectively the productive unit. Now let us suppose that the baker decides to increase the output of buns from 300 to 330. The extra cost involved is the variable cost of the flour, etc., heating of the oven and perhaps a reduction in earnings because the baker has to reduce output of bread to accommodate buns.

If the extra cost per tray of buns is less than 20p per bun it will pay the baker to bake more buns. But if the cost rises above 20p then the last tray will not benefit the baker at all—in fact he or she will make a loss. At this point, only if the price of current buns in local shops rises to a point above the marginal cost of the tray will our baker increase output and then increase prices in turn and cover the additional costs. Thus we can see that the supply curve will in fact mirror the marginal cost curve.

It will not normally be the shape of the whole MC curve because there will be a certain minimum price known as *break-even point* below which income will be less than total costs, and while firms may produce at that level and price for a short time, they cannot do so for long, as seen in Case Study 5.4. The marginal cost curve above this line will be the supply curve for that product because, at each point on that line, the income receivable at the successively higher price levels will be just sufficient to make each extra unit worth producing (Fig. 5.29).

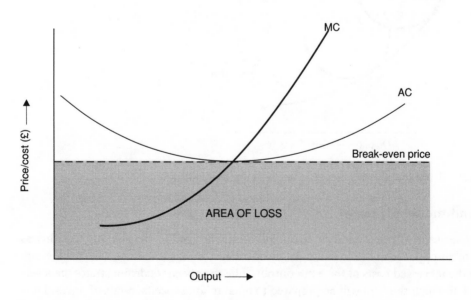

Figure 5.29 Marginal cost pricing and the supply curve.

Firm and industry supply

We have tended in illustrations to use the example of firms. In fact, supply curves can be compiled for firms of all sizes and for whole industries. The supply schedule for a whole industry simply consists of the addition of all the individual firms' supply schedules. No two firms are exactly the same. Some, probably most, will rent their factories or offices but some will own the freehold and their overhead costs will be lower. There will be differences in locational advantages and disadvantages which may be crucial for some industries but, to some extent, affect most firms. This additional feature is illustrated in Fig. 5.30.

Case Study 5.4 —When business is no longer fun!

Price cutting by computer manufacturer Apple has forced the closure of a Diss company with the loss of six jobs and "consolidation" has led to a further eight redundancies at a company at Loddon.

Apple's 25pc price reduction meant that stock held by Diss Computers had to be substantially written down. As a result, directors Mike Milbourne and Andrew Chapel felt a break-even turnover was unlikely to be achieved.

This followed bad trading in September and October despite ending the year in profit in July.

Administrative receivers Andrew Conquest and Geoffrey Harrison were appointed by the Midland Bank following a request from the two directors.

Six sales and support staff based at the company's premises in St Nicholas Street have lost their jobs, while Mr Milbourne and Mr Chapel have been taken on in a sales role by Ipswich-based Getech, which acquired the stock and goodwill for an undisclosed sum.

At Loddon, eight workers have been made redundant at Mussett Engineering.

The company has consolidated two divisions into one set of premises to cut down on overheads.

Source: Extract from *Eastern Daily Press*, 9 December 1992

A look at the article above illustrates at a very practical level the effect of a price reduction on the output in the computer industry. Here a firm has had to close with job losses as a result of a price reduction imposed from outside.

1. What is the significance of the 'break-even' turnover in the decision to cease trading?
2. Are there any substitute products which Diss Computers might have switched to instead of going into receivership?

It should not be assumed that the number of firms in an industry is fixed. Not only will rising prices encourage existing producers or distributors to increase output and sales but other firms will be encouraged to enter that industry either by starting up from scratch or by switching from less profitable lines.

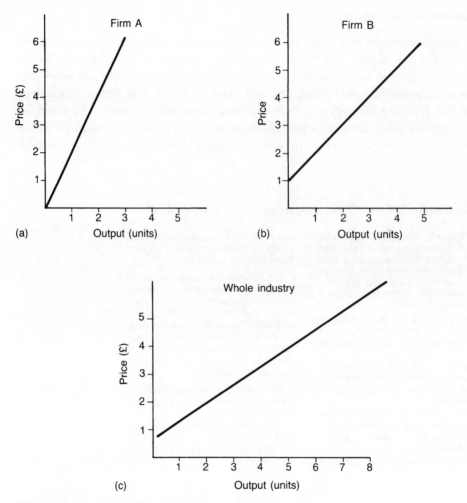

Figure 5.30 Deriving industry supply curves.

A final feature of supply worth noting is that some products are in *joint supply*. In this case they tend to be produced together, usually with one being a by-product of the other. In general, one product is the main profit earner and the other is marketed because it is more profitable to sell it than to dispose of it as waste. Examples include milk, a main profit earner, and the by-product of slurry which is a valuable fertilizer or hydroelectric power and control of water supply. We have already come across the idea of positive externalities which are a type of joint product, albeit one which does not enter the market.

Topic 5.7   Changes in supply

Just as earlier we explored changes in demand schedules so we have to look at changes in supply. It is important to remember that we are not talking about changes in *quantity supplied* which are represented by movements along the curve with output reacting to price, but a change in the quantities supplied at all price levels—in other words, a *shift* of the supply curve.

The shift can take the form of a rightward move if supply is increased at each price level or a leftward move for a reduction in supply. Figure 5.31 shows these two possible reactions and in each case it can be seen that the result of the shift is that at each price level either more or less is produced.

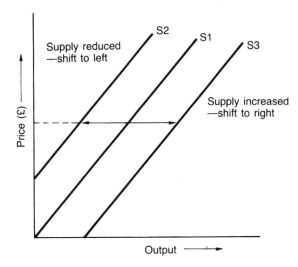

Figure 5.31   Changes in supply.

Changes in supply can be caused by several factors, but the most important are:

1. Changes in the *costs of production*. Costs involved in producing goods or services are rarely stable for long and should they rise, for example, a firm would have to consider seriously the price it would want to charge for its current level of output or, if it was in a perfect market, how much of that product it would be willing to supply at the prevailing price. The most common sources of cost of production changes include:

    (a)   Changes in costs of raw materials and fuels. The supply of many raw materials and fuels is limited and non-renewable. As a result, as the more accessible sources become exhausted, the cost of extraction becomes higher. We have seen this happen in the coalfields of most of Europe and in the oilfields of the North Sea and many other areas.

    (b)   Wage changes are normally upward and are an important cost element of labour-intensive industries. It is worth noting, though, that wage increases are not the dominant source of price rises that a reading of some tabloid newspapers would suggest.

(c)   The supply of agricultural and horticultural products is particularly influenced by external factors, often beyond human control, such as fire or unusual weather conditions. These influence costs because of their control over the quantity of coffee, tea, wheat, etc. coming onto the market and the prices in turn are influenced by speculators in the commodity markets.

2.   The prices of other goods will influence a firm or industry's pricing decisions. If the price of margarine rises then butter producers probably feel that they can safely increase their prices since they are substitute goods. Motor manufacturers are very conscious of price movements in the market while an increase in petrol prices by one distributor is likely to result in price rises by its main competitors. In other words, producers are mindful of the prices for which substitute products are on sale.

3.   The *government* can be a major influence on prices and therefore on the position of the supply curve. Rationing can provide a legal limit on supply so that the curve will indicate an upper limit to market demand fixed rigidly by the size of population and allocation per person. One of the current problems in Russia and the other former Communist countries is the task of disengaging government control of market supply to create a free market.

One of the most important causes of a shift in the supply curve is taxation. If the government imposes a tax of 50p per packet of cigarettes then the supply curve will clearly have to move upwards by 50p—in other words, at every output level firms will want an extra 50p per packet. They may not be able to receive it all, as we will see in the next section.

4.   Changes in *technology* can produce a shift in the supply curve. This will normally involve a movement downwards or to the right, as technological changes usually mean that a firm can supply a given quantity of goods at a lower price, since technical or productive efficiency will have improved. The increase in computer usage has been responsible for considerable cost cutting in clerical work in recent years and this has extended to supermarket checkouts.

5.   *Marketing changes* are also responsible for supply curve movements. Some firms find that moving into direct sales reduces costs, compared with distribution through retail outlets. However, there may be a need for increased advertising. In many countries forms of cooperative marketing have reduced costs of distribution for the individual firm, especially in agriculture. In cooperative marketing firms join together to market and promote their products. The Danish bacon industry, for example, was revolutionized many years ago as a result of cooperative marketing. In the UK the Milk Marketing Board did a similar job for dairy farmers. This all means that a given quantity of produce can be brought to the market at a lower price than previously.

There are other influences on the supply curve, including the activities of speculators in many markets, changing motives of entrepreneurs and management and attitudes to profit in particular lines. For example, a product may be sold as a 'loss leader', its extra low price attracting customers and so encouraging other purchases. A price reduction may also be introduced to increase market share, as happened when *The Times* newspaper reduced its price considerably in September 1993.

Topic 5.8   Determining prices

At the beginning of this chapter we introduced the idea that supply and demand are important because, among other things, they are responsible for determining prices, at least in competitive markets. Case Study 5.5 below is a good real-life example and the reader might like to refer to it for a moment. The undertaking business, we will assume, was happily existing with stable prices until it was faced with a change in demand—which led to the existing prices being too high for the level of demand. Undertakers had to reduce prices to find the new price. The price level which undertakers and mourners are looking for is the *equilibrium* price or, as it is sometimes known, the *market-clearing* price. It is the price level at which output and demand are both satisfied. Figure 5.32 shows a possible equilibrium position for mobile phones.

Why is it that the point where the demand and supply curves cross is the only position for an equilibrium or market-clearing price? The key is in the meaning of those two terms. Equilibrium means a position of balance. In other words, at that point there is price stability with no forces moving towards change. The term 'market clearing' implies that at that point the whole of the available output is bought or 'cleared' by the customers who are willing to buy at that price.

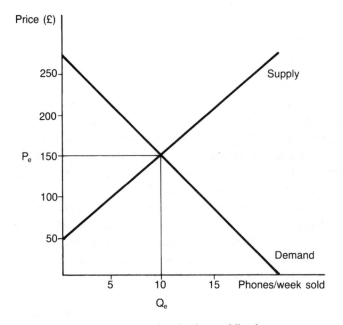

Figure 5.32   Supply, demand and price: mobile phones.

Case Study 5.5—This business is a dead loss!

Armitage & Cotrell are established undertakers with a reputation for tasteful and quality funerals and arrange a high proportion of funerals in the small northern town where they are situated. The nature of their business is regarded as a bit unusual and it is not easy to recruit new staff. It has, however, always been a steady business since, when people die, they need to be buried—a classic case of perfectly inelastic demand, one might think.

However, two things have recently jolted Armitage & Cotrell out of their complacency. One of these is the lack of deaths in the area of late—fewer people seem to be passing on now than used to be the case. In case it be thought that this is the result of the local tipple, recently turned into a real ale, it would appear to be a national trend. The number of deaths in recent years has begun to fall. There has been a $9\frac{1}{2}$ per cent fall in deaths nationally in the ten years from 1980 to 1992 and although there is a year-by-year variation, the trend is clear.

Second, the recession has hit the death industry like every other aspect of life! People are no longer able or willing to bury Grandad in a de-luxe coffin with white marble headstone and enough limos to stretch all the way from the Town Hall to the cemetery. Reluctantly, they choose the cheaper alternatives.

As a result, the funeral directors of the UK are facing a change in demand and are having to offer more cut-price services instead of the luxury burials and cremations which, of course, bring the largest profit margins.

1. Explain what has happened in the funeral industry using supply and demand analysis.
2. Can the undertakers do anything (legally!) to increase demand?

We can demonstrate this by redrawing the graph with alternative prices inserted (Fig. 5.33). At price X suppliers and retailers would be very happy because this is higher than that which they would need to persuade them to produce at the equilibrium level. In fact, at that price they would be prepared to supply Q_1 of phones. However, the market does not like that price and customers will only be willing to buy Q_2 of phones per week. In other words, if that price persists there will be surplus phones left in shops, and producers and retailers will have to reduce prices to dispose of them.

If the price is at Y, then we get the reverse problem. At this price level customers are happy because the price is such that people who previously thought that a mobile phone was a bit of a luxury are now saying, 'Well, I think I could afford one at that price'. Some cutting-edge yuppies might even get themselves a second set! However, the manufacturers are not prepared to produce many at that price. If that is all that they can get, many firms will switch to other products and only the most efficient or supply-inelastic firms will continue to produce and the reduced output will so restrict supply that prices can be increased.

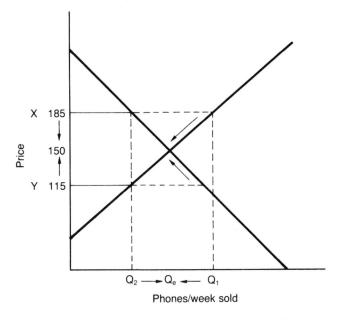

Figure 5.33 Supply, demand and price: moving to equilibrium.

In the end the equilibrium price is that at which suppliers will provide all that the customers are prepared to buy and customers will buy all that producers are willing to sell. The market for phones is 'cleared' and there is stability in the system.

What happens when demand changes?

Let us go back to our case study on the funeral 'industry'. The complaints made by the funeral companies are concerned with changes in demand. The various factors mentioned in the case study have produced a shift of the demand curve to the left. Let us see what happens in such a case (Fig. 5.34).

The equilibrium position above assumes that at an average price of £3000 there will be demand for nine funerals per week in a particular town. Now let us bring in the recession producing a need for low-budget versions of most things, including grandad's funeral, plus the fact that people are living longer and the death rate is falling. The effect is a shift of the demand curve for high-quality funerals to the left producing a new equilibrium price of £1600 and provision of seven funerals per week at that price.

Now let us suppose that the undertakers decide to have a vigorous advertising campaign. They can hardly expect to be able to increase deaths but they can try to persuade people to take more expensive arrangements. They might even push deep-freeze treatment as is happening in the USA. The result will be that the demand curve will now move rightwards again and may even move to the right of the original curve. This would produce a shortage of undertaking facilities and prices would rise, inducing overtime and new firms entering the industry.

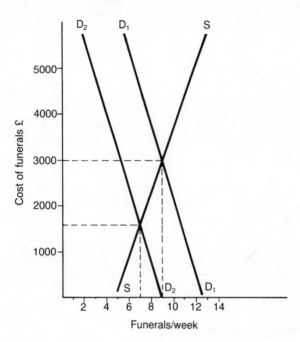

Figure 5.34 Market for high-quality funerals in one town.

We have, in other words, changes of demand which produce movements of the market-clearing price along the supply curve. Unless the undertakers manage to do something little short of instigating mass homicide they are victims of demand changes and have to adjust prices as short-term demand slides up or down their supply curve.

What about supply curves?

The same feature can be seen in the case of supply changes. Look at Fig. 5.35. Here we have the supply and demand for cacti from a garden centre. If we have an initial position which gives an equilibrium price of £1.50 per cactus, assuming an average for all plants, the position might be as shown in Fig. 5.35. Now let us assume that the local producers have a bumper harvest—young prickly shoots appear in abundance and since they cannot be eaten or used to feed chickens the only way they can be disposed of is to be sold through the garden centres. The supply curve moves to the right since at the current price more will be supplied than previously as there is a glut.

What happens to the price? It falls because the supply curve moves down the demand curve. Demand has not changed so the demand curve is not changed, but the supply curve has. Should there be an epidemic of cactus disease then the reverse situation will prevail. There will be a leftward move of the supply curve because at each price level less can be supplied. This will result in movement up the demand curve until a new equilibrium price is created.

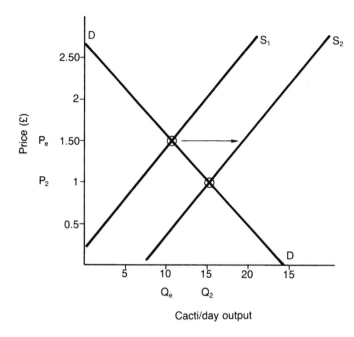

Figure 5.35 Supply curve shifts: cactus plants.

What about the effect of a tax?

One important factor which will shift a supply curve, as suggested in the previous section, is the imposition of a tax. If a firm finds that the government insists on it handing over a certain sum of money per unit sold or a certain percentage of the purchase price, then this will affect the supply curve. The firm will want to add the tax to the price.

It will not, of course, always be able to do this and the question of who actually pays in the end is largely determined by the elasticities of supply and demand. This is an area which will be looked at here but examined in more detail in Chapter 14. We can see what happens if we assume that when a tax is imposed a firm's supply curve will shift. In which direction will it move? If for any level of output the firm has to pay money to the government, with no changes in costs, it will move the curve upwards. The firm will want to increase the price by the full amount of the tax.

Now most textbooks use the example of a tax of £x per unit, e.g. £1 per bottle or 50p per gallon. However, it is more normal to have a tax which imposes a levy in the form of a proportion of the purchase price—the sort of tax known as *ad valorem* or value tax. The most important tax on commodities currently throughout Europe is of this type—Value Added Tax or VAT.

Figure 5.36 shows the effect of imposing VAT or any other *ad valorem* tax on a good. The supply curve will move upwards (often described as 'to the left') but, of course, it

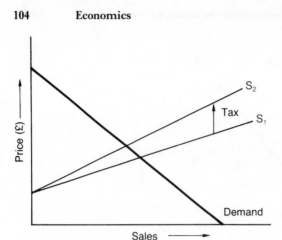

Figure 5.36   Imposing VAT on carrots.

will not be parallel to the original supply curve since the amount of tax due will increase with price.

It is worth noting two things about this move. The first is that a new equilibrium price is found which is *not* the one we might expect if the producer simply adds the tax to the old price. The *incidence* of the tax (i.e. the question of who actually pays it) falls partly on the consumer and partly on the producer. The new equilibrium is at a level less than the full tax, but at that price level the producer will be prepared to supply only a smaller quantity of goods. This feature is discussed further in the treatment of the tax system in Chapter 14.

The second feature to note is that with this tax imposition there is a loss of consumer surplus (see above) so the tax really results in a loss of benefit to society as a whole (Fig. 5.37).

The effect of elasticity

When we studied elasticity earlier in this chapter price was mentioned from time to time, but at that stage we did not bring in both demand and supply curves together on the same diagram. Elasticity is important for our present investigation, however, since it determines the degree to which a shift in either curve will affect prices.

Consider (for the last time) the funeral case study. The demand for funerals of some sort is largely inelastic. If a member of the family dies there is no choice in Western society but a funeral. Burial or cremation are options but DIY in the back garden is regarded as not only eccentric but also illegal. So while demand for trimmings and extras can vary, largely with income, perceived social status or level of life assurance, the actual number of funerals is a direct result of the death rate in the previous 10 days.

As a result, the demand curve in Fig. 5.34 was drawn as relatively steep. Whatever the price, a funeral of some type is a necessity. In view of the specialist training, vehicles and

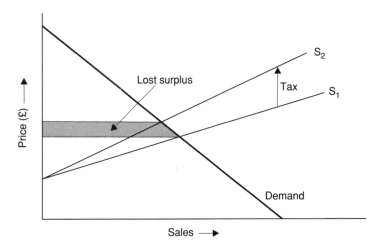

Figure 5.37 VAT and lost consumer surplus.

unpopularity of the job, supply is also relatively inelastic in that that undertaking is not a profession which many people would enter lightly.

Now if we look at inelastic curves we can see that a move of either curve will produce only a small change in output/consumption but a large change in price. Why is this? The answer is largely in the factors which influence elasticity, especially substitutes. Whatever the undertaker charges, all the client can do is move to the cheaper 'no-frills' end of the range. There still has to be a funeral. So the undertakers, despite the complaints in the article reproduced in the case study, have a fairly strong position in the market. They are not in such a strong position, though, if they wish to move into other markets because the undertaker has few alternative uses for the hearses (taxis or crew buses are unlikely!), black suits and expertise with wreaths.

Consider, however, relatively elastic demand and supply. If both have relatively flat curves then a shift of one will produce a large change in output/consumption but less in price. This is logical if one considers the nature of the curves (See Fig. 5.38 (b)) since they cover only a small price range but a large quantity range. High elasticity usually means that there are a number of substitutes, so any change in price or profit could lead to a move by either consumer or producer to other lines.

Elasticity is important in dealing with the question of who actually pays a tax which is imposed on a product. Whether VAT or a unit tax, the degree to which the producer or retailer has to pay the tax depends on elasticity. If demand is perfectly inelastic then the whole of the tax can be passed on to the consumer—who cannot or will not buy a substitute product. On the other hand, a totally elastic demand will result in the producer or retailer carrying the full tax. The reader should refer to Chapter 14 for a more detailed treatment of tax incidence.

We will look further at the influence of elasticity in the cobweb theory on p. 107.

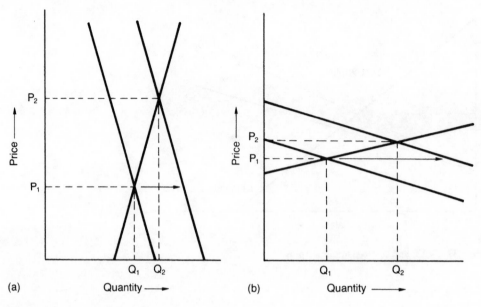

Figure 5.38 Relative elasticity and curve shifts. (a) Relatively inelastic curves. (b) Relatively elastic curves.

What about artificially fixed prices?

In practice, the free market situation which we have largely assumed so far is less common than might be thought from reading economics textbooks. Restrictions on price can be the result of the existence of only one or a few suppliers (see Chapter 6) or of government policy or some other outside organization.

In recent years there has been a lot of fuss in the press about ticket 'touts' at such events as Wimbledon or the football Cup Final at Wembley. Yet an economist would probably recognize the 'tout' as performing a normal free market economic function. Figure 5.39 assumes a provincial tennis tournament and prices are not indicative of admission costs to any actual event.

The situation which prevails in much of European agriculture as a result of the Common Agricultural Policy and the guaranteed farm price system is one of fixed prices higher than the equilibrium. As a result, there are the famous wine 'lakes' and grain 'mountains' in warehouses all round the Continent. The only way in which the high prices can be maintained is for someone—presumably government bodies—to buy up the surplus or for farmers to be subsidized to produce less or for artificial restrictions to be put on output as with the milk quotas.

A price which is fixed below the equilibrium will produce either shortages or some form of rationing. The Russians are wrestling with pricing problems at the moment as under Communism they had low fixed prices with rationing and queues. Now there are higher prices and no queues because people cannot afford the goods.

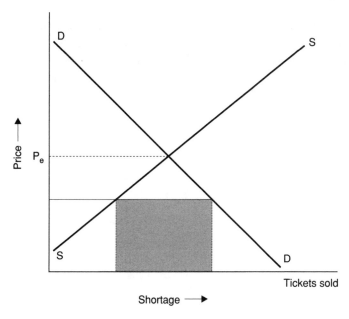

Figure 5.39   Artificial prices and tennis tickets.

Topic 5.9   The cobweb theory

Some of the features of elasticity and price interference are typical of agriculture. It is an industry which in many ways is close to the definition of a perfect market with a large number of suppliers and customers yet no one supplier or customer is able to have any influence on prices. Yet it is far from being free in that most countries have strong government regulations, pricing structures, subsidy policies and other restrictions which affect the industry. In addition, while trade unions are traditionally weak in farming, there are strong organizations of farmers, especially in the UK and France, to lobby politicians and marketing organizations like the Milk Marketing Board, which hold almost a monopolistic position in the marketplace.

The main problem with farm products is that both demand and supply exhibit steep curves with almost complete inelasticity in the short term. Supply is subject to weather and other factors outside the farmer's control and the short term in farming is a relatively long time—perhaps 9–12 months to switch from one type of crop to another or one type of animal to another with an even longer time to switch from arable to livestock or vice versa. Similarly consumers' food tastes change slowly. The result is a feature often called the *cobweb*.

The cobweb theory, developed by M. Ezekiel, illustrates very well the problems experienced by the farming industry and a few other producers, facing relatively inelastic demand schedules while themselves having few options in the short term and not too many more in the long term. There are two types of cobweb—unstable and stable.

Unstable cobwebs tend to show increasing deviation between supply and demand. In Fig. 5.40 we assume the situation for potato growers. Equilibrium price and output in the long term is at the point where the long-term supply and demand curves cross—giving P^e and Q^e. Now let us suppose that the nation's spuds are hit by disease one year and as a result the number of potatoes getting to the shops is reduced to Q_1. At output Q_1 the price is P_1. Why is this?

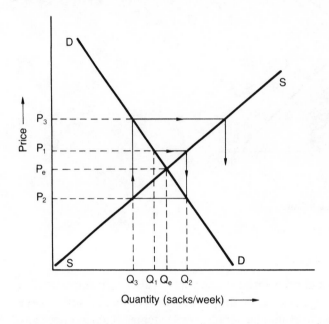

Figure 5.40   The cobweb: potatoes.

Price in the shops today is determined by the short-term supply and demand curves, not the long-term ones. The short-term supply curve is shown in Fig. 5.41. It is vertical and so perfectly inelastic. Why? Because if disease decimates the crop there is nothing farmers can do to replace the stricken plants, and output to the shops and market stalls is the volume of good-quality potatoes. It will take another 12 months to get another crop in the fields, longer if a period of chemical treatment of the fields is needed.

Let us now return to Fig. 5.40 and our cobweb. If the price is now P_1, farmers are interested in getting back into potatoes for next year, so they do what they have to do to kill the offending bugs and plant disease-resistant seed potatoes. The next year, output is at the level which farmers aim at for P_1 but this is not the level of output which will clear the market. They are too expensive for consumers and while chip shops may find they can still sell chips, enough customers switch from mashed or baked potatoes to other vegetables to result in a surplus. At output Q_2 the price on the demand schedule is P_2. So faced with a surplus, farmers cut back for the next year and switch into sugarbeet or turnips until output falls to Q_3. This is the output level which farmers would move to if prices are P_2. However, on releasing a meagre Q_3 volume of potatoes onto the market,

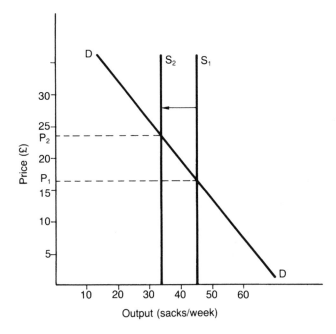

Figure 5.41 Short-term potato supply and demand.

there is a grave shortage because households will buy enormous amounts at the new price, P_3.

This could go on for ever in theory. It does explain one of the reasons why farmers usually receive some form of government aid and encouragement to form marketing associations (there is in fact a Potato Marketing Board) and build up surpluses. If governments or international bodies like the EU buy up surpluses at guaranteed prices and then release the stockpiles gradually or release them to Third World countries (rarely done!) this helps. It also explains why farmers are not likely to make a decision on one year's price change only.

A *stable* cobweb works in the opposite direction with the alternation of price and output changes moving from the initial situation of change back to a long-term equilibrium. What is the difference? It is back to the matter of relative elasticity. In the unstable system the demand curve is steeper than the supply curve. For a stable cobweb the reverse applies as seen in Fig. 5.42. The reader is advised to follow that graph through and compare it with the unstable situation.

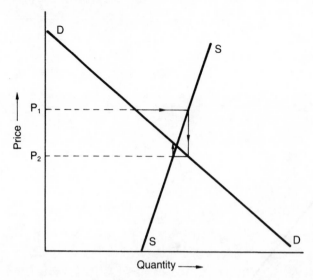

Figure 5.42   Stable cobweb.

Advanced Study Topic 5.1   Measuring elasticity

Measuring elasticity presents some problems which are not immediately obvious. The formula is straightforward, as we have seen, but how do we measure proportional changes in prices and quantity? There are two main problems:

1. In the case of a straight-line demand curve, if we measure elasticity assuming a fall in price, it will give a different answer from a measurement between the same points assuming a rise in price. For example, if price falls from £5 to £4, giving an increase in demand from 2 units to 4 units, then the change in price is 20 per cent and in demand is 100 per cent. This gives an elasticity of 5—or to be more accurate we call it '−5' as the relationship is negative and not positive. However, if we measure an increase in price and a fall in demand, the resulting elasticity is 0.5 because the change in price is 25 per cent and in demand 50 per cent.

    The usual solution to this problem is to take an average of the two proportions and so arrive at an elasticity which holds good—in general—for movements in both directions. It is possible to measure elasticity at a point but this involves calculus and is beyond the scope of this book, even in an Advanced Study Topic.

2. The second problem is how to cope with a curved line. A straight line has a constant slope but a curved line does not and this presents problems. Two possible solutions graphically are to select as small a distance as possible along the curve and to draw either an arc on the inside of the curve or a tangent to the outside of the curve. Using an arc between two price levels, for example, we can apply the usual straight line

measurement of elasticity with its advantages and disadvantages. If we use a tangent and it is possible to extend this to both axes, there is a simple method of calculation available. We can calculate elasticity by measuring the lengths of the tangent above and below the point on the curve which we are interested in. The formula for demand elasticity is:

$$Ed = \frac{\text{Length of segment below the point}}{\text{Length of segment above the point}}$$

Clearly if the point is half way along the tangent, then $Ed = 1$ and we have unitary elasticity.

Figure AST 5.1 illustrates these techniques.

(For further reading, see Samuelson and Nordhaus, Ch. 5.)

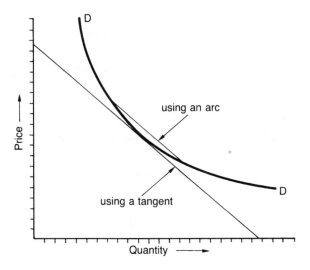

Figure AST 5.1   Measuring elasticity of a curve.

Advanced Study Topic 5.2   Combining budget lines and indifference curves

It is possible to take the analysis of the budget line and see how we can combine this feature with indifference curves. In the case of our student, we can take a budget line showing affordable combinations of hired videos and bought chocolate bars. If we also look at the student's indifference curves we find that there are infinite combinations of utilities but only one curve has the budget line as a tangent. If an indifference curve bends inside the budget line it will cut it in two places but there is always an indifference curve which is to the right, i.e. which gives a higher level of satisfaction until one is reached which just meets the budget line at one point. This point represents the combination of videos and chocolate which give most satisfaction within the budget which our student has.

This point represents the equilibrium position for the student—the combination of goods which gives maximum utility within the constraint of the budget. Should the consumer's income rise then a new budget line can be drawn parallel and to the right of the old one, and a new equilibrium point will be found on a new indifference curve.

For further reading on this topic see Begg *et al.*, Chapter 6, or Samuelson and Nordhaus, Appendix 6.

Essay questions

1. Why is it important to take elasticities into account when using supply and demand curves to analyse economic problems? (*Source*: The Associated Examining Board, November 1990)
2. Explain why the prices of primary products such as agricultural produce, raw materials and energy are often unstable (*Source*: The Associated Examining Board, November 1992)
3. What determines the slope and position of a market supply curve? Why might these change over time? (*Source*: Oxford and Cambridge Schools Examination Board, June 1992)
4. What would be the effects of a marked shift in UK consumers' tastes towards vegetarian food *both* on prices and quantities in
    (a) Goods markets.
    (b) Factor markets? (*Source*: University of Oxford, June 1991)
5. Use the concepts of elasticity to analyse the effects on the market for foreign holidays brought about by:
    (a) A fall in the price of aviation fuel;
    (b) A fall in domestic hotel prices;
    (c) An increase in domestic interest rates.
    (*Source*: University of Oxford, June 1992)
6. Assess the impact of a general increase in real incomes on the prices and quantities purchased of:
    (a) Beer and wine;
    (b) Petrol and cars;
    (c) Beef and its by-product, leather. (*Source*: University of Oxford, June 1993.)

Chapter 6

Firms and markets

Introduction

We have moved from a study of basic demand and supply with elasticity to the costs involved in production and have thus made a start on what economists call the 'theory of the firm'. Firms, however, function in systems of exchange known as markets and as markets take different forms we find that the basic goals and criteria in production decisions can differ from market to market and so from firm to firm.

As we have seen in Chapter 5, firms and industries tend to move to a position where there is an *equilibrium* level of output and of price. This price level is sometimes known as the market-clearing price to indicate that at that level all output will be consumed. There will be no surplus unsold stock (other than that in the process of distribution, display or short-term storage) and no excess demand with shortages. Economists consider that both individual firms and whole industries tend to move towards equilibrium positions.

We can thus see equilibrium as a situation in which two opposing forces are in balance—the effective demand of consumers, 'demand' in this case meaning a want with the means to purchase; and, on the other hand, there is the supply which is issued by producers and the agents of distribution such as shops. Our study of supply and demand has indicated some of the ways in which these forces operate and especially in the factors which influence the strengths of both forces.

At this point it will be useful to review our understanding of the motives of consumers and suppliers. In Chapters 2 and 5 we have considered the concept of utility which lies behind many of the decisions of consumers. We assume that people typically act in order to maximize their satisfaction from purchases and other activities. We assume that they opt for low prices rather than high ones, for maximum satisfaction rather than minimum, and that they think in a rational way.

Alternative motives for demand

Most of these motives are true to some extent, but it should be noted that there are many exceptions and for some industries these can be important. Alternative motives for purchases can include:

- *Status* and *reputation* or 'street cred' as it is often known today. Many people buy goods which are clearly expensive rather than cheap and in many cases of little better quality than lower-cost alternatives. Many people choose their model of car because of the status they think it gives them and the same goes for their house and clothes.
- *High quality* of goods is often regarded as more important than price especially by people with bad experiences with cheaper versions. Many people have preferred Japanese cars because of their reliability compared with the products of British firms. Brand loyalty is important here as people often stick to the company and brand they know best.
- *Fear* and *concern* are key motives sometimes. Some industries sell with a strong fear element and while cost may be important the customer buys in order to get protection of some sort. Burglar and smoke alarms are examples and so is insurance. In fact in some areas of the insurance industry, especially life assurance and pensions, price is not something the client worries about and the reputation of the company is more important. With motor insurance, on the other hand, there is a greater concern with low price.

Alternative motives for supply

Producers and distributors also have mixed motives and not all aim at maximizing profit. Indeed, there has been quite extensive research in recent years on the motivating factors for firms, especially large ones. In many of the larger public limited companies there is a divorce between the owners, the shareholders and the managers who effectively run the firm. Provided the dividend pay-out is adequate and there are no obvious predator firms, the management team is often content to pursue other objectives. Small firms have often had very mixed motives in any case.

The following are typical aims and objectives, other than simply profit, of firm owners and managers:

- *Marketing objectives*   Many firms are led by the marketing department and the marketing director is given high prominence. This is largely the result of the great importance of marketing in making sales out of which the profits come. In the course of company growth marketing departments can see objectives in terms of increase in sales, especially increasing market share, while individuals within the department may aim to break targets, especially if they are paid by commission or bonus.
- *Moral objectives*   There are moral, religious and charitable objectives for some businesses which can lead to considerable success, and Oxfam with its famous chain of second-hand shops comes to mind. Oxfam, however, is a charity despite the success of its shops, and perhaps we need to look at commercial enterprises with a need to make a profit to see the importance of the moral motive. An example can be seen in Case Study 6.1 below, which features the Body Shop. There has always been a clear profit-seeking motive with The Body Shop and its franchises but there has also been a strong moral emphasis which has caught the mood of an environmentally

conscious generation. Case Study 6.1 indicates that where The Body Shop has pioneered, the largest chemist chain is following. The question is whether Boots are moving into this type of product for ethical reasons or because The Body Shop has shown that it is profitable.

- *Prestige* Just as some customers aim to buy goods for status so do some entrepreneurs and managers look to prestige. Small size and high reputation may be the main objective of a number of family businesses in such trades as bespoke tailoring, antiques, high-quality furniture or bookselling. In times of economic hardship these are the ones which suffer but many survive if there are reserve financial resources from the owners.

- *Satisficing* is a word used in management studies to describe the attitude found in many firms of aiming for the minimum performance necessary to maintain managerial jobs and status quo rather than the maximum profit, which may require more risk and effort than would ideally be liked. Large organizations can develop a liking for the status quo. In the past this has been a problem with firms which have been founded for reasons other than pure profit such as the cooperative societies and some old mutual friendly societies and insurance companies. It could also be added that employer–employee relationships and the creation of job satisfaction among employees is an objective of many firms, especially the Japanese and some European companies.

- *Loss-making subsidiaries* are common in many cases where there is a group of companies with some making profits and others making convenient losses which can be set against tax.

- *The owner's interest* is a common motive in small family firms where an angler might start a fishing-tackle shop or a housewife a small direct sales business such as an Avon agency because she is interested in cosmetics or likes visiting neighbours.

Case Study 6.1—Good for the body or for profits?

One of the success stories of recent years in the business world has been The Body Shop. Founded by Anita Roddick, the franchise has established a firm reputation as makers and sellers of environmentally friendly cosmetics. No testing on animals; no allergy producing chemicals; no waste on fancy packaging. In selecting franchisees, Roddick has insisted that they share the vision for environmentally sound products and are not just trying to jump on the bandwagon to make a fast buck.

However, someone is trying to do just that. The success of The Body Shop and a few local imitators had persuaded the larger stores to consider such products and Boots has taken the lead with its Natural Collection. Sold alongside more conventional cosmetics, Boots' version appeals to those who prefer the lower prices of the pharmaceutical superstore. Yet the question remains—and is asked by The Body Shop—whether the Boots product and those of other major stores is of the same quality as the original. The Body Shop claims a long history of research and dedication to the principle of environmental conscious products and its commercial success has been built on an awareness that many of the cosmetic buying public have sympathy with this position. Quality, not price, has always been its hallmark.

However, with Body Shop sales falling and the Boots' natural cosmetic sales rising fast, the question needs to be asked—is quality enough to maintain a business in the profits to which it is accustomed?

1. Are the objectives of Boots' management significantly different from those of The Body Shop?
2. If the demand for natural products were to fall considerably, would The Body Shop have a significantly different approach to the problem compared with Boots?

Topic 6.1   Forms of markets

Introduction

Boswell wrote that, among other things, 'London is to the grazier a cattle market, to the merchant a huge exchange . . . .' This description of eighteenth-century London gives a picture of the two types of market that are of special interest to the economist:

1. *The market place*, where buying and selling takes place on a particular site.
2. *The 'larger' market* which is more a sphere of interest involving all buyers and sellers of a commodity or service.

A market is simply a collection of people or institutions who wish to buy or sell whether they meet in a confined area or communicate worldwide.

The marketplace

Markets take numerous different forms—for example, a stock market, a street market, a livestock market or the money market. The word 'market' can be used in the 'wrong' sense as an economist would see it. For example a supermarket or a hypermarket are not proper marketplaces in that while there are many buyers, most of them in front of you at the checkout, there is only one seller.

Markets are frequently linked together with one market kept supplied by other markets. Distributors will link large commodity markets with local wholesale markets which in turn supply the retail markets. Figure 6.1 also shows links between markets for goods or *product markets* and the markets for the factors of production or *factor markets*.

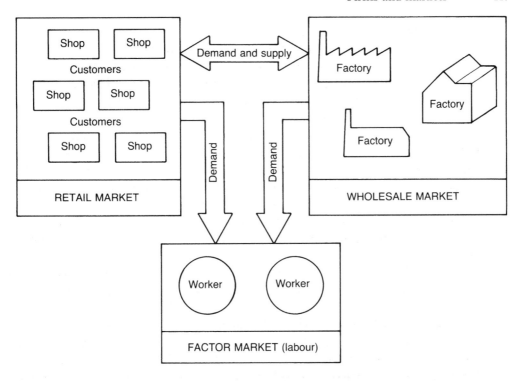

Figure 6.1 Interconnected markets.

So a shop in the retail shoe market, for example, will obtain assistants from the labour market (via job centres, newspaper advertisements or a card in the window, for example), finance from the bank (money market) and a new computerized till from the shop equipment market. In each case we are not speaking of traditional markets in specific places but linkages between buyers and sellers.

In some cases separation of markets is important. There is a feature called *price discrimination* (see p. 130) which depends to a large extent on parallel markets for the same good being separated from each other either physically, legally or in communication.

Types of market by product

Some markets are distinctive and in many cases well known as associations of buyers and sellers for particular commodities. Examples of these include the following:

- *The financial markets*, which tend to be found in the world's large capital cities such as London, New York and Paris. London is especially well known for its financial institutions which were the pioneers of certain ways of trading in financial products. Some are markets with specific geographical locations such as Lloyd's of

London (featured in Case Study 6.2 on pp. 119), the insurance market or the old Stock Exchange, before it changed to a computer-led market.

There are markets for financial futures which involves buying shares and other financial assets at an agreed price for delivery at a future date. There are money markets dealing in foreign exchange and the discount market for bills. Details of these markets will be given in Chapter 12.

- *Commodity markets* exist which include not only traditional places like Covent Garden and Smithfield but auction rooms and telephone, fax and computer links between dealers in cereals, coffee, tea, gold, copper and a range of basic raw materials. Dealing in many of these is by samples rather than by taking full loads to auction. In fact, in many cases they change ownership while they remain in the same warehouse.

    London still remains the world's principal centre for commodity markets in spite of all the political and economic changes that have taken place since Sir Thomas Gresham was responsible for the building of the Royal Exchange in 1571. Although many plantations and mines throughout the world have been nationalized or are controlled by indigenous companies, London is still regarded as the main market for wholesale commodities.

- *Retail markets* include traditional local provision markets like the famous one at Norwich, London's street markets and markets in many country towns up and down Europe. It also includes retail shops of all sizes. The distinctive characteristic of the retail market is that it deals with the distribution of finished goods to ordinary households—food, clothes, durable goods, domestic cleansing chemicals, etc.

- *Property markets* can exist at the level of the humble domestic house bought and sold through local estate agents to the large commercial properties bought and sold through national and international dealers, often to developers or pension funds. Property is different from other products in not being moveable. It is also in units which do not easily change their form and have the potential for lasting a long time.

Types of market by competitive structure

Economists tend to divide markets less by types of commodity or location and more by the ways in which firms and buyers compete with each other. The rest of this chapter will examine how firms and the markets in which they operate tend to reach and settle on optimum levels of output and market-clearing prices.

We will be looking at the following types of market:

- *Perfect markets*, which exhibit a feature known as perfect competition. Often regarded as an ideal, especially in classical economics textbooks, perfect markets are difficult to find in real life but are useful concepts as an ideal against which to measure real-world markets.

- *Monopolistic markets* are distinctive in having only one seller, although legislation on monopolies extends the term to markets which could include four or five large firms. Monopoly has been regarded as a type of market failure and modern governments tend to legislate to prevent it, yet with the recent privatization of most previously state owned industry in the UK, Italy, Russia and other countries, the presence of large private monopolies is with us to a greater extent than ever.

- *Imperfect markets* are a very common form of market. They vary in form from the *oligopoly*, where competition to supply is between a few large firms, to markets where there are a large number of firms of all sizes, competing with products which carry a brand or trade mark and differ slightly. An example of oligopoly is the soap and detergent market and of more diverse imperfect competition is the computer industry. The latter type of market situation is often called *monopolistic competition* and is not to be confused with pure monopoly.

Topic 6.2   Perfect markets and perfect competition

Perfect competition is a system of resource allocation found in perfect markets. As noted above, there is some doubt as to whether such markets actually exist in practice. One of the closest, the Lloyd's of London insurance market, is featured in Case Study 6.2.

Case Study 6.2—Lloyd's of London as a market

Lloyd's is one of the leading specialist financial markets in the world, acting as a means of buying and selling insurance. Insurance is a means of 'risk transfer' which means that if a business or an individual is concerned about the possibility of something happening to them or their possessions which will cause a financial loss, then insurance will fund that loss in return for a regular payment called a premium.

Whereas insurance companies operate from offices scattered throughout Europe, Lloyd's forms a market almost in the traditional sense. Like provision markets in many towns, it is located in a specific place and is even inside a building. Buyers and sellers meet inside that building to make transactions in close proximity to each other so that most people know what is going on in the 'market'.

However, lest anyone thinks that they can 'pop in' to Lloyd's next time their motor insurance is due, we need to modify the idea that buyers and sellers meet. Strictly speaking, their agents or representatives meet, because Lloyd's is a very exclusive market and trading on it is confined to those who are accredited. The 'sellers' are really a large group of wealthy people called *names* who are formed into *syndicates*. The names contribute some funding but guarantee a lot more to provide the 'cover' should a large claim come in. The syndicates are really run by full-time professional members known as *underwriters*, who sit in long benches or 'boxes' in the Room at Lloyd's. They negotiate on behalf of their syndicates and when a contract of insurance is agreed they sign a piece of paper called a *slip*.

The buyers are even more remote. The ultimate buyer, i.e. the firm or individual wanting insurance, has no connection with Lloyd's at all. Clients wanting insurance cover will go to a *broker*. If that broker is accredited with Lloyd's they are known as *Lloyd's brokers* and will try to arrange insurance cover inside Lloyd's with underwriters. If the broker is not a Lloyd's broker then they will contact one on the client's behalf, so there may be two firms involved as 'intermediaries' between the client and the underwriter.

Lloyd's specializes in large risks—ships have been a major subject of insurance since the institution began in a coffee bar in the seventeenth century, but it also covers aircraft, oil rigs, large commercial risks and some smaller lines like motor and house insurance. These last items are dealt with rather differently from the large concerns and syndicates offering such personal cover usually act rather like insurance companies.

If a broker receives a request for insurance then a representative of the brokerage will go round the underwriters until one is found who will agree to take part of the risk. The slip is signed for that part of the risk and once a 'lead' underwriter is found, others can usually be persuaded to take a percentage of the risk. Much depends on personal judgement of underwriters and persuasive powers of brokers but they all are well known to each other and the relationship between premium and risk is known across the market.

1.   Which of the conditions of a perfect market does Lloyd's meet?
2.   Consider the likely effects on the market of one underwriter increasing premiums by 30 per cent if others do not do the same.

The conditions for perfect competition

Perfect competition is said to exist if certain conditions are met. Basically, it can be defined as the conditions which exist in a market where no one consumer and no one firm can influence market prices. To achieve this state certain conditions are necessary:

1.   There must be a large number of buyers and sellers.
2.   No one buyer or seller can influence the price prevailing in the market—firms are known as 'price takers'. If a firm is a price taker it means that the price of the good or service is fixed by the forces of supply and demand and the individual firm cannot influence that price.
3.   The product is homogenous or uniform in nature. In theoretical analysis we assume a standardized potato, a regulation carrot or a uniform-quality shoe. It is quite difficult to achieve this in reality.
4.   There is perfect knowledge and information throughout the market.

5.   There is free access to the market for new firms and buyers, and ability to leave the market without restriction.

Apart from being price takers, firms can sell as much as they want at the prevailing price and sellers can buy as much as they want. In other words, there is no point in reducing the price as it will not help sell more goods—a firm can sell all it can produce at the equilibrium or market-clearing price. This produces a distinctive horizontal demand curve as seen in Fig. 6.2.

> A *price taker* is a firm in a perfect market which cannot influence the prevailing price but can sell all it can produce at that price.

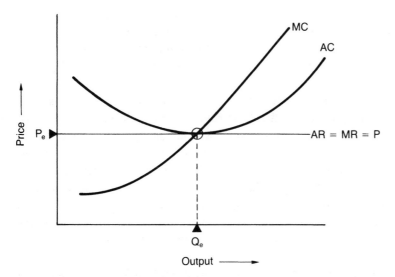

Figure 6.2   Equilibrium under perfect competition.

How do firms determine output?

If firms cannot influence price they can at least make a decision on the level of output. The major question we need to answer, then, is how do firms do this?

We need to return to the matter of costs which were introduced in the previous chapter. By way of recall, we can summarize relevant costs to a firm as:

- *Fixed costs (FC)*   Costs that do not vary with output (e.g. rent and rates). Sometimes management salaries are also included in fixed costs.
- *Variable costs (VC)*   Costs of producing one unit of output and which vary with the volume of production (e.g. wages of direct labour, raw materials).

- *Average costs (AC)*   Total costs (TC) divided by the number of units produced.
- *Marginal costs (MC)*   The cost of producing an extra unit.

The theory of the firm, which is the subject of this chapter, largely uses the costs listed above together with the concepts of average revenue (AR) and marginal revenue (MR). Applying the characteristics of these costs and revenues we arrive at the likely position of stability for firms in the different types of market—basically, the *equilibrium* output and price positions.

The entrepreneur in all types of market will try to attain an equilibrium position because all businesses like stability and certainty rather than change. One of the major principles in the theory of the firm is that this equilibrium, in all markets, is found where marginal costs and marginal revenue are the same, i.e. where

$$MC = MR$$

Figure 6.2 illustrates the situation prevailing under conditions of perfect competition. It is possible to compile schedules showing the types of cost and revenue for given levels of output, but it is usually found that the shorthand illustration of a graph is the best way of explaining situations. So we now need to use Fig. 6.2 to explain why $MC = MR$ in the context of perfect competition.

One of the main purposes of distinguishing between the different types of cost is that a firm will continue producing, at least in the short run, so long as the prime or variable costs are covered. If the firm is able to pay the workers' wages at the end of the week and meet the bills for raw materials, electricity, etc. then production will continue. It does not require much insight to realize that if the labour force were not paid on Friday, then the workers would not report for work on Monday morning. If the factory gates are shut temporarily, the fixed costs still have to be met because the rent, for example, still has to be paid whatever the level of output. Accountants, in fact, calculate a trading profit based on revenues minus variable costs and then regard the surplus as the *contribution* to fixed costs.

Why is it that an equilibrium level of output is reached where $MC = MR$? The immediate answer is that this is the point where the firm maximizes profits, so it is inevitable that if we assume profit maximization as the prime motive of the entrepreneur, then this will be the position desired. What is not so obvious is why that position should be where *marginal* costs and revenue meet.

Basically, a firm will, at the end of the year, calculate profits in terms of total revenue less total expenses, or in the usual shorthand:

$$Profit = TR - TC$$

As we often prefer to work in 'per unit' figures it is usual to translate this in terms of *average* revenue and costs, i.e.

$$Profit per unit = AR - AC$$

So, this being the case, we return to the question 'Why is profit at its maximum where *marginal* revenue and cost are equal?' The reason is really very simple. A typical firm will try to increase output on the assumption that the more it produces, the more it sells and the greater will be the total profit. Our typical firm will have some costs fixed, at least in the short term, and so if it adds an extra unit of output these overheads can be ignored because the addition of the extra unit is not changing them. It is, of course, increasing variable costs because extra workers' time and probably extra raw materials, electricity, etc. will be needed.

Now if the extra income from the sale of an additional unit is greater than the marginal cost of producing that unit, it must be to the firm's advantage to increase output by this extra unit because it will add to the firm's profit. But if the firm goes past the point where $MR = MC$ then the cost of the extra unit is more than the revenue it produces and the firm would be inviting financial trouble if it pushed output beyond this point. On the other hand, if it retreated to an output level below the point where $MR = MC$ then it would be missing out on some profit which is available. As a result, the equilibrium level of output for the profit-maximizing firm is where $MR = MC$.

The firm in perfect competition will see its revenue and cost curves as shown in Fig. 6.2, which should be studied carefully. The following points should be noted:

1. MR = AR = price. Since the firm under conditions of perfect competition only produces a very small part of the total supply and can in no way influence the price, whether it sells one unit or a thousand, it will gain the same price per unit. The curve representing this is a horizontal line and is also the demand curve since it represents AR or price for different levels of output. Since price does not vary with output under perfect competition, the AR and price remain the same whatever is produced.
2. MC = AC at the point of equilibrium. At first, the average cost will be higher than the marginal cost because MC does not contain any part of fixed costs (overheads); MC includes only such variable costs as wages, primary products and power. In contrast, AC includes the cost of the factory, plant, machinery, rent, rates, etc. However, when the MC curve cuts the AC curve, the AC curve will begin to rise. The underlying principle involved can be seen easily by using the analogy of cricket. If a batsman scores more runs in one innings than his average for the season, his average is bound to be pushed up. If he has had 10 innings and scored 1000 runs then his average will be 100. If, however, in the next innings he scores 111 then his total of runs will be 1111 for 11 innings and his average will be 101.
3. If MR = MC and, at the same time, MR = AR and MC = AC, then at the equilibrium output point MR = MC = AR = AC. The output of the entrepreneur producing under conditions of perfect competition will, therefore, be when this four-term equilibrium occurs. Some students, glancing at Fig. 6.2, may ask 'Where is the firm's profit?' The answer is that the producer's profit is *normal profit*, included in the average costs of production. This level of profit is just sufficient to induce the entrepreneur to stay in the industry and is included in the basic costs of running the firm. The equilibrium firm under perfect competition will

find no advantage in changing its output and its average cost of production will be at a minimum. Similarly, the equilibrium industry under perfect competition will have no desire to change its size. Perfect equilibrium exists when every firm in an industry is making normal profit.

Normal profit is the level of profit which is just enough to ensure that an entrepreneur is willing to stay in a particular market. It is the profit level where AR = AC.

All this is hypothetical. In any market, however close it may come to perfection, there will be some firms operating at higher costs than others. These differences will be caused by such factors as differences in management efficiency, use of a new invention giving a short-term advantage to one firm or local variations in costs or prices.

As a result, if in the short term firms gain abnormal profit, other firms not yet providing that good or service will enter the industry, which shows the importance of the condition of free entry as a characteristic of the perfect market. We can also say, as a result, that given freedom to leave, should losses result for more than a very short-term period, some firms will leave and turn their energies to some other product or service.

The Lloyd's market discussed in Case Study 6.2 indicates some of these characteristics (Fig. 6.3). In the prosperous 1970s and early 1980s Lloyd's produced ample profits and many of the syndicates made large profits. It was not difficult for agents to recruit new 'names' to provide the financial backing for insurance. However, losses in recent years as a result of climatic disasters, earthquakes and high liability awards by courts have not only threatened names with bankruptcy but have also discouraged new entries to the market.

The perfect market is seen as an ideal with its notion of consumer sovereignty and open competition between firms. The consumers get what they want because their demand changes will give price signals to producers and if consumers want a product or service and have the means to pay for it they will get it. They are thus 'sovereign'. Competition between the many firms will keep prices low and at the point where there is just normal profit available for the entrepreneur.

Topic 6.3   Monopoly

What are the monopolies?

The basis of supply under monopoly is governed by two conditions:

1. *A single producer*   The supply of particular goods or services must be controlled by one producer only or by a group of producers acting with a unified policy. As was noted earlier in this chapter, the term is often used less rigidly than it perhaps should

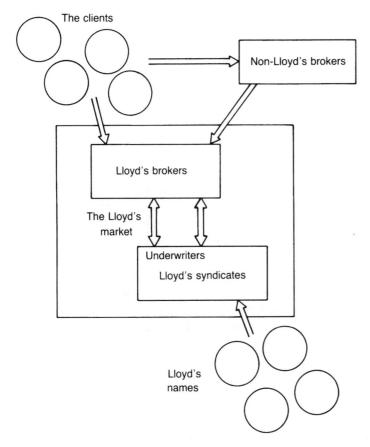

Figure 6.3   Lloyd's of London as a market.

be and 'mono-poly' does not always mean literally *one* producer or outlet. In European Union and UK legislation the term can be used of a firm with a significant proportion of the market and not in the sense in which we use it in economic theory.

2. *Restriction of entry*   A monopolist can restrict entry to the market by other firms. In one sense it is possible to describe a local fishing tackle shop as a 'monopoly' if it is the only one for miles around but it operates in a contestable market—if prices rise unreasonably or service deteriorates, then there is nothing to prevent a rival shop opening and taking away customers. What monopoly power there is, is severely limited.

The monopolist is in a strong position to maximize profits by supplying a smaller quantity to the market than would be the case under perfect competition. A monopoly can gain considerable economies of scale and thus may operate under lower unit costs than an equivalent firm in perfect competition; but because there is no competition and no threats of new entrants to the market, the firm does not necessarily produce at the level of the lowest point on the AC curve.

One important feature of the monopolist, then, is that such a firm can restrict output to up its prices. However, the firm cannot control both output *and* prices since it cannot force consumers to buy a set volume of output at a specified price. The monopoly can fix either the price or the output level but not both. It still has to face a downward-sloping demand curve and so can only increase sales by lowering price. Similarly, if it wishes to clear the market, it can only increase prices by reducing output.

Monopolies in the strict sense are actually quite rare and generally have been confined to the state monopolies and those held by the privatized industries. Even then there are usually a few independent firms operating, perhaps under licence as with private coal mines or in a brave attempt to provide an alternative, as is the case with Mercury as the opposition to British Telecom.

Manufacturers who market heavily branded goods or produce a commodity which is desired because of the manufacturer's name attached to it find a degree of monopoly power even though, strictly speaking, there are substitutes. This might be the case for car firms making popular models like Ford. For some years IBM had such a position in the computer market that most users regarded—perhaps unjustly—the products of rival manufacturers as somehow a little inferior.

The percentage of the market controlled by a producer is unlikely to be 100 per cent but as Professor Nevin has commented:

> To say that a firm does not have a monopoly because it produces only 95 per cent and not 100 per cent of the total supply would clearly be unrealistic . . . The essential point about monopoly, then, is that there ceases to be a distinction between the firm and the industry. (*Source*: Nevin, *Textbook of Economic Analysis*, Macmillan).

A good example of a monopoly is British Rail. There are a few private railway lines but they tend to be of tourist interest only and practically all commercial lines of any importance have been under the control of British Rail since the Second World War. Before nationalization they were public companies operating monopoly services in specific areas. Railways are often described as a 'natural' monopoly because the cost of setting up rival lines is too prohibitive. Even where there have been rivals they have followed different routes as in the case of the Canadian Pacific and Canadian National transcontinental routes or the rivalry between the old LNER and LMS on the London-to-Scotland journey.

Even the privatization of passenger services is unlikely to provide real competition since it is impractical to have rival trains racing along parallel tracks! The result of the railway monopoly is seen in Case Study 6.3, which features reactions to poor services and fare rises in early January 1993. The message the newspaper article gets across is simple—there is little the average passenger can do because there is only one provider.

Case Study 6.3—On the right rails?

British Rail prior to privatization was a joke! In fact, next to the weather, it was probably the most popular conversation starter in the country. The complaints from passengers were many. Trains were often late and sometimes cancelled. Electrification of many lines may have speeded up journeys but made them more liable to disruption from weather, vandalism and accident. Trains were often dirty and the quality of the rolling stock was very varied. Meanwhile prices continually rose throughout the 1980s and early 90s.

Contrasts were made with the French state-owned network as well as private companies operating in other countries. The problem with the railways is that it is very difficult not to have a monopoly situation. Very few pairs of cities can effectively be linked by more than one line and so competition in terms of competing tracks is not economic. It is possible to operate competing private companies operating trains but not possible to have, say, two rival companies both operating the 10.30 from Paddington to Bristol!

Whether a state or private monopoly, the railway services have considerable power in relation to the consumer. Producer sovereignty gave British Rail considerable power over prices and train times. With few substitutes other than overcrowded roads, commuters had to put up with what was on offer. Some bus companies operated competing services on inter-city routes but on most journeys over 100 miles they could not offer the speed of the train. They could compete on price and comfort but many travellers, especially business people, had a decided preference for rail travel. In the circumstances, however the customer complained, the provider of the services was in control.

1. Discuss the possible substitutes available for a commuter travelling from Brighton to London each day and facing a 30 per cent price rise.
2. Describe, using a graph, the effect on possible rail prices of a decision to 'chop' two out of eight trains between two cities.

Monopoly profits and output

Let's see why monopoly can be such an attractive option to the provider. First, we will look at the monopolist's demand and cost curves. The demand curve for the monopolist is significantly different from that for the firm in perfect competition. Figure 6.4 shows the average and marginal revenue curves for the monopolist and illustrates the equilibrium price and output.

Compare Figs. 6.2 and 6.4 at this point. They indicate the revenue and cost curves of a firm under perfect competition and monopoly, respectively. Note the differences:

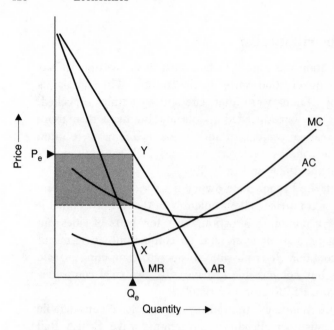

Figure 6.4 Equilibrium under a monopoly.

1. Under monopoly, the AR curve slopes downwards from left to right illustrating the point made earlier that the monopolist can sell more at a lower price, but under perfect competition AR is fixed by the free interplay of market forces of supply and demand.
2. Under monopoly, the MR curve is always to the left of the AR curve; the two curves are not synonymous as in a perfectly competitive market. The reason for MR being less than AR can best be illustrated by a very simple table:

Table 6.1 Marginal revenue and costs in monopoly

Quantity demanded (m)	Price ($£$)	TR ($£$)	AR ($£$)	MR ($£$)
1	10	10	10	
2	9	18	9	8
3	8	24	8	6
4	7	28	7	4

It can be seen that as MR falls it pulls AR down also.

Now we can introduce the cost curves in Fig. 6.4. The marginal cost curve cuts the average cost curve at the lowest point as for perfect competition, since the mathematical logic of the situation remains the same. The equilibrium output will remain, as with perfect competition, at the point where the marginal cost curve cuts the marginal revenue curve. This is shown in Fig. 6.4.

The position:

$$MC = MR$$

is a feature of all markets because it rests on the simple logic that any other position will produce dissatisfaction and loss of profits. A position to the right will lead to a situation where the goods purchased in excess of Q_e will be produced at a loss since the marginal costs exceed marginal revenue. A position to the left of Q_e will result in revenue exceeding costs and should the firm stay at such an output level then profit will be lost. Of course, we are assuming a profit-maximizing motive.

It is important to note that while Q_e marks the equilibrium *output* level on Fig. 6.4 we cannot just read off the vertical axis opposite point X to get the price. The crossing of MC and MR curves marks equilibrium output and *not* market-clearing price. Why is this so?

We have seen that for the monopolist the marginal and average revenue curves diverge compared with perfect competition where they are identical. The AR curve is the demand curve for the product so the equilibrium price will be related to this curve and not just the cost curves. In fact it will be on the AR curve immediately above X. $MC = MR$ fixes the output at Q_e and Y is the point on the demand curve which corresponds with Q_e of output. Therefore P_y marks the equilibrium or market-clearing price.

What is the profit level for the monopolist here? It is found in the shaded area under the line $P_y - Y$. At output Q_e and price level P_y, the profit is found as the difference between the average revenue and average cost at that output level. If this is multiplied by the number of items produced we get the total profit as the shaded rectangle. This gives considerable surplus profit over and above normal profit in the marginal cost price.

The ideal position for efficient allocation of resources in Fig. 6.4 would be where $MC = AR$. Since MC represents the supply curve and AR the demand curve, this corresponds to the equilibrium price position where demand and supply curves cross. At this point the marginal cost of producing the last item equals the price and so is worth producing. If a monopoly produces at $MC = AR$, however, it can only continue in the long run if this point is above the average cost for that level of output.

Marginal cost pricing is an important concept which is regarded as denoting the price and output levels which correspond to maximum efficiency. It is most often used as a measure of the degree of market failure in monopolies and of efficiency in state-owned industry. What is important is to distinguish between short-run marginal cost pricing and such pricing in the long run, when the cost of new capital and perhaps land has to be considered.

The existence of surplus profit for the monopolist has been a cause of concern not only for economists but also for politicians. There has been a feeling that the state monopolies at least should attempt marginal cost pricing and monopoly has been regarded as an example of market failure. As a result, most countries have laws and regulations to control monopoly. Because these usually embrace markets with a small number of suppliers rather than just one, this approach will be examined later in this chapter.

One feature of monopolies which has attracted much attention is the ability of many large companies to exercise *price discrimination*. This term refers to the ability of a firm to charge different prices in different markets. For the monopolist this is a way of maximizing profits by treating each market as a separate entity. The vital ingredient in establishing such discrimination is that the monopoly firm must be able to prevent reselling from one market to another and, preferably, to keep each market in ignorance of what is going on.

Some products cannot be resold on because their very nature implies that they are used up on purchase, as with many services and restaurant meals. Reselling can also be difficult if the markets are geographically separated. It is easier if discrimination is between consumer markets and producer markets as has been the case in the European motor industry. Success in this type of discrimination depends on the firm's ability to control, by legal or financial means, on-selling from the cheaper market to the more expensive one.

> *Price discrimination* occurs when a firm has the ability to charge differing prices for the same product in different markets.

Topic 6.4   Imperfect competition and oligopoly

What is imperfect competition?

If we look at the reality of so much of business in Europe and North America, we can appreciate that while in terms of numbers most firms are small, most markets are dominated by a few large companies, many being multinationals. We see that most of our processed food, cleaning chemicals, white goods, electricals, motor cars and the petrol to drive them are produced by a few large firms. Not only is this the case but it is also most likely that our weekly groceries will be largely purchased in a supermarket belonging to one of perhaps half a dozen large chains; our money is kept in one of about eight large banks or a similar number of national building societies, and when we buy a car we may have a very limited number of dealers to go to if we want a particular model. If we become 'hooked' on a particular brand of cornflakes or beer, then we limit our potential suppliers in a market to fewer firms than exist in total.

An imperfect market can be characterized by the following features:

1. *A limited number of buyers and sellers*   We can see two particular situations in the market:
   (a) *Duopoly* is a situation where two sellers effectively constitute the market. An example is sugar supply in the UK which is for all practical purposes a duopoly of Tate & Lyle and the British Sugar Corporation.

(b) *Oligopoly* is a situation where there are a few sellers (the word comes from the Greek *oligos*) although more than two. It is very common and includes the soap powder and detergent market and the motor trade. Some oligopolies exist in the retail markets. For example, we increasingly see the grocery trade dominated by a few large supermarket chains such as Tesco, Sainsbury's and Asda. While there are a few large firms there are too many to constitute oligopoly or duopoly. This is a very common situation in European markets as some large firms, by merger and take-over, actively seek larger and larger market shares and the market changes composition over time.

2. *Monopolistic competition* We saw that one of the characteristics of a perfect market was the existence of uniform products. If goods are differentiated in any way then manufacturers have a type of monopoly over a particular brand. Loyalties develop towards certain makes and model of cars, certain washing powders and specific cereals, jams and other products. The same thing can happen with banks, insurance companies and brokers and solicitors. Where a strong personal service is important, loyalty to people can produce almost a 'brand' image which to some people can be seen as unique.

Imperfect competition exists when there is a limited number of firms supplying a market and where at least some of them have a significant impact on total supply and on price.

Equilibrium for an imperfect market

Imperfect competition, as we have seen, means that a firm faces competition from a few firms of probably similar size. There may be 'small fry' in the market but they are not of great significance. The grocery business has seen great efforts by the large supermarkets to put the street-corner shop out of business with considerable success but those small local shops which have survived have modified themselves into convenience stores and now the large chains fight among themselves for market share and greater profits.

In imperfect (including monopolistic) competition the firm faces a falling demand curve in much the same way as the monopolist. Output can be increased only if price is lowered and the firm cannot, at the same time, determine both its output *and* the price of the goods. The MR curve falls below the AR curve, which is also the demand curve (see Fig. 6.5).

As with the monopolist and the firm in a perfect market, an equilibrium output is found at the point where MC = MR. Here output is balanced and any movement to right or left will result either in a loss from the next unit of output or in a loss of total profit. As we have seen, there may be non-profit motives and reasons why a firm might settle for a different position but the profit objective is generally the common feature of successful firms and is assumed for most of this analysis.

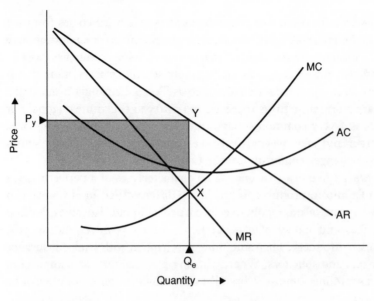

Figure 6.5 Equilibrium under imperfect competition.

If output is fixed at Q_e (Fig. 6.5) then we can find the market-clearing price by extending a line upwards to the demand (AR) curve. This locates P_e as the short-run equilibrium price with a surplus profit as the rectangle between the AR and AC curves. In theory, the level of surplus profit attracts other firms to the industry and the long-run demand (= AR) curve becomes steadily flatter until the surplus profit is eliminated. In practice, it does not normally happen like that. In particular, successful profit making is more likely to lead to a firm being taken over by a conglomerate wishing to diversify than it is to lead to mass entry of small new competitors.

What about the oligopolist?

In oligopoly there are very few firms, perhaps between two and six. In fact most of the anti-monopoly legislation in the UK regards the state of monopoly as commencing with a 25 per cent market share—effectively an oligopoly situation. In many respects oligopoly is regarded as just as much an evil as monopoly because it is so easy for a few large firms to work together with price-fixing and production-limitation agreements. At a formal level such associations are called *cartels*.

> An *oligopoly market* exists when there are only a few firms supplying a market and each one has a major contribution to total supply. A *cartel* exists when oligopoly suppliers agree to fix prices or output levels.

While the oligopoly faces a downward-sloping demand curve it is constantly mindful of the likely tactics of its rivals. Again this can be seen in the grocery trade where the giant supermarket chains are reported to be looking over their shoulders at each other and the price tactics adopted.

In fact, oligopolists are less competitive on price than monopolists or the firm in a free market. They would rather compete on brand image and spend money on TV advertising to stimulate demand. One theory of oligopoly is that of Paul Sweezy, and he saw the oligopolist as facing an unusually shaped demand curve as shown in Fig. 6.6. Sweezy saw the oligopolist as preferring stable prices rather than fluctuating ones. If prices do rise, then the oligopolist's managing director reckons that rival firms will keep their prices steady and sales will be lost. So the demand curve above the oligopolist's position (A on Fig. 6.6) is relatively elastic. However, it is supposed that if our managing director reduces prices then other firms will do the same and there will be little change in demand. This is what is expected to happen in Case Study 6.4.

The result is a 'kinked' demand curve with a change in slope at the current output/price position. This in turn produces a sudden fall, usually called a *discontinuity*, in the marginal revenue curve. Marginal costs can vary between the upper and lower limits of the discontinuity and the equilibrium position with its kink at A will remain.

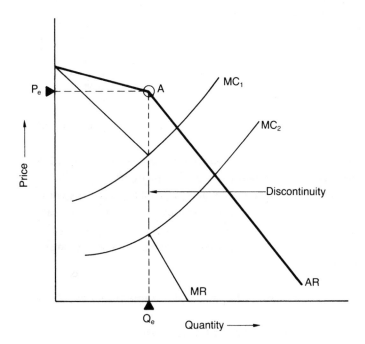

Figure 6.6 Oligopoly equilibrium and the kink.

Case Study 6.4 — Giving credit in a contestable market

Christopher Page *takes a look at the world of credit insurance and finds a surprisingly bullish market*

Recession is a double-edged sword for credit insurers, according to Barbara Bennet of Trade Indemnity, the UK's biggest domestic credit insurer. On the one hand, credit insurers have customers beating a path to their door. On the other, claims go up and the risks customers present may not be those that insurers want to cover.

The difficulties credit insurers have had over the past few years are illustrated by Trade Indemnity's figures. In 1989 it was notified of 2,590 company insolvencies. In 1992, 7,527. Ms Bennet expects it to fall by only 10% in 1993.

Trade Indemnity was virtually a monopoly supplier of domestic credit insurance 10 years ago, and the Government's Export Credit Guarantee Department (ECGD) handled exporters' needs. Now the ECGD has been sold to NCM, which is moving into the domestic market as Trade Indemnity moves into the export market. According to Brian Squibb,

sales director of the Credit Insurance Association (CIA), there are now 18 companies offering credit insurance in the UK.

But rates have not softened, despite this competition. "Reinsurers have to charge a realistic premium for their risk – it's in no one's interests to have a price war," said Ms Bennet. Clive Hilton, director of insurer AMA, which underwrites for Aegon, predicts that if rates do soften as the economy comes out of recession, some companies whose capital bases have suffered from high claims may find it very difficult to rebuild their reserves.

Even with all the difficulties, insurers and brokers are bullish about the prospects for growth in the market. Colin Foxhall, chief executive of NCM, said the company had sold 300 new policies in 1992. Turnover remained roughly static because premiums are based on sales, which have slowed, but Mr Foxhall was pleased to stay still in a market going backwards.

Simon Risebrow, UK manager of Namure Insurances of Credit, said his company is investing in new technology and systems in the UK and the Continent that will improve Namure's service in Europe.

But will the demand for credit insurance evaporate when the recession is over and companies are not so concerned about the possibility of customers not paying up?

Andrew Neill, international director of CIA, said people tend not to ditch credit insurance once they have bought it. "It's a hard sell, but a very loyal customer," he said. Mr Hilton added that after such a tough recession it could be a long time before businesses are confident enough to do without protection.

Most policies sold by insurers protect a company's whole business – a whole-of-turnover policy. This spreads risk for insurers and keeps premiums down. There are also policies that let companies protect themselves against part of their business or even a single customer.

(*Source*: *Insurance Age*, February 1993)

Insurance Age is a professional free paper for the insurance industry and so the article contains some technical terms which may need explaining.

Credit insurance is an insurance contract in which the insured receives compensation in the event of the debtor in a credit agreement being unable to pay. *Reinsurance* is the procedure by which insurance companies, having insured a firm or person, will in turn take out insurance with another company for part of the risk. Points to consider are:

1. What was expected to result from the increased competition in credit insurance?
2. Why did competition enter the industry in the first place?

Many economists cast doubt on the concept of a kinked demand curve for the oligopolist. For one thing, it explains only the tendency for oligopoly prices to be stable or 'sticky' and not how the price reached this point in the first place. It also makes some assumptions about the strategies of firms which face few competitors that are in conflict with the existence of cartels or attempts on many occasions to form cartels or otherwise bring some collaboration to the market. Economists interested in game theory emphasize the tendency of oligopolistic companies to cheat on any agreement if they think they can get away with it.

Can anyone join in?

One of the chief features of monopolistic and oligopolistic markets is the great difficulty facing any firm that wishes to enter the market. In many cases this explains the lack of real competition. One only has to consider British Telecom as an example. BT was for many years a state-owned monopoly as far as the telephone system was concerned. Gradually independents entered the market for handsets and other equipment but these items were subject to BT approval for connection to the telephone system. Following privatization, the provision of a phone system was opened to other firms.

However, only Mercury has made any real attempt to compete with BT and there are considerable difficulties here. To attain viability there has to be much expensive equipment installed and even though BT has by law to allow link-up to the grid, Mercury has to build callboxes which often duplicate those of BT, and in order to succeed at all has to charge a price lower than BT, which keeps profits low.

We see here some of the problems of entry to a market where barriers exist. These barriers include:

1. Significant *economies of scale*, as in the case of BT. These produce what is sometimes called a 'natural monopoly' with high costs of operation. Firms without sufficient venture capital and a lot of confidence in the market will not wish to face the cost of entry.
2. *Legal restraints* can also restrict entry, although sometimes an illegal 'black' market can exist alongside the official one. Examples of legal restrictions include those imposed by the Financial Services Act on insurance and investment companies (see Chapter 12), the Law Society on solicitors and the actions of the Monopolies and Mergers Commission (see Chapter 7).
3. *Restrictive practices*, despite legislation in many countries, can still limit access to a market. Suppliers can restrict access to goods to approved dealers or retailers and control prices. Although this is becoming weaker following legal changes in many countries it is allowed within the EU and is common in the motor trade.
4. *Irrecoverable costs* such as licence fees and initial advertising costs can also be a problem. These are sometimes known as 'sunk costs' for obvious reasons.

5. *Natural advantages* can convey a monopoly or oligopoly position in a market, for example a harbour whether owned privately or by the state, or the landowner of an area which is the sole source of scarce minerals.
6. *Invention* gives an initial monopoly to the inventor or the person or company holding the patent rights. The length of time for which this lasts will vary from one country to another but has been responsible for getting a market leader established in many areas. Good examples are Microsoft in computer software and IBM in hardware.

A recent theory by W.J. Baumol has suggested that the cost of exit from a market is also important. A firm will not be keen to enter into a line of production or a service requiring the investment of a lot of time in staff training or money on equipment if they are locked into the market. If things do not go well they may want an easy escape route. If exit as well as entry is easy then should prices rise above marginal cost, thus giving surplus profit, new firms will enter the market.

This analysis led Baumol to put forward the idea of *contestable markets*. A contestable market is one which may or may not have a large number of producers—it may even be in a state of monopoly—but entry and exit are both easy, so that should prices move ahead of marginal costs new entrants will emerge. Baumol saw that a key feature of such markets was the presence of potential entrants who were essentially temporary competitors but nevertheless would enter the market if profits were there but leave rapidly if they faded.

This way of approaching markets is similar to the thinking behind the privatization of state monopolies which has been going on in the UK now for some years and is also experienced in Spain, Italy and other European countries. If there are no legal barriers to entering a market, and no great expense of entry or exit, then the mere threat of independent players will ensure that prices are kept on or only fractionally above marginal cost.

> A *contestable market* is a market with few barriers to entry and exit, and even if it is currently a monopoly other firms are free to enter if they wish.

Examples of such markets include private car hire (where normal cars can be used, so anyone with a reasonably roomy vehicle can enter the business), bus services and financial services. The last industry is not really contestable in all forms and all countries. Life assurance and investment in the UK, the USA and a number of European countries has major legal and regulatory entry barriers. However, one example can be given from the less regulated market for general insurance and this is discussed in Case Study 6.4 on pp. 134.

Cartels and anti-competitive practices

One feature of oligopolies is the tendency for firms to come to agreements to maintain price levels with the intention of maintaining high surplus profits. A formal agreement is known as a *cartel* but informal agreements can also be effective, ranging from closely debated agreements on prices or sales volume negotiated at board level to informal agreements between top executives between the second and eighth tees on the local golf course! The effect can be to turn an imperfect (especially an oligopoly) market into a monopoly.

Examples of such agreements include OPEC (the Organization of Petroleum Exporting Countries), which successfully produced the massive increase in oil prices on two occasions in the 1970s. OPEC is well organized and is perhaps the world's best example of a formal cartel. In the UK for many years there was a less formal but still organized agreement between the majority of motor insurers to keep premiums at a high level. The break-up of this arrangement seemed good at the time but experience of competition has led to premiums being based on over-optimistic claims assumptions in order to keep competitive. The early 1990s have seen a readjustment upwards of premiums to compensate for this.

Collusion relates to the kink in the demand curve for the oligopolist. Whether Sweezy's interpretation is correct or not, it certainly illustrates the high degree of uncertainty in markets with few firms, and there is considerable pressure for the larger players to discuss common interests and come to an agreement which will provide some security.

Cartels and other means of collusion have been unpopular and regarded as a form of market failure. Governments in most Western countries have legislation and legal controls on both straightforward monopolies and on combinations of firms which are regarded as a threat to the market forces. It has especially been a source of much EU legislation and many European court decisions. For those wishing to look at cartels further there is additional discussion in Chapter 15 and in Advanced Study Topic 6.1.

Advanced Study Topic 6.1 — Price theory and cartels

If there is collusion between firms it may not be just out of fear but also in order to obtain the benefits known as *joint profit maximization*. This can be illustrated in Figs. AST 6.1 (a) and (b). We assume that there is a market with five motor firms each producing 100 cars per week. If the market were perfectly competitive then equilibrium output and price would be where the demand curve (= average revenue) crosses the supply curve (= marginal cost). This would lead to an output of 500 cars at an average price of £10 000. However, by colluding in a cartel they effectively form a monopoly and equilibrium output is fixed where MC = MR and a price is charged which is found by looking at the position of the AR/demand curve at that level of output.

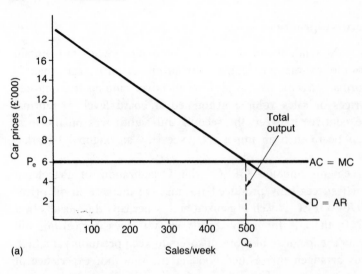

(a)

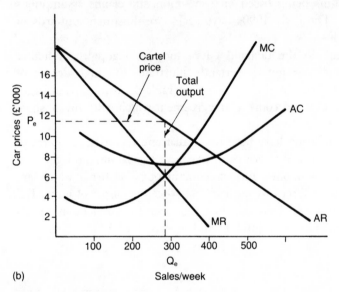

(b)

Figure AST 6.1 Joint profit maximization.

The efficiency loss indicates the degree of market imperfection in a situation of collusion between firms. Output is restricted and price is higher than would be the case if perfect competition prevailed.

The danger is that the success of such a cartel depends on each firm keeping to the agreement. In many cases each firm will be looking to maximize its own profits or market share in the long run and will seek strategies to 'cheat' on the agreement. Modern economics is interested in this type of ploy, which is studied under the name *game theory*.

For further details (including game theory) see Begg *et al.*, Chapter 10.

Essay questions

1. If economies of scale are so significant, why are there so many small firms in the economy? (*Source*: The Associated Examining Board, November 1992)
2. (a) Why do firms advertise?
   (b) Critically discuss the view that advertising promotes market imperfection and is against the interests of consumers. (*Source*: The Associated Examining Board, June 1992)
3. 'The long-run supply curve is the envelope of all short-run average cost curves.' Explain why. Why is it generally considered to be U-shaped? (*Source*: Oxford and Cambridge Schools Examination Board, June 1992)
4. 'If normal profit is the reward to the factor enterprise, then abnormal profit must be recognized as nothing other than ecomomic rent.' Discuss. (*Source*: Oxford and Cambridge Schools Examination Board, June 1991)
5. Are product differentiation and advertising wasteful economic activities? (*Source*: Oxford and Cambridge Schools Examination Board, June 1992)
6. Define a market and explain why markets can improve economic welfare. Discuss how the Single European Market is intended to increase the economic welfare of member states. (*Source*: Northern Examinations and Assessment Board, June 1992)
7. Why do economists lay stress on marginal rather than average costs and revenues in explaining a firm's price and output decisions? Discuss how the costs of measures to improve the quality and supply of water in Britain might affect its future price. (*Source*: Northern Examinations and Assessment Board, June 1991)
8. Explain the circumstances in which firms would operate at an output such that:
   (a) Marginal revenue is constant and is equal to marginal costs, which are rising;
   (b) Marginal revenue is constant and equals marginal costs, both being less than average costs;
   (c) Marginal revenue is zero, but marginal costs are positive and rising. (*Source*: University of Oxford, June 1993)

Chapter 7

The firm and industry

Making firms grow

We have so far discussed at some length the equilibrium conditions for firms under the different types of market which can be found and the ways in which the revenues and costs of firms combine to produce market-clearing prices and stable levels of output. However, most firms' owners and managers are not content with a static equilibrium but seek growth and development. The result is that in most industries there are firms that are in a state of growth as well as some in decline and some that are stable. Decline is not usually something which a firm aims at, but it tends to come about as a result of loss of a market, inflexible technology or management or else the existence of recession. Growth and stability are usually prime objectives and in this chapter we intend to look at how firms grow and the effect of this growth on industry and the regional setting in which these industries function.

What is the optimum size for a firm?

The answer to this question will depend to a large extent on the motive for growth, but if we assume a profit-maximizing firm, the optimum size will be that which gives the firm the lowest long-run average costs, given a particular level of technology.

We can look at optimum size from a number of angles. In our earlier discussion of types of firm we saw the advantages of the limited company in obtaining finance over partnerships or sole traders. If a firm is in a line of business which requires regular injections of capital such as heavy engineering, then optimum corporate size will be at the larger end of the range.

This might be linked to technical optima. In some branches of engineering equipment is large, complex or expensive, and if this is combined with processes that use mass-production techniques then a large size is likely to be the best. However, smaller and specialist engineering requiring high skill and close attention to details and specific requirements will produce a smaller optimum size. Many local garages survive because the owner can give close attention to the vehicles of regular customers and many car owners prefer this to the fast 'while you wait' operation.

Distribution is another area where there may be an optimum size of operation for a firm. In some businesses personal service counts for a lot and while ownership may be remote, the local outlet needs to be small and tightly managed. The survival of the local shop, often as a 'convenience store' as opposed to the giant supermarkets, is an example of an optimum which is not necessarily the same for every player in the industry. Insurance broking is another example. Some people go for the new direct dealing operations but more prefer someone they can talk to and an office they can visit.

Economies of scale

One of the main criteria for a firm in reaching its optimum size is the effect of economies of scale. A brief description of economies of scale was given in Chapter 5 but we need to look at it in more detail here. It is important to remember that economies of scale is not to be confused with increasing or decreasing returns in the *short run*. The term *economies of scale* is used by economists for long-term effects by which all factors are increased and the scale of operation in total grows. If this results in lower costs per unit then we call it economies of scale; if costs per unit increase we can speak of *diseconomies of scale*.

Economies of scale are those reductions in cost which occur in the long term as a result of increasing the level of all inputs.

Topic 7.1   What determines the size of firms?

Why do firms grow?

We have already seen in the previous section that firms *do* grow even though there are several reasons why small firms are viable and indeed important. What reasons are there for this growth?

1. The advantages of *economies of scale*. We noted earlier that technical economies cannot always be achieved but some industries such as steel production can only operate with a large plant size presupposing major capital input. There are other economies in any case which come with size and this issue will be examined in some detail below.
2. Ambition by firm owners and managers to achieve *larger market share* and even to gain monopoly status. Profit may be the motive but it is often suggested that more personal aims are behind some of the acquisitions and mergers that characterize many growing firms. This is especially apparent in the newspaper trade, which has seen the rise of a number of major entrepreneurs owning several papers and journals—such as Rupert Murdoch and the late Robert Maxwell.

3. *Diversification* for security is a motive with some firms which have sought to move away from too much dependence on one industry. This has produced the large conglomerates like British American Tobacco (BAT) and the Hanson Trust (see Fig. 7.1).

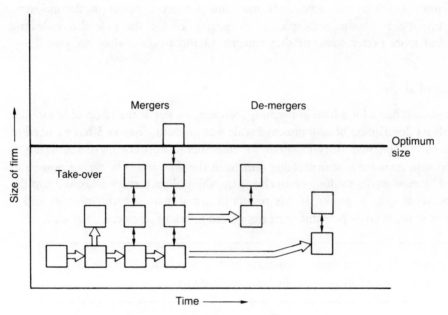

Figure 7.1   Model of corporate growth.

In Chapter 5 we mentioned the division of costs into fixed and variable. It will be recalled that fixed costs do not vary with output, and so if production is increased the variable costs (raw materials and workers' wages, for example) will rise but fixed costs like rent and senior management salaries will stay the same. This gives us a situation as shown in Fig. 7.2.

Figure 7.2 shows the costs of producing plastic garden gnomes. There is a fixed cost consisting of rent of the workshop and the lease on the managing director's Mercedes. An order from a large local garden centre means that there is a lot of activity to increase output. The rent and hire-purchase on the Merc cost the same but a lot more is spent on wages (overtime), materials and moulds. As a result, the *total costs* increase along with output.

In the short run we have established that increasing the use of one factor against fixed factors produces diminishing returns, but what about the situation in the long term when factors are all variable? To look at this we have to consider costs per gnome (see Fig. 7.3).

Here we notice that as output increases, the size of the fixed costs in the cost of each gnome will fall. If rent is £100 a week and we produce 10 gnomes then the price of each gnome has to include £10 for rent. On the other hand, if we produce 200 gnomes in the same workshop, then each gnome has to pay only £5 towards rent. It is a common

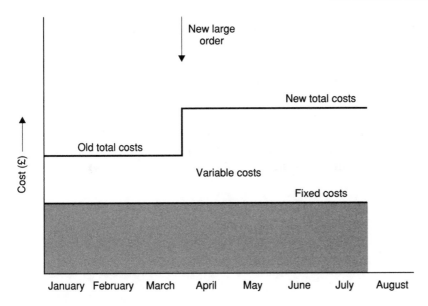

Figure 7.2   Fixed and variable costs: garden gnome production.

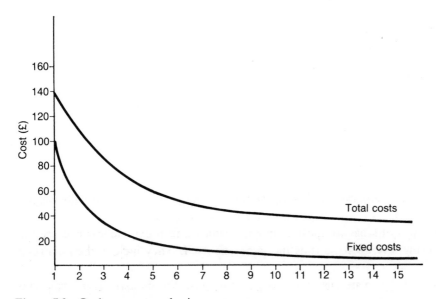

Figure 7.3   Garden gnome production: costs per gnome.

observation that even the variable costs become less per unit as output increases for technical and financial reasons which will be discussed below.

We have already seen (Chapter 5) that short-run average costs tend to form a graph which is U-shaped. At first, costs fall and then rise again as marginal costs first fall and then rise. We can see the long-term average cost curve as a series of short-term curves. After all, as output increases then successive changes will need to be made to plant—larger premises may be hired, new machines employed with greater capacity, etc. With each change there will be a new short-term AC curve and together they produce a larger U-shaped curve.

The lowest point on this long-run average cost curve can be seen as the level of optimum output (Fig. 7.4). At lower production levels full economies of scale have not been experienced, but if production is increased then diseconomies set in and costs rise. In fact, recent studies by economists suggest that the long-run AC curve is more L-shaped than U-shaped and that firms manage to grow without experiencing any significant degree of diseconomies of scale.

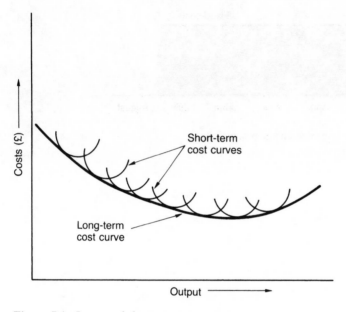

Figure 7.4 Long- and short-term average costs.

What produces the economies and (supposed) diseconomies? We can normally classify scale economies under two main headings: *external* and *internal*.

External economies of scale are those economies which a firm experiences because the industry is growing, even if it remains the same size itself. They include the following:

1.   Lower costs of raw materials or components because the industry is growing and supplies have become more efficient.
2.   Improved training facilities, especially if provided by local colleges. In cities where there are several firms in the same type of business local colleges and even the local university may put on specialist courses. Examples are Birmingham, Sheffield and Newcastle for engineering and Bournemouth University for financial services.
3.   Improvements in technology as a result of the combined research efforts of larger firms in the industry. Despite patent laws and attempts to keep research secret, technological advance soon becomes common property, as IBM has found to its cost.

Internal economies of scale are those which occur within a firm as it grows and they can be seen to include the following:

1. More economical use of land, buildings and equipment. If a firm doubles its output it is unlikely that it will require twice the amount of land area; new storeys may be added or more efficient use made of existing buildings.
2. Greater specialization. A small firm cannot make full use of specialization or division of labour or afford specialist capital equipment. A street-corner shop is unable to buy an electronic checkout system.
3. More use of specialists. A large firm will find it worth while to employ highly paid administrators and professionals such as accountants and maintenance personnel which would be out of reach of smaller firms. Really large firms can train their own specialist staff.
4. Market research. A large firm may indulge in market research. Expert staff will analyse statistics and data relating to the trade and conduct field surveys and product tests.
5. Nationwide advertising. Large companies can afford to spend a lot more on advertising than smaller concerns, especially using national TV as a medium.
6. Attractive to investors. The ability to raise funds either by issuing shares or borrowing enables larger firms to compete in larger markets, invest in up-to-date plant or develop new products. Much of the benefit from the closer European integration and the reality of the 'common market' is going to larger firms which can spend time and money in cultivating new customers in foreign countries.
7. Better facilities for workers. Employees of larger firms may enjoy superior welfare facilities than those provided by small firms. They may have works' canteens, recreation facilities, pension schemes and perhaps uniforms provided.
8. Bulk buying. A large firm will normally get better terms because it buys raw materials, fuel, etc. in bulk. This economy may be double-edged because if the firm is also selling in bulk it also will be expected to offer a discount.

To the above we could also add an economy which has become increasingly recognized as important and is known by the term *learning effects*. With an increase in output workers at all levels learn new techniques and as output increases so they become more skilled with experience and knowledge. This occurs not just at the shopfloor level but also in the administrative offices. If our imaginary gnome producer got much larger then a computer might be installed. At first, this 'newfangled' equipment might be a puzzle to the experienced secretaries and managers and only the employee on Youth Training seems to know how to use it (and prefers to play games on it in the lunch hour!). In time, accounts, sales and many other things are put on the machine and it becomes central to the company's operations.

Finally, it is important to note that economies of scale can operate at the level of the firm itself or at plant (factory) level. It is the firm which benefits from purchasing economies but it is at the plant level that such economies as division of labour and larger machinery operate.

Diseconomies of scale can also operate although, as we noted earlier, some economists now consider that they are given too much prominence. Costs can rise with increasing scale and, on the whole, they tend to occur in management rather than on the factory floor. They include:

1. Problems of control and coordination, especially if the firm diversifies into a number of products to avoid risk or increases the number of plants. This explains a number of management buy-outs as large firms try to divest themselves of subsidiaries which are either not profitable or too remote to control properly.
2. Problems of communication, so that instructions, company policy or sales themes fail to reach all those who they should. We have all experienced large firms—banks seem especially prone—advertising a service or an attitude of mind whereas the customer may find that the local branch is oblivious to the new idea.
3. The firm becomes impersonal and top management find themselves remote not only from the customer but also from the workers in the factory. This can produce a sense of alienation in the workforce. Current good practice among managers is to make a determined effort to involve workers in decisions and to visit factories and offices on a regular basis.

It can be seen from the above comments on large commercial organizations that the smaller firm has some advantages. There are in fact good reasons why so many small firms survive against the pressure of larger corporations. The main reasons are:

1. In many areas of commerce, especially service industries, the personal touch is important and clients/customers like to be able to see 'the boss' rather than some minion. This especially applies if the service is technical, like accountancy, law or insurance.
2. The same personal touch can be important in keeping the loyalty of the workforce, and where continuity of staff is important the larger firm with frequent staff turnover can be at a disadvantage compared with the smaller unit. Small size also aids communication between staff.
3. Some firms do not achieve many economies of scale and may even get diseconomies at an early stage. There is a lot of logic in the fact that the majority of our newspaper sales are from small shops and delivery units rather than from supermarkets. In many areas of business the market area which is most cost efficient is relatively small.
4. In some industries tight control and monitoring of work is important. This is one reason why the building trade has maintained a number of small local firms, often doing small but high-quality jobs which the larger firms would not want. Many master builders find that as the firm grows, the quality of work slips.
5. Many business people prefer to keep their operations small for personal reasons.

Topic 7.2   Corporate growth

Assuming that a firm decides that its optimum size is larger than it experiences at present, it will seek to grow. This growth may involve a change in corporate status, especially if more capital is needed. In this way many large firms can look back to humble beginnings and growth from perhaps one man and his vision. So began Sainsbury's from one grocery shop, Boots from a chemist shop in Nottingham, Marks & Spencer from a stall in Leeds market (see Case Study 7.1), and many a prestigious financial institution began with one merchant lending a few sovereigns to a friend in need—for interest, of course!

As a firm grows it may continue in the line of business with which it began but it may seek to develop links with other processes in that industry or with totally different lines of business altogether. These approaches become very apparent if a firm decides to grow not just by internal changes but also by buying existing firms. The examples mentioned earlier all largely grew internally and over a long period of time, but some business leaders prefer more rapid growth and achieve it by mergers and take-overs. As a result, we have a few very large firms which are known as *conglomerates* and operate over a very wide range of activities.

How do firms grow if they wish to acquire another 'off-the-peg' firm? We will look first at the direction of growth and later at the methods used. Economists usually see three general directions for growth:

1. *Vertical integration*   The iron and steel industry provides one of the best examples of vertical integration. A large firm may organize everything including mines, blast furnaces, rolling mills, right up to the steel mills producing the final product. It is more economical to keep the metal in a molten state and not allow it to cool down and harden with the expense of reheating to make it workable. It is also possible to make full use of by-products such as coke, coal gas and cement. As a result, the separation of iron producers and steel producers which once was the norm half a century ago has been replaced by fully integrated plant. A modern example of vertical integration is found in the poultry industry, which has not become highly mechanized. Vertical integration allows the careful planning of each stage of production. Many of the stages could be separate firms but it is more beneficial to be integrated. Vertical integration is also common in the licensed trade where most public houses are owned by breweries and serve mostly their brewery's products. Many petrol stations are owned by refiners and some motor manufacturers have bought retail outlets.

> *Vertical integration* is the merger of firms or processes by acquisition of other enterprises at different stages in the productive or distributive process.

2. *Horizontal integration* Many firms prefer to keep to one process rather than purchase suppliers or outlets. Apart from enabling the firm to grow within techniques and processes it is familiar with, horizontal integration enables a firm to eliminate rivals by combining with them. Horizontal integration occurs when there is a merger between two firms which are at the same stage of production or distribution and involved in the same market. There have been a number of mergers between building societies recently as they strive for increasing economies of scale and access to larger 'tame' markets. In 1993 there was a major merger between Leeds Permanent and National Provincial, for example. Most of our breweries are the result of mergers between rivals and the same goes for many motor manufacturers. The current British manufacturer, Rover, for example, has developed with many name changes over the years and mergers between such marques as Austin, Morris, MG and Rover. Many mergers are multinational, for example Volkswagen's merger with the Czech firm Skoda.

Horizontal integration is the merger of two firms at the same stage of production or distribution and selling in the same market.

Case Study 7.1—The growth of 'Marks & Sparks'

The centre of most high streets in the larger towns and cities of Britain is dominated by three stores—Woolworths, Boots and Marks & Spencer. Various local department stores, including the John Lewis Partnership group and the clothing chains, are also prominent but the 'big three' are long established symbols of the city centre. All three are also examples of how businesses grow from small beginnings to become national or even international chains. Woolworths started in the USA as a one-price, low-cost store; Boots began as a chemist's shop in Nottingham; and Marks & Spencer plc began life as a pair of feet selling haberdashery door to door.

Michael Marks was not only an itinerant salesman but an immigrant from the distant—and to Victorian society, strange—land of Russia. To cope with the limitations of a foreign language he fixed the price of all his items at one penny (in the 1880s this was still a useful coin!)—a similar tactic to F.W. Woolworth. Hard work brought success, and Michael Marks moved up to the dizzy heights of a stall in Leeds market. Needing finance for expansion he went into partnership with Tom Spencer, thus forming one of the most famous duos in British business. They expanded in other local markets and bought shops but, seeing a ready market for low cost reliable retailing, were ambitious for even faster growth. As a result, the partnership changed into a private limited company.

Eventually, Tom Spencer retired, and he and Michael Marks died to be succeeded by Simon Marks and his brother-in-law, Israel Sieff (later Lord Sieff). A further push for growth came after a visit to the USA gave Simon Marks a chance to see American retailing operations which were much more advanced than those in the UK. The company went 'public' by opening its shareholding to all. This financed the purchase of not only more stores but larger and more prestigious buildings.

Now 'Marks and Sparks' usually occupies the freehold of a key site in the centre of most cities and has an enviable reputation as a quality retailer of clothing and food. It has expanded into Europe, especially Spain and France and so has become truly multinational.

Questions to consider

1. What were the reasons for the changes in company status which have marked the history of Marks & Spencer?
2. What were the advantages for Marks & Spencer of growth by buying *new* stores rather than purchasing an existing chain of shops?

Lateral and conglomerate integration

The two directions we have discussed have both assumed that a firm wishes to expand within an industry or at least stick with its close relations. Many firms, however, see growth as an opportunity to diversify, and large firms with a diverse range of activities are known as *conglomerates*. They include some of our largest companies like British American Tobacco, which includes among its subsidiaries two insurance companies, and Unilever, which has branched out from soap powders and detergents to animal feeds, packaging, food and many other areas.

There is a slight distinction between the terms lateral and conglomerate integration in that lateral movements are seen to be into different products or services but where there is some degree of similarity. The creation of Next from a merger of the gents' outfitters Hepworth with the ladies' clothes shop Kendalls is one example. The purchase of Scottish Mutual, an old-established life assurance office, by Abbey National Bank (formerly a building society) is another.

Mergers and take-overs

Having looked at some of the directions of growth, we can examine the methods used. Any serious newspaper reader will be used to the words 'merger' and 'take-over' because they are common enough on the City pages. Just about every day, someone somewhere in Europe is thinking of buying another firm. The motives may be to benefit from economies of scale, but in some cases they may be a lot more personal between the leading players. Some researchers have concluded that many managers are more interested in rate of growth or market share rather than in profit as such and some even seek to settle old scores against business rivals by a purchasing strategy.

There is a difference between a *merger* and a *take-over*, although sometimes it is very blurred. Many take-overs are officially called 'mergers' because it sounds better and is less unsettling to staff, especially to key managers. A merger takes place when two or more firms agree to come together as one body or, sometimes, to create a new company in which they both have shares. Occasionally, the merger is on equal terms with economies of scale as a prime objective, perhaps in order to protect the business from overseas competition.

A take-over is less negotiated. Subject to certain rules established in the stock markets or government rules which most European states have on monopolies (see p. 153) any firm or individual can buy a public limited company by the simple device of buying a majority of its shares. Under the rules of the International Stock Exchange in London, a take-over has to be formally announced and cannot be done by stealth, although over time a company can gradually acquire shares in another. In fact the *predator* company rarely has to buy a majority of shares in its victim. It may find that it has support from large shareholders and can gain an effective majority at any meeting of shareholders and thus control the board.

What usually happens is that a predator will buy a few shares (up to 5 per cent is permissible or the Stock Exchange must be given notice and information). This gives the predator some access to the victim as a shareholder and rights to speak and vote at meetings. It may find a general poor performance by present management yet sees considerable potential for the future. If there is generally some unrest among share-holders, especially institutions such as pension funds, then the task is easier. If a formal bid is made, the Stock Exchange is informed and shareholders are offered a certain price for their shares. This is usually higher than the existing price and so is tempting but will still be low enough to make the purchase viable to the predator.

Sometimes the board of the victim firm will resist the take-over but in many cases they may see advantages in the move and may agree to recommend to the shareholders that they accept the offer. In this way some key directors may stay on in the new situation, perhaps in figurehead positions.

Take-overs and unequal mergers are not necessarily evil although they can get a bad press, especially if they threaten to produce a high market share for one firm or the key individual concerned is an abrasive business 'tycoon'. If market share is likely to be a cause of concern then the Monopolies and Mergers Commission may step in (see p. 154).

A *merger* is a coming together of two firms to form a new business with an agreed allocation of assets in the new business. A *take-over* occurs when one firm or person buys a majority shareholding in another company, usually against the wishes of the board of the 'victim' firm.

Case Study 7.2—Insurance crosses frontiers

The insurance industry is becoming increasingly multinational, after being of all types of business the most insular. British insurance companies and the Lloyd's market have been prominent as earners of foreign exchange but reluctant to take on board overseas capital. Some have ventures abroad—the Prudential for example, but only recently have foreign companies begun to buy British or to merge with UK offices.

Two recent examples are worth a closer look. Equity & Law was formed in 1844 as a life assurance office with particular interest in the legal profession. In order to satisfy solicitors and barristers, investments had to be very sound and the company needed to establish high standards. It became one of the most prestigious life offices in the UK.

In 1970 Equity & Law began to establish branch operations in other parts of Europe, especially Germany and the Netherlands. Life assurance has a different history in continental Europe compared with the UK and product emphasis has had to change but the story has been one of success. An international arm opened also in the Isle of Man to benefit from offshore tax advantages. At the same time Axa, a large French insurance company, was expanding into the UK selling motor, house and business insurance and the two merged with Axa purchasing Equity & Law which is now a UK subsidiary of the French parent. Axa are also in the American market owning the life assurance corporation 'The Equitable'.

A similar development saw the merger in 1993 of the Dutch insurance company Aegon with the UK's Scottish Equitable. Again, it was the British company which was bought to enable the continental parent to establish a life assurance and pensions arm in the UK. Aegon owns 100 per cent of the Scottish Equitable shares but it did not have to bid for them. The Scottish office was a *mutual* company, i.e. it was owned not by shareholders but by policyholders, so the merger involved getting agreement of policyholders to 'de-mutualize' and the new shares were wholly bought by the new parent. A £40 million injection of capital was made into Scottish Equitable to support growth.

1. What are the advantages to Equity & Law and Scottish Equitable of being 'taken over' by a foreign company?
2. Is it important that a subsidiary company is part of a large multinational conglomerate?

Case Study 7.2 shows examples of agreed take-overs which benefit both sides. Equity & Law, an old-established British life assurance office, was bought by Axa, an old French insurance company which has been using the open frontiers of the EU to expand across Europe and operates in the UK as an insurer of motor, house and small commercial risks.

This case study also brings to light one final technical term we need to examine when we look at corporate growth—*multinational*. Many of the largest companies in the world have operations in more than one country and the term 'multinational' is used for them. This does not just mean that they sell goods in several countries—a company can be an exporter but not be a multinational. Rather, it implies that they have factories or offices and a corporate identity in more than one country. For example, Nissan is a Japanese company but has an operation in the UK which has a British corporate identity—Nissan UK Ltd, a wholly owned subsidiary of the Japanese corporation.

In fact, the British motor manufacturing industry is a good example of multinational operation. For over half a century Ford UK has operated as a subsidiary of the Ford Corporation in the USA but its main competitors were traditional home-grown firms such as Standard-Triumph (itself a merger) and the various components of what is now called Rover. Then there was Vauxhall, which became part of another American company, General Motors.

> A *multinational* is a company which has subsidiary or associate companies in several countries.

The UK also acts as host not only to Nissan but also to another Japanese firm, Toyota, which has factories in the UK as a way of avoiding EU restrictions on non-European imports. In fact, Toyota has manufacturing plant in ten European countries, including Monaco (which manufactures the door handles).

A high proportion of the world's largest firms are multinational and many are American—not only Ford but oil giants like Esso and Amoco, IBM, Coca-Cola and the Kellogg Corporation. Increasingly, larger companies in Western Europe are multinational, although in the context of the increasing integration of the EU it is to be expected that most European companies of any size will be operational across Europe and so be technically multinational. On the other hand, it may be doubtful how long we can regard a company which is operating across the EU as 'multinational' in the light of closer integration of the European economy.

Topic 7.3   Market failure

In Chapter 3 we briefly touched on the question of *market failure* and here it would be useful to explore this concept in a little more detail. What is meant by this term?

We can start with our old friend Adam Smith, who made reference to the market in *The Wealth of Nations* in which he used the phrase 'invisible hand' to describe how market forces led naturally to economic growth (see Chapter 1). In recent years a number of economists such as Friedrich Hayek and Milton Friedman have returned to this concept and advocated the virtues of a 'free' market system. Evidence from recent history has certainly tended to lend support to the idea that wealth is created better by the market than from state direction. Both in Europe and in Africa the socialist states have had great difficulties in producing prosperity compared with those that have followed market principles.

Table 7.1 Comparative economic growth

Country	Annual change in GDP 1994 (%)	Country	Annual change in GDP 1994 (%)
USA	3.4	Egypt	1.5
Canada	3.0	Kenya	2.5
Germany	1.9	Hungary	1.0
France	1.6	Poland	4.5
UK	3.0	India	4.8
Denmark	3.5	Brazil	3.0

Note: These figures are mid-year estimates.
Source: *Barclays Bank Economic Review* (3rd Quarter) 1994.

However, most economists and politicians recognize that market systems do not provide all the answers. They may produce economic growth but can be very poor at achieving other objectives such as an even distribution of wealth or high employment. The former Soviet Union may have experienced a much lower rate of economic growth than the USA or the UK but it managed to achieve, at least in theory, full employment, and the liberalization of the new Russia has produced almost as many problems as it has solved in economic terms.

The failure of markets takes a number of forms. In Chapter 3 we looked at the problems of externalities, i.e. benefits or costs faced by third parties outside the system. Here we look at two other problems. One concerns the restrictions on markets as a result of monopoly and cartels and the other is the need for public and merit goods.

The problem of monopoly

We have already seen in the previous chapter that monopolistic firms control a number of markets. They are price makers rather than price takers and they are able to receive surplus profit. Much the same applies to oligopolists, especially when they work together in cartels. In fact the UK legislation, as we have seen, regards 'monopoly' as a 25 per cent market share.

It is interesting that even in countries where the concept of a free market is strong, there have been laws and regulations to control price discrimination and monopoly power. In the USA a degree of control goes back as far as 1890 with the passing of the Sherman Antitrust Act. This made it a criminal offence to attempt to 'monopolize any part of the trade or commerce among the several States or with foreign nations . . .' The Clayton Antitrust Act of 1914 developed this and the USA has always since taken a strong approach to monopoly and oligopoly power.

In the UK regulation came much later with the very mild Monopolies and Restrictive Practices Act 1948 which created the Monopolies Commission, but successive Acts of Parliament produced a tighter regime. In 1973 Parliament created the Director-General of Fair Trading and in the same year the Monopolies and Mergers Act gave the Director-General the power to refer suspect cases to the Monopolies and Mergers Commission. It is this Act which redefined 'monopoly' as a 25 per cent market share. The Competition Act 1980 gave the Director-General powers to investigate matters of product pricing and to include state-owned industry in his or her brief.

The European Union has also been strongly in favour of restricting the powers of major market leaders. There is a Director-General for Competition and strong activity against unhealthy mergers and growth, based on Articles 85 and 86 of the Treaty of Rome.

There are those who argue that economies of scale and natural market forces may mean that full Pareto efficiency will only come if there is a degree of cooperation between leading firms or the creation of monopoly. Yet the ability of the monopolist to enjoy surplus profit rather than apply marginal cost pricing would suggest that efficiency is likely to fall rather than rise. Research has tended to indicate that mergers, for example, have not been sought especially for any economies of scale. In any case, there are considerable dangers in having too much production in too few hands and Case Study 7.3 explores the benefits of one of the more recent attempts to introduce competition where there was a state monopoly.

Before leaving the problem of monopoly power and its control we might ask the question 'Have the control strategies been successful?' One way we can measure the degree to which any industry is dominated by a few firms is the concentration ratios. The conclusion probably is that despite the legislation and the various control bodies in many industries there is still a high concentration of market share in a few firms.

Case Study 7.3—When monopoly power wanes

One of the classic monopolies in the British economy for many years has been British Gas. Previously a public corporation with responsibility for the supply of gas to domestic and industrial concerns, it also was a major developer of North Sea reserves and active in other parts of the world. The corporation was privatized in 1987 as part of the Conservative Government's programme of creating free markets in as many areas of the economy as possible, even energy supply.

British Gas plc inherited the old public corporation's monopoly position but various reports and recommendations from the Monopolies and Mergers Commission (the latest in August 1993) sought to see the enterprise decentralized and opened up more and more to competition. However, gas has not proved an easy product to compete with, since supply requires a fixed infrastructure of pipes with a high safety cost while the exploration and development side has very high capital requirements with profits a long-term prospect.

The selling-off of assets and markets has had an effect on British Gas's profits. Table 7.2 shows what the current cost of pre-tax profits have been.

Table 7.2   The current cost of pre-tax profits

Year	Pre-tax profit £ million	Year	Pre-tax profit £ million
1986*	800	1990	1 063
1987	1 059	1991	1 469
1988	1 008	1992	846
1989	1 054	1993	(613)

*This year is the last year of public ownership

It can be seen that profits before tax rose slowly but gradually until reaching a peak in 1991; but the following year, fell and, in 1993, the company recorded a substantial operating loss (in accountacy convention a loss or negative figure is indicated by placing it in brackets). In 1993, turnover increased but most of the profit was in overseas areas and exploration and gas supply in the UK suffered a loss.

This coincided with a change in market domination brought about by government insistence on increased competition. Some assets were forcibly sold and the company re-structured. Market share of the commercial contracts market fell from 51 per cent at the end of 1992 to 27 per cent at the end of 1993 while in the domestic tariff market, the share fell from over 95 per cent to 74 per cent. It is still the dominant company, especially in the supply of non–contract gas, but official policy is to bring in competition. The effect on profit levels can already be seen.

It might at first be thought that this is bad news for British Gas shareholders. However, since most of them are also customers, they will benefit from lower prices if competition succeeds. In any case the company will become more streamlined and with the existing market status and expertise, will be in a strong position to resist competition, provided that the government allows it to do so.

The following questions could usefully be considered:

1. What economies might be achieved by British Gas plc as a result of the gas market becoming more competitive?
2. To what extent is gas supply a 'natural' monopoly?
3. Is loss of market share a serious problem to British Gas?

Public and merit goods

A second example of market failure is the way in which market economies fail to produce some goods and services which are regarded as either essential or at least highly desirable. In Chapter 3 we mentioned these and gave them their technical names—*public goods* and *merit goods*. It may be recalled that the term 'public goods' refers to goods or services which, even if fully consumed by one person, can still be consumed by another. They cannot be confined to 'private' consumption. In addition, it is impossible to exclude any other citizen from use of a public good.

Defence is the classic example. If the UK is defended against attack then we all benefit. Even the pacifist benefits, although perhaps not liking the way in which the country is saved from invasion. No-one can be excluded from the peace and security and we can all have our fill of peace without anyone else having less as a result.

The government therefore takes over the task of providing defence. There have been some private armies in past centuries. In the Middle Ages, the European nobility had private bodyguards, often illegally, but when their kings went to war they used troops which were raised for the occasion from peasants and gentry and paid for from taxation. In every recognized country the state takes over responsibility for defence as no private company could provide this service. There is no method of charging people money without insisting on everyone paying—essentially, therefore, raising money by taxation.

Table 7.3 shows the levels of defence spending by the UK government in recent years. It can be seen that, on the whole, there has been a fall in defence spending as a proportion of total domestic expenditure. This indicates a slight decline in its importance compared with other areas of the economy, largely thanks to the ending of the 'cold war'.

Table 7.3   Defence spending in the UK

Year	Total expenditure (£ million)		% of total domestic expenditure
	Actual prices	1990/91 prices	
1980–1	11 182	21 082	4.48
1981–2	12 607	21 382	4.59
1982–3	14 412	22 683	4.75
1983–4	15 487	22 997	4.75
1984–5	17 122	23 904	4.84
1985–6	17 943	23 870	4.63
1986–7	18 163	23 044	4.24
1987–8	18 856	22 660	3.86
1988–9	19 072	21 674	3.56
1989–90	20 755	22 297	3.67
1990–91	22 298	22 298	3.69

Source: CSO, *Key Data 1992/93*, HMSO.

Public goods tend to have a relatively settled level of spending since there is a generally agreed level of 'output'. One growth area, however, is in environmental works such as sea defences, preservation of areas of natural beauty and national parks. Global warming is likely to produce increasing danger from coastal flooding and erosion in the next hundred years and most works required to combat this will be in the area of public goods.

Inevitably, when dealing with such cases it is important to consider whether coastal defences might be merit goods instead. A merit good is a commodity or service which could be provided by the market and often is but not in sufficient volume to satisfy a community's idea of adequate provision. Classic examples are education and health care. Both can and are provided by the public sector but the bulk of the provision is by state bodies. Some social service benefits are similar in type. Pensions, for example, are provided by the state at a basic level but many people also benefit from employers' pension schemes or personal pension plans provided by insurance companies.

Some economists cast doubt on the existence of merit goods, seeing them as simply special cases of market goods. It has been argued that such 'commodities' as education or health would be underconsumed in a market system simply as a result of lack of information on their benefits, and some would be underconsumed because the state sees positive externalities which the individual does not. Education, for example, will provide a country with highly qualified workers and a good health service will reduce absence from work due to illness or injury.

Topic 7.4   Location of industry

We can look at the location of industry by asking three questions:

1. What forces persuade firms to locate factories or offices in some places and not others?
2. What is the significance of concentration of industries in certain areas?
3. What role can the government play in relieving the problems of regions with economic difficulties?

Location theory

The modern theories of location were developed by American economists Losch, Weber and Isard and provide an area of overlap with human geography. Figure 7.5 shows the four main influences on industrial location:

- The pull of power sources such as coal or electricity
- The pull of raw materials such as iron ore or sheet steel
- The pull of the market
- The pull of skilled labour

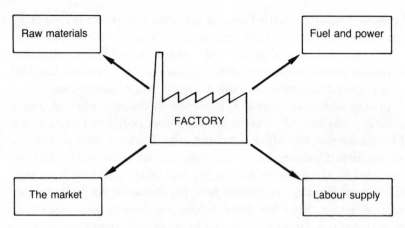

Figure 7.5   Influences on industrial location.

Power sources have had an enormous influence on the siting of our oldest-established industries. Until the nineteenth century, industrial siting was governed to a large extent by water and steam power and the textile industries relied at various stages on both of these. Later many staple industries were sited in the north of England because of their proximity to the coal that was used to generate the steam power. Since the advent of electricity, in the latter part of the nineteenth century, the source of power is a factor of decreasing importance, as within any one country costs of electricity from the grid varies little (if at all) with location. The piping of natural gas is also cheap on distribution and North Sea gas has not had the pull on industry that coal had two centuries previously.

Raw materials remain vitally important as attractions to industry. Two aspects especially are important. One is the issue of 'weight loss'. If raw material loses weight in production so that the firm is paying to move a lot of material which is not being used then it will try to locate as near as possible to the source of this material. This explains an apparent paradox that in the iron and steel industry it is low-quality ores that have attracted the blast furnaces at Corby and Scunthorpe whereas the high-grade haematite of Sweden and Labrador has proved more transportable and is carried long distances to be smelted.

A second feature is the existence of 'break of bulk' points. If materials have to be changed from one form of transport to another, e.g. from ship to rail, cost savings can be made by siting the factory at this point. This especially helps to make ports into large industrial centres, as water transport is relatively cheap but transport by rail or road is more expensive. The growth of Rotterdam as an oil-refining and storage centre for Europe is based on this feature.

The market exerts a pull on firms, especially if the end product is heavy or perishable and thus expensive or difficult to transport. Most market gardening, specializing in fresh fruit and vegetables, tends to be found around the major cities, although there are some specialist areas like the Vale of Evesham and the Netherlands. The large urban centres like Paris and London provide huge markets for firms supplying a wide range of goods and thus urban growth tends to produce further growth.

The labour market can also exert a pull on firms. This is less important when the skills required are generally available, but in some industries where special skills are needed it costs a lot less in retraining and recruiting to locate where the labour is. The Ruhr is known worldwide as a steel-producing region, Sheffield has a high reputation in stainless steel, Houston, Texas, in oil technology and the 'City' of London in financial services.

Other locating features include special climatic and soil conditions for the farming industry and access to government or local authorities for companies which tender regularly for public contracts.

The common feature in most of these influences is the cost of transporting materials, people or finished products. Transfer costs for material objects depend on distance, weight and perishability. For industries like iron and steel, tinplating or chemicals it will cut production costs considerably if a location near the major fuels or raw materials can be obtained. Some firms which provide services or produce only light products for international markets have locations near airports to facilitate the movement of top executives.

Finally, some locations get such a reputation for particular industries that any firm wanting the stamp of quality will look to these areas as ideal locations. It is difficult to imagine any cutlery firm locating outside of Sheffield or Rotherham in south Yorkshire. A watch firm in Switzerland has a clear advantage in reputation over one from Birmingham and wine connoisseurs tend to prefer the produce of France or Italy to that of the UK—for reasons of tradition rather than objective evaluation of the product!

Significance of regions

We all know that certain regions specialize in certain products, services or processes. This fact is of some significance, however, when we look at the economy of Europe and note that while some regions have attracted new industry and have grown relatively prosperous, others have stagnated and have seen considerable unemployment.

Where heavy industry using specialist labour, for example shipbuilding on the Tyne or Wear, has seen loss of orders and closure of production units there is often severe unemployment. People are not always willing or able to move area. Older workers especially are liable to find themselves with skills no-one wants and unless they can get retraining it is difficult to get a job elsewhere. It requires considerable courage and savings to move area before a new job is secured.

Some regions suffer from lack of demand for products of a major employer if the firm becomes inefficient and costs are too high. In other cases a whole industry may find that its products are not competitive in world markets, as happened with the British car industry, or even that the product is no longer required. This last feature is a problem with the coal industry.

In many cases technological change means that the factors which originally influenced location no longer apply. The coalfields, as we have seen, attracted a lot of heavy industry in the eighteenth and nineteenth centuries when coal was a major fuel. With the general use of electricity, industries are more 'footloose'—in other words, unless there are heavy raw materials firms can locate in many areas without serious cost implications. In practice, this means that in a free market situation they will tend to home in on the market, i.e. the large cities.

Technological change can also lead to some old-established firms using out-of-date equipment and lacking the competitive edge. This is especially relevant when we look at the problem in a European or even a world context. The UK steel and vehicle industries, for example, have fallen behind the Germans and the Japanese in technology, and as a result have suffered from higher costs and an inability to compete in world markets.

The exposure of East European countries to Western market forces has seen a similar problem, especially for the former East Germany which, on integration with West Germany, became part of the EU. Older and slower productive processes which were adequate in a planned economy are proving a costly burden in a free market one.

Many countries have regions which have experienced pronounced growth compared with others. In the nineteenth century it was the regions on the coalfields and near the major ports which grew rapidly—for example, Birmingham and Merseyside in England, Duisberg and the Ruhr in Germany, or Pittsburgh in the USA. More recently growth has been in lighter manufacturing such as cars, producing growth in such cities as Turin, Detroit and Coventry. In the UK, a pronounced growth of the South-east, centred on London, has been a prominent feature and one which has been regarded as somewhat of a problem by a succession of governments.

One key feature of the growth of South-east England (including East Anglia) has been the importance of service industries in this growth. In particular, the financial institutions have been important players in the growth of employment and wealth in this area. The recession of the early 1990s has struck hard at these tertiary firms. The old division of Britain into an industrial, depressed and largely unemployed North and a prosperous, white-collar South is far less prominent than it used to be.

Government intervention

Successive governments have shown considerable concern about the two problems of a drift to the South-east and large-scale unemployment in areas of traditional heavy industry. The result has been a high level of intervention to reduce migration to the South-east and to increase employment in 'black spots'. In other European countries similar problems have appeared and, in addition, there are a number of areas of considerable poverty. Most of these are predominantly rural.

As far as the UK is concerned there has been government intervention in regional development since the creation of the Special Areas in 1934, although enthusiasm for such action has varied as the political nature of the governments has changed. In general, intervention in the UK has involved designating certain areas as deserving of special help. They have generally been known as 'assisted areas' and have included two main types:

1. Development areas, which with various changes of definition and significance have had a continuous existence since 1934, are the main recipients of aid. For a number of years they included territory which was given the title 'Special Development Areas' but these were abolished in 1984.
2. Intermediate areas were set up after 1969 as a result of the Hunt Report with the intention of forestalling decline in areas which were not quite bad enough to merit the prime title above, but which were moving in that direction.

In addition, Northern Ireland has been set aside for special treatment.

Governments have developed various devices or 'instruments' to deal with the regional problem. The general approach has been a 'stick and carrot' one—in other words, policies have been used which attempt to attract industries to assisted areas and others which seek to prevent industries from beginning or expanding in the south-eastern counties. The methods which have been used include:

1. *Industrial development certificates*   These were required by any firm wishing to build a factory or extend an existing one, above a certain size. They were issued by the Board of Trade and attempted to prevent large-scale development in areas of comparative prosperity as a 'stick' to persuade firms to locate elsewhere. They were abolished in 1981.
2. *Regional selective assistance*   This replaced the Regional Development grants in 1988. The change of name is significant in that after 1988 the government wished to exercise much more discretion in regional aid to encourage newer growth industries rather that just support any firm which happened to move into an assisted area. The government maintained that many firms were being given support when they would have moved into the assisted area in any case.
3. *Regional enterprise grants*   These are available for smaller firms which are investing in new plant and seeking to develop. An interesting feature is the subsidy given to firms to use management consultants with the intention of ensuring that firms gaining public finance get the best advice available.
4. *European funds*   The EU's Regional Development Fund is a major source of finance. The EU's strong regional policy has been a holding factor on the Conservative government's wish to reduce aid to regions. There has been criticism that some EU funding to regions has produced simply a reduction in support from the national governments. Recently more EU funds have been earmarked for approved projects. Indeed, the major decisions on regional support are now taken at EU level rather than by national governments and an initiative by a government on behalf of one of its regions can fall foul of EU rules.

The question needs to be asked as to whether or not regional policy has been a success. Regions that just miss out on aid and even those that are prospering are liable to resent the support for the poorer areas coming from the taxes they pay. For example, in northern Italy there has been considerable resentment about aid to Sicily and Naples. Has the money been well spent?

This is difficult to answer with certainty since we do not know what the situation would have been without assistance. In the UK the number of jobs created in assisted areas has been over 400 000 with an estimated average cost per job of over £50 000. One problem has been the limited multiplier effect (see Chapter 9). If a job is created then the employee will in turn spend the new income on goods and services locally. This will help to create further jobs and these will in turn produce fresh spending and hence jobs. In the end an investment of £500 000 in ten jobs may result in not just ten initial jobs but a number of other jobs also.

The problem is that the multiplier effect is not confined to any one region. The newly employed worker may spend money on goods from other regions or even from overseas and local firms may not benefit much at all. There has also been a problem in the way the grant system has been administered. Not only was it, before 1988, giving automatic grants without considering the likely benefit from the firm concerned, but grants were largely confined to the manufacturing sector. In fact, the growth industries in the UK in the last thirty years have been, as we have seen, in the tertiary sector, especially financial services which do not normally qualify for grants. However, it is significant that while many financial services firms are relocating away from London they are choosing other locations in southern England such as Bournemouth, Swindon or High Wycombe rather than northern cities, with a few exceptions.

There has been some move of government offices into assisted areas. For example, the Inland Revenue collection department is at Cumbernauld in Scotland, the driving licence office (DVLC) is in Swansea and Girobank was sited in Bootle.

Essay questions

1. Carefully explain how diminishing marginal returns and decreasing returns to scale affect a firm's production costs. (*Source*: The Associated Examining Board, June 1991)

2. (a) Carefully explain why a firm may charge different prices for the same product.
   (b) Discuss whether such a pricing policy is in the interest of the firm's customers. (*Source*: The Associated Examining Board, November 1992)

3. Either: (a) Examine the argument that the benefits from monopoly can exceed the costs,
   or   (b) Show the effects over time of a change in market demand on the equilibrium of a firm in monopolistic competition. (*Source*: Oxford and Cambridge Schools Examination Board, June 1991)

4. Either: (a) What is the significance of small businesses in the British economy? Is government policy promoting or hindering their development?
   or   (b) Account for the growth in the number of referrals to the Monopolies and Mergers Commission since 1987. Does this trend suggest that

competition policy is more or less effective than previously? (*Source*: Oxford and Cambridge Schools Examination Board, June 1991)

5. Are there any advantages to monopoly and disadvantages to competition? Discuss what gains there might be, if any, from the abolition of the monopoly of the Post Office to collect and deliver letters. (*Source*: Northern Examinations and Assessment Board, June 1992)

6. Why is competition in an industry thought to be desirable? Discuss the likely economic effects of policies to introduce competition into the supply of public sector services such as education and health. (*Source*: Northern Examinations and Assessment Board, June 1991)

Chapter 8

Factor markets

We have so far looked at supply, demand, prices and markets with examples, for the most part, of markets in goods or services. These are sometimes known as *product* markets. There has, however, been the occasional reference to markets in the factors of production and we need to devote a chapter to looking at the special situations in these *factor markets*.

Topic 8.1   Factors of production

We have from time to time, and especially in Chapter 2, mentioned the factors of production as elements that are brought together by firms in order to make or distribute goods or to provide services. Here we need to look at these factors a little more closely and especially to examine the rewards they gain for providing inputs into the productive and service processes. These rewards, as we shall see below, provide the income for a country's people, and the study of this income is known as *distribution theory*.

In Chapter 2 the four factors of production were introduced as inputs and we can recall that they are:

- Land, using a very broad definition to include natural resources
- Labour—the people who work in the firms which engage in production and services
- Capital—basically machinery and equipment but the term is also extended to include money capital
- Enterprise—the initiative and risk-bearing element, sometimes known by the French word 'entrepreneur'.

Factors of production are *inputs* into the productive process and are used in various combinations. (A method of finding the best combination is shown in Advanced Study Topic 8.1.) They constitute the costs of production so that both fixed and variable costs are the expenses which have to be met to use the factors. We can represent this in the form of a diagram representing inputs in the steel industry (Fig. 8.1).

The factors receive earnings which are often called 'rewards' or 'factor income' by economists and it is these earnings which are the concern of this chapter. To be accurate, the earnings are received by the owners of the factors so all earnings are ultimately

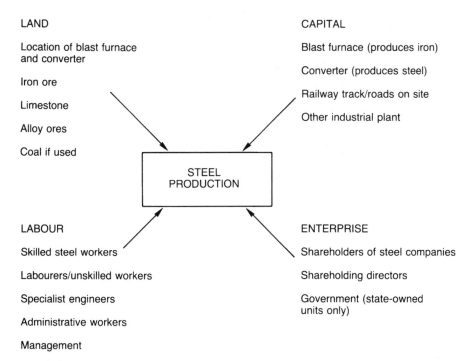

LAND

Location of blast furnace
and converter

Iron ore

Limestone

Alloy ores

Coal if used

CAPITAL

Blast furnace (produces iron)

Converter (produces steel)

Railway track/roads on site

Other industrial plant

STEEL
PRODUCTION

LABOUR

Skilled steel workers

Labourers/unskilled workers

Specialist engineers

Administrative workers

Management

ENTERPRISE

Shareholders of steel companies

Shareholding directors

Government (state-owned
units only)

Figure 8.1 Inputs into steel production.

received by someone. It is important to appreciate that, apart from labour receiving the reward of wages, the other factors have owners who receive payment for use of their assets. Distribution theory looks at the principles that determine the proportions by which factors get the earnings from the business.

The risk element in business

Before turning to examine the earnings of the factors we should look briefly at another financial aspect of the use of these inputs. We have already seen that one of the functions of enterprise is risk bearing, but in one sense labour and the owners of capital can also take risks. Some risks, called *pure risks*, can be covered by insurance or by the firm laying aside a reserve; other risks, called *speculative risks*, are fundamental to business and cannot be insured. These risks include the possibility of gain and profit as well as of loss or break-even.

Speculative risks include the chance that a firm will make a loss because its products go out of fashion or that the world economy will go into recession and so reduce demand. These are risks which all factors have to face—the entrepreneur stands to lose the business if insolvency results or poor profits if the ultimate indignity is avoided. Labour may lose their jobs and the owners of capital may not get paid their interest.

Insurable risks include some legal requirements such as insurance for commercial vehicles and employer's liability insurance. In addition, the firm can take out cover against fire, theft, public liability and loss of profits arising from these risks. The cost of risk is really an element of cost, whether it is a reserve to meet possible loss or the known cost of an insurance premium.

Topic 8.2 Distribution theory

The term *distribution theory* is used to describe the study of the income earned by the factors of production. These incomes have special names in economics which may be slightly different from the use of the same words by the 'man or woman in the street'.

Economists usually refer to factor incomes by the following names:

Land   rent
Labour   wages
Capital   interest
Enterprise profit

Factor markets differ from product markets in a number of ways and the different terms used for the prices of the factors, as listed above, is one of them. It is not really an error to refer to the 'price' of labour, but the term 'wage' is better. However, the reader should take a note of the way in which these terms are used.

Rent includes not only rent paid to a landlord (and most commercial and industrial property is in fact leased from a person or another company) but can also be used for the opportunity cost of land that is owned. If capital has been invested in the purchase of land then there is a loss of interest that might have been earned had it been invested in, say, a bank account.

Wages include salaries, commission, fees and other forms of payment. The fine distinction between types of earnings which can be so important in the social interaction of workers is not significant in economics.

The word 'interest' is not only used to include interest paid on borrowed money capital but can also be applied to any payment for leased equipment—sometimes called 'rental' in commercial circles. In fact, just as most land is rented, so much equipment is leased for the same reason—it helps cash flow not to tie up too much money capital in fixed assets.

A further peculiarity of factor markets is that demand for factors is always *derived* demand. Some demand in the products sector is also derived—for example, there would be no demand for petrol if people did not own vehicles but where factors are concerned demand is always derived. The entrepreneur will consume quantities of the factors according to the demand for the goods or services being provided. For example, a shoe firm may employ new workers if demand for its shoes is increasing, or at least

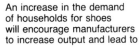
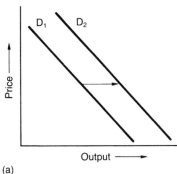
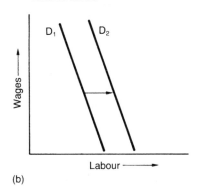

An increase in the demand
of households for shoes
will encourage manufacturers
to increase output and lead to

an increase in the demand
of shoe manufacturers for
labour, especially that
which is skilled

(a)

(b)

Figure 8.2 Derived demand: products to factors.

the management think that there is likely to be expansion in demand in the near future. It
may also acquire additional machinery and even expand the factory space (Fig. 8.2).

Not only is demand for factors derived but the demand for one factor is interconnected with that for the others. Factors do not exist in isolation. Consider the example of
the shoe factory. In increasing the workforce, management will have to increase the
number of machines available and perhaps also the floor space. The only exception to
this would be in a situation where there was high unemployment and machinery and
space were already there.

Why are some factors paid more than others?

It is a matter of common observation that some workers are paid more than others; some
land attracts a higher rent than others and some machinery costs more than others. This
is one of the fundamental questions in the theory of distribution, and to understand the
answer we need to apply some ideas already used in studies of product markets.

We can use the concepts of margin and average to understand how demand for a factor
is related to the price of that factor and the quantity already consumed. Saxon
Enterprises Ltd, we will suppose, makes printed circuits and demand is increasing.
The company decides to employ additional labour and finds that if one extra worker
is employed then an extra 100 circuits per week can be produced. This figure of 100
circuits is the marginal physical product of labour (abbreviated to MPP)—the extra
output resulting from employing the extra worker (Table 8.1).

However, in itself this figure is of limited use, especially if the 100 circuits include
many different types. If Saxon Enterprises is to decide whether the move is worth while
it has to convert that figure into something which it can use to compare with the wages
paid to the latest worker. To do this it finds out the additional revenue gained from this
extra output—the *marginal revenue product*.

Table 8.1   Output for Saxon Enterprises

Workers	Printed circuits	Marginal product	Average product
0	0	0	0
1	50	50	50
2	120	70	60
3	220	100	73
4	300	80	75
5	365	65	73
6	415	50	69
7	460	45	65
8	495	35	62

> *Marginal revenue product* is the value to the producer of any additional output from using an extra worker or other factor of production.

The problem is that we cannot just multiply the physical output by the price. If the firm is in an imperfect market then it can only increase sales by reducing price, and if it reduces the price of the marginal output it has to reduce the price of all goods on sale. The marginal revenue will then include an element of loss of earnings on items already produced. For a firm in perfect competition, we know that marginal revenue and average revenue are the same (and identical to the demand curve), so we *can* use price. The firm can sell as many goods as it wishes at that price so the marginal revenue of each additional item sold is the price.

As a result, we can conclude that marginal revenue product will be calculated in one of the following ways:

Perfect competition: MRP = MPP × price

Imperfect competition: MRP = MPP × price − loss

The use of a money value enables us to draw a graph to express a typical MRP curve as in Fig. 8.3. If we plot a marginal revenue product curve we see that it is somewhat concave to the origin of the graph. MRP increases initially as extra workers produce increasing levels of output through division of labour and other improvements, but in due course diminishing output per worker takes over. Diminishing marginal product can be seen here as another version of our old friend diminishing marginal returns.

We can now begin to get some insight into how a firm decides its level of factor inputs. In general, any firm will employ additional workers, machines or factory space provided that the marginal revenue product of the addition exceeds the marginal cost. Workers will be employed to the point where MRP = the last worker's wages plus employer's

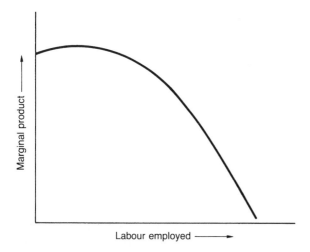

Figure 8.3 Marginal revenue product (labour).

National Insurance; land will be occupied up to the point that MRP = the rent of last square metre leased; machinery and equipment will be used until MRP = the lease rent or interest. One can even extend this to the entrepreneur who will get involved in additional risks until the MRP of the last project just covers the cost in money, hours and worry expended on it. This is more difficult to calculate than in the case of the other three factors but is real nevertheless, and it may be that some of the business executives who commit suicide as a result of stress have taken on one project too many.

We can thus see the MRP curve as the effective demand curve for the factor. At each point on the curve, the firm (or industry) is prepared to pay in wages or other reward the equivalent of the MRP for each additional factor unit put to work. Given a supply curve on the graph and we can derive a price for the factor (see below).

We have already seen that the factors work not in isolation but together. We can consider the link between them to be the *production function*, which is the combination of factors needed to produce the maximum output. For example, a farm may produce maximum milk given 40 acres of grazing, two workers on 40 hours a week and 20 tons of silage (Fig. 8.4).

Any firm is using factors at the optimum point when the marginal product per £1 spent is the same for each factor employed. If this were not so it would pay for the firm to invest in more of the factor which produces the highest marginal product. The more expensive factors clearly need higher marginal product in order to be employed; and so this can be expressed in a formula as:

$$\frac{\text{MP labour}}{\text{Price labour}} = \frac{\text{MP land}}{\text{Price land}} = \frac{\text{MP capital}}{\text{Price capital}}$$

This is called the *least cost rule*.

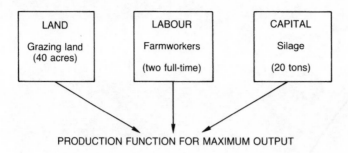

Figure 8.4 Production function: dairy farm.

Factors and economic rent

In Chapter 5 we introduced the concepts of transfer earnings and economic rent. These are especially important in the factor markets and help to explain why some factors are paid a lot more than others. Why, as was revealed recently, is a top insurance executive paid £6 million a year as salary and a junior clerk in a small brokers only £5000? Why is prime office land in a large city centre worth £1000 per square metre per year whereas the same sum would purchase the use of half a mountain in some parts of Scotland or Wales?

Let us look again at transfer earnings and economic rent, using land as an example. Figure 8.5 shows the supply and demand schedules for farmland on a steep hillslope.

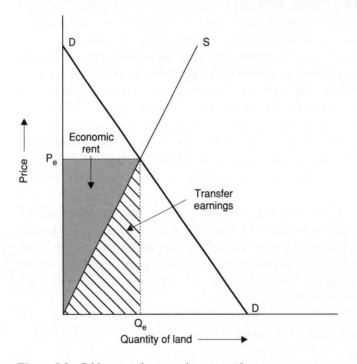

Figure 8.5 Cabbage-patch economics: economic rent.

The landowner has cleared bracken and gorse from open moor and established a small field rented out to a local farmer for growing cabbages.

We can see in Fig. 8.5 the transfer earnings which are the minimum earnings required to keep a factor in a particular task. In this case it is the rent required to persuade the landowner to lease the land for growing cabbages. It is low because the only alternative is to keep the land as rough grazing or, at best, a grouse moor. If in fact the landowner gets paid more than this, say equilibrium rent P_e, then the surplus is *economic rent*. It is important to distinguish between economic rent in this context and *rent* in the everyday meaning or the meaning as a reward for use of land. In this latter sense transfer earnings can be described as 'rent' but they are not economic rent.

Suppose that a neighbouring golf club offers to lease the land for a rent three times the current level, and to stop this happening the tenant farmer agrees to pay a higher rent. Then the extra rent earned by the landlord is economic rent. If a sudden shortage of cabbages increases their price and the landowner, seeing that the tenant farmer is making a lot of money, raises the rent the landowner can make short-term excess income until more land is brought into cabbage production over the next couple of years. The short-term excess is known as *quasi-rent*.

Topic 8.3   Labour and wage theory

The price of labour

In this and the next three sections we will look at one factor in detail—the factor labour and the aspect of distribution theory which deals with labour, i.e. *wage theory*. Most of the basic concepts have been discussed in the previous two sections but we need to examine them a little more closely in the context of what is arguably the most important of the factors. Much of our discussion here can be applied to land and capital also.

Nominal and real wages

What is important at this stage is an understanding of the difference between *nominal* and *real* wages. This lies at the heart of much collective bargaining between trade unions and employers. *Nominal wages* are wages expressed in money terms but *real wages* are wages in terms of the goods and services the money will buy. You may get a pay (or grant) rise of £500 in one year. The nominal increase is £500 but if the prices of your normal purchases have risen by the same amount then your real increase is nil.

Why do wages differ?

One of the key features of the earnings of people as they give their skills and energies to employers is the variation in payments. Why are doctors, for example, paid more than labourers? There are numerous reasons why wages differ and one or several of the following reasons may apply in an individual case:

1. *The scarcity factor*   The supply of a particular type of labour may be restricted in relation to demand. In particular, if demand for new skills suddenly increases, perhaps as a result of the growth in demand for a new type of product, there can be a temporary shortage. Such short-term shortages are really examples of economic rent being earned. Until recently there has been a great shortage of computer experts as the growth of information technology in businesses and homes has been phenomenal.

   An extreme form of scarcity is the uniqueness of certain individuals such as leading football or tennis players, comedians or film stars. If talent is unique in some way then the individual may earn what is sometimes called *rent of ability*.

   Scarcity can also be the result of the difference between *specific and non-specific labour*. A labourer's work is general and non-specific—most people could do it if they were in good health. On the other hand, a surgeon has very specific skills and few people can do that sort of job.

   Another cause of scarcity is training and education. The reader of this book is presumably hoping either to gain qualifications in economics or to improve their knowledge of the subject and the end result will be the ability to command higher wages. You will have knowledge that most other people do not have. The more specific the training and education, the higher the likely rewards, although it needs to be said that however long the training, if there is no demand for those skills and learning there will not be much, if any, advantage in money terms. Some very highly qualified people were made redundant in 1992 and 1993 as a result of the recession hitting professional jobs.

2. *Collective bargaining* can be an important determinant of wage levels. The power of trade unions and professional organizations is important in ensuring that employers pay what is considered by the workers to be an adequate wage. However, it needs to be said again that the power of the unions is only strong if there is a genuine demand for the skills of their members, which in turn usually depends on there being a demand for the goods or services they produce. Some key workers have bargaining power without union help if they have special skills—perhaps the ability to persuade the 'boss' to give them a rise. Sales staff in smaller firms are often quite skilled in that area.

3. *Benefit to society*   Some jobs are paid more than others because they are considered to be worth more to society as a whole. This has been a factor in determining public sector wages, although it is less important as more of the public sector becomes privatized or profit-making trusts take over.

4. *Wage differentials*   Even within the same type of job there can be differentials according to experience or levels of responsibility. Teachers, for example, gain increases in wages annually up to a certain limit and head teachers are paid more than the classroom teacher.

5. *Other factors*   Other influences on wages include regional variations which can be important in the case of jobs of a casual or non-specific nature. Discrimination on

sexual or racial lines has also been an element although legislation and increased public awareness of the problem has reduced its level considerably.

Theories of wages

Individual wage differences have such varied causes that it is useful to know some of the basic underlying theories of wages, each of which contains some aspect of truth. We will start with a brief look at two traditional theories before moving on to spend most time on the more modern approach. Students using more than one textbook sometimes find difficulties with wage theory as no two books seem to follow the same approach. The presentation here is intended to make the different ideas as straightforward as possible, and integration with other modern textbooks should not be difficult.

Traditional wage theories

Some classical economists were fond of the *wage fund theory* of wages. This held that there was a limited fund for wage payments and one group could only gain an increase at the expense of others. There is an element of truth in this approach, but few economists would now see the issue in terms of a fixed fund.

Other classical economists held the *subsistence theory*, which was first put forward in the eighteenth century by François Quesnay, leader of the French Physiocrats. It was developed by Thomas Malthus as part of his theory on population. The subsistence theory considered that supply of labour would always exceed demand and so workers would compete with each other for jobs, thus reducing wage levels to subsistence level, i.e. just enough to live on, and to provide enough energy for work.

The market theory of wages

In modern economics there are two predominant viewpoints of how wages are formed. They are not really alternative theories but are rather complementary ways of approaching the processes by which the labour markets move towards equilibrium wage and employment levels. The market or 'classical' theory forms the basis of our study of how these objectives are achieved.

Just as the price and equilibrium level of purchases of a good such as baked beans is determined by supply and demand, the factor markets also depend largely on supply and demand analysis. In principle, there is no difference between one can of beans and one hour of labour in producing that can. Both the can and the worker are part of a process involving demand and supply.

Figure 8.6 illustrates the way in which the market theory operates. If we assume that we are looking at the market for computer operators then we can draw demand and supply curves representing the wage-related demand by firms for computer operators and the wage-related desire of qualified operators to seek employment. In both cases the

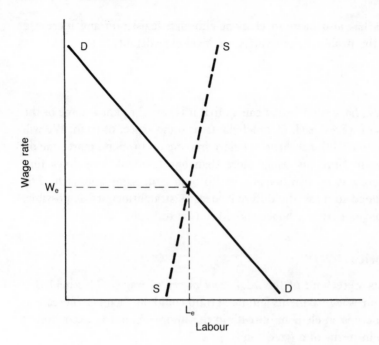

Figure 8.6 Wage equilibrium for computer operators.

shape and slope of the curves depend on the degree of elasticity which in turn is a reflection of the degree of perfection in the market.

Labour markets can be divided into perfect, imperfect and even monopolistic markets. The conditions for a perfect factor market are the same as for a perfect goods market, and this includes freedom of entry and exit, perfect knowledge of job availability and wages, and a uniformity between workers in ability. We would assume that each firm and each worker is a 'price taker' in the market and cannot by themselves influence wage rates. In theory, if workers hear that wage rates are higher in a firm round the corner from the current workplace then they will 'hotfoot it' round to the personnel manager of that rival firm.

A point which needs clarification at this stage is the definition of 'wages'. In economics the price of labour is labelled 'wage rates' and the assumption, for the sake of simplicity, is that this is expressed, in the UK, as £x per hour in sterling. The term 'wages' is intended also to include salaries, commission and fees, and although many methods of payment are not measured per hour worked the principle is the same.

However, it is not as simple even as that. Wages really should be labelled 'remuneration' because the reward for labour includes not just the contents of the weekly or monthly wage packet or bank transfer but also a number of other employee benefits. These can include employer's contributions to a pension scheme, a company car, free or subsidized lunches, a house, free travel and many other 'perks'. At most elementary and even intermediate levels in economics these distinctions are ignored, although students reading this book as part of a business studies or professional course may need to be aware of it. Case Study 8.1 explores pensions as part of pay.

Finally, it is also worth noting that while, for the sake of simplicity, we regard wages as equivalent of the average cost of labour, the employer does, in reality, have additional costs such as employers' National Insurance and the costs of recruitment and training of new staff.

Case Study 8.1—Your pay is a pension!

All workers look forward to the end of the week or month when they receive their pay. The payslip is examined with great interest and disgust often expressed over the deductions made from gross pay. Most of these deductions are for tax and National Insurance but in many cases a deduction appears which is for an employer's superannuation scheme.

In most cases an employer's superannuation scheme will involve the employees paying contributions through deductions from their pay. In most cases it will also, however, involve the employer making some contribution. In the traditional statutory schemes set up for teachers, health workers and former government corporations like British Telecom the employee's contribution is set at 6 per cent. Most employers 'chip in' between 5 per cent and 7 per cent.

As an addition to pay, this pension input is important. It provides for pension payments after retirement and, in most cases, for a lump sum on retirement day. However, employers have good motives for setting up superannuation schemes and contributing to them. For one thing it helps to secure staff loyalty since transfer from one scheme to another, while possible, is not simple and employees feel that they have a long-term stake in the company. Years ago, a 'pensionable job' was considered to be a distinct cut above one without such benefits. The pension scheme will probably include widows' benefits so avoiding any appeals from bereaved families of dead employees for financial consideration. Finally the scheme is a valuable tax perk for the firm. Contributions can be set against tax and with investments being tax free, the scheme can frequently acquire a useful cushion. Some schemes, like British Telecom, have had such periods of surplus that the firm has been able to take a 'contribution holiday'—in other words, a period when no contribution is made at all.

Benefits are usually based on the employees' salaries and years of service—for example, 1/60th of final salary for every year of service. One reason for this is that it takes into retirement the divergence between the higher-paid executive and lower-paid manual or clerical worker. However, the law permits a maximum benefit of two-thirds of final salary, which is one reason why many workers are opting out of employers' schemes for personal pensions which have no limit.

Personal pensions invest contributions and benefits are paid from the fund which accrues. Some employers' schemes are based on this principle also.

1. Consider why an engineering firm of 1000 employees might wish to set up a superannuation scheme.
2. In what ways would a superannuation scheme encourage a worker to stay with the employer?

Demand for labour

Unlike the case in the market for goods, demand for factors is from firms and not individuals, assuming that our definition of a 'firm' includes one-person businesses. This demand is essentially a *derived demand* in that the number of workers required and the hours of work needed will depend on demand for the product or service which the firm is involved in putting onto the goods market. If a firm is making ice cream it will find that, apart from normal seasonal variations, an exceptionally hot summer will produce an unusually high demand for ice cream. In turn this may mean that the firm will need to take on more workers than expected to cope with this demand.

Derived demand refers to the way in which the demand for a factor of production ultimately depends on the level of demand for the good or service being produced.

A further aspect of demand is the *marginal productivity theory*, and we have spent some time in the previous section looking at the idea of marginal productivity of factors. One of the key ideas in neo-classical economics has been the marginal productivity theory of labour, which puts forward the suggestion that the wages of a worker are equal to the marginal revenue product of the last worker taken on.

Figure 8.7 illustrates how the demand curve for labour reflects, in a simple example, the productivity in money terms of each additional worker taken on. An employer, it is assumed, will only take on an additional worker if the marginal productivity of that worker covers the wage paid. Thus the MRP curve for labour is effectively the demand curve for labour.

In fact the marginal productivity theory is now less popular. Apart from difficulties in measurement, it is often pointed out that the theory is a description of equilibrium level of labour used in the market and not of wage-level determination. Many economists claim that it is the marginal productivity of a worker which determines whether or not he or she is employed and not the wage level. Another criticism is that factors are mutually

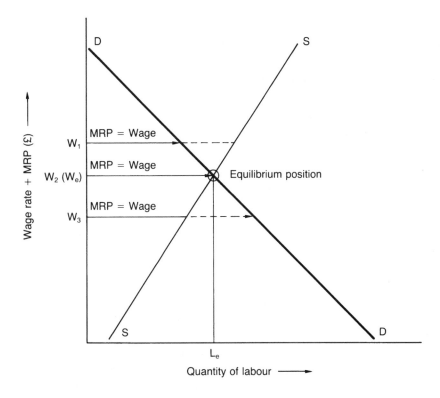

Figure 8.7 Market theory equilibrium.

dependent and it is difficult, if not impossible, to measure how much of an increased output comes from the extra worker and how much from simply longer use of a machine.

The supply of labour

The supply curve for labour rises, as does that for goods, to the right. The higher the wage rate, the more labour will come forward. The supply of labour can be increased in two main ways:

1. Existing employees can work overtime or, with a bonus incentive, work harder.
2. Additional workers can be recruited.

Usually both of these operate. An increase in wage rates will induce unemployed or casually employed labour to seek permanent work and will also create an incentive for existing staff to work longer hours.

As wage rates rise, potential employees and existing workers considering working longer hours will be making comparisons, perhaps without realizing it, of the opportunity cost of the proposed work. If more hours are given to work, fewer hours are given to leisure and a worker will consider the utility of work versus the utility of leisure when deciding whether or not to work more hours. The extra earnings will have to compensate for loss of leisure and so we all, in that situation, will be putting a monetary value on our leisure time.

One interesting feature of the supply curve for labour is that it can become backward-sloping at higher wage rates. This takes place when the higher-paid workers decide that the marginal utility of their reducing leisure time is greater than the wage rate offered. Should a rise occur in wage rates, they may decide to work fewer hours and keep their total earnings the same to increase leisure time (see Fig. 8.8).

Wage equilibrium

The equilibrium wage rate can be seen in the classical theory as established by the interaction of supply and demand curves for labour, just as the equilibrium price of a good is determined by the supply and demand schedules for that good. This is shown in Fig. 8.7. Wage rate W_2 is the equilibrium wage where supply and demand are in balance. Other wage levels will produce either a surplus of supply leading to unemployment or a surplus of demand.

As we have seen, if wage rates are comparatively high more labour will be forthcoming as existing workers take up overtime and reluctant workers offer themselves for jobs. However, firms will find that it is cheaper to use other factors. Thus wage rates will fall towards the equilibrium as some workers settle for jobs with wage rates increasingly closer to the equilibrium. A similar procedure, but in reverse, will operate if wages are below the equilibrium. In an effort to get hands on machines, employers will bid up wages.

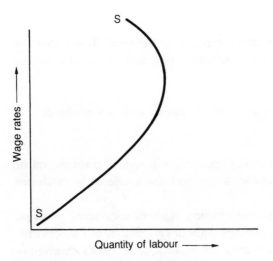

Figure 8.8   Supply curve for labour.

Bilateral monopoly and wages

The assumptions of a free market which underlie the market theory of wages do not apply in much, perhaps most, of the real labour market. Firms may not be faced with a large number of workers operating independently and workers may well not be faced with a large number of firms also acting independently. In the real-world situation, especially in any one locality, there may be only a few or even one employer of a particular type of labour, and the workers may not act independently because they are members of a trade union.

We have to consider, therefore, the case when two monopolies face each other. Strictly speaking, the employer, or trade association if there is one, would be known as a *monopsony*—a monopoly buyer. The firm or association has no competition in the labour market and can set wage rates without fear of being undercut by competition. Many firms are in the position of having a local monopsony—in other words, they have competition in other parts of Britain and Europe but within commuting distance of their factory or office they are the only large user of particular types of labour. Examples would include General Accident as an employer of insurance personnel in Perth or Fiat in Turin as an employer of car-assembly personnel.

Collective bargaining

Where a bilateral monopoly situation arises, wages tend to be fixed as a result of a process known as *collective bargaining*. This involves stages of negotiation between the two parties (hence the term 'bilateral'), which are the employer and trade union representatives—and, if necessary, further processes of conciliation and arbitration. These processes are explored in more detail in the next section. Here we can concentrate on how collective bargaining influences our conclusions on the determination of wages.

If we consider the market theory of wages we can see that should a wage rate be agreed which is different from the equilibrium position then there will be a lack of stability in the market. Disequilibrium which results from bargaining is often held responsible, especially by politicians, for rising unemployment. In Fig. 8.9 we can see how a fixed wage rate at W_x will lead to a surplus supply of labour—at that rate workers are very willing to increase their work yet the firm is not willing to employ as many workers as there were before. At that rate the firm is paying more than the equilibrium rate, and if the original level of employment is maintained the cost of labour will exceed its marginal revenue product.

However, there may be reasons why the firm can pay the higher rate. Long term it will not be happy with the situation but in the short term it may wish to avoid the cost of redundancy payments or laying off trained and experienced workers. It may fear being short of trained staff when an increase in demand is just round the corner.

The firm may prefer to make cost cuts elsewhere such as in obtaining cheaper equipment or moving to a lower-cost site rather than upset labour relations. One common reason given for increasing wage rates like this is the agreement to introduce

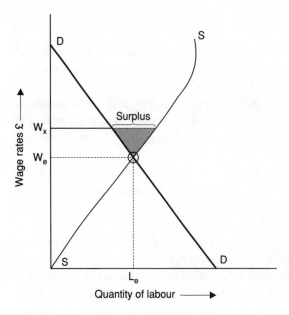

Figure 8.9 Bargaining and wage levels.

improved techniques of working or better equipment which will increase productivity. If this happens, the demand curve for labour will move to the right, and if the firm and union have made the correct calculations it will come to rest at the new wage level.

If these conditions apply in a competitive market it may be that even without there being a bilateral monopoly situation, wage agreements may be made that are above the equilibrium rate. Sometimes, though more rarely in a competitive market, an agreement may be made to fix a wage rate below the equilibrium. This will probably prove unstable in the long run or even in the short run. If a firm is expanding—and remember that the demand for labour is a derived demand—then it may desperately need extra labour and only by increasing wages above the official level, or providing 'perks', will the firm manage to increase labour inputs and so the output of goods.

However, if a firm or association of firms faces an upward-sloping supply curve for labour there is a further explanation of how they will find a stable wage rate and level of employment. Consider Fig. 8.10, which shows the supply and demand for labour in a market where there is a monopsony employer. The demand curve is, as we have seen, also the marginal revenue product curve. It is downward-sloping because increasing the use of any one factor will invoke the operation of diminishing marginal returns. If the firm faces imperfect competition in the sale of its products then any increase in output following an increase in labour will involve a reduction in price, which in turn will further reduce the marginal revenue product of labour.

The supply curve is also the average cost curve for labour for the firm. Each level of wages represents the wage per person employed, assuming for the sake of simplicity that all workers are uniform in status, skills and work requirements. However, if the firm

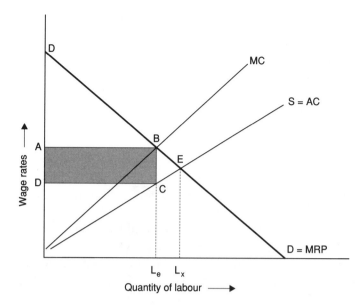

Figure 8.10   Employment and wage rates: monopsony buyer.

increases wages in order to employ an extra worker it will need to pay extra to all the others, so the marginal cost of the extra worker will be greater than the average cost. Hence Fig. 8.10 also shows an upward-sloping MC curve. As with the product market and the firm operating in monopoly or monopolistic competition, the key point is where marginal cost equals marginal revenue. Where MC = MR, the firm finds the equilibrium level of employment.

It will be noted that this level is less than the level that would prevail if we accepted an equilibrium at the free market point where the supply and demand curves cross. It is also a lower wage rate because the wage rate that is appropriate to this reduced level of employment is that where the supply curve is immediately below the point where MC = MR. In other words, the pattern is similar to that in the product market for a monopoly market—MC = MR fixes the level of supply.

In summary, under bilateral monopoly situations, the level of employment and the wage rates will tend to be less than those which would prevail in a competitive market. There is, however, a *zone of negotiation* which enables the trade unions to push the wage rate higher than this equilibrium level. This zone is represented by the rectangle ABCD on Fig. 8.10. The role of the unions and how negotiations or bargaining are carried on is the theme of the next section.

Topic 8.4   Organization of labour

We have already seen the importance of trade union representation as the key to workers negotiating wage levels that may be higher than would be the case were the free forces of supply and demand allowed to operate. Although a detailed knowledge of trade unions is no longer a priority for examination courses at this level, we do need to look briefly at their role in negotiated bargaining.

What are the aims of trade unions?

Trade unions exist for five main reasons:

1. *To improve pay and working conditions*   Some people mistakenly think that this is the *only* aim of unions, which is not the case at all, but it is, nevertheless, one of their main objectives.
2. *To safeguard jobs*   Some industries have been severely affected by redundancies in recent years and the unions have been at the forefront of the fight to preserve jobs. Widespread protest led by the two miners' unions met government proposals to stop working at a large number of coal mines towards the end of 1992, and as a result of these efforts a review and, in some cases, a reprieve was earned.
3. *To offer monetary benefits*   These include sickness and accident benefits, unemployment and strike pay. As state social security benefits have provided more financial aid for workers, this role of the trade unions has diminished in importance.
4. *To liaise with the government and employers' representatives*   Discussions between union leaders and ministers or government departments are common, although less frequent than was the case in the 1970s. There are also working relationships with the appropriate employers' bodies, trade association and the Confederation of British Industry.
5. *To participate in political organizations*   The Labour Party began its life as the political committee of the Trades Union Congress and many unions sponsor Labour members of Parliament. Unions are also represented on many national bodies including the Monopolies and Mergers Commission and on local industrial tribunals.

What are the main types of trade union?

Trade unions vary enormously in character and approach and this needs to be taken into consideration. Some have traditionally been formed by workers in a particular industry and are known as *industrial unions*. The National Union of Mineworkers and the Democratic Union of Mineworkers are examples, as they cover a wide range of types of worker employed by British Coal. There are advantages for the employer in this type of trade union as there is usually only one body to negotiate with.

Craft unions also have a long history and in some respects have similarities to the medieval guilds. Their members all have a particular skill or craft. The textile industry has traditionally included a large number of craft unions for the different specialist skills. Standards of work and training are often important concerns of these unions.

In the last thirty years there has been a considerable growth of so-called *white-collar unions* which bring together clerical, scientific and managerial workers. In the 1960s many such workers felt that they were missing out in the pay stakes because they were less organized than their 'blue-collar' colleagues.

Finally, some of the largest trade unions are *general unions* which embrace a wide range of industries and crafts. In many cases they have been produced by mergers between smaller unions. Just like firms, trade unions can achieve economies of scale by merger!

It is also important to consider the trade unions operating together, which they do through the Trades Union Congress. The TUC is the body which represents over three-quarters of trade unions in the UK. Founded in 1868, it is a highly respected body representing the trade union movement in discussions with governments and employers' bodies such as the Confederation of British Industry. It has little power and authority over member unions although it does advise in the event of disputes between members or unofficial strikes.

The TUC is affiliated to the European Trade Union Confederation (ETUC), which attempts to unite the trade union movement in Europe. Many European unions have stronger political or religious attachments than the TUC, which generally supports the Labour Party to which, as we have seen, it gave birth. One significant trend is the likely increasing power of the ETUC in negotiating with the large multinational companies.

The TUC has an employer's counterpart which has already been mentioned in passing. The Confederation of British Industry (CBI) has an important role in the national discussions with government and union leaders on the economy, legislation and the needs of industry. Other bodies representing firms include the Industrial Society and small firms organizations.

Topic 8.5   Industrial relations

In spite of the commonly held view that the UK suffers from very bad industrial relations, our record compares favourably with those of the USA, Canada and Italy, although it is worse than Germany and Japan. It is the unofficial strike which is so disliked by employers because of its effect on planned production programmes, and especially if it is simply a sympathy strike rather than over a dispute within a firm.

As Fig. 8.11 shows, the number of days lost through strike action has fallen since the days of the 'winter of discontent' in 1978–9, and with increasing unemployment in the 1990s industrial action has become far less of a prominent feature of the economy. A major contributory factor has been the legislation on industrial relations which Parliament put on the statute book in 1980, 1982 and 1984. These laws provide public funds to support the election of trade union officers and deal with control of 'closed shops', i.e. agreements that all workers have to belong to a specific union. The 1984 Trade Union Act sought to limit secondary picketing and made strike action unlawful unless it is approved by union members through a secret ballot.

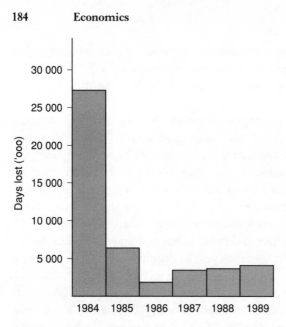

Figure 8.11   Days lost through industrial stoppages. (*Source*: *Annual Abstract of Statistics*, HMSO, various years)

The power of trade unions is a vital aspect of the bilateral monopoly theory and any weakening of this will give the employers comparatively greater power. However, the lesson of Japanese companies has not been lost on European firms. Most firms in Japan adopt a paternalistic approach, with the intention, on both sides, that a worker has a job for many years, probably life, and is looked after by the employer. In return there is strong loyalty and job commitment. The opening by Japanese manufacturers of factories in Europe, such as the Nissan factory near Sunderland, is helping to provide an atmosphere of cooperation rather than confrontation.

Collective bargaining

In normal circumstances relations between trade unions and employers are conducted in an amicable manner. Collective bargaining, as it is known, is the process by which problems over pay, conditions of work, redundancy or training can be the subject of discussion and negotiation. There has been increasing legal recognition of unions and the rights of employees to join unions. Many contracts of employment specifically give the employee the right to join a union and the Social Charter of the EU, introduced in 1988, gives unions a specific place. The aim of this charter is to enable workers to enjoy equal rights across the EU in view of the mobility of labour now enjoyed.

Some collective bargaining has been institutionalized in bodies such as the former Wages Councils, which for many years controlled wage levels for lower-paid workers, joint councils between employers and unions and the Advisory, Conciliation and Arbitration Service (ACAS). This body will act as an intermediary in collective disputes where a trade union is confronting an employer or in personal disputes, for example between an employee unfairly dismissed and the former employer.

There is much greater security of jobs following employment legislation and even job applications have to be dealt with in certain ways or the law may be breached. The following rights are among those now available to employees:

1. Employees must not be discriminated against on the grounds of sex as established by the Equal Pay Act 1984 and the Sex Discrimination Act 1975. There are considerable rights to sick and maternity pay and leave. Women are now entitled to leave of absence to give birth. At present, UK law is less generous than European law. In fact a European Court judgment of 1980 against a British firm forced the changes in UK law which gave women equal pay and other rights. There are wider maternity rights and recently the European Court has had to make judgments on equal rights over pensions.
2. Similarly, there must be no discrimination on the grounds of race (Race Relations Act 1976). Race and sex discrimination cannot be practised in engaging staff nor during employment. It is illegal in advertising for staff to restrict applicants on racial or—with a few exceptions—on sexual grounds.
3. Rights to redundancy pay and due notice have been established through legislation so that after a period of 2 years' continuous employment a firm cannot dismiss an employee without adequate notice and redundancy pay. There are a few exceptions, such as gross misconduct or dishonesty, when employees can be dismissed without notice.
4. Legislation such as the Health and Safety at Work Act 1974 and subsequent minor additions control heating, lighting, hours of work, provision of first aid and protective clothing. As a result, workplaces are much more comfortable and safer than they used to be.

In the event of a dispute, especially over dismissal, the Industrial Tribunal, which is part of the court system, will hear cases and adjudicate between employers and employees. The tribunal conducts its proceedings in a more informal style than the county court and legal representation is not necessary.

In some cases neither the law nor negotiation provides a solution to the problem and unions seek stronger action. Usually this takes the form of one of the following:

1. A restriction of working hours, such as a 'work to rule' or overtime ban. In this way a firm is prevented from increasing output or even from maintaining current levels of production or services. It was used with great effect against British Rail because of the complicated rule book and frequent accepted short-cuts that are normally taken.
2. A restriction on work procedures. Sometimes a trade union may instruct its members not to take part in some process or to work with a particular person.
3. A strike is total withdrawal of labour. If a strike is the end result of a proper ballot of members then it is an official strike but some stoppages are the result of unofficial or

'wildcat' strikes. Sometimes strikes are difficult to enforce if workers are reluctant and the union will employ some members to stand by works entrances as 'pickets'.

Topic 8.6   Can wages be controlled?

It is not only employers who might wish to keep wage increases down but this may also be official government policy. The reason lies mainly in the link between earnings and inflation, as expressed in the Phillips curve (see Chapter 13). In practical terms, if wages are to be controlled so also must prices, so the end result is a 'prices and incomes policy'.

Apart from controls during the Second World War there have been a number of attempts to control incomes and prices, as shown in Table 8.2 Except for the late 1960s and early 1970s, such a policy has been voluntary rather than compulsory, but in 1966 the Wilson government brought in the first statutory prices and incomes controls. At other times persuasion was the method used and the 'social contract' negotiated by the Labour government of the late 1970s with the TUC was a high-profile

Table 8.2   Prices and incomes policies 1948 to 1979

Date	Minister responsible	Duration	Main policy
1948–50	Sir Stafford Cripps	2 years	Control of prices and wages in three phases
1956	Harold Macmillan	10 months	Government's moral authority plus Council on Prices, Productivity and Incomes
1961–63	Selwyn Lloyd	2 years	Wage freeze with $2\frac{1}{2}$ per cent norm followed by a $3\frac{1}{2}$ per cent norm. Establishment of National Incomes Commission (NICKY) and National Economic Development Council (NEDDY)
1965–69	Harold Wilson	4 years	First statutory controls in 1966. Complete pay and prices standstill for 6 months followed by a $3\frac{1}{2}$ per cent norm
1972–74	Edward Heath	2 years	A 'freeze' followed by successive relaxation of controls in second and third phase. In phase three, wages linked to cost of living
1974–76	Harold Wilson	2 years	A voluntary incomes policy combined with a social contract agreed with the TUC
1977–79	James Callaghan	2 years	Continuation of social contract. The first time a British government had attempted four stages of an incomes policy. The final stage involved a 5 per cent ceiling on pay increases

example. Since 1980, controls have been more subtle but even the monetarist administrations of Margaret Thatcher and John Major have not flinched from recommending limits for the private sector and unilaterally imposing them on public sector employees.

In general, however, monetarists have resisted prices and incomes policies as an unwarranted interference with market forces whereas Keynesian economists have supported its use to enable tax changes and other demand stimulants to be used to reduce unemployment. In general, prices and incomes policies have not worked, and under the new European integration it is unlikely that they would be brought in by a national government without a great deal of thought and consultation. As freedom of labour movement becomes a reality in Europe, such a policy would have to be decided by the authorities in the EU and it would be difficult to get agreement on such a course of action.

Various difficulties have stood in the way of success in bringing in wage and price restraint. It is difficult to control both elements, especially prices. Whenever the policy is introduced there will be some groups who claim that they are being unfairly treated because they were just due for a rise in pay and others will claim to need special treatment because of staff shortages. In this respect some employers may be as willing to give pay rises to key workers as are the workers themselves. Finally, a basic objection is made to the whole idea of such a general policy on the grounds that it interferes with the free interplay of economic forces (Fig. 8.12).

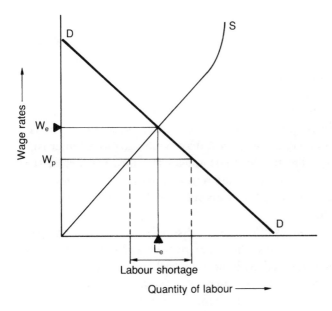

Figure 8.12 Incomes policy: effect of upper wage limit.

Topic 8.7   Rewards for other factors

We have explored distribution theory in some detail so far in the context of the labour market. In part, this is an example of how income is determined for a factor assuming that parallel processes are at work with the other factors. It is also partly in recognition of the importance of labour as the human factor and as the factor that is easiest to adjust in the short term. However, we do need to take a brief look at the distribution of income to the other three factors, to point out both similarities to the distribution of labour and the differences.

Land and rent

The reward of land is usually called rent, but there is a potential confusion here because we have also come across the term *economic rent*. The reader will recall that this describes the payment made to a factor of production over and above the transfer earnings required to keep that factor in its present use. It can be applied to any factor, and when used of labour is sometimes called 'rent of ability', as it is earned by specially talented and able people whose services are in short supply.

It is distinct from rent as applied to the earnings of land, although there is a connection in that rent of land can be seen as payment for use over and above the payment required just to keep the land in farm use as opposed to reverting to nature. We can therefore use it as a starting point as it demonstrates the key feature of land as a factor, i.e. its comparatively inelastic supply.

Land is, for most purposes, fixed in amount. Each year some land is gained from marshes or the sea but other land is lost, and it is now predicted that global warming will reduce further the amount of land available. However, this is still very small as a proportion of the total landmass. If we regard the sea as a 'land' type resource giving up fish, providing tidal power and allowing access to resources such as oil below the seabed, then the world total is fixed.

However, one of the characteristics of land is its enormous variety in quality— probably greater than that of labour. Some land is of very little use at all except as a means of getting from one place to another—the great deserts, for example. Other land, however, contains fertile soil and a climate which encourages farming. Yet further land may contain valuable minerals or have a prime location in relation to trade routes. Even some apparently poor-quality land may have the assets required for a large airport, such as the marshes off the Essex coast.

Rent is determined largely by the forces of demand and supply but in most European countries there are laws, rules and regulations which may restrict land use. For example, in the UK the 'green belt' planning restrictions limit industrial and residential land use around large cities. Land can be improved, and discovery of gold in Alaska and oil in Texas provided windfall rents or selling prices for some previously impoverished land-owners. Agricultural land can be drained, ploughed or otherwise improved.

However, on the whole, land is fixed not only in quantity but also, in the short term, in quality. The result is a very inelastic supply curve with price fluctuations almost entirely the result of changes in demand. In Fig. 8.13 we can see the effect on rents, in theory, as a result of the recession in the UK in the early 1990s. The failure of many businesses and the high rents in inner cities, like London, resulted in empty office blocks and rapid revaluation of the prices of such properties.

It can be seen in Fig. 8.13 that the supply of office premises is comparatively inelastic in the short term. The 1980s were boom years with the growth of office-using firms such as banks, insurance companies and brokers, stockbrokers and money dealers. This demand for central city properties had pushed up prices and property speculators and developers had built large new office blocks, including—with government encouragement—the vast London Docklands project. However, come the recession, many offices remained empty and demand totally slumped.

One thing to note about this result is the distinction between property prices and rent. Property values dropped considerably and many collective investments in property funds showed their first loss over a 12-month period in twenty years. On the other hand, this did not have an immediate effect on rents, despite the prediction in Fig. 8.13. Rents, or payments for use of the properties, were protected by law and lease contracts. Even if a firm were to leave premises, they would in all probability continue to be responsible for rent payment until they could find a new tenant. Thus, unless the tenant became bankrupt (and a number, of course, did), the landowner did not suffer loss of income.

What is more, commercial rents in the UK are traditionally drawn up as reviewable after a set number of years, usually three or five. Further still, the normal clause inserted is that rents will be reviewed 'upwards'—with no obligation on the landowner to concede

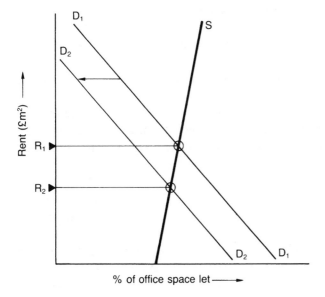

Figure 8.13 Commercial rent in the recession.

a lower rent, even in a sticky market. Whether, of course, a landowner would maintain a high rent in the event of a prolonged slump is another matter, but property owners have a great optimism in the ultimate value of 'bricks and mortar' and may be willing to bide their time.

A study of the recession illustrates an interesting question often asked of land rent. Is it a cost to put into the melting pot when considering the price of goods or services or is it itself determined by the market for goods or services for which it is used? The reader who wishes to pursue this question further is invited to study Samuelson (p. 266).

Capital and interest

The subjects of interest and investment will be dealt with again later in this book, and for the moment we will look at two features of the rewards available to capital. To an economist, capital is fundamentally the equipment or 'plant' used in production or service provision. To the man or woman in the street it means money saved or invested. In fact, the two terms are closely linked, because it is the money invested which purchases the equipment.

Equipment, machinery and industrial plant are sometimes known as *capital goods* to distinguish them from *consumer goods*. Practically all manufacturing and service industries have some capital, ranging from the ladder and bucket of your local window cleaner to the vast equipment in a nuclear power station. These capital goods cost money.

A large proportion of capital goods are leased rather than owned and sometimes the payment is known as a 'rental' and not 'interest', which can be confusing. To economists, *interest* is the payment for capital irrespective of what it is called by the providers and users of the equipment. Some equipment may be purchased by the firm but even if it is, we can still regard the opportunity cost of the purchase price as a form of interest payment. If a builder takes £10 000 from a building society account to invest in a new truck he is losing the interest he would have gained on that money and gaining a depreciating asset. The loss of interest is an opportunity cost and it is the cost of acquiring the truck.

The interest or return on capital investment can be seen as being determined by both the forces of supply and demand and the marginal productivity of that capital. It is also related to the timespan of any investment and the expected earnings over this timespan.

Loanable funds theory

This is the 'classical' theory of interest rates in which the forces of supply and demand for available money ('loanable funds') are regarded as the determinants of interest rates. If households have money which they wish to save rather than spend they will be tempted to save more of it if interest rates are high rather than low. As interest rates rise, so households with savings already invested may invest more, and those currently spending or hoarding will be tempted to save through a bank or other institution, so releasing funds for lending.

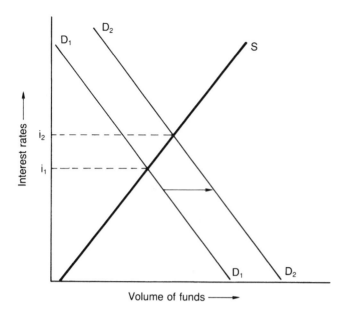

Figure 8.14 Loanable funds theory.

At the same time, there are firms which need to borrow money in order to invest in equipment. They are looking for as low an interest rate as possible, and if rates are low then they are likely to borrow more. The equilibrium level of interest rates and corresponding volume of funds available is set at the intersection of supply and demand curves (Fig. 8.14).

It can be seen that an increase in demand for funds, for example by a government wishing to borrow to invest, is liable to increase interest rates. This is a topic which will be examined further at the macro-economic level in Chapter 15.

Marginal efficiency of capital

The loanable funds theory, as explained rather briefly above, does not answer all questions. In particular, it does not answer the question 'Why should a manufacturer borrow at interest rate *x* per cent?' In other words, what actually shapes the demand curve for loanable funds?

John Maynard Keynes developed the marginal efficiency of capital (MEC) theory to help explain this. He considered that interest rates were largely determined in the money markets, and the entrepreneur then related investment needs to these rates in deciding whether or not to borrow.

The MEC theory is a development of the marginal productivity theory explained earlier for all factors and which is especially used in connection with labour. If we take the marginal and average physical products (in this case of capital) and from them produce the marginal and average revenue products then we can express these figures as percentages of the investment. So the marginal revenue product of £10 000 invested in three computers, for example, might save jobs and time to the extent of £6000 over 5 years. This can be expressed as a percentage of the investment which in turn can be compared with the interest on the funds borrowed to purchase the equipment.

One important feature of the MEC, however, is that it falls as more and more capital is employed, in response to the principle of diminishing returns. Many students forget that this principle applies to any factor, not just labour. In order to be willing to use more and more capital the rate of interest payable on the money borrowed will have to fall. One reason is that usually it is the most profitable projects which are invested in initially and then less profitable. Chapter 9 will investigate this more fully. In Fig. 8.15 it can be seen that the slope of the curve makes the foundation of the demand curve for capital.

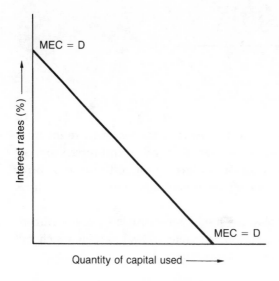

Figure 8.15   Marginal efficiency of capital.

Net present value

One problem with applying MEC to assess whether a project is worth while or not is that the payback is not a single lump sum as soon as the project is completed. Earnings from investment usually come in over a period of time. Yet to calculate correctly the value of this stream of income we cannot just add up the annual sums as if they are equal. At the start of a project the value of future income is less than its face value for two reasons:

1. There is a waiting factor involved. If I do not receive the money until a year has passed I am deprived of its use for a year and may even have to borrow.
2. Inflation might occur in that year and make the value of the earnings even less.

To counteract this problem we have to calculate the value in present-day terms of those future payments. This sum is known as the *net present value (NPV)*, the process is called discounting and the rate we use is known as the discount rate. It is usually the same or related to the current general interest rate.

If future earnings over the lifetime of the equipment, plant, road or whatever is under consideration, is greater when reduced to NPV than the interest outgoings on borrowed money, or interest lost on a firm's own reserves, then the project will go ahead. These concepts were introduced in Chapter 3 in connection with externalities.

Enterprise

Few textbooks consider the entrepreneurial factor when looking at distribution theory. Admittedly, it is difficult to apply, as the typical business executive who may own a firm earns from the profits of the firm and may well have varied motives, including a longing for power. However, there is certainly some relationship between earnings and effort. Many entrepreneurs are very capable of achieving success with one company or one line of business, but as they diversify or acquire new firms their degree of success diminishes. This is not a firm rule, and some top business 'tycoons' thrive on work and expansion, but it is a common feature among smaller local owners of businesses.

Topic 8.8   Why are some people unemployed?

There are many reasons for unemployment:

1. *Structural unemployment* is caused by changes within the economy such as switches in demand. Vinyl records are out and compact discs are in. If different skills are needed for CD manufacture than for the old-style record then unemployment and redundancy may result. Changes in supply and demand, and consequently in work opportunities, is a frequent situation in industries catering for the ever-changing fashion industry.
2. *Frictional unemployment* takes place when there are unemployed workers with a specific skill in one region but a shortage of these workers in other regions. For instance, there may be a large number of unemployed people in north-east England, but vacancies for people with their skills in the south-east. The term 'friction' refers to the slow way in which such inequalities are evened out by migration. The problem of persuading workers to take jobs in other countries of the European Union is an example of a new type of frictional unemployment. It also applies to slow movement between types of job wherever located.
3. *Seasonal unemployment* may take place if there is a suspension of workers because of changes in the weather or because a particular job is available only at certain times of the year. Examples of the first type include building, agriculture and fishing, although usually only casual workers are rendered jobless by temporary weather problems. The second type of seasonal unemployment is found in the holiday

trade. Some workers may find it possible to link seasonal jobs, for example by having a job at a holiday camp or a vineyard in the summer and working at a sugarbeet factory in the winter.

4. *Casual unemployment* is a decreasing feature and tends to be found among migrant workers such as gypsies and casual labourers.

5. *Residual unemployment* is the term used to describe the basic level of natural unemployment already discussed above.

6. *Technological unemployment* occurs when new processes and technology render older labour-intensive methods obsolete. In recent years computers have taken over many routine clerical jobs and computer-controlled robots now do the work previously done by thousands at car factories such as Ford at Dagenham or Fiat in Turin.

7. *Disguised unemployment* is really *underemployment* when people have a job in name but are not used to the full. It has been typical of the planned economies of Eastern Europe, and one of the major problems in Russia and its neighbours is the creation of actual unemployment where it was previously non-existent. Even in a market economy, however, it is possible to have employees not working to the full, especially for parts of the year. Work may be seasonal but many employers would rather pay employees to drink tea for most of the day than make them redundant and have to chance what the job centre will bring a few months later. This is a common feature of farms, especially in more traditional societies, where the family land is considered as able to support all members of an extended family.

The above causes of unemployment will exist even if there is an equilibrium in the labour market, i.e. a stable average wage rate and labour supply. There are some very important causes of unemployment, however, which result from a lack of equilibrium. Usually, average wage rates are higher than the equilibrium level would be if supply and demand for labour were the sole feature determining wages. We could now just mention briefly three causes of unemployment arising from disequilibrium:

1. An *increase* in the supply of labour. This usually takes place slowly but can have an effect on specific industries or occupations. In a number of developing countries it results from a general increase in population, but in Europe and North America it is usually significant when certain types of skill become very common, perhaps as a result of an earlier shortage. It is possible that the computer industry will be facing this problem in a few years' time as increasing numbers of computer-literate students come onto the market.

2. *Cyclical unemployment*—often known as 'demand-deficient unemployment'. This type of unemployment is associated with a reduction in demand during the recession part of a trade cycle. It was very significant in the 1930s and in the recession at the beginning of the 1990s.

   Governments often claim that cyclical unemployment is outside their control, yet governments of all political views aim to keep unemployment low and are unhappy when it is high. Keynes introduced policy techniques for dealing with this type of

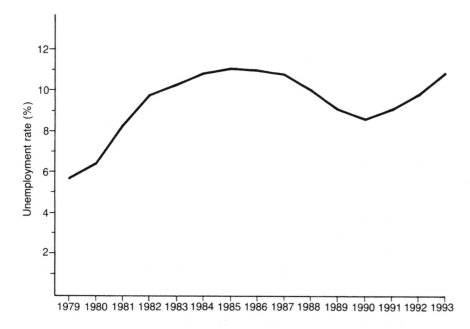

Figure 8.16   Unemployment in the EC 1979–93. (*Source*: Eurostat, *Basic Statistics*.)

unemployment although they are now considered by many economists and politicians as ineffective in some quarters. Figure 8.16 indicates how unemployment has a
tendency to be cyclical in form, and suggests that this may be one of the major causes
of the problem.

3. *High wage unemployment*, sometimes called 'classical unemployment', is the type
    which is often blamed by the tabloid press for loss of jobs. It occurs when union
    power enables wages to be pitched at a level higher than equilibrium in real terms or
    when government incomes policies fix wage increases that are higher than inflation.
    Basically, workers then become too expensive and firms will substitute machine
    technology and cut back on labour. It has been said that one person's pay rise is
    another's redundancy letter!

There is a strong relationship between unemployment and inflation, which will be
discussed later in Chapter 13.

Advanced Study Topic 8.1   Combining the factors

In Advanced Study Topic 5.2 we looked at combining indifference curves and budget
lines in order to study ideal combinations of consumer purchases. We can use a similar
technique to examine the ideal inputs of factors of production.

For the sake of simplicity it is best to look at the situation where the firm is faced with two variable factors only. The principles apply when more are brought into the picture but we need computer simulation to illustrate the decisions. If we combine two factors which will produce the same level of output, and link them together, we obtain a curve which is known as an *isoquant*. This is shown in Fig. AST 8.1. It is possible to draw any number of isoquants on a graph, each one representing a higher level of output and so higher levels of input of the factors.

Now just as the individual has a budget line, so the firm has cost restrictions which can be expressed as a straight line, known as an *isocost* line (see Fig. AST 8.1). This shows those combinations of the factors that are affordable.

The most cost-effective combination for the firm is that which occurs where the isoquant for its required output level has the lowest possible cost combination—in other words where the isocost line is tangential to the appropriate isoquant. Alternatively, if the firm is restricted on costs then it can choose a combination of factors that will give it the maximum output for its cost restriction, points L and C on Fig. AST 8.1.

In reality firms rarely do work out the combinations with isoquant and isocost lines, but the concepts help us to understand what happens when firms apply costing analysis to their output levels and make the decisions over levels of output and the factor inputs

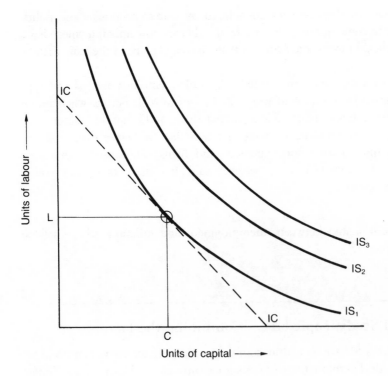

Figure AST 8.1 Isoquants and isocost lines.

which are suitable for that output level. The shape of the isoquants will depend to a large extent on the technical requirements for factor combinations, and these can change over time.

For further reading see Begg *et al.* Chapter 11 (appendix).

Essay questions

1. Assess the case for and against replacing national collective bargaining with an alternative system such as regional bargaining or profit-related pay as a method of determining wages. (*Source*: The Associated Examining Board, June 1992)
2. Consider the view that substitutability of factors is the prime requirement for the success of the market as an allocative mechanism. (*Source*: Oxford and Cambridge Schools Examination Board, June 1992)
3. Outline briefly the causes of differences in the wage rates paid to workers of different age, sex, race and skill in different industries and occupations. Discuss the possible effects of the introduction of a national minimum wage in the UK. (*Source*: Northern Examinations and Assessment Board, June 1992)
4. Outline the factors which determine the structure of wages in the economy. Explain whether or not there are any economic reasons why, despite equal pay legislation, on average, women are paid less than men in Britain. (*Source*: Northern Examinations and Assessment Board, June 1991)
5. What economic effects may trade unions have on the wages and employment of:
    (a)   Their own members;
    (b)   Non-unionized workers?
    Can the actions of trade unions raise the rate of inflation? (*Source*: University of Oxford, June 1992)
6. Why might economic rent be regarded as an unnecessary payment? If this is so, why are property rents high in city centres? (*Source*: University of Oxford, June 1992)

Chapter 9

Macro-economics: national income and accounting

Introduction

The national income consists of a collection of goods and services produced in a certain period (usually a year) and reduced to a common basis by being measured in monetary terms. Income is a *flow* and not a stock of goods existing at one time. This distinction was made in Chapter 2 and illustrated in Fig. 2.1. The national income is concerned with additions to the nation's wealth—with new machines rather than with all the machines existing in a factory or with new cars rather than with all the cars on the roads. The national income for the UK was £407 899 million in 1992 at market prices. This figure and those for other European countries will be examined in more detail later.

Topic 9.1   Uses of national income statistics

National income figures are especially important in helping us to analyse the following situations:

1. Measurement and comparison of economic growth over *time*. We can compare periods of history for which figures are available. In doing this we need to be aware of certain possible problems such as:
    (a) The effect of inflation—so real not nominal changes need to be considered.
    (b) Methods of collecting data and accuracy can vary over time—this is a problem faced especially by economic historians.
    (c) Populations change over time so comparison is usually made on a per capita basis.
    (d) Quality of goods can vary over time.
    (e) Some GDP can involve military expenditure.
    (f) Externalities are not taken into account.
2. Measurement and comparison of economic growth and wealth between countries and regions. Again there are some snags:
    (a) Comparisons need to be made on a per capita basis.
    (b) Countries differ in accuracy of statistics.
    (c) The problem of using a common currency and what exchange rate to use.

Topic 9.2   The flow of income

The concept of national income has become very important in the last half-century as a result of the increasing role of governments in attempting to manage the economy in the interest of establishing an equilibrium position and maintain a high level of employment. Keynes became dissatisfied with the prevailing view that the economy naturally tended to produce a full employment equilibrium in a free market economy. Here we begin to look at some of the concepts which Keynes and later economists have used to investigate equilibrium national income and employment.

Stocks, wealth and flows

There is an important distinction between the national capital stock (the nation's wealth) and the income which flows from that stock. As was seen in Fig. 2.1, part of the income is used to deal with depreciation and the rest produces *net* investment in order to increase the stock, or is consumed. The size of the stock of capital determines the level of national income/output in the following year and so if growth is to occur (defined as increase in national income) then net investment has to occur in order to increase the stock.

Circular flow of income

To understand this concept we need first to look at the national accounting identities and recognize that

$$\text{National income} = \text{national product} = \text{national expenditure}$$

or as it is usually expressed:

$$NY = NP = NE$$

The circular flow is illustrated at its simplest if we consider a simple economy consisting just of firms producing goods and households which provide factors of production and spend earnings on goods. In this case all the earnings of households are spent on goods and services provided by the firms. This money earned by the firms goes out as earnings to the factors of production (wages for labour, etc.) and this provides the income for households to spend. Figure 9.1 illustrates this simple idea.

We can complicate this basic model a little if we consider that households will *save* some of their money and these savings will disappear from the circular flow as a *leakage* or *withdrawal*. However, those savings will not usually be placed under the floorboards but will be the source of new *investment* by firms. This investment will include both planned (*ex-ante*) investment and actual (*ex-post*) investment. For example, if households spend less than all their income firms may well produce more than will be consumed and

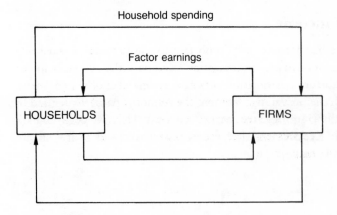

Figure 9.1 A simple two–sector economy.

will accumulate stocks of unsold goods which are regarded as investment. Figure 9.2 illustrates this more realistic model.

> *Ex-ante* investment refers to that investment which is planned in advance. *Ex-post* investment refers to the investment level which actually takes place in a specific period of time and is quantified afterwards.

The total for *savings* must always equal the total for *investment*. The logic behind this is that as income (Y) is 'spent' on consumption plus savings and this expenditure (E) consists of the money spent on consumption plus that invested, it follows that savings

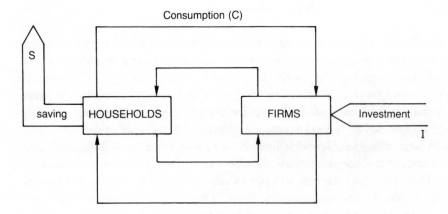

Figure 9.2 Circular flow with investment/savings.

must equal investment (I). Expressed in simple mathematical shorthand we can say:

$$Y = C + S \text{ and } E = C + I$$

Therefore

$$S = I$$

We can also add other leakages and injections—for example, there is government expenditure (G) as an injection but taxation (T) as a leakage. We can then introduce foreign trade adding exports (X) to injections and imports (M) to withdrawals. So a full equation of identity would be:

$$I + G + X = S + T + M$$

If we include exports and imports we are describing an 'open economy'—if we exclude them it is called a 'closed economy'. This distinction is important in establishing our assumptions.

A *closed economy* is one where the flow of money is confined to the households and firms within that economy. An *open economy* is one where there is money leakage through imports and injections as a result of exports.

Topic 9.3 How is national income measured?

As we have already seen, we can look at the cycle of flow of income and see the factors and the goods they produce and also the flow of money—factor incomes and spending (Figs 9.1 and 9.2). It would be possible for an economy not to use money and markets and to distribute goods to the factors on some other basis, but over most of the world some form of money economy is used.

It is this use of money which enables us to measure national income because otherwise it would not be realistic to add up output of cars, milk, carrots and saucepans, add in services like tourism and retailing, and get any meaningful figure. Now we have also seen that one feature of the model is that there is an equality—in fact, an *identity* between the income which the households earn and the spending they make on goods and services. If we want to measure national income using this simple model we can measure factor incomes, household expenditure or the value of output.

However, before we see how we actually do this we have to clarify three aspects of our definition of national income.

What is included in national income?

If we look at a set of official statistics like Eurostat's *Basic Statistics of the Community* or the HMSO publications *Key Data* and *Annual Abstract of Statistics* we find 'National Income' only as a general heading, if at all. The figures are usually headed by one of three other terms—GDP, GNP and NNP. What are these strange abbreviations? They are actually part of the more accurate definition of national income.

Gross domestic product (GDP) measures the expenditure of both UK residents and foreigners on goods produced within the UK within a certain year, or alternatively it may measure the value of UK output in a year. In many ways it is the simplest measure of national income and is probably the most widely used.

Gross national product (GNP) goes a stage further. GDP measures factor incomes from the UK economy but some of the UK economy is owned by foreigners. Much property is owned by overseas residents as are a number of firms and so some income disappears overseas. The reverse also occurs, in that a number of British firms and residents receive income from overseas. When these two flows are taken together we get a figure called *net property income from abroad*. If this is added to GDP we arrive at GNP.

Net national product deals with a second problem. The original flow diagram (Fig. 2.1) indicated that some income does not actually increase wealth but replaces worn-out capital. In normal accounting terms this is called *depreciation* but for the national accounts it is entered as *capital consumption*. In many respects NNP is the real measure of national income but, as mentioned earlier, GDP is more commonly used as it is easier to calculate (Fig. 9.3).

Although the methods of calculating national income vary between countries, as does the accuracy of data collection, all countries aim at producing these three definitions and statistics published for comparisons by the United Nations, the World Bank and other international agencies also use them as standards, usually quoted in US dollars (Fig. 9.4).

What are market prices and factor cost?

A look at any set of national income statistics will reveal one or both of the two terms 'factor cost' and 'market prices'. The figure which was given at the beginning of this chapter for the UK national income was said to be 'at market prices' but at the time this term was not explained. So what do they mean?

If we add up the value of all the goods and services produced in a country we might simply count up the prices to the consumer—the price charged over the counter or in the showroom. The task is difficult enough as it is but at least we know what we are after using this method. It does, however, carry a problem. The prices we pay include, in many cases, indirect taxes like VAT and excise duty or, in some cases, are lower than they should be as a result of subsidies from governments or the EU. To arrive at a more realistic figure, therefore, taxes and subsidies are often removed from the figures and the result is national income at *factor cost*.

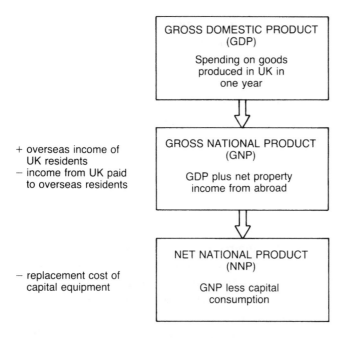

Figure 9.3   National income determination.

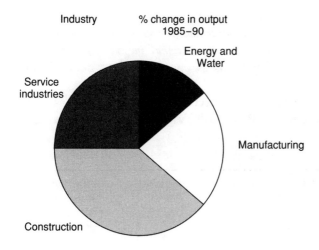

Figure 9.4   GDP by industry of output (*Source*: CSO, *Key Data* 1991, HMSO).

One of the reasons factor cost is a better method of presenting national income figures is that it removes differences in taxation and subsidies when we are comparing one country with another or one year with another.

> *Factor cost* is the term used for the presentation of national income figures taking *market prices* and adjusting these for indirect taxes and subsidies.

What is real national income?

One of the advantages of national income figures is that they enable us not only to measure incomes but also to compare one country with another and also the progress of any one country over time. We have just seen that this is one advantage of using factor cost rather than market prices as the basis of our calculations. It is also a reason for looking at *real* as well as *nominal* national income.

Let us take the figures for the UK for 1981 and 1991 as examples. In 1981 GDP for the UK at factor cost was £218 755 million and rose to £514 594 million in 1992. Now we might think that this is good going and congratulate ourselves as loyal British citizens on an excellent job—certainly the governments in the 1980s were doing that! Yet were we better off *to the extent that those figures suggest*? Not really. We need to consider whether the GDP in 1992 represented greater wealth of goods and services than 1981 and did not just measure inflation.

Between 1981 and 1992, prices rose by 66 per cent and this has to be taken into consideration when looking at the rise in GDP. If we recalculate GDP using a measure of inflation then we often refer to that measure as the *national income deflator*. Using the deflator we can recalculate GDP in real terms as opposed to just nominal ones (Table 9.1).

In presentation of national income figures where several years are compared, as in the *Annual Abstract of Statistics* for the UK, GDP is usually valued at the price level for a

Table 9.1 Inflation and real GDP 1993

Country	Inflation (%)	Real GDP Growth (%)	Country	Inflation (%)	Real GDP Growth (%)
UK	1.6	1.9	USA	2.9	3.0
France	2.1	−1.0	Turkey	66.0	7.3
Germany	4.2	−1.3	Australia	1.8	3.3
Italy	4.2	−0.7	Japan	1.2	0.1
Denmark	1.2	0.5	Canada	1.9	2.4

Source: *Barclays Economic Review* (Second Quarter, 1994)

particular year to aid comparison. So data may have a footnote such as 'at 1985 prices' or similar wording.

Calculating national income

There are three ways of calculating national income based on the circular flow of income. We have to intercept the flow at some point and take a statistical snapshot of its size, and the three approaches should, in theory, come up with the same answer.

The output method attempts to measure national income by making a valuation of all goods and services produced in the UK (GDP) and then calculating capital consumption to arrive at NNP. Now at first this might seem simple. We can send civil servants in their grey suits round all shops, factories and farms to find out what has been produced and sold and to come back with their clipboards full and feed the data into a computer. However, it is not nearly as simple as that!

Calculating national income by product carries some problems:

1.   In the first place there is the danger of double-counting. It is a truism that the output of one industry is the input of another. The coal industry is mainly concerned with the output of coal but for the electricity industry, coal represents an input. If British Coal is asked to tell the Central Statistical Office what the value of its output was in 1994 it can do so—but only a small proportion of that output is then bought by households. Most of it goes into further production. If we ask the electricity industry for a total value of its output then an element in the prices for electricity will be the cost of coal. If we add the value of electricity to the coal we will have double-counted. In turn, some electricity users will be factories which in turn will make a product, etc. What in fact is counted is not the price of the finished product of a producer but the *value added*, i.e. the difference between a firm's revenue from sales and the costs of the raw materials and fuel it has used.
2.   A second problem is that the value of services needs to be added to the total and this necessitates calculating the value of banking services, accountants and solicitors. A particular problem arises with those who are dealing not with new goods but second-hand ones. The second-hand car dealer does not contribute the price of the car to national income but the difference between that price and the cost of the car to the dealer. This is the value added for each car.
3.   A third problem is counting the value of those who have no tangible output nor even a marketable service. Most of these are public employees such as police, teachers or civil servants, and income is really the only way of valuing such work.

A study of Fig. 9.4 will indicate the make-up of GDP by output and the different sectors of the economy which have to be measured to achieve the final figure. One significant feature is the large size of the construction industry in GDP terms.

The income method is in many ways the easiest to visualize and on which to collect information. It totals all the personal incomes of everyone in the country. Since the

Inland Revenue, at least, is keen to get accurate information on all incomes, the data should be obtainable, but this method also has its problems:

1. One problem is that of *transfer earnings*. This term includes social security benefits and other payments from National Insurance or taxation. They are all characterized by the fact that they are not rewards for work done and are simply a transfer (via the government) of part of one person's gross wage to another person who is in need of assistance. If these payments were included there would be some double-counting.
2. Some people are paid 'in kind'. For example, farmers and farm workers may consume some of what they produce, company directors may have a company car and other perks may be available. To be accurate, the value of these benefits should be included.
3. Workers have certain expenses of their business, such as business travel, which should be deducted from national income calculations.

Table 9.2 presents the national income accounts for 1991 using the income method, and the reader is advised to study it carefully.

There are many different types of income and all present their problems when it comes to measuring them. Table 9.3 indicates the main types and the proportion which is taken in statutory and other deductions. Wages and salaries are nearly all paid under a tax and National Insurance system called PAYE (Pay As You Earn) which makes data collection easier.

Expenditure is the third method of calculating national income. It totals all consumption on food, clothes, housing, fuel, etc. All spending on services and investment must also be included. After all, what is not spent out of income must be saved or invested. Account must also be taken of the expenditure of central and local government.

One problem with this method is how to deal with semi-finished goods which clearly have not been sold and so no spending has been made on them. This problem is dealt with by making a valuation of stock in hand and adding it in. Another problem is the presence of taxation in total spending, and this has to be deducted. Otherwise a government could produce a paper increase in national income simply by putting up indirect taxation.

A final problem with the expenditure method is that it cannot take account of exports. Goods and services exported enter into both output and earnings calculations but clearly not into the expenditure method. On the other hand, this method will account for imports which the other two will not. The result is that all methods have to attempt to find out the *net income from abroad* to add to the value of national output.

A final point to note about the use of all three methods is that while in theory the final figure for GDP or GNP should be the same whichever method is chosen, this is not the case. Inevitably, in every country of the world, inaccuracies and delays in data collection mean that errors creep in. The existence of 'black' markets or the hiding of income or output figures for tax evasion cause similar problems. In fact, some people regard unofficial trading as one of the main causes of the discrepancies.

Table 9.2   National accounts (GDP) 1992

	£ million
Income method	
Income from employment	341 009
Income from self-employment	58 060
Gross trading profits (companies)	64 574
Gross trading surplus (public corp.)	1 813
Other government GTS	89
Rent	46 846
Consumption of non-trading capital	4 207
Total Domestic Income:	516 598
less stock appreciation	−2 216
Statistical discrepancy	212
Gross Domestic Product (factor cost)	514 594
Expenditure method	
Consumers' Expenditure	382 696
General Government Final Consumption	132 378
Gross domestic fixed capital formation	−1 992
Value of increase in stocks	92 892
Total Domestic Expenditure	605 974
Exports of goods/services	139 827
Total Final Expenditure	745 801
less imports of goods/services	−149 164
Statistical discrepancy	−472
Gross Domestic Product	596 165
Net property income from abroad	5 777

Table 9.3   Household income 1991

Sources of income	% of total income
Wages and salaries	58
Self-employed income	10
Rent, interest and dividends	9
Private pensions, annuities	9
Social security benefits	12
Other current transfers	2
Direct Taxes, etc.:	
Taxes on income	14
National Insurance	3
Pension contributions	2
	£ billion
Total Household Income	497
Total Household Disposable Income	404

Source: CSO, *Key Data 1993/4*, HMSO.

There are also errors produced in the process of calculation, rounding of figures and some inevitable lost information. These are usually entered on the accounts as 'Statistical discrepancy'. However, provided a consistent approach is adopted, national income is a valuable measure of the economic health of any nation. A persistent fall in GDP is the official indication of a recession and a rise in GDP in real terms measures growth.

Topic 9.4   National income, consumption and savings

Having looked at the nature of national income and how it is measured we need to examine the model of equilibrium national income which includes the component parts of aggregate demand and supply. The concept of an 'equilibrium' is a regular theme in economics as we search for stability in economic affairs. Much of the analysis presented here was developed by Keynes and economists in the 1940s and 1950s working on Keynesian principles.

The key issue at the root of this analysis is the problem raised by Keynes of achieving full employment equilibrium. The older 'neo-classical' viewpoint (followed by today's monetarists) believed that the operations of a free market, through the price mechanism, will automatically produce an equilibrium of full employment of all the factors of production. Keynes saw the likelihood of this mechanism failing, with possible permanent unemployment of factors and demand-pull inflation (see Chapter 13).

Goods and other markets

At a macro-economic level individual consumers and producers are added together to produce an aggregate demand and supply. We can see that if we were to total all the demand and supply schedules for all goods and services we would obtain figures for the total demand for and supply of all goods and services in the UK. We then recognize that if we can do this, we see three major markets emerging which are interrelated—the *goods* market; the *factor* markets (including the important market for labour); and the *money* market. The first two are sometimes referred to as the 'real' markets and it is those on which we will concentrate.

Equilibrium national income

The equilibrium level of national income/output within the goods market is achieved when the *planned* (or *ex-ante* as it is sometimes called) aggregate money demand (AMD) of all economic agents in the economy in the current period equals the income produced in the previous period. By definition, this income must equal total output since all factor incomes are the result of output and in a closed economy, such as is described below, national output and income are equal. Because of this we can see that if planned consumption is equal to actual output/income then the economy is in equilibrium.

> *Equilibrium national income* is the level of output or income in an economy at which planned expenditure equals actual income produced.

Consumption, savings and investment

Our look at consumption and savings starts with a simple two-sector economy, rather as we did with circular flow of income. We assume that the economy consists of just households and firms. The analysis considers the way consumption increases with an increase in income. There are other forces which might influence the levels of consumption, but it is normally considered that income level is the most important.

However, if we assume a very low level of income (even no income at all) then there will be some basic consumption even if this involves using reserves of savings or borrowing (known as 'dissaving'). This level of expenditure is usually known as *autonomous* consumption. As income rises consumption will increase above this level and this is called *induced* consumption, i.e. it is produced by some other influence acting on it. This applies whether we look at an individual household or at the country as a whole.

> *Autonomous consumption* is that level of consumption by an economy which takes place irrespective of the level of national income. *Induced consumption* is that level of consumption which rises with the level of income.

This consumption is usually represented as a straight line on a graph. The vertical axis represents planned expenditure or *aggregate demand*; the horizontal axis represents income or output (they are the same, as we have seen) or, if we are looking at individual households, the horizontal axis might represent disposable income. The straight line is often represented by the usual linear formula:

$$C = a + bY$$

where $C =$ planned consumption
$a =$ autonomous consumption
$Y =$ income/output
$b =$ the slope of the line.

This slope is very important and represents the proportion of any extra pound of income which is spent on consumption goods and services, as opposed to being saved. It is known as the *marginal propensity to consume* (MPC). Some economists argue that the MPC decreases as income rises, producing a flattening curve, especially for individuals.

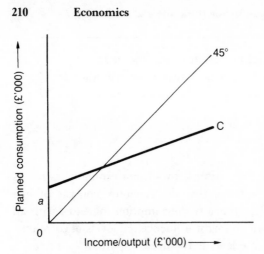

Figure 9.5 The consumption function.

On the other hand, applied research in both the USA and the UK indicate that the MPC may be constant. The line plotted on the graph is known as the *consumption function* (Fig. 9.5).

> The *marginal propensity to consume* (MPC) is the proportion of any extra income received which is spent on goods and services as opposed to being saved. It is represented by a line known as the *consumption function*.

The graph is normally drawn in such a way that the vertical and horizontal scales are identical and a 45° line is drawn to represent the location of equilibrium between income/output and expenditure/demand. The consumption function begins above this line and eventually crosses it. The consumption between planned consumption of '0' and the consumption function is the autonomous consumption. At the point where the consumption function crosses the 45° line income = demand, i.e. all income is spent. A further line can be drawn crossing the horizontal axis immediately below the point where the consumption function crosses the 45° line and which represents savings. Figure 9.6 explains this in a diagram with which students should become very familiar. We can therefore also speak of a *marginal propensity to save* and of a *savings function*. Since income has to be either spent or saved, we can say that:

$$MPC + MPS = 1$$

$$\text{or } Y = C + S$$

These are *identities* rather than mathematical equations.

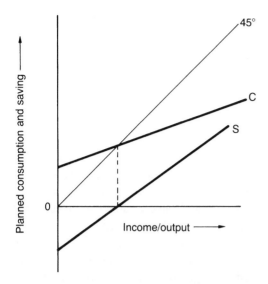

Figure 9.6   Consumption and savings.

A look at Fig. 9.6 will bring out the fact that the savings function is negative when consumption is in its autonomous phase, i.e. when *dissavings* are operative; is zero when consumption = output/income; and becomes positive as income rises above this equilibrium level.

> The *marginal propensity to save* (MPS) is the proportion of any additional income that is saved as opposed to being spent on goods and services.

We can also use the concept of an *average propensity* to *consume* (APC) or to *save* (APS), which is:

$$APC = \frac{\text{Total consumption}}{\text{Total income}}$$

There are, however, some other influences on consumption which include:

- The level of *wealth* in a household, including house values and the values of shares and other assets which will also influence how much people plan to spend and to save.
- *Inflation* is also important. If inflation is anticipated then people may well buy in advance but inflation also reduces personal wealth in real terms and, on the whole, the latter outweighs the former, so inflation tends to produce a reduction in consumption.

- Availability of *credit* and interest rates are also important factors affecting consumption.

Theories on consumption/savings

There are three main theories on the relationship between consumption (and savings) and income:

1. *Keynes' theory*   Keynes developed the consumption function concept but was concerned that MPC is likely to decline as incomes rise with MPS increasing, and that this would reduce demand for goods and services and have an adverse effect on the economy. Experience has indicated that MPC tends to be constant.
2. *Modigliano* and *Ando*: life cycle theory   This theory suggests that consumption depends less on income and more on a combination of life style and the age of individuals. The level of consumption will change throughout a person's life as various needs arise.
3. *Friedman: permanent income hypothesis*   According to this theory, spending is based on a person's concept of average income over a lifetime subject to changes in wealth, incomes, interest rates, etc.

Investment

So far we have looked at households and their consumption but if we consider aggregate demand for the whole country we appreciate that part of the expenditure planned involves investment goods by firms. The determinants of investment will be examined later. For the moment it is sufficient to note that investment demand is normally regarded as being autonomous as far as income/output is concerned, and so on the standard graph it is represented by a horizontal line parallel to the horizontal axis. If we wish to describe aggregate demand as opposed to just household consumption then we need to add investment to the picture.

This is usually done by drawing a further line parallel to the consumption function line on a graph relating aggregate demand (vertical axis) and income/output (horizontal axis), as shown in Fig. 9.7.

Equilibrium national income

The analysis so far is leading us to an analysis of the equilibrium level of national income. The equilibrium condition for the model is represented by the equation:

$$Y = C + I$$

Note that this is *not* an identity (like $Y = C + S$) as it may not always hold true.

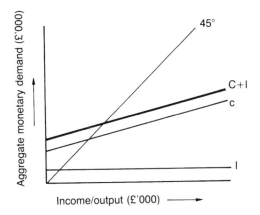

Figure 9.7   Aggregate demand: consumption and investment.

To demonstrate equilibrium graphically we usually use a diagram which shows the equilibrium point as being that where the aggregate monetary demand (AMD) crosses the 45° line. If we assume that aggregate supply responds rapidly to any change in demand then the 45° line can be seen as representing the aggregate supply function. So at the equilibrium point:

$$\text{Aggregate demand} = \text{aggregate supply}$$

If we bring in the lower or savings part of the diagram as in Fig. 9.8 we can see that at this same level of income/output the injection of investment equals the withdrawal of savings. So we can say that at the equilibrium point:

$$\text{Planned savings} = \text{planned investment}$$

$$\text{Planned leakages} = \text{planned injections}$$

Any position either side of this equilibrium will lead to either an excess of planned demand over output or an excess of output over planned demand. So in Fig. 9.8, Y_e represents the equilibrium point for consumption and investment.

Adding other sectors

As with the cycle of income, we can complicate the simple two-sector economy by adding in the government sector and considering exports and imports. So far, we have compiled an aggregate monetary demand identity as:

$$\text{AMD} = C + I$$

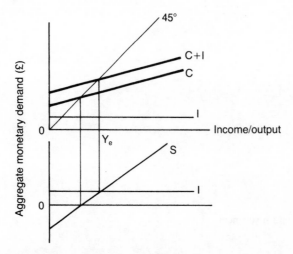

Figure 9.8   Equilibrium national income.

If we add the injections of government spending and export demand and the leakages of taxation and import demand we can extend the identity to:

$$AMD = C + I + G - T + X - M$$

When AMD is the same as total income we have a state of equilibrium which can be represented by:

$$Y = C + I + G - T + X - M$$

or $\underset{\text{leakages}}{S + T + M}$ $=$ $\underset{\text{injections}}{I + G + X}$

In other words, when equilibrium exists two equations are satisfied:

$$\text{Income (Y)} = AMD$$

and

$$\text{Leakages} = \text{Injections}$$

See Fig. 9.9.

If exports and imports are introduced we then describe the situation as an 'open' economy as opposed to the 'closed' economy when domestic demand and output only are considered.

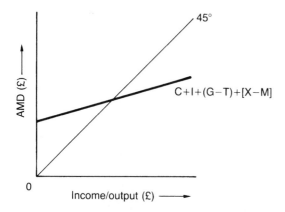

Figure 9.9   Aggregate monetary demand: four-sector open economy.

Equilibrium national income and employment

If equilibrium national income is at the right point to employ all the labour force then the economy is in balance. However, if the equilibrium national income is less than the level of income required for full employment then it is not in balance—in fact, there will be a deficiency in demand in the economy resulting in unemployment. Keynes regarded deficient demand as the main cause of unemployment.

In this situation a graph will show a *deflationary gap* between the AMD line representing the equilibrium national income level and that which it would have to be in order to produce full employment. If, on the other hand, the equilibrium income level is above that for full employment then demand is greater than that which can be catered for with the available labour force at normal rates and an *inflationary gap* will appear.

This is shown in Fig. 9.10. The student may like to consider recent fluctuations in the UK economy in the light of this analysis and see how often deficiency in demand is regarded in the press, as well as by academic economists, as a major cause of recession.

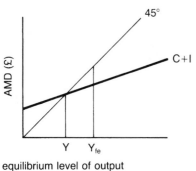

Y = equilibrium level of output
Y_{fe} = level of output for full employment

(a)

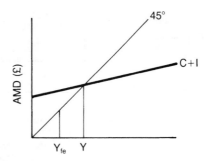

Y = equilibrium level of output
Y_{fe} = level of output for full employment

(b)

Figure 9.10   (a) Deflationary gap. (b) Inflationary gap.

Topic 9.5   The multiplier

Basic information

The *multiplier* is a concept developed by R. F. Kahn and was extensively used by Keynes. In the context of national income it expresses the idea that even small changes in total spending may well lead to relatively large changes in the equilibrium level of net national product (NNP) (Fig. 9.11).

For example, if the government were to inject an additional £10 million of investment into the economy this would result in more people being employed and other factors being used. This in turn would generate income for the factors used—wages, for example. These earnings would in turn be spent, so generating further factor uses and factor earnings. Of course, not all income is spent as some is saved. We have already seen that the proportion of any extra income being spent on final goods (consumption) is known as the marginal propensity to consume. This can be represented as:

$$\text{MPC} = \frac{\text{The change in consumption}}{\text{The change in income}}$$

If MPC = 0.8, then 80 per cent of the extra earnings generated will be spent as opposed to being saved. Thus for each increase in extra spending there are several stages of further earnings generated which in turn will increase aggregate demand. This is illustrated in Fig. 9.12.

The ratio between the original change and the final increase in national income is called the *multiplier* and can be expressed mathematically as:

$$\text{Multiplier} \ (k) = \frac{1}{1 - \text{MPC}}$$

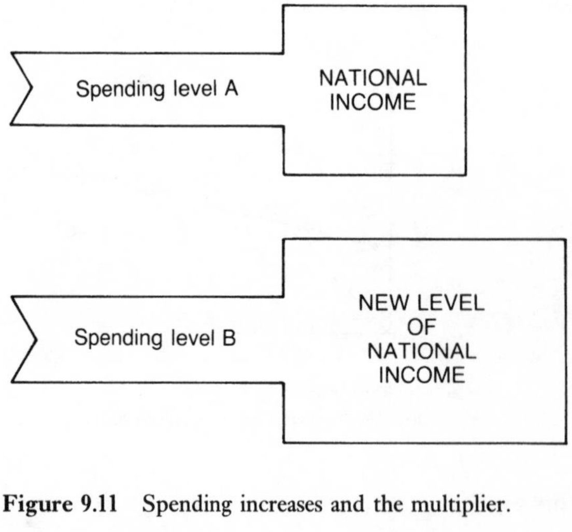

Figure 9.11   Spending increases and the multiplier.

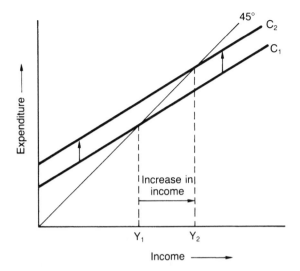

Figure 9.12   Spending increases and multiplier.

which is more simply

$$k = \frac{1}{\text{MPS}}$$

since MPC + MPS = 1. As a result if the MPC is 0.8 and an investment of £10 million is made the multiplier effect will be:

$$\frac{1}{1 - 0.8} \times £10 \text{ million}$$

$$= 5 \times £10 \text{ million} = £50 \text{ million}$$

The multiplier is 5 and the final total increase in national income is £50 million.

The multiplier is often seen in the form of the investment multiplier. In this case we see that the effect of an increase in investment or some other autonomous expenditure is to create further expenditures along the line—this is sometimes known as 'crowding in'. This can be expressed in graphical form using the normal expenditure/income graph. It is also interesting to look at the savings element using the Keynesian Cross diagram (Fig. 9.13). It can be seen that a decrease in the savings function produces a proportionately greater increase in income/output. A multiplier effect is also evident if there is a reduction in savings since this, by definition, will provide an increase in consumption.

An increase in savings will produce a more than equivalent *fall* in consumption. This is known as the 'paradox of thrift' in that while saving is considered good on an individual

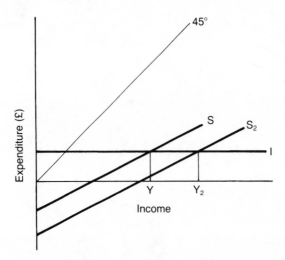

Figure 9.13 Investment multiplier. Downward shift in savings function from S to S_2 leads to a greater increase in income/output (Y to Y_2).

level it is not necessarily good for the economy, since it involves a reduction in demand. This is especially a problem if there is unemployment in the economy.

It is worth noting that the multiplier effect can be seen in a number of other areas of economics. For example, there is a tax multiplier, an employment multiplier and a credit multiplier.

Topic 9.6   Investment and the accelerator

Finally, we need to look a little closer at the investment aspect of our analysis of national income. As we have seen, investment by firms is part of aggregate demand along with planned consumption by households, and we have assumed that the level of investment is autonomous of changes in income.

Keynes saw capital investment as being influenced mainly by the expectations and confidence of the business community rather than by interest rates, which had been the key feature of the classical *loanable funds* theory. This theory saw interest rates as the key factor influencing both savings on the supply side of funds and investment on the demand side. The lower the interest rates, the less attractive saving as a whole would be and the keener business people would be to borrow and invest.

Keynes developed a concept called the *marginal efficiency of capital theory* which took the approach that when business people decide to invest they consider future expectations of the returns to be obtained from purchasing land, machinery, etc. The return from such investment can be expressed as a percentage known as the *internal rate of return* and in turn this expresses in numerical form the *marginal efficiency of capital*. In

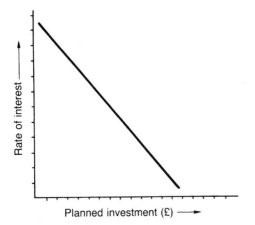

Figure 9.14 Planned investment and interest rates.

other words, the MEC is the return available from the last or marginal investment project contemplated.

The MEC can be used to produce an *investment function* which indicates the level of planned investment in relation to interest rather than to income as in our earlier model. It falls to the right because as interest rates fall, more investment projects become viable as options (Fig. 9.14).

The accelerator

Although interest rates and expectations of capital efficiency and business prospects have both been regarded as factors determining investment levels, there is one theory which does relate investment more closely to income and output. This is the accelerator principle.

This concept rests on certain assumptions, the key one being that business decision makers relate the levels of investment to the output they are about to produce, which in turn relates to demand. An increase in demand, even if expected rather than real, will produce an increase in investment. What is more, this increase in investment will be proportionately greater than the increase in demand and output.

To see why this is so we need to look at an example and to note a key feature of investment. To produce goods of, say, £1 million, capital equipment and 'plant' is necessary. The ratio between these two, the *capital:output ratio*, is crucial to the working of the accelerator.

Let us look at a simple example. We will consider a small motor manufacturer in the 'special jobs' part of the market. The manufacturer's output is small and cars are advertised as 'hand-made' but there is still need for some machinery, especially a hoist. Each hoist will take five cars a year, and there are four hoists in the workshop. We can see in Table 9.4 what happens if orders begin to flood in.

Table 9.4 The accelerator in the motor trade

Year	1	2	3	4	5
Expected output	20	25	40	40	35
Hoists needed	4	5	8	8	7
Hoists in workshop	4	4	5	8	8
New hoists needed	–	1	3	0	0

The ratio between hoists and cars is an example of a capital:output ratio. This determines the number of machines or expenditure on capital equipment needed for a specific volume of output. The reader will note that if orders are expected to increase and so additional output is planned, then there will be additional investment in new capital equipment. In Table 9.4 an increase in car output from 20 to 25 per year in year 2 leads to an extra hoist being ordered; an increase to 40 cars the next year results in hoist purchases of three. In other words, an increase in output of 60 per cent results in an increase in capital investment of 200 per cent (see Fig. 9.15).

In fact the above figures are rather simplified. In addition to new equipment, most firms have to spend on replacing worn-out machinery, so each year there will be some spending on capital equipment which is simply making up for that which has worn out. Sometimes we insert this factor into Table 9.4 for accuracy. The reader should note that acceleration occurs when there is *growth* in expected sales. If expected sales remain the same then demand for new hoists falls to nil.

Following on from this conclusion we can see that, apart from 'acceleration' of investment spending when there are changes in demand and planned output by firms in an upward direction, there is also accelerated decline. The above figures show that as soon as planned sales fall, no new equipment is ordered. What is more, one can expect that the surplus of existing plant over that needed at the new lower level of production in

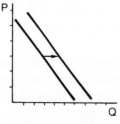

(a) Increase in demand
    (real or perceived)
    for consumer goods

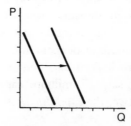

(b) Manufacturer increases
    demand for machines
    by greater percentage than
    the increase in output
    of consumer goods

Figure 9.15 Stages in the accelerator.

year 5 will serve the replacement needs of that year—so no extra equipment will be bought at all.

From this analysis it can be seen that the accelerator is an important part of the cycle of boom and recession which characterizes modern economies. If over a number of years there is a sustained increase in demand then there will be a greater level of increase in the output of firms making capital equipment. However, in times of recession, when demand and output fall, the suppliers of equipment will be hit very hard.

In fact, the accelerator tends to work with the multiplier in amplifying the effects of additional spending and investment and both fuelled, to a large extent, by the expectations of business leaders and the urgings of government.

We can see that the accelerator is often viewed as working in tandem with the multiplier. The latter will produce an increased demand which will in turn result in increased demand for capital goods of much higher value. The demand for capital goods can be seen as a *derived* demand, following on from planned demand for consumption goods. However, the increase in production of capital goods results in further income generation and further real or expected demand. Thus a spiral of increasing demand and output is created.

Keynes put it well, in one of his lighter, but still profound moments, when he wrote:

> If the Treasury were to fill old bottles with banknotes, bury them at suitable depths in disused coal-mines which are then filled up to the surface with town rubbish, and leave it to private enterprise on well-tried principles of *laissez-faire* to dig the notes up again (the right to do so being obtained, of course, by tendering for leases of the note-bearing territory), there need be no more unemployment, and, with the help of the repercussions, the real income of the community, and its capital/wealth also, would probably become a good deal greater than it actually is (*The General Theory*, Macmillan).

This combination of multiplier and accelerator is often seen as the basic engine room of trade booms with rapidly accelerated output and employment, but it may also explain the rapid nature of the decline into recession which usually follows the boom. Thus these two concepts are important and topical elements in our study of macro-economics, although the theories are not without their critics (see Advanced Study Topic 9.1).

Topic 9.7   Aggregate demand and supply

We have looked at one way of determining equilibrium national income which uses the 45° diagram. We considered aggregate demand related to the level of national income. There is, however, another way of exploring this equilibrium by using aggregate demand and supply schedules which relate consumption and output to price levels. This is called 'aggregate demand and supply analysis' or sometimes simply AD/AS.

It is also often called the *classical model* of analysis with the 45° approach as the *Keynesian* model. In fact we do not choose one or the other according to whether we follow Keynes or not, as both are relevant but under different circumstances. The Keynesian model assumes that prices and wages are fixed, and is thus very useful in

Figure 9.16 What shall we do with the unemployed? (By permission of *Punch*.)

the short run especially for examining the multiplier effect or the liability of demand increases to cause short-term inflation. The classical model is more appropriate in the longer term when prices and wages can change, and this is the situation which we will now investigate.

Aggregate demand

At its simplest, aggregate demand is simply the total of all micro-economic demand schedules. So if we add all the demand curves for goods and services, relating consumption to prices, we can derive a total or aggregate curve. However, in reality it is a little more complex.

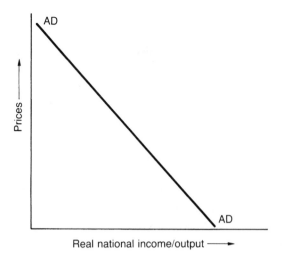

Figure 9.17 Aggregate demand.

To start with, we usually change the horizontal axis from quantity demanded to real national income. This is logical, because the total of demand is equal to total output of final goods and services and this in turn is equal to national income in real terms. So we can draw a graph as in Fig. 9.17. The demand curve slopes downwards to the right, just as the micro-economic demand curve, but the reasons are not identical. As the curve measures total demand there is less scope for substitution of products but other influences become important. The reasons for the slope are as follows:

1. As prices rise so domestic demand/output/income will fall because while consumers cannot substitute home-produced goods they can import more. So increased domestic prices will produce an increase in imports at the expense of home goods.
2. Interest rates are closely related to prices, and an increase in prices is likely to mean also an increase in interest rates which will result in a fall in demand for 'high-ticket' items such as motor vehicles, houses and capital equipment.
3. An increase in prices has the effect of reducing the value of not only cash but also bank accounts, bills and other savings of money.

The spending power of such liquid wealth is reduced because of the price increases and so wealth in real terms falls.

Aggregate demand is the total of the demand schedules from all markets in the economy.

Aggregate supply

In the case of aggregate supply there is the problem that economists differ in their idea of the shape of the curve and the relationships between prices, costs and output. Figure 9.18 shows a somewhat different shaped curve from the typical micro-economic supply curve. It is still true that the higher the price level, the higher the level of output, but the curve is certainly not the sum of all micro-economic curves.

The inverted L-shape reflects the way output can be changed at different levels of real national income. Below the maximum potential level of income there is spare capacity so firms can increase output without corresponding cost increases. On reaching the level of income corresponding to full employment, no further expansion is possible and any attempt to increase output results only in increasing costs (= prices) without any increase in output. There is an intermediate zone which is curved and in this zone some firms can expand and others cannot.

If we superimpose the AD curve on this we can see how supply might change as AD increases—for example, as a result of a reduction in taxation or an increase in the money supply. Figure 9.19 shows what might happen if AD increased over time. From AD_1 to AD_2 there is an increase in output but not in cost or prices. However, from AD_2 to AD_3, as maximum potential output level is approached, costs and prices will increase because firms can only increase output if prices rise sufficiently to cover the extra costs. Beyond AD_3, output cannot increase and any further increase in AD will simply result in increased prices, i.e. inflation.

The above curve is not, however, the picture every economist uses in an analysis of macro-economic equilibria. It represents a composite which is found useful by most economists. Classical economists and modern monetarists prefer to see the AS curve as vertical on the grounds that aggregate output cannot be increased just because of an increase in AD. It is based on the views of the nineteenth-century French economist

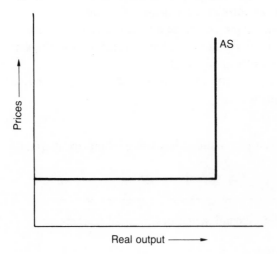

Figure 9.18   Aggregate supply (Keynesian).

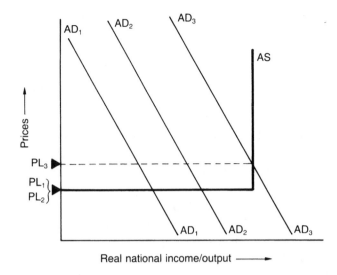

Figure 9.19   Aggregate shifts and price levels.

J.B. Say that supply will create its own demand. The level of supply is therefore, according to this view, determined by forces other than demand. The economists of this school of thought recommend that economic growth comes from increasing output and advocate policies which encourage this. As a result, this approach is sometimes called *supply side economics*.

Figure 9.20 shows this approach alongside the opposite—a completely horizontal supply curve. This represents a view put forward by Keynes that the level of output

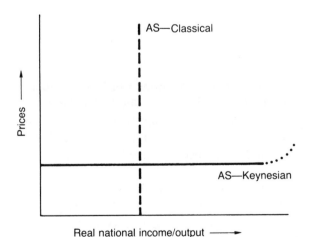

Figure 9.20   Aggregate supply in short term: two theories.

is largely determined by the level of demand. So if the economy is at a level below potential, particularly below the full employment level, then output can increase without inflation.

A third approach is to see AS as an upward-sloping curve, more like the micro-economic supply curve. The argument here is that most economies are somewhere below maximum output/full employment level and output can be increased in response to a growth in demand, but there will be some increase in costs and so in prices.

The point of maximum potential output is worth looking at in more detail. This is usually regarded as the full employment level, but the term 'full' is interpreted as the point not where everyone has a job but where the economy has reached the 'natural' level of unemployment. Ideas on the position of this level vary, but 6 per cent unemployment is often considered as the likely position.

As we have seen, economists tend on the whole to see that there are advantages in all approaches and for most examination purposes below degree level a composite AS curve as shown in Fig. 9.18 is safe to use. It is often felt that the vertical curve represents the true long-term position and the horizontal and curved sections are more a short-term situation. This assumes that, in the long term, economies will tend to perform at something like the full employment/maximum output level.

Topic 9.8   Economic growth

The term *economic growth* is widely used in textbooks, newspapers and wherever people meet to 'put the world to rights', but there is not always clarity on what it means. Basically, economic growth is an increase in national income, usually measured by GDP, but it has wider implications. If GDP increases it is usually assumed that so will employment rates, incomes and general prosperity.

Problems with measuring economic growth

One of the problems in measuring economic growth lies in knowing which figures to use. We can, of course, simply use GDP as printed in official statistics, and for the most part, this is what the newspapers do. It is perhaps a little more realistic, however, to measure GDP per head, a concept we have already come across when looking at wealth (Chapter 2). We should also be sure to account for inflation by using figures for GDP that have been calculated at constant prices.

In fact, many of the statistics used for growth measure not GDP as such on a year-by-year basis but the rate of GDP growth. The idea is that an economy is moving in positive directions if GDP is actually growing rather than stagnating or even falling. In fact, a fall in GDP (or 'negative growth', as it is sometimes called) is an indication of recession (see below).

Potential economic growth

While GDP statistics measure actual growth in an economy it is more difficult to assess potential growth. A country will have a potential determined by the production possibility curve and a shift to the right of the curve will indicate a general increase in potential productivity. Of course, most economies at any particular time will probably be at a point *within* the PPC and so not be achieving full potential.

The growth of GDP will depend on a number of factors which will vary from country to country and from one region to another. Together they are sometimes called the *production function*. This means that output is a function of:

Capital
Labour
Land and natural resources
Technical and scientific knowledge

An increase in any of these factors will increase the potential for growth, although whether growth will actually take place depends on other features such as the growth of demand. Businesses will not produce if no-one will buy, although there is some element of truth in Say's Law that supply generates its own demand. Investment and an increase in production of capital goods has been frequently used to 'kick-start' an economy before now.

Growth and the trade cycle

The level of national income varies enormously over time. In fact a pattern of growth and decline, boom and slump is a common feature of economic history. Figure 9.21 shows the changes in real GDP for the UK from 1921 to 1991, and it can be seen that there is anything but stability. The figures measure not GDP itself but growth rates, so that years such as 1940 and 1973 show exceptional growth not just high GDP. In fact, the case of 1940 is a warning not just to assume that growth in output means increased happiness—the existence of war or state-directed production of capital goods, as in Stalin's USSR, will induce growth but may not make the ordinary person feel much better.

Although GDP has tended to rise, even in real terms, for most industrial nations it is the rate of growth which is regarded as significant. The changes in growth tend to conform to a pattern which is often known as the *trade cycle*. Figure 9.22 illustrates this feature. Not only are there fluctuations in the long run but there are also smaller variations within a long-term trend. These smaller variations are often known as the *business cycle*. If an economy is on the highest part of a cycle it is said to be experiencing boom conditions and the bottom of the cycle is known as a slump. The arm of the cycle between boom and slump is known as *recession*. In other words, during recession an economy has stopped growing in real terms.

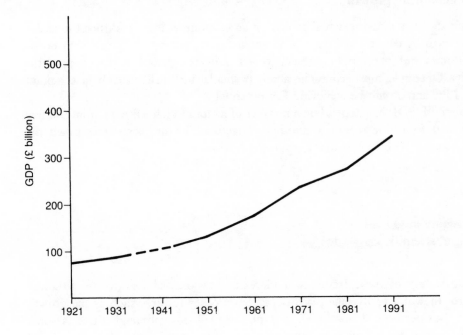

Figure 9.21   GDP for UK (factor of). (*Source*: CSO, *Annual Abstract of Statistics*, HMSO, various years.)

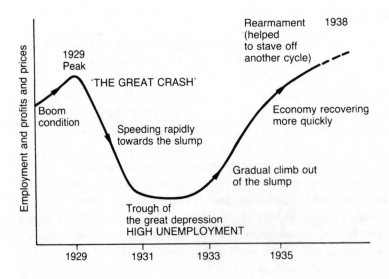

Figure 9.22   The trade cycle.

As we will see in Chapter 15 and in Case Study 9.1 governments are actively concerned with economic growth. If a democratically elected government presides over recession it will be unpopular and may face defeat in an election; if it presides over growth and boom it may be able to declare, as did one previous British prime minister, that 'you never had it so good' and win an election in style. In fact there is some doubt as to whether individual governments can influence the trade cycles as most, including the slump of 1991–3, tend to be worldwide.

People tend to like growth and boom not because the person on the number 7 bus gets excited about graphs in the *Financial Times* but because of the knock-on effects in real life. Growth means increase in output and this means jobs. If there is an increase in demand for labour it will probably also mean an increase in wage levels. More jobs and higher wages mean increased consumer demand, so that there is more incentive for firms to invest and increase output. The multiplier/accelerator twin effect is important here in increasing both the speed of growth and the speed of decline. Some of the output may be exported, although there has been a tendency in the UK for booms to increase consumption of imports, with unfortunate effects on the balance of payments.

Economic growth rates show considerable variation from one country to another and poses the questions 'Why, if trade cycles tend to be worldwide, is there so much variation from one country to another? Why do we see China, Malaysia and Chile experiencing high growth of real GDP while the USA, Germany and France show low growth rates and the UK and Sweden have "negative growth"?' To some extent, we can relate growth rates to growth potential here. Most European nations and the USA and Canada have established mature economies, probably at the boom peaks producing near to potential. On the other hand, countries with less developed economies have underused resources, and with new technology coming in from Europe and the USA these resources acquire a potential considerably higher than capital and labour skills will currently achieve. As a result, input of investment capital or reorganization of the economy will see strong growth.

Theories of economic growth

Since the days of Adam Smith, economists have been concerned about economic growth and it is a popular theme in the press. Many theories have been developed to explain growth, trade cycles and policy instruments which can be used to change them, but examinations at 'A' level or of a professional nature tend not to require detailed knowledge of them. For the interested reader, some treatment of these ideas is given in Advanced Study Topic 9.2.

Case Study 9.1—Unemployment in a recession

Recession is traditionally associated with low GDP growth, low inflation rates and high unemployment. This is natural if we consider what a recession is. The poor per capita growth in GDP is, in fact, a common definition of recession and rapid growth is seen as boom. This is associated with reduced output and a reduction in investment in industry. The accelerator works rapidly in reverse!

The recession of the early 1990s took some people by surprise, as it followed a particularly prosperous boom during which many European citizens, especially in the UK, got used to buying shares in enterprises which had previously been publicly owned and seeing themselves as part of an economic bonanza. Along with increases in home purchases, including the right to buy rented accommodation, and a renewed interest in personal financial planning ordinary folk ignored warnings from various 'dismal Johnnies' of disaster to come.

However, the recession of worldwide proportions, which western Europe was experiencing from 1990 to 1994, was especially notable for the high and persistent level of unemployment which is likely to be above acceptable levels until the end of the millennium. After falling to under 8 per cent at the beginning of 1990, unemployment rose to $10\frac{1}{2}$ per cent by the end of 1992 and running at over 3 million. For the Conservative government of John Major this was an awkward political issue, especially as his attempts, both as Chancellor and as Prime Minister, to reduce inflation was seen as largely responsible for the problem.

Why was unemployment so high and why by the beginning of 1994 had it only declined by very marginal amounts? Some of the answers lie in the changing nature of the UK economy. The onset of recession saw a reduction in imports which is a normal feature since with many people out of work, demand for goods of all types fell dramatically. However, exports fell also, from an annual change of about 5 per cent in 1990 to a negative change in 1991. Significantly, manufacturing output fell by alarming proportions.

One of the significant features of the unemployment of the 1990s recession was the way it hit the south of England. It was the yuppies in the service industries which were, for the first time for many years, facing the dole. Financial services, which had grown prodigiously in the 1980s suffered dramatic problems and retailing faced a downward roll in custom producing many insolvencies, mergers and cut-backs. The building trade was devastated along with the white collar associated professions such as architecture and surveying. Insurance companies, like the Prudential, which has eagerly bought up estate agents chains by 1992–3 were desperately selling them off.

Previous recessions tended to produce an eventual bounce back in employment and hence of demand because it was manufacturing industry which saw the possibilities of overseas markets and had high expectations of future growth. Increased investment produced a demand for producer goods such as machines and in turn jobs were created. Unfortunately, the UK had by 1990 become dominated by service industries and manufacturing was not in a position to respond rapidly to new prospects. The coal industry was facing terminal decline, steel industry and heavy engineering was still closing plant and a high degree of structural unemployment prevailed. Many firms in those industries which were seeing potential, especially the 'HighTec' areas, were reluctant to take on unemployed workers over 40 and preferred to train young graduates and school leavers.

What was the answer? To some, increased public investment in industry was seen as the panacea but to others, especially the monetarist economists, this was seen as a likely cause of increased demand driven inflation and high interest rates as a result of increased government borrowing. Was closer integration with Europe the answer, as the Maastricht Treaty fought for acceptance among the peoples of western Europe? There were those who advocated increasing education and training to give workers the technical skills, although the job adverts were still head hunting accountants and management personnel. The economists were left divided and as puzzled as anyone else but there was a general conclusion that this was different from what had gone before.

1. Consider why the recession increased unemployment and why this in turn prevented economic growth.
2. Is education and training a feasible solution by itself, to the problem of recession?

Advanced Study Topic 9.1   Criticisms of accelerator/multiplier theory

The accelerator and multiplier combined can be seen as the engine behind economic growth but the theory is not without its critics. In particular, it can be seen that it does rest on the assumption that business decision makers depend on past experience. It assumes that if anticipated demand remains constant then firms will not increase investment, but if there is an accelerating growth in output then firms will invest.

In many respects the theory assumes that business leaders are not very clever. It considers that entrepreneurs do not recognize a business cycle, are naive about the causes of growth and respond immediately to potential growth by large volumes of investment. In practice, business leaders are more circumspect, as the government of John Major discovered in trying to 'talk up' a recovery from recession in 1992–3. New investment is often introduced more slowly and experienced 'captains of industry' recognize that false signals may be generated.

For further discussion of the accelerator/multiplier concept and its weaknesses the reader should refer to Begg *et al.*, Chapter 31, pp 551–553.

Advanced Study Topic 9.2   Theories of economic growth

Economic growth has been a theme in economics since the beginning of the subject as a modern discipline. Adam Smith was very interested in economic growth and placed emphasis on the importance of labour as the key to development. The Labour Theory of Value was the cornerstone of this theory which considered that as population grew so total output would rise. If technology improved, then output per head might rise also. Malthus, however, considered that population growth would produce a reduction in wealth per head, on the assumption that land is fixed in quantity.

Since Britain, especially, grew rapidly in prosperity in the nineteenth century, the idea that population growth would result in a reduction in prosperity clearly was not the full story. As we have already seen, the predictions of Malthus proved unfounded, but the problem with most early economists was that they developed their ideas on the assumption that the economy was primarily agricultural.

The Neo-Classical theory pioneered by Robert Solow in the 1950s recognized the importance not of land but of capital. He saw one of the keys to growth as the increase in capital through investment and the concept of *capital deepening*. This term is used to refer to the increase in the amount of capital per worker which is available. If capital increases at a faster rate than labour supply, then there will be more equipment or industrial plant available per worker and an increase in per capita output. This does not impose the limits on growth which the classical economists considered to be the main problem.

Other important influences on economic growth are the level of education and training of the working population and the level of technology. These are reasons why most governments place a lot of emphasis on education and research, and in some cases seem to place more importance on the university sector than on primary educational provision.

Economic growth and political action

Economic growth is one of the normal objectives of any government but where it is achieved it may be at a price. In the case of some countries such as Turkey the price is inflation; others achieve it by increasing the gulf between the rich and the poor; and it may involve opening an economy to foreign capital and what some people call 'economic imperialism'. Economists may be called upon to work in many different types of political background in attempting to achieve economic growth.

Economic growth is an important area of economics and students interested in further study of it are recommended to consult Begg, Chapter 30; Samuelson & Nordhaus, Chapter 30; or Dornbusch & Fischer, Chapter 10.

Essay questions

1. Discuss the view that the costs of economic growth outweigh the benefits. (*Source*: The Associated Examining Board, June 1991)
2. (a)   Distinguish between the national income multiplier and the accelerator.
    (b)   Discuss their significance for a government's macro-economic policy.
    (*Source*: The Associated Examining Board, June 1992)
3. Either (a) Explain what is meant by the consumption function and show how it is used in the calculation of the multiplier, or
    (b) How does fiscal policy affect the level of national income?
    (*Source*: Oxford and Cambridge Schools Examination Board, June 1991)
4. Compare output and productivity as indicators of the economic growth of the economy. Explain in your view how, if at all, the kinds of measures required to stimulate economic growth in developing economies might differ from those required to stimulate growth in the UK. (*Source*: Northern Examinations and Assessment Board, June 1992)
5. Explain whether or not you regard a high growth rate as a desirable economic objective. Discuss the implications of growth for (a) Britain and Europe and (b) the less developed world. (*Source*: Northern Examinations and Assessment Board, June 1991)
6. Discuss the role of the multiplier in the execution of government economic policy. How will the size of the multiplier change if:
    (a)   Consumers decide to save more of their incomes;
    (b)   Direct tax rates decrease;
    (c)   The propensity to import increases? (*Source*: University of Oxford, June 1993)
7. Explain whether or not you regard economic growth as a desirable objective of economic policy for any government. Compare the obstacles to achieving a satisfactory growth rate in the UK with those in countries such as Ethiopia and Chile. (*Source*: Northern Examinations and Assessment Board, June 1993)

Chapter 10

International economics

So far, we have studied the subject of economics in the context of an internal market system, and except for some reference to exports and imports in Chapter 9 there has been no discussion of why or how we might wish to exchange goods and services with overseas countries. We have worked on the assumption that the economic system with which we are concerned is that of the European Union or, even narrower, the UK. Now, however, it is time to look at the world as a whole and how we relate, in economic terms, with other nations. We will also examine the formation of the European Communities and the reasoning behind their existence.

Topic 10.1 Comparative costs and advantage

The fundamental logic behind the willingness of one country to trade with another lies in the principle of *comparative advantage* or, as it is sometimes called, *comparative costs*. It is also the logic behind the movement of goods and services between regions within a country, a fact that is sometimes forgotten by students. The movement of cheese from Somerset dairies to Yorkshire delicatessens or of Nebraska wheat to New York bakeries are based on just as much comparative advantage as they would be should the cheese go to Iceland or the wheat to Canada.

To understand how the principle works we first have to distinguish between *absolute* and *comparative* advantage. We can do this best using imaginary examples. There are also two ways in which the principle can be explained, and textbooks differ in the approach used, which can be very confusing to students. To try to clarify this issue we will here use both the cost and the advantage approaches.

Absolute advantage

Absolute advantage occurs when a country or region can produce a good or service at a lower absolute cost than another. As a result, it is said to have an advantage in producing that good or service. Suppose that we go back in time and assume that the merchants of London in 1500 wish to explore trading with France. They consider that they may be able to produce wool cheaper than France can, and an investigating committee of the guilds in the City comes up with the figures in Table 10.1.

In Table 10.1, if we look at the cost of producing a standard bag of wool or flagon of wine we see that England has an absolute advantage in producing wool and France in producing wine. Clearly, if costs of transport were not more than the difference it would be cheaper for the citizens of London to buy imported French wine than Chateau Brixton, or for the citizens of Paris to buy their wool from England rather than from the local sheep runs.

This example assumes production of a standard amount of each product and examines how costs of production (assuming that the costs are just labour) differ. There is an alternative way of examining the problem found in some textbooks in which we keep the costs constant and examine the output. In the case above we can rewrite Table 10.1 as Table 10.2.

In this case we assume a full 8-hour day and look at what can be produced in that time by one person. The same absolute advantage appears as it did with Table 10.1. For wool a typical day's work will produce two bags in England compared with the French two and for wine a French day's toil will result in eight flagons of wine as opposed to a meagre 1.6 flagons in England.

> *Absolute advantage* exists when one country or region can produce a commodity or service with a lower cost than another country or region.

One fundamental reason behind the willingness to trade, given this position, is the existence of our old friend opportunity cost. If there is full employment of resources in England then if an extra bag of wool is produced there will be an opportunity cost in

Table 10.1   Costs of producing wool and wine

	Worker/hours of labour in production	
Commodity	England	France
Wool per bag	2	4
Wine per flagon	5	1

Table 10.2   Output of wool and wine per worker/hour

	Output per worker per 8-hour day	
Commodity	England	France
Wool (bags)	4	2
Wine (flagons)	1.6	8

terms of wine because some vineyard acreage will have to be given up to keep the sheep necessary to produce that extra bag. Using the figures in Table 10.1, to produce an extra bag of wool requires 2 worker/hours and this will mean that two-fifths of a flagon of wine (two worker/hours out of the five needed per flagon) will have to be sacrificed.

Now if this extra bag of wool is sent to France in exchange for wine, it might be more worthwhile. How much wine would we get? Well, the French need four worker/hours to produce a bag of wool but only one for a flagon of wine, so if they were to get English wool instead of the local fleece then they might be willing to give up four flagons of wine for it. The opportunity cost of one bag of wool for the French is four flagons of wine.

In producing the above argument we ignore differences in quality, the patriotic virtues of 'Buy British' or 'Buy French' and transport costs. To cover the latter there will need to be a reasonable difference between the costs and not just a marginal amount.

Comparative advantage

So far, the logic behind trade seems indisputable. However, the difficult part is to come. Most students can see the reasoning behind trade based on absolute advantage but it is more difficult when we consider another approach. *Comparative advantage* looks not at absolute costs but at relative costs—in fact, at the opportunity costs mentioned above. Consider the alternative possible results in Table 10.3 of our London guild international committee. We have changed the figures and the wool production in France now costs only two worker/hours per bag compared with England's three worker/hours per bag. The wine figures are one worker/hour for France and four for England. You might conclude that, as a result, France would export both wool and wine to England and we would have to raid the royal treasure chests to pay our way! However, if we look closer we can see how trade can still pay in both directions.

Suppose that there are 60 worker/hours available in both countries and workers were divided equally between wine and wool. They would now be producing the amounts shown in Table 10.4. England has 10 bags of wool and $7\frac{1}{2}$ flagons of wine and France has 15 bags of wool and 30 flagons of wine. Is it worth while for them to trade? Surely not as far as France is concerned! Yet if we look again at the figures we see that the opportunity cost of England producing one flagon of wine is approximately 1.33 bags of wool. If the

Table 10.3 Comparative costs of producing wool and wine

	Worker/hours of labour in production	
Commodity	England	France
Wool per bag	3	2
Wine per flagon	4	1

Table 10.4

	England		France		Total output
	Worker/hours	Output	Worker/hours	Output	
Wool (bags)	30	10	30	15	25
Wine (flagons)	30	$7\frac{1}{2}$	30	30	$37\frac{1}{2}$

30 vineyard and winepress workers were to switch to wool then we could have 20 bags of wool in total but no wine. We would be well clothed but rather thirsty!

In France the opportunity cost of one flagon of wine is half a bag of wool. In other words, in terms of wool, wine is cheaper in France than it is in England. This we are not surprised at! However, if we look at wool we see that should one worker switch from wool to wine to quench English thirsts, 0.75 a flagon on wine is gained, i.e. the opportunity cost of one bag of wool is 0.75 of a flagon. In France, however, a similar move would show the surrender of two flagons of wine to produce a bag of wool, which is an opportunity cost of two flagons per bag.

In other words, surprising as it may seem at first, the cost (i.e. opportunity cost) of wool is lower in England (0.75 flagon) than in France (two flagons). So it would be better for England to concentrate on wool production and France on wine. If the two agreed to adjust the days of labour between the two goods, we could get the total output shown in Table 10.5.

Now if England devotes all labour to wool and France 10 workers hours to wool, a total 'world' output is 30 bags. In the case of wine, England gives up any attempt to produce it and France produces all wine, giving a total of 40 flagons. So the combined output for both countries is increased by five bags of wool and two and a half flagons of wine. Each country specializes in the produce for which it has a comparative advantage, i.e. where opportunity cost is lowest.

> *Comparative cost* refers to the principle that countries or regions may trade with each other if the relative or opportunity cost of production of goods is different.

Table 10.5

	England		France		Total output
	Worker/hours	Output	Worker/hours	Output	
Wool (bags)	60	20	20	10	30
Wine (flagons)	–	Nil	40	40	40

Topic 10.2   Terms of trade

We have seen how absolute and comparative advantage can explain why countries trade with each other and international trade is based on those two ideas. However, the question still remains whether countries will trade in specific products and whether or not a country will be primarily an exporter or an importer.

One of the tools we use to help with these questions is the concept of *terms of trade*. These express a relationship between the prices of a country's imports and the prices of its exports and are calculated by dividing export prices by import prices and multiplying by 100. A certain year is taken as the base year. If the index is under 100, the terms of trade have moved against a country, but if the figure is over 100, then the terms of trade will have moved in that country's favour, compared with the base year (see Fig. 10.1).

> The *terms of trade* of a country refers to the figure which represents the relative movement of the prices of exports and imports.

In common language we speak of the 'favourable' movement of the terms of trade if export prices have risen relative to import prices. It is not strictly accurate to think of 'favourable' or 'unfavourable' terms of trade in any absolute sense, as it is only the changes that mean anything in economics.

Figure 10.1 shows the terms of trade for recent years and it might be helpful to see how it is compiled. It uses the index figures for import and export prices, using unit value as an indicator of 'price'. The formula used is:

$$T = \frac{P_e}{P_i} \times 100$$

where T is the terms of trade index and P_e and P_i are, respectively, the price/value indices for exports and imports. The reader may also see reference to the gross (barter) terms of trade which uses volume instead of values and the *income terms of trade* which measures the degree to which income from exports has resulted in increased imports. It is sometimes known as the 'capacity to import'.

Topic 10.3   Balance of payments: current account

The term *balance of payments* refers to the accounts which place payments for imports alongside receipts for exports and capital money flows between one country and another. So if Germany imports goods from overseas such as French wine and exports Volkswagen and Audi cars, lager and electrical equipment, its balance of payments will indicate whether the money received from exports exceeds or not that paid for imports,

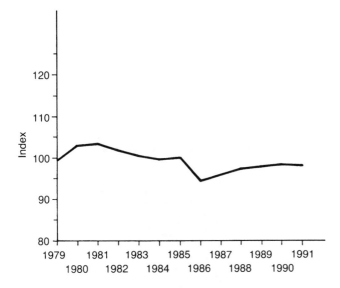

Figure 10.1   Terms of trade for UK: 1985 = 100. (*Source*: CSO, *Annual Abstract of Statistics*, HMSO, various years.)

and whether there is a positive or negative flow of money of a capital nature or official payments.

The presentation of the balance of payments in the UK has changed from 1987 but, as some older statistics in the previous form are still being used, it will be helpful to outline both systems. They have one item in common, and that is the *current account*, so we will look at this first of all.

> The *balance of payments* refers to an account which places money flow out of a country alongside money flow into that country.

The current account is the best indicator of the UK's or France's ability to pay their way in the world. Figure 10.2 gives an indication of recent trends in the UK's balance on current account and it measures the value of UK exports and imports on a year-by-year basis. The balance may be compiled for a calendar year or a financial year, and represents the most commonly accepted measure of balance of payments performance for any given year, however chosen. In fact, the figures never do 'balance' exactly as there is always a favourable or unfavourable difference at the end of the year. Normally, if earnings from exports exceeds payments for imports we describe the balance as being 'favourable'.

The current account is divided into visible and invisible trade. The term *visible trade* is used to describe movements of goods which are tangible, such as cars, wheat or coal. The net value of visibles is known as the *balance of trade* because it measures values of transactions which involve 'trade' in the normal meaning of the word.

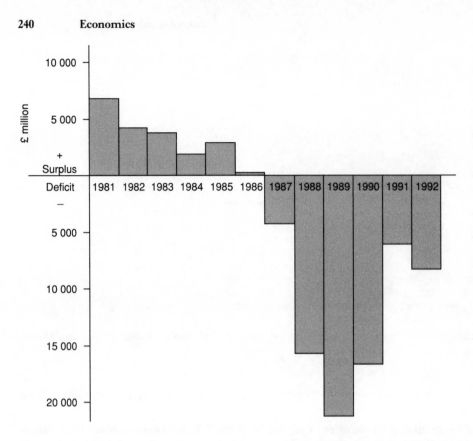

Figure 10.2   UK balance of payments current account. (*Source*: CSO, *Key Data 1992/3*, HMSO.)

Invisible trade include services and payments of dividends, interest, etc. The UK has always been strong in invisible exports such as insurance, banking, shipping and, more recently, tourism, whereas Russia and Canada have been more important for visible exports.

> *Visible trade* refers to movements in goods, i.e. items which are tangible and physical. In contrast, *invisible trade* refers to trade in services and benefits which are not easy to see in tangible form.

Visible trade consists of a number of items which represent a most important component of the economy of any country. The actual items will vary from country to country, and Table 10.6 shows the main items for the UK while the pie charts in Fig. 10.3 indicate some major items for exports and imports for two European countries. In looking at such statistics you may come across the initials 'fob' and 'cif'. The former means 'free on board', which refers to the value of goods when they are shipped, and the latter term means that cost, insurance and freight are included in the values.

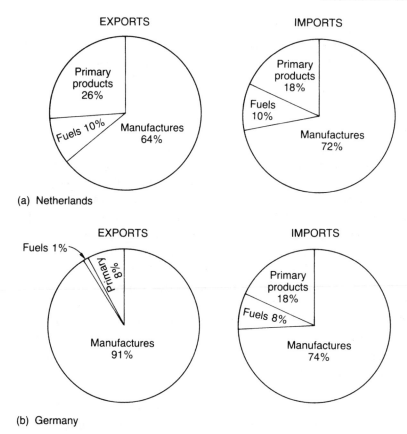

(a) Netherlands

(b) Germany

Figure 10.3 Exports and imports: The Netherlands and Germany. (*Source*: World Bank, *World Tables 1992*, John Hopkins University Press.)

Table 10.6 Visible trade UK: main items (1991)

Class	Values of: exports (£ million)	Imports
Food, beverages and tobacco	7 749	12 326
Basic materials	2 013	5 065
Fuels	7 144	7 582
Manufactures	86 058	92 103
Chemicals	13 784	10 973
Total	104 816	118 867

Exports valued fob and imports cif.
Source: CSO, *Key Data 1992/93*, HMSO, Table 7.2

1. *Raw materials* For many industrialized nations these are mainly imports and sustain manufacturing industry. They could include metals such as iron ore, copper or bauxite (aluminium); foodstuffs such as wheat, tea, coffee and sugar; or rocks such as diamonds. For many countries raw materials represent valuable exports and some countries, especially in the Third World, rely rather too heavily on one or two raw materials for overseas earnings (see Chapter 15).

2. *Manufactured products such as cars, machinery, washing machines and refrigerators (white goods) and electrical goods and equipment* Traditionally, these have been the main earners of the countries of Western Europe or North America, but over the last 30 years there have been serious inroads made into this pattern by Japan and a few other rapidly developing countries such as Taiwan. Figure 10.4 indicates the pattern of visible exports and imports for one major industrial product. It should also be noted that the leading exporter (Germany) is also the leading importer. This is not unusual for industrial products, especially where there is a range of different qualities and types of product. The UK both exports and imports oil.

3. *Foodstuffs* are also manufactured but can perhaps be treated separately. Most of our food today is processed in some way or other from the humble loaf to complex oven-ready meals. Many countries have built up an expertise in taking grains, milk or meat and manufacturing edible products which command a place in worldwide trade. Danish butter and bacon; French wine and cheeses; and Italian pasta are all significant in international trade.

4. Finally we should mention *fuels*, which are highly significant, especially oil. The regularity with which an oil tanker runs into difficulties and spills oil on some unfortunate coast reminds us of the vast trade in this essential commodity. Coal is

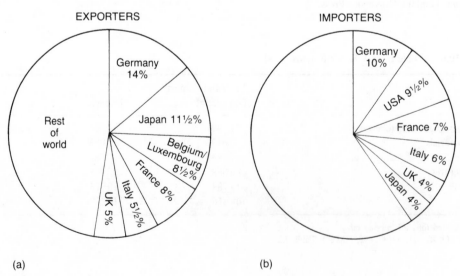

Figure 10.4 Major trading nations in iron and steel 1990: percentage of world total. (*Source: Gatt International Trade* 1990–91, Volume II.)

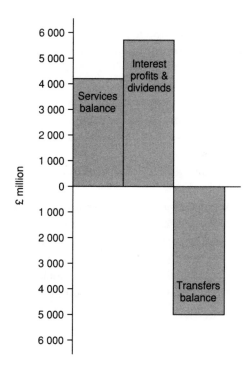

Figure 10.5   Invisible trade: UK 1991. (*Source*: CSO, *Key Data 1992/3*, HMSO.)

less important as it is more common in consumer nations and is heavy but there is nevertheless considerable coal movement within the EU.

Invisible trade includes a number of items which are not obvious as trading items (Fig. 10.5). The USA and the UK are the world's main earners of invisible income but some small nations depend very heavily on this area (for example, Hong Kong and the Cayman Islands). The main invisibles are as follows:

1. Interest, profits and dividends are the largest net overseas earnings of the UK although they also comprise a large part of the invisible imports sector. In fact, in recent years the difference between the earnings from these sources and the payments out has been small. In many respects they reflect past investment overseas or past investment in the UK. Official statistics divide this category into private and public investments. In other words, they include shares in companies, loans to companies or loans or investments to or by governments.
2. Shipping and civil aviation are important, and in this context consist of the carriage of passengers and freight and the earnings from this activity and not to the sale of ships and aircraft.
3. Insurance services are a strong source of invisible exports to the UK. The Lloyd's market features very heavily here in offering insurance cover to a high proportion of

the world's ships and such major items as oil rigs and major civil engineering projects. Some other countries of Europe also have strong insurance interests which appear in their invisible export figures—including The Netherlands, Switzerland and France.

4. Banking and other financial services are important earners for some countries and significant 'import' items for others. Again, London acts as a major centre for banking and financial services. British clearing banks have offices and business centres overseas and foreign banks have branches in the UK. European banks are increasingly becoming international in character and a number of significant mortgage lenders in the UK are owned by overseas banks.

5. Tourism and the holiday industry is a vital invisible export in many countries. What is 'exported' is the country itself—weather, scenery, tradition and facilities. It is a reminder that exports and imports are not all they seem because a family going from Germany to Spain on holiday are *not* a German export! They are importing Spanish hospitality. If in doubt, the student is recommended to consider which way the money is flowing—if money is leaving a country then the item bought is an import.

Topic 10.4   Capital flows and the balance sheet

Apart from movements in goods and services, we also need to consider movements of capital. Students often have difficulty in deciding what movements are classed as 'liabilities' and which as 'assets' in accounting balance sheets, and accountants dealing with company accounts always use the flow of actual money as the key in doubtful cases. As we indicated in the previous section, doubts on the balance of payments account can also be resolved by considering the direction of the flow of money. If money flows *out* of a country it is paying for an import, even if that import involves something or someone going overseas. Similarly, a flow of money *into* a country will imply that an export has been made.

However, when we come to look at capital movements we find that we need to revise this simple rule. If money comes into the UK and it may not be paying for goods or services it could be a *capital movement*, perhaps a loan, and so will be a liability of the UK to an overseas nation. As a liability it means that we owe someone overseas a capital sum or debt. We also probably owe interest but payment of this is part of the current account as it is payment for the loan, i.e. for a service. If we send money overseas it is probably an investment or loan to someone in another country, i.e. an 'export' of capital. The foreign recipient then owes us the capital and it is a UK asset.

Movements of capital can be simply investment or borrowing—buying shares in another country, investing in a project or lending to foreign residents. A UK resident buying a retirement property in Spain is taking capital out of the UK, and a Dutch company buying shares in a French company is likewise moving capital out of The Netherlands. Cash flows like these are often called *autonomous* movements because they are generated from outside the sphere of international trade. The lender and borrower are not concerned with how the business affects the balance of payments.

Some movements, however, are made by the government in order to deal with deficits or surpluses elsewhere on the balance sheet. These are often called *accommodating* movements, and because of the involvement of the government are usually referred to in formal accounts as 'official financing'. They are necessary if, for example, there is a deficit on current account and so we are wanting to buy more foreign currency to pay for imports than we have earned on exports. The government in this case will move reserves or borrow from, for example, the International Monetary Fund (IMF) in order to 'accommodate' the deficit.

It is in this area that there has been changes in the way the accounts are presented. Before 1987 the current account was shown first and then a section dealing with 'Investment and Other Capital Flows', and this was followed by a third section headed 'Official Financing'. The figures for 1980 in Table 10.7 will serve as an example.

In line with the greater emphasis on the current account and the tendency of the government of the 1980s in the UK to leave balancing flows more in the hands of the international banks, the 'official financing' has been merged with the investment capital to form a briefer item 'Transactions in UK Assets and Liabilities'. Table 10.8 indicates the new approach.

The appearance of a balancing item reminds us that accounts by nature have to balance, yet it is very difficult, if not impossible, to collect all the data required for an exercise like this without errors or omissions.

It is also important to note that a deficit on the assets/liabilities part of the account is not a matter of great concern. This is because the movement of money out of a country (i.e. the creation of an asset) is entered as a debit item, as if it were an import because of the direction of money flow. This means that a large amount of overseas investment by

Table 10.7 'Old style' balance of payments: Balance of payments; UK 1980

	£ million
Visible Balance	1177
Invisible Balance	1567
Current Account	2763
Investments and other capital transactions	−649
Balancing item	−742
Balance for official financing	−1391
Other transactions	−1081
Drawings/additions re official reserves	−291
Total Official financing	−1372

Source: *Annual Abstract of Statistics*, HMSO, 1982

Table 10.8 'New style' balance of payments: Balance of payments; UK 1991

	£ million
Visible Balance	−23 840
Invisible Balance	4 714
Current Balance	−19 126
Transactions in Assets	−20 780
Transactions in Liabilities	26 030
Net transactions	5 249
Balancing Item	1 072

Source: CSO, *Key Data 1992/93*, HMSO, Table 6.3.

banks in, say, the UK could produce a large debit item, but in fact in future years will produce a stream of dividends or interest for the invisible section of the current account.

We have concentrated on the UK in this section as it is easier to understand the principles if we look at a known country with an established record of trade accounting. The same principles, however, apply to other countries. For example, if the reader consults Samuelson and Nordhaus (p. 672) the US balance of payments will be found, and although there is some difference in names, the basic format is similar to our older method of accounting.

Topic 10.5   Trends in the UK balance of payments

It would be useful to look at how the balance of payments has changed in recent years in the UK. Again, we choose our own country as the example since it would be impossible in a text of this size to cover all nations, even in Europe.

Table 10.9 shows the UK's balance of payments since 1978 and Fig. 10.6 gives more detail for the last few years. There have been certain significant changes since 1980 and we need to look at these:

1. The visible trade balance has normally been in deficit, but from 1980 to 1982 was in credit. The reason for this movement was that the UK changed from being a net importer of oil to being a net exporter as a result of the growth of oil exploitation of the North Sea. It is significant that oil had been one of the main causes of the persistent trade decifit.

2. Invisible trade shows a consistently healthy positive balance which increased in the late 1980s although it began to dip in the 1990s. The 1980s saw a very busy period of growth in the 'City' markets and in overseas investment. As a result, the 'profits, dividends and interest' section showed a healthy flow of funds. The narrowing later

Table 10.9 UK balance of payments 1970–91

Year	Current Balance (£ million)	Year	Current Balance (£ million)
1978	1 123	1985	3 750
1979	−453	1986	−24
1980	2 843	1987	−4 182
1981	6 748	1988	−15 151
1982	4 649	1989	−21 726
1983	3 765	1990	−17 029
1984	1 798	1991	−6 321
		1992	−8 620

Sources: Annual Abstract of Statistics, HMSO, 1982, and CSO, *Key Data 1993/4*, HMSO.

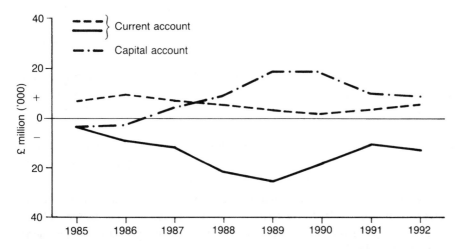

Figure 10.6 UK balances of payments 1985–92. Current account and Capital account. (*Source:* CSO, *Key Data 1992/3*, HMSO.)

is the result of a similar growth of overseas investment in the UK brought about by the buoyant economy of the mid to late 1980s.

3. After 1986 visible trade showed an alarming increase in the size of deficit, mainly as a result of increases in imports, especially of manufactured goods. We can, however, look a little deeper into the past here. Apart from the effect of the changes in the oil balance, the surplus in the 1980s was also the result of the recession of 1979, which drastically reduced imports while exports held up. The problem in the 1980s was related to high inflation, which meant that it was cheaper for the UK to import goods than to buy its own products and, in addition, it was more difficult for UK marketing experts to sell overseas. There was also an increasing integration into the European Community culminating in the Maastricht Treaty ratifications in 1993 and the renaming of the organization as the 'European Union'.

More on surpluses and deficits

It might be questioned how important surpluses and deficits on balance of payments can be to the economy of a country. A deficit or surplus for a few years is not a great problem in itself and difficulties only arise if the trend persists. The problem which can occur for a persistent deficit is that in order to pay for the excess of imports the country has to use up reserves or borrow, perhaps from the IMF. If the exchange rate is floating (see below) then a new rate emerges and this controls the balance, reversing the deficit. However, if the rate is fixed, then a government usually has to take action, including:

1. Deflation—which involves reducing the level of demand in the economy so reducing imports. It may also result in expenditure being switched from imports to the home market as home products become more competitive.
2. Imposing controls such as tariffs. This is no longer such an obvious option in view of our membership of the EU, GATT and other trade agreements.
3. Devaluation or a reduction in the official exchange rate. This makes exports more competitive and imports more expensive. For example, if £1 is worth $1.80 then a book worth £2 in the UK would be sold for $3.60 (plus carriage costs) in the USA. If sterling were devalued to $1.40 then the same book would sell for $2.80. The publisher would still get £2 but the American reader would pay less for the book.

The problem with devaluation or a deflation where it is hoped that there will be a switch of expenditure is that it may not be as effective as is hoped. Much depends on the price elasticity of the exports and imports of the country making the policy change. In the short term it is likely that demand schedules, especially for capital goods, will be relatively inelastic and this could mean that for a time the deficit gets worse. This is known as the *J-curve effect* from the shape of the curve measuring balance of payments surplus and deficit (Fig. 10.7).

The J-curve effect is an example of the importance of a principle known as the *Marshall–Lerner condition*. This states that it is necessary, for devaluation to be successful, that the demand elasticities of imports and exports should exceed unity. This is sometimes expressed as:

$$E_x + E_m > 1$$

> The *J-curve effect* occurs when devaluation or deflation results in a short-term deterioration of balance of payments before the longer-term improvement.

It is sometimes popularly thought that a balance of payments surplus is always a good thing, but a persistent surplus can carry problems. These include the following:

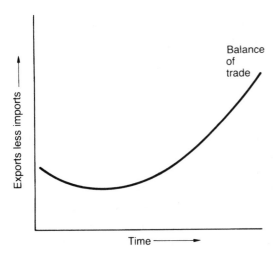

Figure 10.7   The J-curve.

1. A surplus for one country means that some other countries have a deficit and they may be tempted to impose tariffs, devalue their currency or take other steps to reduce the foreign penetration of their markets. We have seen this sort of action by EU member countries against Japan in recent years.
2. The oil-based surplus of the early 1980s led to a rise in the exchange rate of sterling and the currency of other North Sea oil nations (Norway and The Netherlands). This in turn made UK exports less competitive and increased the level of imports. Manufacturing industry in The Netherlands was especially hit and faced increasing difficulties. As a result, this is sometimes known as 'Dutch disease', although the problem also appeared on the UK side of the North Sea.
3. A persistent surplus means that there is a shortage of a country's currency on the foreign exchange markets, and so either the value of that currency will rise or the authorities will have to release reserves. If a currency increases in value then exports will be less competitive, and if reserves are released the money supply will be increased.

Topic 10.6   International liquidity

The word 'liquidity', in an economic context, refers to the means of payment for goods. Cash is the most liquid of all assets because it is generally acceptable as a form of purchasing power and other means of payment have varying degrees of liquidity in relation to cash. International liquidity is more complex but is based on the same principles. Except in the rare case of international barter, if citizens of France wish to buy machinery from Germany then they have to obtain German currency—the deutsch-mark. German producers do not want French francs because they cannot pay their workers or other factors of production in francs. Liquidity in this case is the ease with which French customers can purchase marks and the price they may have to pay for them.

Exchange rates

Some students get worried at the thought of exchange rates as they seem so mysterious and complex. In fact, there is no great difference between an analysis of the rates of exchange for currencies and that for the price of butter! A currency can be seen as a commodity and its price in a free market is subject to supply and demand, like every other commodity. Figure 10.8 illustrates how the Spanish peseta might be priced in sterling. The demand curve reflects British and other sterling holders' demand for Spanish goods and services—perhaps notably Spanish sand and sun. If the pesetas are expensive you don't get many for your £100 spending money on your holiday and you may only get four nights in the hotel instead of eight. You might be attracted by a cheaper deal in Greece.

So the demand curve slopes down to the right as a normal demand curve—the cheaper pesetas are, the more of a Spanish holiday (or trainers or cars) you get for your money, and the more you will therefore want Spanish currency. The supply of pesetas in total is relatively price-inelastic but there will be many banks and currency dealers willing to release pesetas in exchange for dollars, marks or sterling should the peseta rise in value and give them a chance to make a profit.

In Fig. 10.8 we see how the interplay of supply and demand produces an equilibrium level of peseta release on the world markets and an equilibrium price or exchange rate.

> The *exchange rate* of a currency is the price at which it can be bought or sold and in a free market is determined by the forces of supply and demand.

Now let's look at what might happen if the demand for pesetas increases. Perhaps a series of wet summers in the UK makes more people seek the sun of the Costa del Sol or Spanish wines may become popular. Demand for currency is essentially a derived demand. So the demand curve shifts to the right and the price of pesetas rises (Fig. 10.8).

However, this may produce problems for the purchasers. If the peseta is now more expensive, you will need more sterling or deutschmarks or guilders to 'buy' pesetas. The Spanish hotelier still wants to be paid the same rate as before for a night's stay, so you end up paying more out of your hard-earned sterling wages. Table 10.10 gives an example.

On 1 June there are 50 pesetas to every £1 coin. The pound sterling is worth 50 pesetas and each peseta is therefore worth 1/50th of a pound, i.e. 2p. The Spanish hotel wants 500 pesetas for a night's stay and at this rate the cost would be £10

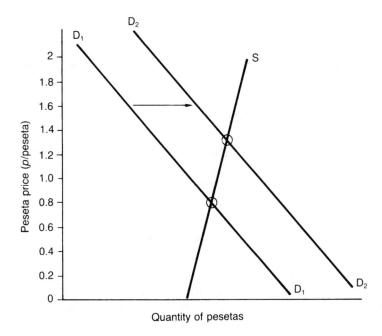

Figure 10.8 Demand shift for peseta.

Table 10.10 Possible exchange rate changes

Date	Pesetas/£1	Hotel rate per night (pesetas)	Total bill (£)
1 June	50	500	10
1 July	25	500	20
1 August	40	500	12.50

(500 × 2p = 1000p = £10). So you book your holiday and save up! But as you get on the plane at Gatwick news comes through that the exchange rate has risen or 'hardened'. The peseta has increased in value and is now worth 4p—so you get 25 pesetas to each £1 coin. The hotel (too busy serving seafood dinners with wine to notice exchange rates!) still wants 500 pesetas. At this stage it has no reason to change the price. However, you now find that the stay is costing you £20 because you get only 25 pesetas per £1.

There are a number of problems as a result of the changes in exchange rates which would be produced if free market conditions prevailed or, to use the popular term, the currencies *float*:

1. There is clearly a lot of uncertainty in that not only does the tourist not know for certain what the cost of the holiday will be but the business traveller speeding across Europe to sign some fantastic deal does not know what the sums will be at the end of

the journey. Rates rarely do change that quickly, but the possibility is certainly there, and if goods are being bought or sold by negotiations over a period of several weeks, fluctuations in exchange rates can be very significant.

2. If a country is efficient and its economy begins to grow and produce competitive products it will find that the exchange rates are liable to move against it. Suppose that Denmark is able to increase sales of Danish bacon at lower prices than anywhere else in Europe and orders come in from all over the place. Assuming that a free market in currency prevails, people will be buying Danish bacon and wholesalers will be asking their banks to find Danish kroner. Demand for kroner will rise (i.e. the demand curve moves to the right) and, as a result, the value of the kroner will rise. The households in Bristol, Brussels or Berlin will have to pay more per kroner and so more per rasher of bacon. As the price of Danish rises so British, Irish or Dutch bacon becomes more competitive and the Danes lose their market edge.

    In general, a low exchange rate will help a country to export and a high one will restrict exports but make imports cheaper. Why is this? If your currency has a low value you can get more foreign cash for each unit of home currency than you would if the value were high. If the pound sterling is worth $US 2 (exchange rate £0.5 to the US dollar) you can buy American jeans worth $40 for £20. However, if the American jeans manufacturers are so successful that demand for dollars pushes up the rate to £0.8 then you will only get $1.25 to the pound. Your jeans are now going to cost you £0.8 × 40 = £32. You decide to try Marks & Spencer's own brand. The reverse applies if exchange rates rise—it becomes cheaper to import.

3. A floating and therefore variable exchange rate has the dual problem of discouraging investment in a country and yet encourage speculators. The foreign exchange markets include a number of dealers who hope to make fast profits by buying currency at a low price and selling at a higher one. As a result, money may change hands and cross borders (by electronic transfer rather than in bags of coins!) in large amounts and at great speed, yet it is not for investment but is 'hot money' which is effectively passing through.

The basis of the floating or free market approach to currency is that exchange rates will settle at a ratio in proportion to the price levels in different countries. Suppose, for example, that a sample 'basket' of goods in Portugal costs 100 escudos and the same basket in Spain costs 130 pesetas. The currencies will exchange at a rate of 1:1.3 if we can ignore transport costs. A change in price levels in one country will clearly produce a change in this rate.

This is known as the *purchasing power parity theory* of exchange rates, but it is doubtful whether it has more than a very background influence. For one thing, while a basket of typical goods may be similar in Spain and Portugal they would be very different between Spain and Norway. The advantages of a floating currency can be briefly summarized as:

1. The currency becomes self-regulating. Market forces continually adjust the currencies value in international terms so that it is rarely out of its natural rate for long.

2. It removes exchange rates from government responsibility so that they cease to be a target of policy.
3. It is often considered to be a condition of achieving worldwide economic efficiency.
4. It safeguards an economy against the importing of inflation.

In general, there is no firm confidence in the inevitability of free or floating systems and nations have for centuries attempted to find alternative methods of stabilizing rates. We now turn to look at some of these.

The gold standard

According to Euclid, if two things are each equal to a third thing then they must be equal to each other. This principle of logic was the basis of a system of international liquidity which prevailed for many centuries in Europe and was based on gold. When most coins were made of gold or silver their value was automatically equivalent to the value of the metal. Coins in cheaper metals and notes had a fixed ratio to the gold and silver coins and were exchangeable for gold. However, debasement by mixing base metals with the precious ones and rising prices made this simple system unworkable. It was replaced by a system in which gold was held in bulk by governments and moved in reaction to currency price changes. This was known as the *gold bullion standard*.

> The *gold standard* is a method of stabilizing currencies by using the value of gold in or backing each currency as a unifying factor.

The rules of the gold standard acted as a self-correcting method of adjusting surpluses and deficits in the balance of payments, and in the gold bullion form which operated between 1925 and 1931 were basically very simple:

1. If gold came into Spain as a result of success at exporting, then Spain would increase its money supply. This would cause some degree of inflation (see Chapter 13) and so raise the price of the goods produced in Spain. Its exports would rise in price and the balance of payments surplus would disappear.
2. If Spain was a net importer it would lose gold and should deflate its currency. This would create cheaper home-produced goods and so increase exports.

Unfortunately some countries, notably the USA and France, hoarded gold without adjusting their money supply and in the end the gold standard collapsed. Gold now accounts for only a small proportion of international reserves.

Exchange controls

An alternative to the gold standard and to a free market in currency is a rigid exchange control system. At one extreme a government could simply decree that its currency would exchange at a specified rate with others or more usually with a major international currency like the US dollar or the pound sterling. The problem with this is that it does not really work except in a planned economy, because if the official rate is out of line with the market rate then a 'black' market will develop.

Usually, where this approach has been used by Western governments there as been an official rate which the government has promised to guarantee by buying and selling currency itself. This is known as a *pegged* system, i.e. the exchange rate is pegged at the official level. It is usually backed up by physical controls, i.e. limits on the amount of foreign currency that can be purchased or limits on the amount of national currency that can be taken out of the country (Fig. 10.9).

Within the countries of the EU there is now no restriction on movements of capital and the physical controls were, in any case, for the UK, abolished as far back as 1979. One problem has been that whatever the rate accepted and agreed by a government, the markets for currency and ultimately the goods and services markets which determine currency demand are not controlled. From time to time the UK rate has been out of line with its market rate to such an extent that governments find that they are buying sterling at a rapid rate to keep up the exchange rate. If demand from the market is slack, the government has to step in, using gold or foreign currency reserves to buy its own money. If reserves are depleted too fast while imports are much stronger than exports then it may be necessary to call a halt to that official rate and to accept a new lower one.

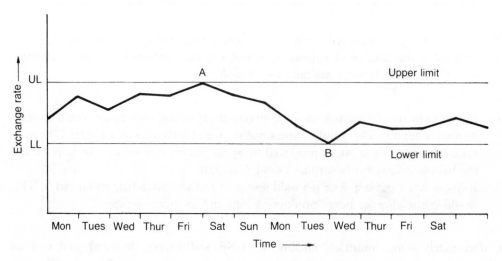

Figure 10.9   A 'crawling peg' system with sterling. At A and B there would be intervention by the Bank of England.

This is *devaluation*, and is regarded as a politically weak move. In 1967 it brought considerable criticism on the Wilson government and in 1992 in the 'Black Wednesday' U-turn by the Conservative administration of John Major the effective devaluation resulting from withdrawal from the European Monetary System (see below) produced criticism from all sides and arguably was the first nail in the coffin of Norman Lamont's career as Chancellor of the Exchequer. It need not be regarded as a disaster, however, since, as we have already noted, a lower exchange rate increases a country's competitiveness in overseas markets.

> *Devaluation* is the reduction in the exchange rate of a country's currency which is given official recognition.

Exchange rates and the IMF

In the post-war Western world a lot of nominal support has been given to the notion of stable exchange rates, largely backed by the IMF. This body has the objectives of encouraging world trade by establishing exchange rate stability, monetary cooperation and orderly exchange arrangements. Short-term credit has also been available and countries have been encouraged to consult and discuss before taking drastic steps to devalue.

Each member of the IMF has to provide a quota, made up of its own currency and gold, and this quota is determined by the Fund and adjusted every five years. The Fund was established in 1947 at a famous conference at Bretton Woods and developed an interesting approach to exchange rate control. This method is sometimes known as the 'adjustable peg' system, which established some stable relationships but did allow a measure of flexibility. Each nation's currency had a fixed rate in relation to the US dollar as well as gold and the US dollar had a basis in gold only. It allowed some flexibility in that the dollar acted as a cushion between national currencies and gold.

The system lasted until 1971, when the Nixon administration in the USA cut the connection between the US dollar and gold. The burden had become too great for one currency. The US dollar had become the international currency. Oil was priced in it, trade was conducted in dollar terms and in some developing countries the US dollar was prized far more than the national currency.

Managed floating

Since 1971 the world's currency markets have generally operated a system of floating which is nevertheless under the close scrutiny and manipulation of governments. This management of 'dirty' floating enables a measure of free market forces to operate so that differences in purchasing power or inflation between countries can alter exchange rates.

Nevertheless, each government has a fixed idea of at least the acceptable range for its currency and by careful buying and selling of its own and other moneys, depleting or adding to its reserves, each government contrives to keep its currency at an acceptable rate.

A degree of floating allows a government to concentrate on other economic objectives and allow short-term fluctuations to take place, automatically adjusting for inflation and balance of payments changes. As we explained above, freedom in rates will lead to stability in trade since excess of surplus or deficit on the balance of payments will be compensated by changes in the currency exchange rate. One might expect that, as a result, currencies would find an equilibrium, but unfortunately there are so many countries and currencies and factors which can disturb an equilibrium—especially the psychological ones which fire the speculators—that stability is still very much sought after.

Figure 10.10 shows the progress of the pound sterling against the deutschmark over a number of years with the key points indicated. Table 10.11 gives the rates in the main period of managed float up to 1990 when the UK entered the Exchange Rate Mechanism of the EC (see below).

The European Monetary System

A possible combination of fixed rate and floatability is to have the rate for a currency fixed between two limits and it is allowed to float between. Intervention is only necessary if the rate approaches the upper or lower limit and looks as if it might breach the 'ceiling'

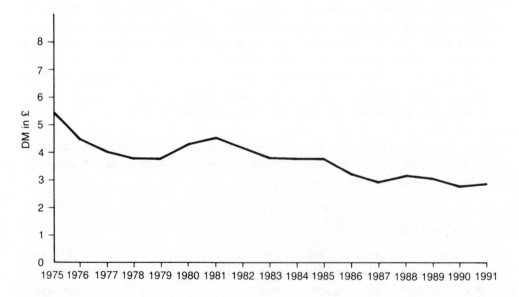

Figure 10.10 Deutschmark against sterling 1975–91.

Table 10.11 Exchange rate of sterling 1986–1993

Year	Annual averages for £ sterling against:		
	$US	DM	ECU
1986	1.46	3.18	1.49
1987	1.64	2.94	1.42
1988	1.78	3.12	1.51
1989	1.64	3.08	1.49
1990	1.79	2.88	1.40
1991	1.77	2.93	1.43
1992	1.77	2.75	1.36
1993	1.50	2.48	1.28

Source: CSO—*Economic Trends*, March 1994, HMSO.

or the 'floor'. The best-known version of this approach is the Exchange Rate Mechanism (ERM) of the European Monetary System (EMS).

Treatment of the EMS in relation to the rest of the European Communities will be postponed until the final section in this chapter. For the moment it is necessary, however, to explain its role in international liquidity. The EMS was set up on 13 March 1979 with the aim of creating a 'zone of monetary stability in Europe', with the later intention of consolidating the system by establishing the European Monetary Co-operation Fund. The essential components of the EMS are:

- A European currency unit (the ECU) to act as a unit of account and to aid in fixing budgets
- An exchange rate and intervention mechanism
- A credit mechanism
- Measures designed to strengthen the less prosperous states in the EMS.

Each of the participating countries has an ECU-related central rate and these rates are used to establish a grid of bilateral exchange rates. In fact, the market has tended to relate itself to the German deutschmark in view of the success of the German economy and the dominance of the independent Bundesbank. The deutschmark has been strong and other European nations have tended to judge their currencies by the deutschmark rather than the artificial ECU. It can be seen that there is a dual system with the ECU itself being valued against a basket of European currencies so that, in reality, each currency is relating itself to the European average. However, if world rates change (for example, the yen or US dollar) then the whole system will change against the outside world—but the rates between each of the European currencies will remain stable. As a result, trade between EU countries can be conducted with relative security (Fig. 10.11).

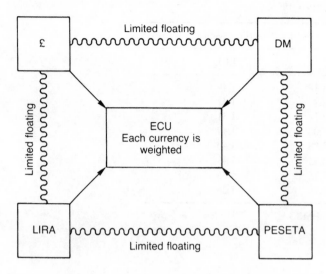

Figure 10.11   The ERM: weighted ECU and currency floats.

The attempt to establish fixed or restricted rates have not yet been very successful and that includes the ERM in the EU. The advantages are stability, certainty and the importance of a degree of discipline on a country's government and economic institutions. However, it is possible to 'import' inflation as exchange rates cannot adjust to price differences and there may be economic problems such as recession and unemployment in a country which has a currency considered out of line. There is also the problem that the exchange rate becomes a prime economic target of government policy which can deflect from other important priorities.

The purpose of these various approaches to exchange rate control is to establish a stability with automatic adjustment in order to encourage free trade. Why, though, is free trade so desirable? This is the question we will attempt to answer in the next section.

Topic 10.7   Free trade versus protection

We have seen the economic logic of free trade—that world efficiency will be increased if countries and regions can all specialize in what they can produce or provide best according to the principles of comparative advantage. However, economic history tells us that for many hundreds of years free trade has been the exception rather than the rule, and that however much economists and many businesses argue for free trade, most governments and some other businesses will maintain the need for protection.

What is protection?

A government can restrict free trade and protect its home industries from foreign competition by a number of means. These include:

- *Tariffs*, where import duties are imposed on goods coming into a country. This will increase the price to the consumer although not necessarily to the whole extent of the tariff. Figure 10.12 indicates the likely effect of a tariff assuming perfectly inelastic demand. Effectively, if the import is a necessity like wheat, then a tariff can probably be passed on in full but if demand is more elastic, perhaps because of home-produced alternatives, then a tariff will be partly absorbed by the importing firm.
- *Subsidies* by the home government is another method of interfering with free trade and one which is less easy to notice. Some subsidies can be in the form of low–cost power or low rents, and thus an overseas exporter attempting to penetrate the home market may not find it easy to see what is keeping home companies' costs low.
- *Quotas* are a third method of restricting trade, especially following bilateral (two countries) or multilateral (a number of countries) agreements.

> *Protectionism* is the theory that it is better for a country to apply tariffs, quotas or subsidies to protect home firms rather than to allow free trade.

Supply and demand analysis can be used further to investigate the effect of tariffs or quotas. In Fig. 10.13 we see the theoretical domestic demand and supply curves for microwave ovens. On top of the curves, representing the domestic schedules, we can see

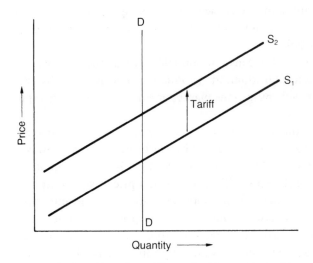

Figure 10.12   Effect of a tariff on price (demand inelastic).

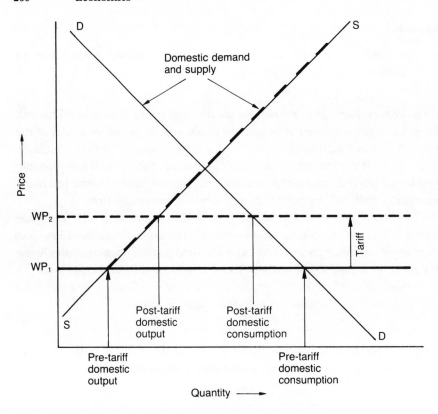

Figure 10.13 Effect of tariff on domestic output and consumption.

the supply curve for the world as a whole. This is a horizontal line at the world price (WP$_1$) since it is assumed that the full domestic capacity can be supplied at that price if required. If a tariff is imposed the world supply curve rises to WP$_2$, with the difference between WP$_1$ and WP$_2$ being the tariff.

The effect on the domestic market is that consumption falls because the new price is too high for some previous purchasers, but domestic production increases because the price is now high enough to entice new firms into the market or existing firms to invest in new plant and increase output.

If we look at quotas instead we see that the same effect—a rise in price and an increase in domestic output—is achieved by a different route. The world price for microwaves (WP$_1$), let us suppose, is the same as in the earlier example, but this time a quota of 10 000 a year is introduced, cutting back supply. This results in a price rise as output is now at a different point on the demand curve. Again, some customers are now out of the market but domestic producers can increase output at the new price. One interesting feature, though, is that while imports have been cut back those overseas traders who manage to be included in the quota get a surplus or 'windfall' profit because they are able to charge a higher price, even though they do not need to.

Why have import controls been so popular?

There are a number of reasons protectionism has been so popular with governments. These include the following:

- *Revenue* Yes, quite simply some governments have seen the chance to make money out of imports. This will especially apply where demand is inelastic and is often justified in the case of luxury items. In the Middle Ages, the barons in the Rhine valley built their castles in such positions that they could control transport on the river and levy duties on passing traffic for the sole purpose of making a lot of money. We can look at this in much the same way as we considered the imposition of VAT in Chapter 5. The principle is the same because, as far as the customer is concerned, a tax has been levied, either *ad valorem* (by value) or a flat-rate tax by volume or weight. The difference is in the mechanics because, typically, the import duty is paid by the importer and in most cases the retailers are not involved. They simply have to pay the importer a higher price and this increase is passed on, in whole or part, to the customer.
- *Protecting infant industries* This is the most common reason for restrictions. Comparative advantage may be fine in theory but it does not help a country which is trying to get an industry established if large multinationals based overseas can use the full benefits of economies of scale to undercut at every turn.
- *Redressing a balance of payments deficit* If a country is suffering from a bad balance of payments deficit one of the simplest ways of readjusting the account is to impose import duties, quotas or insisting on a money deposit from importers.
- *Supporting home industries* It may be considered advisable to impose duties on a relatively permanent basis in order to support weak or struggling industries. In particular, the action may be introduced to protect jobs in areas of high unemployment. The Corn Laws which were a major issue of political debate in the nineteenth century were an attempt to protect Britain's farmers from cheap overseas foods arriving from the New World—but bitterly opposed by the factory owners and town dwellers who wanted cheaper food.
- *Political and military policies* These may move a government to impose duties or quotas or even outright prohibition of imports. There are often restrictions on the import of weapons or of prohibited drugs, and recent years have seen a number of trade boycotts in operation in an attempt to force a country to change its policies. South Africa is perhaps the prime example.

Those in favour of free trade will argue that despite the short-term local benefits of some of the above motives, free trade is a better long-term option. In moving the world towards a higher level of efficiency it can ensure that:

- *Technology* is improved and diffused as firms around the world need to become more efficient.

- *Greater variety* of goods are available for the consumer if there is free trade. The contents of a typical greengrocers will indicate the amount of imported food which enables us to eat more than typical British foods.
- *Higher standards of living* are possible because goods are cheaper and so disposable incomes will go further.
- *Employment* prospects are improved as a result of the increase in efficiency in industries where a region has comparative advantage. The problem is in explaining this to redundant shoe workers in Northampton or steel workers in the Ruhr. There are many short-term sacrifices on the route to long-term benefits.
- *Real output* is increased for the world as a whole, so we are all richer as a result. Effectively, GDP per head increases and, as mentioned earlier, the whole world economy becomes more efficient.

How is free trade achieved?

Case Study 10.1 looks at some of the problems. Free trade may be seen by economists as obvious and clearly beneficial but neither governments nor electorates see it that way! The development of free trade has been slow and there is still much to do, although it is on the world agenda.

Case Study 10.1—GATT on a tightrope

In the years following the Second World War a spirit of international coopera-tion prevailed and not only was the United Nations launched from the ashes of the old League of Nations, but new plans were made for making world trade easier. Among the arrangements which came out of the discussions of 1947 was the establishment of a free trade treaty known as the General Agreement on Tariffs and Trade (GATT).

GATT was not an agreement for instant free trade as this would have thrown the economies of many countries into instant turmoil and indeed it created enormous commercial advantages for those nations which had not been deva-stated by war. Primarily GATT was an agreement to talk. The signatory coun-tries agreed to meet regularly to discuss global and more local trading agreements and to have the long-term objectives of removing tariffs and other barriers to trade. Regional tariff zones, like those which a few years later were to develop in Europe, were not considered to be wrong provided that they contributed to the overall objectives. Among the GATT principles are resistance to subsidies and other hidden barriers to trade and the concept of non-discrimination between nations. This latter point may be a little at variance with the policies of the European Union.

GATT has proceeded by a series of discussions usually known as 'rounds'. Each round has had shorter-term objectives and usually been centred around one country or city—hence recent examples have been the Tokyo Round in the late 1970s and the Uruguay Round which was completed at the end of 1993. The latter was very much an 'on–off' affair and several times in 1992 and the earlier part of 1993 its future was in doubt. However, completion was successful in the end.

One of the features of the Uruguay Round was the establishment of GATT as a more permanent World Trade Organization to enable it to monitor free trade on a more regular basis. The agreement also eased industrial tariffs by over a third and planned reduction in subsidies and similar hidden barriers over a 6-year period. There was also an agreement to eliminate discrimination and establish a freer market in services, including financial products. This was one of the 'sticky' areas which held up the Uruguay Round for so long.

Another key issue which caused problems in the discussions in 1992 and 1993 was the problem of intellectual property. The question of ownership of patents and the limiting of the use of ideas and inventions to one country is a very complex one as most countries feel that they ought to be able to make some profits out of inventions. Since most patents belong to the developed countries of Europe, North America and Japan, it is particularly important for the developing countries that intellectual property is not restricted to countries already rich in technology.

GATT involves a lot of talk and a lot of paper! Most countries have some vested interests in protecting their own industries, farmers and financial institutions. While the principle of comparative advantage may be seen as relevant and valid, it is not so easy to apply it in a practical way when jobs and profits are at stake.

1. Can GATT achieve a more prosperous world, easier with regional free trade areas like the EU?
2. Why are hidden trade barriers, like subsidies, considered to be more of a problem than tariffs?

Basically, free trade was a very spasmodic affair until after the Second World War. Some countries like Britain which thrived on commerce favoured free trade on the whole because it meant cheaper raw materials and easier markets for manufactured products. However, while there were occasional gestures and agreements, free trade was not systematically sought until talks in 1947, which resulted in the formation, in 1948, of the General Agreement on Tariffs and Trade (GATT). This was a declaration of intent by most of the countries of the 'free' world. The principles of GATT were:

1. No member country should show trading discrimination against another.
2. If protection of home industries is felt to be essential, it should only be by customs duties and not by fixed import quotas.

3. Consultations should take place when tariff changes are being considered so that traders and trading interests are warned and advised.
4. Negotiations should be held with the intention of general reductions in tariffs and other trade barriers. These are usually known as 'rounds' and the 1990s have opened with the so-called Uruguay Round. Negotiations have been difficult and its obituary has been prepared many times, but slow progress has been made.

One of the difficulties faced by GATT has been the fact that within the general objective of worldwide free trade certain countries have formed free trade areas to implement the idea more quickly. Since 1948, we have seen free trade areas set up for the Latin American states by the Montevideo Treaty; between Australia and New Zealand, the British Commonwealth preferential treatment principles (and similar procedures for French former colonies), a Central African Customs Union and a Central American Free Trade Association.

The most significant events in promoting free trade have, however, taken place in Europe. The 1950s saw the establishment of the European Free Trade Association (EFTA), the European Economic Community (EEC) and the East European equivalent, COMECON. These are the subject of the next section.

Topic 10.8   The European Union

No chapter on international trade and the balance of payments can be complete without a mention of the European Community of which the UK is a (sometimes reluctant) member. Since 1 January 1993 especially, our economic future has been inescapably tied up with that of our neighbours and following the Maastricht Treaty the trend towards a federal Europe seems, whether we like it or not, inevitable. Among other things the Treaty brought about a change of name of the Community to 'European Union'. This is the reason why this book has attempted to see economics in a wider context than just the UK.

The European Economic Community (EEC) was formed as a result of the Treaty of Rome (1957), and from the start set out to be a wider, more integrated, organization than its rival European Free Trade Association and with different objectives to the East European COMECON, dominated by the USSR. Its original six members (France, Italy, West Germany, Belgium, Luxembourg and The Netherlands) have since been joined by the UK, Eire, Denmark, Spain, Greece, and Portugal. Since the independence of the countries of Eastern Europe, East Germany became part of the new united Germany and so entered the EC, and a number of former Comecon countries are likely to be seeking association within the next few years.

The EEC was not the only organization founded by the 'core' countries of Western Europe. The European Coal and Steel Community was founded in 1951 by the 'six' named above as a result of the post-war Committee for European Economic

Cooperation. Euratom was also founded at the same time as the EEC. The result has been some confusion of terms. From the late 1970s the European Commission and its supporters showed preference for use of the title 'European Community', a slight amendment of the earlier plural form 'European Communities'. As there are many joint institutions for the three bodies, it makes a lot of sense to see them as one, but some people feel that there are sinister federalist implications in using 'EC' rather than 'EEC' as a title. Following the signing of the Maastricht Treaty in 1993 the name 'European Union' has been preferred. In this book we have tried to use 'EEC' when referring specifically to the economic arrangements and 'EU' or 'EC' when discussing more general or political issues.

Unfortunately, the Treaty of Rome has political implications and many people are unhappy about the loss of sovereignty involved in membership of the EU. However, it has provided the member countries with a huge market for their products and has stabilized agriculture and encouraged competition. It is significant that the UK's trade with the EU, as a proportion of all trade, increased from 43 per cent in 1978 to nearly 51 per cent in 1988.

Since January 1993 the level of integration has been even greater. All tariffs have been eliminated, creating a single market for goods and services across the Community. There will also be free movement of labour and freedom in previously closed areas like insurance and banking. The European Monetary System, which has already been discussed, was designed to become a pillar of the system and there is a strong current moving in the direction of having a 'hard ECU'—i.e. a single currency. The Maastricht Treaty is aimed at even closer integration, with many politicians seeing it as another step on the route to a federal European state.

The Common Agricultural Policy

One of the main features of the EEC is the Common Agricultural Policy (known as CAP). The EEC was faced on its formation with a community in which over 20 per cent of the population were involved in agriculture and many of the farmers were comparatively poor, farming small amounts of land with very old-fashioned methods. The aim of CAP was to stabilize farm incomes by operating a guaranteed price system which would not produce an undesirably large increase in food prices.

If prices of farm products fall below a specified 'intervention price' then the EEC will buy up production to raise the price levels. It has thus acquired the famous butter 'mountains' and wine 'lakes' which are really reserves that can be released later, perhaps for export. Since 1972 there has also been a programme of guidance for farmers seeking to leave marginal land or to increase the size of holdings on better land.

Administration

One of the unfortunate features of the EU has been the large bureaucracy which has grown to administer it. The European Parliament which has elected members is more of a consultative and advisory body than a legislature but it can dismiss the Commission and reject the Community budget. The real leadership rests with the Commission which is appointed by the member governments but is independent of them. Policy making and implementation are its main concerns. The final power rests with the Council of Ministers, which includes government representatives from all the member states, usually the foreign ministers. On vital matters a unanimous decision is required. The European Court of Justice is the highest court in the EU and deals with disputes on Community Law.

Problems

The Community has been one of the thorns in the side of the Uruguay Round of GATT negotiations. Although in theory any free trade area is better than none, the closer integration of Europe has led to duties being imposed against the outside world with the UK and France negotiating special terms for their former colonies and associates. As far as GATT is concerned, the EU is the equivalent of a country and has proved resistant against offering too much to outside nations.

Essay questions

1. (a) Discuss whether a balance of payments deficit poses problems for the United Kingdom economy.
    (b) Critically compare different ways in which a payments deficit may be reduced. (The Associated Examining Board, November 1990.)
2. What are the main components of the balance of payments accounts? Would the existence of a persistent deficit in the non-oil account create any problems for the development of the economy? (Oxford and Cambridge Schools Examination Board, June 1992.)
3. What are *trade creation* and *trade diversion*? Use these concepts to compare gains from a customs union and gains from free trade. (Oxford and Cambridge Schools Examination Board, June 1992.)
4. Outline the possible causes of deficits on the capital and current accounts of the UK balance of payments. Since 1986, the annual deficit on current account has increased from nearly zero to about £15 billion. Discuss whether or not this matters. (Northern Examinations and Assessment Board, June 1992.)
5. Explain what is meant by the balance of payments and whether or not a deficit on the visible balance should be regarded as a problem by the Government. Discuss the factors responsible for the UK's foreign trade record in recent years and evaluate their importance for the future economic performance of the economy. (Northern Examinations and Assessment Board, June 1993.)

6. Define foreign exchange rates and explain what factors can cause them to fluctuate in the long-term and the short-term. Discuss the merits of the ERM and EMU (a) to its members and (b) to the rest of the world. (Northern Examinations and Assessment Board, June 1993.)

Chapter 11

Money — supply and demand

Topic 11.1   The supply of money

The term 'money', as we saw in the previous chapter, can take on a very wide meaning but when we speak of the *money supply* in economics we normally refer to the issue of notes and coins and the creation of deposits in banks and building societies. The next section will consider further various definitions, but for the moment we need simply to be aware of the distinction between *narrow money*, consisting of currency and current (cheque) accounts, and *broad money*, which includes other types of account and asset. Notes and coins in circulation (including those held by the banks) are also frequently known as the *monetary base* or as *high-powered money*. The reasons for these names will become apparent later in this chapter).

In a modern economic society, the supply of money comprises two main sources (see Fig. 11.1):

1. *Currency*   Currency circulation consists of coins and notes. In most countries the production of coins and notes is under state control if not actually produced by a

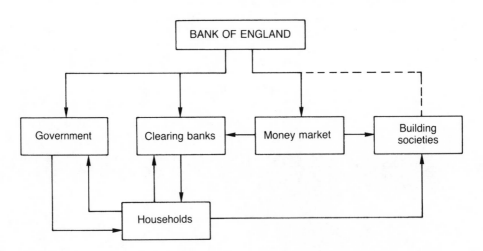

Figure 11.1 Money in the economy.

government department. In the UK strict government control has been in operation since 1931, although before then production of notes was determined by the Bank of England, a private company before nationalization in 1945, according to its reserves of gold. UK coinage is produced at the Royal Mint but despite the fact that we may be more aware of the weight of the coins in the pocket or purse than the notes, as a proportion of currency in circulation coins take decided second place to notes.

Bank of England notes together with Scottish and Northern Ireland banknotes (still legal tender in their own countries) are the most important part of UK currency. The same situation also applies in most other countries, especially those where paper currency is in much smaller values than in the UK.

Both notes and coins reach the public by way of the clearing banks. If the public's preference for liquidity increases, there will be increased withdrawals of notes and coins by the holders of bank accounts. In order to maintain a satisfactory cash float, the commercial banks will obtain more notes and coins from the Bank of England and have their accounts with the Bank debited accordingly.

2. *Bank money*   Figure 11.1 indicates that the total money supply includes deposits held by financial institutions. The student who has little knowledge of the workings of the monetary system may be excused from wondering how financial institutions can hold more 'money' than there are notes and coins in the country. Deposits are increased by the bankers' power to create credit.

It is important to consider how it is that banks can 'create' deposits which could count as money. To do this, we can consider goldsmiths who, two centuries ago, were the main financiers of Europe. Goldsmiths, probably because they owned strong safes and were used to handling valuable items, were often asked to look after deposits of gold and silver, issuing a receipt in return. This receipt evolved into money, and over time money became increasingly divorced from deposits of gold, turning into fiduciary token money.

Eventually the state controlled money issue through the Bank Charter Act 1844 and the gold backing disappeared finally in 1931. Effectively the banks were able to create money by issuing banknotes of nominal value which were accepted even if there was no gold to back them.

The method of distributing this money was through the medium not only of receipts for gold but, more importantly, of loans. The goldsmiths and banks found that if they held enough gold, on average, only a few customers would arrive on any one day demanding their valuables. As a result, they made more profit if they loaned out some of the gold deposited, thus receiving interest. Once the receipts became banknotes, the embryo banks could lend by issuing paper currency. If this happened, then money had been created because not only was there gold in the bank, owned by the person who deposited it there, but there was also paper money lent to a borrower.

Modern creation of money by banks

Today, the gold is not important but the process has been carried a stage further and lending is made on the basis of the cash or high-powered money held by the banks. If someone wants an overdraft or a bank loan they will make the request to their bank and, if granted, the effect will be to create extra money because the borrower will be able to sign cheques on a current account to the value granted by the bank. They have not deposited any money in the bank but have extra to spend.

Of course, if our borrower decides to write a cash cheque for most of the allocated overdraft, actual money will be passed over by the cashier. So the bank cannot just give everyone current account facilities or loans without considering the need for a certain proportion of cash to be held in the bank tills and vaults. Table 11.1 indicates how this might work if we assume that the bank wishes to keep 10 per cent of its deposits as a cash reserve while it lends the rest.

If Table 11.1 is studied we can see three phases which together result in money being created:

1. A deposit of cash in the bank by a customer. Note that the deposit of cash represents an asset in that the cash is now the property of the bank, but a liability in that the bank is liable to pay it back to the customer if the customer requests this, or signs a cheque for the amount.
2. The second stage involves a loan to Bongo Computers of £900. Bongo Ltd's account is credited with £900. No cash changes hands but the bank reckons to keep 10 per

Table 11.1   How banks create money

On 1 February a customer deposits £1000 in Goldmine Bank plc. The bank's accounts will show:

ASSETS		LIABILITIES	
Cash in vaults	£1000	Customer deposit	£1000

On 2 February the bank lends £900 to Bongo Computers Ltd by creating a business loan. The accounts now show:

ASSETS		LIABILITIES	
Cash in vaults	£1000	Customer deposit	£1000
Loan to Bongo Ltd	£ 900	Bongo Ltd's account	£ 900
	£1900		£1900

On 3 February Bongo Ltd writes a cheque for £900 to ABC Software Ltd. who deposit it at the bank. The accounts now show:

ASSETS		LIABILITIES	
Cash in vaults	£1000	Customer deposit	£1000
Loan to Bongo Ltd	£ 900	Bongo Ltd's account	£ nil
		ABC Software a/c	£ 900
	£1900		£1900

cent of deposits in cash to meet customer requirements. Hence £900 is lent rather than £1000, leaving £100 (10 per cent of the original deposit) as a cash reserve.

3. Bongo spends this money on software for its computers and does this by signing a cheque on its current account which is then paid into the bank by the recipient, ABC Software. The bank then has a liability to the original customer and to ABC Software totalling £1900 and this is balanced by assets of the original cash (£1000) plus the £900 loan to Bongo Computers.

The bank has created money—£900 in effect, which has been spent in the economy. It can, however, go further because of the new deposit of £900 by ABC Software. The bank can lend again all but 10 per cent, i.e. £810. So the process can continue for some time—all because one anonymous customer deposited £1000! It can continue in fact until the amount of deposits created amounts to a value of £10 000. These deposits are sometimes called *low-powered money* as opposed to the high-powered cash deposit which started it all off.

High-powered money or the *monetary base* is the notes and coins which are in circulation including that held by the banks. *Low-powered money* refers to the deposits created by the banks on top of the monetary base.

The money multiplier

The value of £10 000 can be calculated because the level of low-powered money created is determined by the *money* or *credit multiplier* and this in turn depends on the cash ratio adopted. The multiplier can be found by the formula:

$$M = \frac{\text{Value of new deposits created}}{\text{Value of original deposit}} = \frac{10\,000}{1000} = 10$$

The smaller the cash reserve ratio, the larger will be M.

It is important not to confuse the money or credit multiplier with the national income multiplier (Chapter 9) despite superficial similarities. They are not related and do different things.

The money multiplier in a multi-bank system

The example above assumes that only one bank is involved but in Western Europe there are in fact many banks. However, the principles remain the same as long as there are a large number of transactions. If Goldmine Bank plc grants a loan or overdraft and Bongo Computers Ltd sends a cheque to a supplier who deposits it in another bank, then that bank has received a deposit against which lending can take place. If we look at the

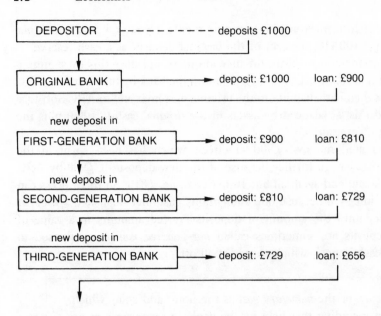

Figure 11.2 Money creation in a multi-bank system.

banking system as a whole, the assets and liabilities show a pattern identical to that for Goldmine Bank by itself. Low-powered money is created by the system and there are enough transactions to ensure that all banks benefit from the process. Figure 11.2 illustrates this.

Finally, the money supply for any country is ultimately in the hands of the government, since it is public policy which determines how much high-powered money is released to the banks for credit creation. The multiplier effect is, as we have seen, very powerful, so the finance minister in a government (the Chancellor of the Exchequer in the UK) has to be aware of the ultimate effects of policy decisions. This aspect of the topic will be explored further in Chapters 14 and 15.

> The *money multiplier* is the ratio between the change in money supply and a £1 increase in the monetary base.

Topic 11.2   What are monetary aggregates?

Official statistics often include tables entitled 'Monetary Aggregates', which are a puzzle to many people, especially as they include headings that look more like motorway signs than economic categories! These tables are, however, among the most important which

Table 11.2 Monetary aggregates 1992

Aggregate	Amount outstanding (£ million)	
	Not seasonally adjusted	Seasonally adjusted
M0	20 586	19 369
Retail deposits and cash in		
M4	374 121	372 369
M4	519 418	518 785

are published and carry a lot of vital information on the performance of the economy. Table 11.2 gives a sample from some recent tables.

The term *monetary aggregates* simply means the supply of money but since, as we have already seen, money can be defined in various ways, there are a number of possible aggregates. They are vital to an accurate control of the economy since money supply is so important in relation to inflation, the level of demand and interest rates. So far, we have distinguished only between narrow money and broad money to illustrate the role of banks in giving credit and so creating purchasing power.

The different definitions of money aggregates or the money supply reflect various degrees of narrowness or breadth in our definitions, but most definitions are relevant to some aspect of the economy. It is crucial that the student of economics appreciates the differences and remembers the most important ones. Table 11.3 illustrates the differences.

The table, even though much simplified, still looks complex. In general, broad money builds on narrow money and adds layers of further expressions of money supply. It is, however, complicated by the fact that some definitions do not lead further. The main stream follows M1 to M3 to M4 and then divides into M4c and M5. In general, all money and deposits included are in sterling except for M4c, when foreign currency is introduced.

> The *monetary aggregates* are the definitions of the total money supply such as M0 and M1.

We can define these for the UK in a little more detail as:

- *M0* This is really the shorthand for the monetary base or 'high-powered money', as it includes cash and notes plus some of the banks' deposits with the Bank of England. Both currency in private circulation and that held in banks' tills are included. One

Table 11.3   Monetary aggregates in the UK

		Narrow money
Notes and coins in circulation with public	Banks' money in tills plus banks' operational balances at the Bank of England	M0
Sight bank deposits with banks (both interest bearing and non-interest bearing) and both retail and wholesale		M1
Private sector retail bank deposits bearing interest plus Private sector retail shares and deposits in building societies plus National Savings ordinary accounts		M2
		Broad money
M1 plus Private sector time deposits and holdings of bank certificates of deposit (CDs)		M3
M3 plus Private sector holdings of shares, deposits and CDs in building societies but *less* building society holdings of bank deposits, bank CDs, notes and coins		M4
plus Bank and building society deposits in foreign currency		Private sector holdings of money market instruments and a range of other types of deposit (excluding those held by building societies)
M4c		M5

complication can cause the student some confusion is that M0 is sometimes also called the *broad monetary base*. This is not to be confused with the term 'broad money' because M0 is in fact very narrow money, but it refers to the inclusion of banks' operational balances at the Bank of England. It is thus 'broad' compared with the narrower base of just cash in circulation and bank tills.

● *M1*   This figure was used as the 'target' narrow definition of money rather than M0 because it includes sight bank deposits, i.e. bank accounts which can be used for payment or immediately turned into cash. However, when the Abbey National Building Society turned itself into a bank the result was to play havoc with M1, and after 1989 the figure was not produced. It also proved to be unsuitable with the changes in financial markets and practices noted below.

- *M2*   This category took M1 and added interest-bearing retail deposits in banks, building societies and National Savings. It was introduced in 1982 to replace M1. The 'retail' deposits are those used by households as opposed to the 'wholesale' deposits, which are owned by firms and especially by financial institutions holding deposits with each other.

- *M3*   This is another abandoned classification and added to M1 private sector time accounts in banks and private sector holdings of certificates of deposit in banks. In other words, it dealt with accounts where notice was required before withdrawal but excluded building societies, which made it increasingly less relevant.

- *M4*   This solved the problem of the exclusion of building society deposits in M3. As it included wholesale as well as retail deposits there was the danger of double-counting, as building societies hold deposits with the banks, so these are specifically deducted to get the final M4 figure.

- *M4c*   This is a figure which takes M4 and adds foreign currency deposits in the private sector. All the other definitions of money are for sterling cash and deposits only. Regular calculation of M4c was abandoned in 1991.

- *M5*   Finally, we have a figure which adds to M4 all other types of deposit which give liquidity such as all but long-term National Savings accounts and many other types of shorter-term loan. It confines itself to sterling deposits. M5 is the broadest measure of money supply but is not now regularly calculated.

In general, measures M0 to M2 are regarded as narrow money and M3 to M5 as broad money. We have discussed some definitions which are no longer calculated, but as students and research economists are liable to come across them in older official statistics and books it is useful to have at least some understanding of the full range.

We have spent some time looking at details of the monetary aggregates in the UK and in a book of this size there is little space for examining the systems in other countries. On the whole, there is a general similarity between industrialized nations, the differences being in how many separate definitions there are. In the USA a simpler system is in operation, with M1 being a narrower definition of money and similar to our own M1 and known as 'transactions money'. American M2 including savings accounts and other assets which are not far removed from being transactions money. If the reader is interested in exploring the American system further, then Samuelson and Nordhaus, Chapter 28, can be consulted.

Some problems arise in attempting to define monetary aggregates. These can be listed as:

1. The changes taking place in the financial markets as a result of deregulatory legislation. In particular, the freedom which building societies have to either formally become banks, as the Abbey National did, or to simply act in the same way as banks, as many large societies now do. A current account can be held as easily

with a building society as with a traditional bank and so the distinctions between banks and building societies become less relevant.

2. The distinction between retail and wholesale deposits has also appeared in Table 11.3. It is now regarded as more important than the bank/building society distinction. Wholesale deposits are not really related to consumers' spending decisions like retail deposits, which are those held by the general public. Wholesale deposits are the result of decisions by banks, building societies, financial institutions in general and some normal firms on investment of cash portfolios. As such, they are not very significant in terms of the money supply to meet demand.

3. The distinction between sterling and foreign currency which was the *raison d'être* of M4c will come under fire in the future as the UK becomes closer to other EU countries. Indeed, the day is probably not too far off when monetary aggregates are calculated in ECUs for the whole of the EU.

With the complexity of money supply definitions it can be difficult to answer the question 'What is the money supply?' Governments vary in the measure which they prefer to target but, on the whole, M0 and M4 have high prominence as narrow and broad definitions, respectively.

Topic 11.3   The demand for money

The demand for money is derived from three main sources:

- Individuals and households for the *consumption function*
- Individuals and business undertakings for the *investment function*
- The government for the *state expenditure function*

These three sources are interrelated with each other and with other economic phenomena. Consumption, for example, is largely determined by disposable income and is dependent upon wages, prices and employment. Investment is related to the rate of interest and preference for liquid assets, i.e. the degree to which firms want ready money as opposed to fixed assets. Government spending is related to political requirements such as defence or social security needs as well as to taxation and the acceptable size of the borrowing requirement.

The basic principle governing the demand for money is that as money is generally acceptable as a medium of exchange, the demand for it increases with income. The second 'law' of Professor C. Northcote Parkinson that 'expenditure rises to meet income' may be humorous but it also contains a basic economic truth underlying the demand for money. If people do not hold money, then they will hold other assets such as gold, diamonds, property or shares. Individuals have to decide in what proportion of money or other assets to hold their wealth. The problem centres round how much money to hold and this will depend on:

- The level of incomes in the economy
- Liquidity preference or the degree of desire for spending flexibility
- Rates of interest
- The state of trade
- Inflationary or deflationary trends in the economy

The demand for money varies with liquidity preference especially. In other words, to what extent do people and firms wish to hold money compared with other forms of wealth?

Keynes suggested that there are three important motives for holding money in the sense of a preference for money over other assets.

1. *The transactions motive*   One demands money to pay one's normal day-to-day bills depending upon the changing patterns of consumption. In a period of sharply rising prices, the amount of money demanded for the transactionary motive increases.
2. *The precautionary motive*   Money is needed to cover any unforeseen problems. Even if no definite purchase is intended, people often carry money 'just in case'. A household may want some cash reserves in case there is something in the sales or for small purchases, whereas a firm will need some petty cash and perhaps a float in the till in the case of a shop.
3. *The speculative motive*   There is a third motive for wanting to hold money rather than assets and this is for speculative purposes. This used to be regarded as a motive for the more prosperous households and collective savings schemes, such as unit trusts and insurance funds with the option of fund switching. However, as a result of the privatization of public utilities and the publicity given to Personal Equity Plans (PEPs), more ordinary people are interested in doing things with their money other than leaving it permanently in the building society.

One aspect of economics which has become a popular area for study in recent years is *portfolio theory*. A study of this theory is really beyond the scope of this book but it is relevant in a consideration of the speculative motive for holding cash or current account balances. The idea is that individuals and collective investment managers try to balance income against capital growth and security against risk. This means frequently switching wealth between assets and encashing one asset to invest in another. Sometimes when extra security is important, cash funds are chosen for short- or medium-term investment to satisfy the need for a safe haven for wealth. For further study of portfolio theory the reader is advised to read Advanced Study Topic 11.1.

Economics textbooks traditionally, for the sake of illustrating this motive, regarded the alternative to money as being the ownership of bonds. Bonds are fixed-interest loans such as government securities (gilts) or company debentures. Although in most cases households will regard interest-bearing time accounts or shares as the alternative to money, the illustration using bonds is still a valid and painless way to demonstrate the role of speculation.

Clearly, if bonds are paying a high rate of interest they will have more potential value to us than cash which does not pay interest at all. Bonds do involve a loss in liquidity, as we lose the ability to buy large items like a car or antique chair at a moment's notice. As a result, we will insist on some interest payment, and the higher the interest, the more attractive do bonds become. It may not surprise us, therefore, to learn that the demand for money varies inversely to interest rates. In other words, if interest rates rise, the astute investor will dispose of cash or current account balances to buy bonds.

However, as so often in economics, it is not as simple as that! One of the problems with bonds is that once a bond is issued, its interest rate is fixed and if we have our wealth in low-interest bonds and general interest rates are high we are not too happy. What is more, should we wish to sell the bond we will have difficulty in securing a purchaser and so the price of the bond will fall. In other words, we can say that if interest rates are high the fixed-rate bonds will tend to fall in value and vice versa. Bond values are in an inverse relationship to interest rates.

Investors appreciate the income to be gained from bonds but they are also concerned about the value of their investment. As a result, if they think that bond prices will fall they will tend to sell to avoid a capital loss. Thus if interest rates are high we would expect investors to prefer bonds issued at the new rates. They will also be interested in existing bonds because they will have a low value but will be expected to see capital gains. If interest rates are low, on the other hand, bonds will be relatively expensive but should rates be expected to rise, then investors may fear a capital loss and turn their bonds into cash before it is too late. This feature explains not only the inverse relationship between interest and demand for money but also the fact that the relationship is not linear.

If we look at the three elements in the demand for money we can use them to express liquidity in a graph, known as a *liquidity preference curve*.

The precautionary and transactions motives for holding money are not related to interest rates and so are represented by a vertical straight line (Fig. 11.3).

The speculative demand is inversely related to interest rates but becomes infinite at very low rates. It is just not worth putting any money into an investment at this level, and

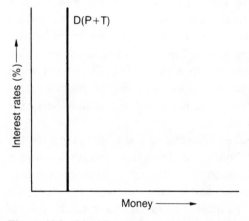

Figure 11.3   Liquidity preference: precautionary and transactions.

in any case, the real speculator prefers to be liquid in anticipation of future interest rate rises (Fig. 11.4). This level was called by Keynes the *liquidity trap*.

Finally we find that the full liquidity preference curve combines all three motives (Fig. 11.5). The minimum level of money required in the economy depends on the transactions/precautionary level and so the curve starts here. However, the slope of the curve is determined by the speculative motive.

Topic 11.4   Theories of interest rates

In Chapter 8 we looked briefly at interest rates in connection with the factor of production, capital. We considered two theories of interest: the loanable funds theory and the marginal efficiency of capital theory. We saw that the former regards interest as the reward for money capital available for lending with the supply and demand for such

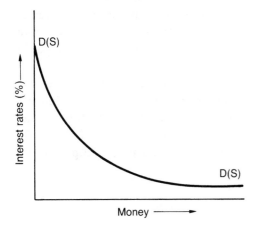

Figure 11.4   Liquidity preference: speculative demand.

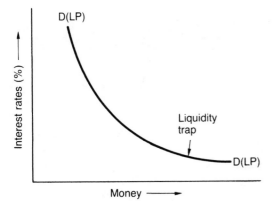

Figure 11.5   Total liquidity preference curve.

funds producing an equilibrium supply and 'price' (i.e. interest) after the classical model of price theory. The latter theory sees the falling efficiency of capital as it is used as the main determinant of the demand curve for capital.

We have now, however, another type of demand curve to look at—the liquidity preference curve. This is specifically the demand for money—cash and current account balances (say, aggregate M1) and not just the demand for borrowings as in the case of the loanable funds theory. As we saw in the previous section, the demand for money is a result of the need to hold cash for either mundane transactions or as an interim measure in the process of shifting investments. It is *not* a demand for funds for industrial investment.

If we return to our liquidity preference curve (see above) we can view equilibrium interest rates as a point where the liquidity preference curve (i.e. the demand for money) crosses the money supply curve. The supply 'curve' is more accurately a straight line since the supply of money is not influenced by interest rates at all. The volume of money available is determined by the government (specifically in the UK, the Bank of England and the Treasury in consultation) and is rarely set in response to interest rates. It can be represented therefore as a vertical line with a relatively fixed position along the horizontal axis, at least in the short term. The main movement is likely to be of the liquidity preference curve.

In Fig. 11.6 we explore how this may operate. Suppose that the demand for money increases, perhaps as a result of an increase in disposable income. Then we see a move of the demand for money from LP_1 to LP_2. As we move from LP_1 to LP_2 with the money supply line M–M remaining in the same position, interest rates will rise. Note that the liquidity trap position stays in the same place—it is the curved and vertical parts of the liquidity preference curve which move.

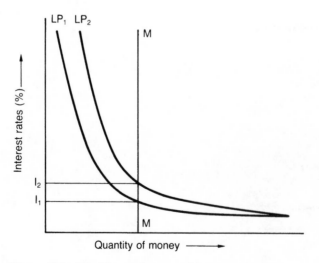

Figure 11.6 Liquidity preference and interest rates.

Why do interest rates rise? If we look back to the previous section we will recall that the real rate of return from an investment is the *yield*, and this is the earnings from the investment as a percentage of the capital value. With fixed-interest bonds there is a relationship between the capital value of the bonds and interest rates, which has an inverse nature. If interest rates rise then bonds lose capital value as people try to replace them with higher-earning investments. Now worth less, the fixed interest paid becomes a higher yield, in line with the rise in interest rates elsewhere. Eventually, despite the fact that its nominal interest rate is fixed, the yield from the bond will become similar to other yields in the market.

If people are moving into money either to spend or to reinvest then this will mean that some of them will sell bonds, or perhaps unit trusts invested in bonds (gilt trusts) and so bond prices will fall and yields rise. The 'standard' interest rate in the London money market is the yield on undated gilts, and so a move out of gilts directly produces interest rate rises in the market. As most people will prefer to lend to the government as a safer bet than practically any other investment, the rates are fractionally lower than others, and if the yield on gilts rises then other borrowers will need to raise their rates in order to borrow. If the government decides to increase money supply then we also see a change in interest.

We can see from Fig. 11.7 that if the money supply (M–M) moves to the right, i.e. increases, then interest rates will fall. Is this surprising? It should not be, since we are now used to the idea that if the supply of any commodity, including money, increases then its price will fall. Money is no different from commodities in this respect and if there is more money around then people are more likely to be satisfied with the provision and will wish to get rid of surpluses by buying bonds. This will, in turn, push down the interest rate because bonds will increase in price, giving capital gains, and so yields will reduce.

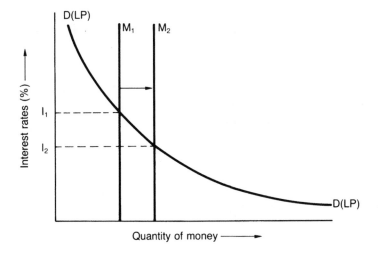

Figure 11.7 Money supply and interest rates.

Interest rates and the City

We will be looking at the money market institutions which are found in the UK in the 'City' of London and those in the European markets in the next chapter. However, we should consider briefly what we mean by 'interest rates', because even a casual glance at the financial pages of a serious newspaper will show that there are many different rates on offer.

Given that interest rates are determined by supply and demand for loanable funds according to the classical theory or by supply and demand for money as a whole in the liquidity preference theory, we need to consider why interest rates vary from one type of loan or investment to another (Table 11.4).

There are four main factors that are considered by a potential investor when thinking of lending or investing capital:

1. *Security of the investment*　We have seen that a sort of 'base' rate for interest is the yield on undated gilts because they are safe government loans. All things being equal, gilts, National Savings and other government-backed investments will not offer exciting interest rates, although the 'all things being equal' is important. As can be seen in Table 11.4, the undated gilts rate is higher than base lending rates and dated gilts would be higher still. Similarly, in much of 1992 and 1993 National Savings were offering high interest on deposits, to the annoyance of the building societies.

2. *Getting at the money*　The second factor is also important. Many of the interbank rates below are intended as short-term lendings, even as short as overnight, and thus involve little loss of liquidity. While gilts can be sold easily, unless the timing is right a capital loss may occur and, in any case, they are more correctly seen as longer-term investments.

   Consider the rates of interest in Table 11.5 which show comparisons for one building society. It can be seen that the longer the period of notice, the higher the rate of interest.

Table 11.4　Sample interest rates from one day in April 1993

	Rate (%)
Base Lending (Barclays Bank)	6
Base Lending (Exeter Bank)	7
Interbank offer rate (overnight)	6
Interbank offer rate (6 months)	$6\frac{3}{16}$
Sterling Certificates of Deposit	$6\frac{1}{8}$
Consols 4pc (undated gilts)	8.52
Leeds $13\frac{1}{2}$% 2006	10.19

Table 11.5 Sample interest rates: Alliance & Leicester as at 23 December 1991

Account	Minimum deposit (£)	Notice (days)	Interest gross (%)
TESSA	3 000	28	11.40
Ninety-day	1 000	90	9.35–11.25
MIDAS	10 000	Instant	10.00–10.60
Instant access	10	Instant	4.40–9.70
Cash plus	25	Instant	4.0–8.0
Deposit	1	Instant	2.0

In the case of some investments you 'get at' your money by selling the asset, so marketability is important. It is considerably easier to sell gilts or local authority bonds, for example, than loans to small companies.

3. *The volume of capital handled*   The building society rates are also graded on the size of investment. In general, the larger the sum involved, the higher the interest rate for investors. One reason for this is the per pound reduction in set-up costs and servicing. It costs no more to process £100 000 in a building society than £1000, or to buy £100 000 worth of gilts compared with £1000 worth. The bank or building society will be prepared to offer a higher rate for large depositors and in the case of gilts or shares while the dividends and yields stay unchanged, brokerage (the charges for buying and selling) will be much reduced, effectively reducing the capital cost of the purchase.

4. *Prospects for capital gain*   Some investments are acquired more for capital gain purposes than for the income. Shares in companies are a good example. While some people do look forward to their dividend cheques from British Gas most of the buyers of shares, and of gilts also, are corporate bodies such as insurance companies, unit trusts, pension funds and professional investors. With the exception of some income-seeking unit trusts and insurance funds, they are, on the whole, looking for capital gains and the yield is less important. As a result, yields on shares can be quite low without investors getting unnecessarily ruffled. Immediately after the stock market crash of 1987, when shares dramatically collapsed in price, there was a rush to gilts for safety. Many astute investors moved into gilts ahead of the pack and after a few months had made considerable capital gains. Yields were insignificant by comparison.

We have not mentioned more subjective factors such as patriotism, which was a prime motive in the purchase of those gilts known as 'War Loan', or tradition, which leads many people to their favourite building society, whatever the rates offered. Convenience of access for the general public also helps National Savings (sold through post offices) and building societies to attract savers. Pension funds will often switch large sums into gilts or cash deposits away from shares for individuals as retirement approaches for safety, and interest rates play little part in the decision. Gilts are also used as a safe haven for insurance 'with profits' funds when a guaranteed bonus has been declared.

All of these factors suggest that any theory to explain the differences between interest rates let alone how the standard rates are determined needs to be hedged about by the 'all things being equal' disclaimer, which is a standard of economists everywhere. One advantage of this part of the subject is that students can in fact exercise their applied economics daily by reading the financial pages of a newspaper and watching how interest rates are changing and noting the reasons given by the commentators. They may also apply their knowledge to their own personal savings!

Advanced Study Topic 11.1   Portfolio theory

Portfolio theory is the branch of economics which deals with the decisions that are made by investment managers in regard to the moneys for which they are responsible. Since large institutions such as insurance companies, pension funds and unit trusts are very large players in the capital and money markets, the ideas on how they manage their investments is significant.

Portfolio analysis rests on the problems of risk and the need for fund managers to decide what level of risk they will accept and then how they will diversify the portfolio in order to satisfy this risk level. The technique is known as Markowitz portfolio analysis, after the economist who developed many of these ideas.

Risk is an element which varies from individual to individual and from one fund to another. Some individuals are 'risk averse'—in other words, they try very hard to avoid risk; others are 'risk seeking'. Unit trusts and insurance funds are usually distinguished largely by the degree of acceptable risk. Extreme safety can be achieved by investment in gilts or even cash funds, while risk can be sought in 'special situations' funds.

Portfolio analysis and risk are not requirements for 'A' level economics but may be a requirement for banking, insurance and management examinations in economics. Those readers requiring more detail are recommended to consult Begg *et al.*, Chapter 14; D. Blake, *Financial Market Analysis*, Chapters 13 and 14; and J. C. Francis, *Investments: Analysis and Management*, Chapter 9.

Essay questions

1. (a) Why are there many different rates of interest?
   (b) How may monetary policy be used to influence the structure of interest rates?
   (*Source*: The Associated Examining Board, November 1990)
2. (a) Explain how the banking system creates bank deposits.
   (b) How might total bank deposits be affected by:
        (i) The government's budget moving from deficit into surplus?

    (ii)   A large-scale sale of shares to the general public resulting from the privatization of the electricity industry? (*Source*: The Associated Examining Board, June 1990)

3.   Examine the validity of the claim that controlling the increase in the money supply merely increases the cost of consumer credit. (*Source*: Oxford and Cambridge Schools Examination Board, June 1991)

4.   'Long-term inflationary pressures can be successfully contained only by control of the rate of increase of labour costs.' Discuss. (*Source*: Oxford and Cambridge Schools Examination Board, June 1992)

5.   What problems are involved in measuring the supply of money in the UK? Explain whether or not you regard the supply of money as an indicator or a determinant of the state of the economy. (*Source*: Northern Examinations and Assessment Board, June 1991)

6.   In what ways may a fall in interest rates increase the growth of consumers' spending? (*Source*: University of Oxford, June 1991)

7.   Is control of the money supply incompatible with the management of the exchange rate? (*Source*: University of Oxford, June 1991)

8.   What effects will an increase in the rate of interest have on the demand for and the supply of money? (*Source*: University of Oxford, June 1992)

Chapter 12

Financial markets and institutions

Topic 12.1 The structure of financial markets

Of all the markets which we might consider studying in some detail, perhaps the best known is the conglomeration of markets known as 'the City'. The financial markets in the UK are overwhelmingly concentrated in the area where the Romans established the city of London, with the flagship institutions being the Bank of England, the Stock Exchange and Lloyd's of London. Although we will take a close look at European versions, it is not jingoistic to state that London is the most important centre for world dealings in money and financial assets, and so we are justified in concentrating largely on the home product.

In looking at the structure of the City we find that there are many separate markets, connected and interconnected and it is usually helpful to classify these markets in three ways:

- Division by product, i.e. the *capital* market and the *money* market
- Division by type of institution, i.e. *bank* and *non-bank intermediaries*
- Division into the *government* or *public* sector and the *private* sector.

Capital and money markets

The capital market deals with longer-term funding for industry and the government, and is dominated by the Stock Exchange, now a computerized market for shares and stock. Many banks are also involved in this market including some specialist commercial mortgage banks. The market brings together firms seeking funding and individuals or institutions (including other firms) which have spare moneys that can be invested relatively long term. These moneys are used to buy 'securities' such as shares or debenture stock in the firm needing the funds.

In order to make it easier to obtain funding these securities are usually saleable to other potential holders which gives them liquidity, and this is especially the role of the Stock Exchange. In fact, the word *security* applies to those financial assets which can be sold on to any buyer as opposed to those which can only be sold back to their originator such as building society accounts. The client firms tend to use brokers, now known as 'market makers' in the case of Stock market dealings (see below), to advise them and introduce them to sources of finance.

The money market deals in short-term money, sometimes so short term that it is called 'overnight' funds! This money is used not for large capital projects but for the financing of temporary transactions or money shortages of both private firms and the government. The banks are active but so are a number of other institutions and the market is dominated by the Bank of England.

Closely connected with the money market, but also having links with the capital market, is the specialist market for the transfer of risks from individual firms to insurance companies or syndicates. This is centred around Lloyd's of London in Lime Street and a number of large insurance companies. We will discuss this market below.

Bank and non-bank intermediaries

When we come to look at the markets as divided by institution we find that there is an amazing variety of financial firms involved in this market. Nearly all of them can be classified as *intermediaries* and this term needs careful definition.

An 'intermediary', as defined in economics, is a body which comes between a person or firm needing to borrow and one with surplus to lend. In most cases the intermediary will 'package' the lending in the form of a standard product such as a bank loan, a mortgage or a bill of exchange. There is a wide variety of these products and collectively economists and writers on financial matters can call them *paper assets, financial claims* or *financial instruments*. Within the markets, although they will usually only have a visible form in the shape of a certificate or other document, they are frequently called 'products' as for manufactured items.

The packaging of financial products is important. Consider, for example, that well-known product, the mortgage, which is a loan to buy a house, factory or sometimes land. If a firm wishes to borrow £1 million to buy a factory site and to pay this money back with interest over 15 years it has to find some person or company willing to part with that amount of money to a total stranger and wait 15 years to get it back. This could be difficult, although private mortgages like this are arranged. Instead of simply acting as a broker and linking those needing money and those with a surplus, intermediaries in the mortgage market such as the banks and building societies will borrow money from individuals in small amounts or on the money market in larger sums. They then package it into mortgages of suitable size and duration for house or business purchase (Table 12.1).

In this way the assets and liabilities in the market are doubled. If John Smith, a millionaire, lends £100 000 to Brown Enterprises, a manufacturer, to buy a factory, then there is created an asset for John Smith and a liability for Brown Enterprises (see Table 12.2). However, if John Smith considers that a safer home for his savings would be in the deposit account at ABC Bank plc and they in turn give a mortgage to Brown Enterprises then the bank has also created an asset and a liability. Smith has an asset in the form of his deposit account and this is also a liability for the bank. Brown

Table 12.1   Selected financial instruments

Instrument	Normal market	Status
Equities (shares)	Capital	Securities
Government bonds (gilts)	Capital	Securities
Bank deposits	Money	Cash account
Building society deposits	Money	Cash account
Bank/building society mortgages	Capital	? Securities
Treasury bills	Money	Securities
National Savings accounts	Money	Cash account
Life assurance policies	Risk/Capital	? Securities
Eurobonds	Capital	Securities
Certificates of deposit	Money	Cash account

'? Securities' refers to instruments that are not normally regarded as securities but can be sold on to third parties.

Table 12.2   Intermediaries; double assets/liabilities

	Assets ($£$)	Liabilities ($£$)
1. Private Mortgage		
John Smith	100 000	
Brown Enterprises		100 000
Total	100 000	100 000
2. Use of intermediary		
John Smith	100 000	
ABC Bank	100 000	
Brown Enterprises		100 000
ABC Bank		100 000
Total	200 000	200 000

Enterprises has a liability to the bank in the form of his mortgage but the bank regards this mortgage as an asset. So instead of there being a £100 000 asset balanced by a £100 000 liability in the system, there are assets totalling £200 000 and liabilities totalling £200 000.

It is important to note that the term 'intermediary' as used by economists is slightly different from the use found in the personal finance pages of the newspapers. The financial services industry, now regulated under the Financial Services Act 1986, uses the term 'intermediary' to apply to the type of institution more traditionally known as a *broker*. As we saw above, a broker also comes between two parties but whereas the large banks and insurance companies can be called intermediaries in the economist's sense they are certainly not brokers. The broker does not package paper assets but has the role of advising clients, whether individuals or companies, and arranging the purchase from a supplier of shares, insurance contracts, mortgages, etc. on behalf of those clients (Fig. 12.1).

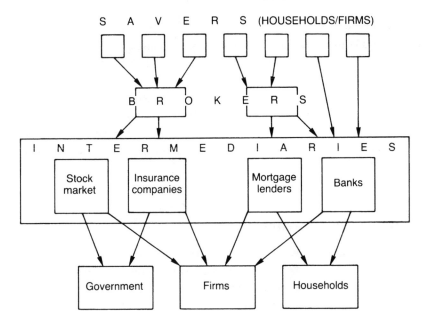

Figure 12.1   Financial markets.

The government

This is an important player in the financial markets both for longer-term loans such as gilts (bonds) or for shorter-term Treasury bills and as the authority behind the Bank of England's dealings in the market. The key to its role lies in the need to borrow for state spending, a need known as the public sector borrowing requirement (PSBR).

The PSBR will be examined further in both Chapters 14 and 15. It is important here to note that it varies from year to year according to the government's need. Even where the government is balancing the budget by raising taxes to meet spending there are likely to be short-term shortfalls of money. Firms and the self-employed pay their tax some time after the end of the year on which they are assessed and with smart accountants they may well keep the inevitable day of payment at bay for some time, perhaps for over a year. Meanwhile, the government needs to pay salaries to civil servants and moneys to contractors for road building, and has many other needs.

The government's borrowing has two possibly harmful effects on the private sector. In the first place, if the government is lent money by the banking system the money supply will increase as the banks pay with cheques on their own resources and create accounts. A second possible effect is that the borrowing activity effectively increases the total demand for loanable funds and so interest rates will rise. This is known as 'crowding out' the private sector and makes borrowing by firms more expensive than would otherwise be the case.

As the government borrowings have built up over the centuries and the amount owed has become very large and constitutes the *national debt* (see Chapter 14). This debt has to be serviced and part of tax revenues goes toward paying interest and capital repayments on the National Debt.

In addition to activities in the money and capital markets, the government also borrows directly from the public through National Savings. These are paper assets sold through post offices and some brokers and accountants and which are aimed at the ordinary public. The public can also buy gilts through post offices, although the range does not include all gilts available.

Topic 12.2   Finance for industry

One of the most important tasks of the financial markets is to provide funding for firms involved in production and services, including farming, manufacturing, leisure, transport and various types of tertiary industries. While some of this is short term and involves the money market, the most important requirements are for longer-term funding and involve the capital market.

At the heart of the capital market lies the Stock Exchange, although in view of recent changes to the way business is conducted the term 'stock market' might be more appropriate. Since the changes known as the 'Big Bang' in October 1986 the market functions through a computer network and transactions are not visible on the floor of the Stock Exchange as they used to be. One of the other changes introduced was an abolition of the distinction between the stock brokers, who dealt with the public, and the stock jobbers, who bought and sold on brokers' instructions. Under the current 'single capacity' rules one firm can combine both functions, and so dealing is frequently between the broking and market-making departments of one firm.

The stock market deals in certain types of security and the main types of security are as follows:

1. *Ordinary shares or equities*   These were mentioned in Chapter 7, when it was seen that the ordinary shareholders are the owners of a limited company with responsibility for electing the board of directors. While many people, firms and institutions such as pension funds do buy shares in order to own and 'have a say' in the running of a company, most share dealing is by those who are buying or selling short term to make a capital gain, improve their income or widen a portfolio of investments.

   Equities are the main assets traded in the stock market and the activities of the 'bulls' who try to profit from a price rise and 'bears' who profit from a fall in price are well known. Ownership of equities is still mainly in the hands of institutions and some large insurance companies and pension funds can each own up to 3–4 per cent of the whole market. There are increasing numbers of smaller investors, however, especially since the government's privatization programme has encouraged share ownership.

The advantage to a firm of raising capital by issuing shares is that there is no requirement to pay back the money received and no guarantees are given of any dividend to be paid. The owner of the shares relies on the 'second-hand' market under the auspices of the International Stock Exchange to liquidize the asset should this become necessary. For private limited companies the ability to sell shares is far more restrictive and will depend on finding someone who wishes to buy into the company. For both public and private limited companies, issuing shares is an easy way to raise money, provided that the company is prepared to see the new share-holders as co-owners with voting rights.

2. For the owners of the shares there is higher risk and no certainty that, even if sold, the shares will fetch the price paid. Of course, many investors are, as we have seen, buying in the hope of making a capital gain but some look to steadier income and security. For these there are *preference shares*, which give the owner priority in the issue of dividends. They too are sold in the stock market.

3. In some cases finance can only be obtained by a firm in the form of a loan which is a specific liability of the firm. For modest sums this is usually achieved by issuing a bond or, as it is usually known, a *debenture*. Debenture stock is usually secured on a particular fixed asset of the company, which will be sold off for the benefit of the debenture holder in the event of insolvency. Interest is paid each year on the debenture until maturity, when the loan is paid back in full.

4. Loans to the government are, as we have already seen, also known as bonds but their specific name is *gilts* (gilt-edged securities). Gilts are issued at a set interest rate and for a specific time span. In second-hand dealings on the stock market they are divided into three groups by the time left to maturity: 'longs' (15 years or more); 'shorts' (less than 5 years); and 'mediums' which lie in between. As in the case of commercial stock, a fixed interest is paid until maturity when the nominal value of the gilt is paid in full. A few gilts do not have a maturity date and are known as 'undated' stock—War Loan is a good example. As we noted in the previous section, the issue of gilts is related to the PSBR and budget deficit.

It should be emphasized that the stock market is largely concerned with securities that have already been issued. New issues of shares and company stock are normally made by merchant banks, especially the accepting houses. It is, however, the existence of the market for 'second-hand' securities which enables them to be sold in the first place. In the case of shares and undated gilts there is no obligation on the borrower to repay the capital invested but the holder knows that they can be traded and, as a result, are marketable. The price will vary from day to day and the stock market is one of the best known for frequent price changes. Every day in the national news and in the press, prices on the London, Paris, Tokyo and New York ('Wall Street') exchanges are quoted using index numbers.

Figure 12.2 indicates some of the variations that can occur in share prices and Case Study 12.1 takes this a stage further. Supply and demand operate as for any commodity,

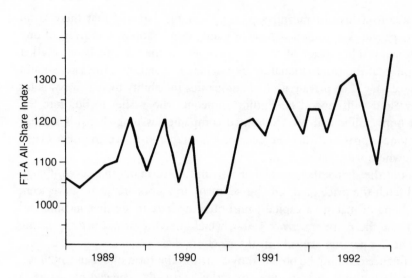

Figure 12.2 Share prices (FT-A Index).

but more than in most markets the price mechanism is 'oiled' by the large number of transactions for speculative reasons.

There are other methods of finding capital investment for industry than shares or debenture stock, such as long-term loans and mortgages or shorter-term overdraft facilities, but these are left for the next section as they are mainly provided by the banks and building societies.

However, there is one institution which provides assistance to firms and which needs further examination and that is the *merchant bank* or *accepting house*. Not all merchant banks are, strictly speaking, accepting houses although the best known usually are. The term 'accepting house' originated from the traditional function which these companies provided of accepting or guaranteeing bills of exchange. The bill of exchange developed as trade grew in the eighteenth and nineteenth centuries as a means by which a manufacturer might obtain supplies without paying for them at the time. It was basically a large IOU which, if acceptable to the recipient, was effectively regarded as payment.

However, the degree to which a supplier would be willing to accept such a bill depended on the reputation of the firm that had drawn it up. Manufacturers and merchants found that if a bill was accepted by a reputable merchant bank then it was not only more likely to be paid on time but if the merchant receiving the bill wished for money before the due date, the bill could be discounted. In other words, it was a marketable asset and could be sold for a sum rather less than the ultimate value.

As the accepting houses made the guarantees they found it in their interest to investigate the creditworthiness and reliability of firms wanting to use bills. They therefore acquired considerable knowledge and expertise which they put to use in giving more general advice and financial assistance to firms. Today the best-known merchant banks such as Rothschilds or Baring Brothers are more frequently associated with the handling of new issues of shares. We can thus see that merchant banks work in both the capital and the money markets.

The problem of small firms

The stock market has traditionally been a source of finance for the larger corporate bodies and even within the number of companies which are quoted on the Stock Exchange, the top 100 have been regarded as especially significant—hence the index of share prices known as the FTSE-100 which measures the share price changes of the largest UK companies. Smaller firms have had problems, however, in obtaining finance for growth. If they are private companies, partnerships or sole traders which outnumber public limited companies many times over, then borrowing can be difficult.

Private companies cannot offer shares to the public and smaller public limited companies may find that as they are not well known share take-up is not easy to secure. To obtain a full quotation by the Stock Exchange a company needs to have been established and be of much larger than average size in terms of shares issued. In addition, small firms find that the banks are not very sympathetic and they have modest overdrafts called in while large companies manage to run up millions of pounds in overdrafts and loans which may be arranged amicably over a round of golf!

From the point of view of the investor, a small firm does represent more of a risk than a large one. For example:

- The small firm is usually involved in a narrower range of activities and so is subject to the market fluctuations of one market instead of enjoying the comparative security of a diverse corporation such as Unilever or Vickers.
- Small firms may lack expertise and while the owners are usually high on enthusiasm and may have technical experience they typically lack marketing, accounting and personnel management experience. For example, a local restaurant may be owned by a gourmet food enthusiast who is an experienced chef but unless expert help is enlisted the chef may well keep very haphazard accounts and have little idea on how to boost the restaurant's image.
- Small firms are usually *highly geared*. The term 'gearing' refers to the degree of borrowing as a proportion of assets. A firm which is highly geared has a high proportion of its funding from borrowing, although in practice much of this borrowing is likely to be directors' loans.

However, from the point of view of the economy small firms can be seen as a positive feature. In particular, there is evidence that small firms are more important than large ones in bringing innovations to the market and that few large firms actually have significantly larger factories than smaller ones. Thus most of the significant plant-level economies of scale are acquired at a relatively low level of operation. Most of the effective growth has been as a result of small firms evolving and much of the apparent growth of larger firms a result of mergers and take-overs.

The Labour government of the 1970s was concerned about this problem and a Committee on the Financing of Small Firms was set to work. The consequent Wilson Report (1979) studied the problem in some detail and set out recommendations, most of which were adopted in the 1980s. The key developments since then were:

1. *A business expansion scheme* (BES) was introduced in 1983 to replace the Business Start-up Scheme which was an attempt made in 1981 to implement one of the Wilson Report's recommendations. The BES allows tax relief on investment in small firms (with a few categories, such as financial services, not being eligible) and relief from capital gains tax if shares are held for 5 years or more.

2. *The loan guarantee scheme* was set up in 1981 and supports applications by small firms to banks and other lending institutions by guaranteeing up to 70 per cent of the loan. Early reports did suggest, however, that a high proportion (20 per cent) of small firms helped under the scheme had ceased trading although it has also proved a cheap way of creating jobs. Small firms have also gained from the grants made under the Enterprise Initiative for assisted areas and the Enterprise Allowance Scheme which assists the unemployed wishing to set up their own business. These are all good examples of 'supply side' policies by governments, which will be discussed again in Chapter 15.

3. Access to the stock market for smaller firms has been made easier by various initiatives by the Stock Exchange. The Unlisted Securities Market (USM) has enabled firms which are too small for a full Stock Exchange listing to be recognized and have shares sold. Unfortunately, it has been used more as a means of enabling owners of small firms to get a valuation of their shareholding, but it has also enabled growing firms to get a toehold in the stock market. 'Over the Counter' (OTC) share 'shops' have grown up outside the Stock Exchange to enable unlisted firms to sell some shares to the public, but the Stock Exchange's Third Market set up in 1987 has been closed as it did not really prove useful to enough companies.

Case Study 12.1—Going public

The privatization programme of the 1980s and 1990s in Europe has emphasized to many people the importance of shares as a means of raising capital for industry. As public corporations or statutory boards the enterprises were dependent on state funding should they need to expand. On privatization in 1984, British Telecom acquired nearly £4,000 million for the half of the company which was sold at the time. British Gas in 1986 acquired over £5,500 million this way. Shares enabled many members of the public to acquire a part-ownership of the companies, a prospect of capital gain and of future earnings.

Yet many of the buyers of BT and BG shares did not want to hold on to them despite the prospects and the limited number they were allowed to hold. Such was the demand for the shares that their prices leapt up and many people 'made a killing' by early sale. The great British public was turned from a nation of shopkeepers into a nation of stags!

This illustrated the power of the Stock Exchange as a means of attracting capital for industry. Not that the stock market itself releases funds to firms, but it does provide a second-hand market for the buying and selling of shares, gilts and debentures. Without the prospect of selling the shares on, many speculators and even smaller investors would have held back from purchase of BT and BG shares and far less capital would have been released.

In order to encourage the growth of public limited companies, the Stock Exchange set up subsidiary markets to cater for smaller or riskier enterprises. The Unlisted Stock Market (USM) was important in this respect and while moves were made to abandon it as too small it has persisted because no alternative has been found. One of the problems with companies getting a 'full listing' by the Stock Exchange is the high level of corporate assets required and many smaller companies desperately need to be able to attract share capital to grow. The alternative is a persistent gulf between the large public companies and smaller private ones.

1. Why is share capital so important to a smaller company?
2. What risks are attached to holding shares in a small company?

Topic 12.3   Commercial banks and building societies

Most of the institutions discussed in this chapter will not be familiar from first-hand experience to many readers of this book but those we look at in this section are the high street banks and building societies. Their part in the financial markets, especially the money market, is of enormous importance. Apart from the creation of credit money as explored in the previous chapter, they hold much of the country's personal wealth in current and deposit accounts, and their credit-creation function does a lot more than just add to the money supply.

The *high street banks* are familiar to us all but are called by many names in textbooks including commercial banks, 'joint stock banks' or 'clearing banks'. This last definition stems from the clearing system for cheques. They grew from the goldsmiths who, we have already seen, played a vital part in the development of financial markets. Their income came largely from interest on loans and various fees and charges.

Over the years the many local banks merged and a few went out of business, leaving us today with a 'Big Four' plus a number of smaller banks. Some of the smaller banks are growing fast as a result of the doubtful public image of the four market leaders and high charges as a result of errors in account handling.

In the last fifteen years the Scottish banks have expanded south of the border, the Cooperative Bank has seen considerable expansion with the facility to use the Coop shops for routine banking facilities, Yorkshire Bank is aiming to become more national and the TSB was—after a legal battle—privatized. The largest single change was the decision of Abbey National Building Society to change status to a bank, which it now is.

> *Banks* are intermediaries which borrow from both firms and households and then make loans. They are often known as *commercial banks* or *high street banks* to distinguish them from *merchant banks* or accepting houses.

The commercial banks operate in both the capital and the money markets and have a number of other fringe activities. Their current functions can be summed up as:

1. Traditional bank account provision include current or cheque book accounts and deposit or time accounts. The latter earn the holder interest but the position regarding current accounts is in a state of change. Most banks operate high-interest current accounts for deposits and cheque payments of a considerable minimum size but some have been paying interest or, at least, waiving charges on current accounts. Others charge quite steeply and all will charge for an account which is overdrawn.

2. The banks tend to be the main routeway to credit cards, with *Visa* and *Access* as the main systems used. In addition, most of them will operate cash dispensers which, by use of plastic cards, enables customers to obtain cash outside normal banking hours.

3. Lending has always been the main source of income for banks, but in recent years the variety of loans has been extended. Traditionally, bank loans have taken two forms:

   (a)   The *overdraft*, which is a short-term (in theory!) permission to write cheques over and above the amount in a current account. Most businesses have an overdraft facility, even if it normally makes a nice profit, as there will always be times when immediate expenditure such as payroll exceeds the income in current account.

   (b)   The *loan*, which is usually longer term, perhaps from 12 months to 10 years. While personal loans are common, the main customers for loans have been businesses and in many cases security is required, i.e. the loan is backed by the factory, office or a director's house, in case of default. More recently the types of loan have been extended with packaged personal loans for car purchase or home extension and, increasingly, mortgages. Mortgages are longer-term loans for purchase of a domestic residence or commercial premises. We will discuss mortgages a little later when we look at building societies. It is worth noting here, though, that the high street banks are keen to get involved in commercial lending and commercial mortgages form a significant feature of their long-term lending.

> An *overdraft* is a temporary agreement for bank customers to sign cheques to a set value above the level of money in their current accounts.

4. Financial services are now offered by most banks although some 'push' them more than others. All account holders know that they will receive mailshots and perhaps selling phone calls from a bank's 'financial consultant' offering life assurance, pensions or investment products. Banks have seen these as major money-spinners on account of the commission to be earned and increasingly have developed their own 'in-house' insurance arms to underwrite such policies.
5. Miscellaneous services include acting as trustees, business consultants, depositories for valuables and documents and share-dealing services.

The price mechanism for bank deposits

An interesting feature of the market for bank deposits is that if we regard a bank (or building society) deposit account as a product, then the demand and supply curves are the reverse of the normal pattern. Consider Fig. 12.3. The demand curve slopes upward to the right instead of down. Why? Because our vertical axis shows the price of the product as its yield, and the demand will increase, the higher the yield. Conversely, if yields are high the banks will be less interested in providing such accounts and may wish to obtain funds by borrowing in the money market.

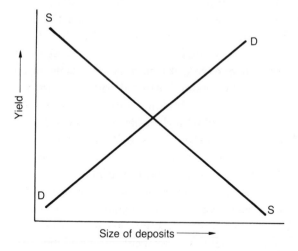

Figure 12.3 'Reverse' supply and demand curves for bank deposits accounts.

The difference from the normal product supply and demand curves arises because the product is provided by the institution (the bank) which would be regarded as the source of demand if we looked at the transaction as one in loanable funds rather than account facilities. In one sense we have simply switched round the idea of what the product is in this type of transaction, but it is an interesting exception to the normal rules of price theory which the reader should keep in mind.

Building societies are a familiar sight in the British high street although they do not have a precise equivalent in the rest of Europe where credit banks take their place. Until the Building Societies Act 1986 the societies had a special place as providers of mortgages for house purchase, funded by many small deposits from individuals. Whether one is a mortgage holder or a depositor (and most people are both), the building society has proved an important institution for the British family.

The BSA enabled the societies to become limited companies, although so far only Abbey National has taken the plunge. The advantages to Abbey National have not been enough to encourage others to follow them. The societies have also been freed to engage in other activities including banking and have taken full advantage of the growth in financial services.

A typical building society will now be involved in:

- *Deposit account* provision, which has been the main use of the societies for the average citizen. There are usually a range of types of account for different levels and paying different interest rates.
- *Current accounts*, which are common with larger societies such as the Halifax and Nationwide Anglia and operate in much the same way as the banks, although usually without the automatic charges. Cheque books are available and cash dispenser machines are common.
- *Mortgages*, which are the other major product of the building societies. For the most part, these are for domestic house purchase although some societies are developing commercial mortgage departments for lending to businesses, especially for the purchase of freeholds on shops. One important feature of mortgages is that they break the traditional 'rule' of lending in that the bank or building society is 'borrowing short and lending long'. In theory, this exposes them to risk. It is normally advisable for an intermediary to try to match the term for the money borrowed with the term for lending. In borrowing short term, as in the case of building society accounts, the societies are open to a 'run' on their funds. Most of their depositors can gain access to their account money either immediately or with no more than 6 months' notice, but the society cannot ask for the mortgage to be repaid before the agreed term is completed, which can be as long as 30 years with a pension-linked mortgage.

In fact, of course, one of the main reasons for the existence of the banks and societies as intermediaries is that they can engage in *maturity transformation*, which is the name given to this process. They survive because the number of depositors is very large and the law of large numbers operates so that banks and societies can calculate fairly accurately how much money is likely to be withdrawn at any one time.

- *Financial service* products such as life assurance and other insurances are being sold by a number of societies for the same reason that the banks have followed this route. Building societies have perhaps a little more excuse to move into this area since a mortgage has traditionally had an insurance policy associated with it, but in recent years some societies have been selling insurances in their own right. In many cases mortgages are only granted if the borrower is prepared to take out an endowment policy through the society or house insurance so that the society earns extra commission. Some societies also deal in share transactions.

> A *building society* is a firm, often a mutual, which traditionally specializes in offering savings accounts to attract funds which it lends out as *mortgages* for house purchase.

From the discussion in this section so far we can see that the traditional differences between banks and building societies have broken down and for many transactions the two institutions are identical. We noted that the Abbey National's cross-over from one to the other wrecked the existing money aggregate categories and the developments have further made the traditional distinction between 'bank' and 'non-bank' intermediaries rather meaningless.

The *other mortgage institutions* might be mentioned here. Prominent are the specialist mortgage banks which provide mortgages and perhaps other loans but not normal banking facilities in the UK. Instead of getting their funds from many small accounts like the banks and building societies, which is expensive, they tend to borrow on the money markets and by obtaining funds of many millions of pounds at a time the rate they pay and the administration costs are reduced.

Some of these mortgage banks are UK subsidiaries of foreign banks. For example, among the larger players are the French bank BNP and the Canadian Imperial Bank. Others specialize in commercial lending, often of a particular type. The Agricultural Mortgage Corporation (AMC) specializes in funds for the purchase of farm land and property, on which most other lenders are not keen.

Other institutions active in the mortgage market are the brokers. Many insurance brokers are involved in this type of work and there are some specialist mortgage brokers such as John Charcol, the largest firm in this part of the market.

Topic 12.4 Dealing with risk

This section looks at the financial aspects of risk and the market which deals with this— i.e. insurance. Some examination boards may not require a detailed treatment of the subject although for those reading this book as part of studies for professional examinations or the economics content of Business Studies, it will be more important.

Risk is an essential feature of life. The moment we are born we are faced with risks and some risks have financial consequences and some do not. This section is concerned with the former. Unless there are financial consequences of a loss there is no need for a financial market to deal with the problem. So losing your economics notes may be a minor tragedy but it is doubtful if they have any monetary value, whereas if they were lost because they were in a mislaid briefcase then the briefcase has money value.

Risks which have a money loss can be dealt with by transferring the financial consequences of the risk to a firm that is prepared to pay compensation should the risk occur—in other words, *insurance*. However, in order for a risk to be insurable it also needs to be a *pure* risk as opposed to a *speculative* one. Speculative risks carry the possibility that you may not only lose something of value but may also gain profit from it. So a shopkeeper selling clothes has two types of risk: the risk of having stock which is no longer fashionable but, equally, which may stay in fashion for some time and the risk of the stock going up in flames. The first risk is speculative and the second is a pure risk. Only pure risks are insurable.

Insurance is one aspect of financial markets which most of us come into contact with in our late teens—usually when we get a motorcycle or car and have to insure it. Students may also need to insure personal belongings, and on renting or buying a house or flat further insurance becomes essential. However, the real economic importance of insurance tends to be with the coverage of risks attached to business. Without insurance most firms would not be in existence because the risks would be too great to make an entrepreneur willing to chance investment, or at least not without much higher profit margins.

Insurance works on a principle often called a 'pool'. If each of 1000 plumbers runs the risk of customers suing for negligence then each one faces a possible ruinous liability. However, if they transfer this risk to an insurance company then the company will use the law of large numbers to calculate the chance of any one plumber being sued. It will then calculate the likely loss in a year, add its administrative costs, and this sum is paid by the plumbers with each one making a contribution called a *premium*. In insurance language the plumbers will have 'exchanged the uncertainty of a large loss for the certainty of a small one'. Most plumbers will consider this money well spent!

Insurance companies and *Lloyd's syndicates* are involved in accepting the transfer of the financial consequences of a risk in return for a payment called a *premium*.

The insurance industry is not only important for risk transfer but the premiums are invested and, as a result, there is a large source of funds for industry. Figure 12.4 shows some of the range of investments typical of the industry. A total premium income of £65 billion (1991) means a lot of money to invest, although some of the premiums will go into administrative costs.

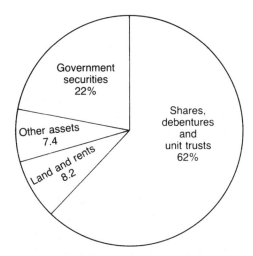

Figure 12.4   Invested assets of UK insurance companies. (*Source*: Association of British Insurers, *Insurance Statistics 1987–1991.*)

Of particular importance for investment are the life offices and pension funds, where the invested money is intended to build up a fund for the client. In this case the client is not only buying insurance against a risk but is also using an insurance or pension policy as a means of saving for the future.

The insurance industry is divided into two groups of products, i.e. life and pensions business, on the one hand, and other insurances, usually known as 'General Business', on the other:

1. *Life assurance*, or 'long-term business' as it is sometimes called, deals with the uncertainty of the timing of death—not with death itself which is, of course, certain. Life assurance has had rather a bad press as a result of stories, many exaggerated, of high-pressure sales staff lurking on the doorstep or in banking halls. It is, however, a vital product since untimely death can cause not only sorrow but also considerable financial loss. If a married man dies while his family is young and there is a large mortgage on his house, the difficulties faced by his wife can be enormous, and the death of a wife, even if she is not earning, can also cause financial difficulties for the husband. The life assurance and pensions business is now heavily regulated since the passing of the Financial Services Act 1986 and this aspect will be discussed in more detail in Chapter 15 as an example of government regulation.

2. *General business* consists of 'short-term' business which is usually insurance with annual renewable premiums as opposed to life and pensions, which are contracts for a number of years and with, usually, monthly premiums. Motor and house insurance are the most common types of General Business purchased by households, but for businesses there is cover for fire, theft, storms and the important areas of public and employer's liability. Employer's liability insurance is compulsory for all employers, whether they are incorporated or not.

The structure of the insurance market

The insurance industry in Europe shows a remarkable variety in the form in which it is sold. We need to look at it from a European perspective more, perhaps, than most industries because of the high degree of integration of European firms in recent years. Many British insurers are owned by European parents including Axa Equity & Law and Norman (French); NIG Skandia (Swedish); and Gresham Life (Dutch). Nevertheless, there are considerable differences between the UK and European insurance industries which we need to remember.

Figure 6.3 in Chapter 6 gives an indication of the structure of the marketplace. It is important to note the role of the broking institutions, which may range from large Lloyd's brokers such as Sedgwick's to the small-town agent. This is where the first difference between the UK and many other countries shows itself. Most UK brokers deal with more than one company, at least for General Business, with perhaps up to 40 or 50 agencies typical of busy broking offices. Many are increasingly 'tied' to one life office following the strictures of the Financial Services Act and the regulations which followed, but few are tied to motor and house insurance. In contrast, French brokers tend to be agents for one company only for all products.

Lloyd's of London is also unique to the UK and, as a result, transacts business from all over the world. Some details of Lloyd's appear in Chapter 6, where it is used as a case study of a market. It is a market under considerable strain, however, as a result of heavy losses from earthquakes, storms and increasing terrorist activity, and its future may lead it into changes in structure and procedure.

Insurance companies can be divided into life offices dealing with life and pensions business only, General Business companies and a few giants which deal in both types of product. These are known as *composites*. Most large insurance companies such as General Accident, Norwich Union and the Prudential are composites. The industry is dominated by large companies and of over 800 companies authorized by the Department of Trade to conduct insurance business the leading ten insurers produce most of the business. Small companies survive by offering either significantly cheaper premiums or specialist products.

A feature of insurance companies, especially on the life side, is the existence of a form of incorporation known as the 'mutual'. Again, this is not really found much in Europe and has developed especially in the UK. The owners of the company are the policy holders although, in practice, they tend to be run by self-perpetuating boards with the general support of the workforce who are the policy holders most able to attend the AGM!

Topic 12.5   Other financial institutions

There are a number of institutions which do not fit neatly into the categories so far discussed but which are important in Europe's financial world.

Discount houses

The principal financial institutions in the money market, apart from the central and clearing banks, are the discount houses. These institutions are unique to the London market and are not found in other countries, but they have helped to give the British government a special way of dealing with the financial institutions and controlling money supply and lending.

The main purpose of the discount house is to buy or 'discount' bills of exchange and Treasury bills or bonds. They also hold other assets including sterling certificates of deposit and cash. In fact the proportion of their assets represented by Treasury Bills has fallen significantly, as can be seen in Fig. 12.5. Like so many institutions in the financial markets, the discount houses are changing their patterns, diversifying and looking at new ways to make money.

The traditional function of the discount houses has been to act as intermediaries between the Bank of England, representing the government, and the rest of the market (Fig. 12.6). They borrow and invest short-term money, the investment traditionally being in Treasury bills. If the government wishes to sell bills, the Bank of England will sell to the discount houses and they have the particular responsibility to cover the weekly Treasury bill tender. As they deal in short-dated government stocks, they provide a medium through which the Bank of England influences interest rate movements.

This is because the discount houses buy bills with money they have borrowed 'at call and short notice' from the banks. This is very short term, even 'overnight' money, and as a result carries very low interest. Any interest which the banks make is better than keeping the money in accounts or in the vaults. The discount house makes a profit by

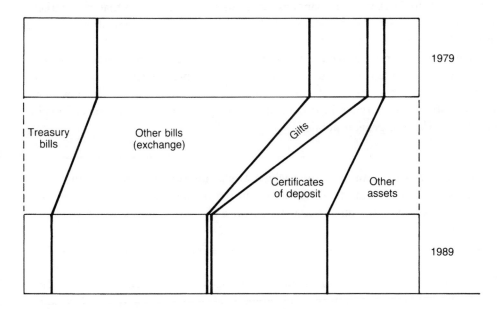

Figure 12.5 Assets of discount houses. (*Source*: CSO, *Annual Abstract of Statistics*, HMSO, 1991.)

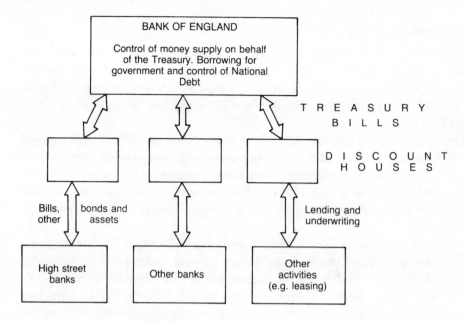

Figure 12.6 Discount houses and the banking system.

using this 'cheap' money to buy government bonds, which, of course, then form secure and liquid assets. There is an understanding with the Bank of England that if the discount houses are unable to borrow enough money to purchase the bonds each week, then they can borrow from the Bank, although at a higher rate than they would from the rest of the market. If this happens, the newspapers will report that 'the market is in the Bank'. This does enable the Bank of England, however, to control interest rates since it is the 'lender of last resort'.

As mentioned earlier, the discount houses are now moving into other areas of business and are much more widely involved in lending and borrowing to a range of institutions in the market, including using certificates of deposit. They are essentially, however, a 'wholesale' rather than a 'retail' institution in that they deal with other financial institutions and not with the general public.

A *discount house* is an institution which acts as intermediary between the Bank of England and other institutions in the money market. It discounts bills, especially Treasury bills with short-term loans (see Fig. 12.6).

Finance houses are specialists in medium-term loans for purchase of goods such as washing machines, cars or furniture. Their traditional product is a hire-purchase agreement by which a consumer can obtain goods, usually with a deposit paid, and then pay over a period between 12 months and 5 years by monthly instalments. Although familiar to the average household for purchase of larger consumer goods, the finance houses are also strong in the commercial field. Much industrial and commercial equipment is leased, not bought, with the finance companies actually owning the machinery. This is better for a firm than purchase outright as it helps with cash flow and saves depleting capital. It also makes replacement of out-of-date equipment easier and, as a result, has become the norm for computers, copiers and company cars.

As with much of the rest of the financial services industry, changes are taking place here also. Many finance houses are taking on more normal banking products such as mortgages and personal loans while offering deposit accounts.

Collective investments are financial instruments in which the investor buys units in a fund and the fund in turn is invested in a range of securities or other assets. This arrangement gives the ordinary saver greater security than investment in, say, one company's shares or one type of gilt. As the sums invested tend to be small—typically between £1000 and £10 000 at a time—the costs are less than would be the case if the money was divided into very small amounts to achieve the same investment spread oneself. Chapter 11 mentioned portfolio theory, which studies the way people and firms seek to develop a spread of investments to balance the aims of income, capital gain, safety, liquidity, etc. In theory, a collective investment will do this for you.

There are three main types of collective investment:

1. *Unit trusts* have been in existence since M&G launched the first in the 1930s. The investor will buy units in a trust which in turn will invest the money in assets of particular stated types. The investors choose a trust which conforms to their financial objectives. For example, a UK Equity Income Trust would be invested in UK shares expected to produce high dividend income but not necessarily highest capital gain. There are trusts investing in overseas shares in 'special situations' which are usually small companies that may do well, and in gilts. Units have two prices, a price at which they are bought and a lower one at which they are sold, the difference being the managers' earnings. Unlike shares themselves, units in a trust are not securities as they can only be sold back to the managers and not to a third party.

2. *Investment trusts* are similar in operation to unit trusts but the trust is actually a company and the investor buys shares in that company. As a result, the pricing of units is rather different. In the case of a unit trust the units are valued according to the valuation of the assets in which they are invested, but an investment trust's shares may vary in price like those of any other company. They are thus often considered more risky.

3. *Investment bonds* are not to be confused with normal fixed-interest bonds such as bills or gilts. They are actually life assurance policies in which the life cover is the value of the investment. They operate in an almost identical manner to unit trusts but carry some of the tax advantages which belong to life assurance policies. They are also able to invest in property, which is prohibited to unit trusts.

Unit and investment trusts and investment bonds are all under the authority of the Securities & Investment Board and are subject to the Financial Services Act which increases some of the costs of administration. Most life assurance offices operate unit trusts as an alternative to life assurance savings policies, including investment bonds, but investment trusts are separate. There are a number of unit trust management groups which are not involved in life assurance and some, like M&G, which have moved into life assurance from unit trusts.

Derivatives are products that are 'derived' from other more fundamental assets. The main ones are futures and options.

- A *future* is a contract in which a commodity or shares are to be delivered at a future date for a specified price. It enables buyers of large amounts of raw materials to obtain supplies at a known cost and for sellers to be ensured of a sale. Futures contracts can be sold on or traded and there is an active market in existence to do this.
- An *option* is an agreement to take an option to buy specified assets or commodities at a future date. Unlike a future, it is not a binding contract on the buyer, who may decline to take up the option. If the option can be sold on to a third party then it is known as a *traded option*.

Topic 12.6   Central banks

Central banks control the banking system of a country and frequently act as the state bank and main means of exercising economic control. The role of state banks is currently a matter of some debate with the German Bundesbank seen as a model for the future on account of its independence from the German government. Before looking at the European scene, however, we will consider the Bank of England.

The Bank of England began as a private company which was incorporated by royal charter in 1694 with the initial purpose of lending money to the government of the day. This gave the bank one of its basic functions right from the start—holding and managing the National Debt! It continued to act as a normal bank among all the other similar institutions in the eighteenth and nineteenth centuries but acquired a particularly close relationship with the government, and the Bank Charter Act 1844 recognized its position as the key bank for the British financial system. It functioned not only as the government's bank but also as the bank for other banks—in other words, it was the bank where the other banking institutions kept their own accounts and where they could borrow money in times of financial stress.

The Bank of England became the sole institution in England and Wales to issue bank notes and was the custodian of the nation's gold and foreign currency. In 1946 it was nationalized, which really only formalized the existing close cooperation between the government and the Bank.

The functions of the Bank of England

The Bank consists of the Issue department and the Banking Department. It has a number of key functions as the central bank to the UK economy:

1. *Issuing banknotes*   The Issue Department of the Bank is responsible for printing banknotes (but not coins). At one time the value of notes was related to the amount of gold in the Bank's vaults, but increasingly a fiduciary element was used to extend the limit and now there is no specific gold backing at all. To maintain the note issue in a clean condition the Bank also retrieves worn notes for destruction and replaces them with new ones.

2. *Carrying out monetary policy*   It has become one of the chief functions of the Bank in recent years to control the money supply on behalf of the government, for reasons which will be discussed later. The Bank ensures that the rest of the banking system has sufficient cash to meet its day-to-day obligations. It does this by buying or selling Treasury bills and this in turn has an influence on short-term interest rates. The Bank of England influences the balances which the other banks have deposited with it by buying or selling securities in the open market, and since credit creation by the banks is dependent on the amount of their deposits, this activity influences the degree of lending in the economy.

    One important element of monetary control is the level of interest rates. In the past the 'bank rate' was the key rate for the whole system and other banks' rates were closely related to it. The *minimum lending rate* which replaced it was closely related to the Treasury bill discount rate, usually $\frac{1}{2}$ per cent above that rate. It was set and made public for weeks at a time, so giving the market a level of certainty.

    After 1981, however, this arrangement ceased and the Bank now controls interest rates on a much more flexible basis 'in the market'. This enables the government to control lending interest rates by fine-tuning the short-term market interest rates— basically the rate at which the Bank will lend to the discount houses and other banks.

    A brief mention should be made of the requirements for other banks to make deposits with the Bank of England. The *special deposits* have been used from time to time in the past as 'frozen' deposits which act as a form of security for the system and a means of restricting bank lending. For a time in the 1970s 'supplementary deposits' were required. These were non-interest-bearing deposits in a system often known as 'the corset', which had the aim of restricting the lending powers of the banking system at a time when bank lending was reaching astronomical proportions.

3. *Borrowing for the government*   The Bank acts as the means by which the government borrows to finance its spending. Chapter 14 discusses the need for borrowing and the circumstances in which the government will borrow. Related to this is the Bank of England's original activity of managing the National Debt on behalf of the government. It keeps records of stockholders and makes interest payments to them.

4. *Advising the government*   The Bank acts as the government's financial adviser and works closely with the Treasury. The Governor of the Bank of England is regarded

as a key person in the City and the holder of that office has the 'ear' of the Chancellor of the Exchequer and Prime Minister.

5. *Supervising the financial community*   The bank supervises the banking system and has power to investigate banks which it considers are being improperly run or are run by people who are not considered suitable. The controversy over the collapse of the Bank of Commerce and Credit International was a case in point, with many people blaming the Bank of England for not intervening properly.

6. *Acting as bankers' bank*   Any central bank of maturity will act as the other bankers' bank, holding their cash reserves. The banks write cheques to each other to deal with debits on the clearing system, using their Bank of England accounts, and if short of money they will go to the Bank for assistance. The Bank also deals with the discount houses for the sale of government bonds and acts as a lender of last resort. Any bank, if short of money, can request a loan from the Bank of England but the interest charged is rather higher than the normal market rate, so it is a habit the other banks would prefer not to cultivate!

7. *Looking after the pound*   The Bank of England acts for the government in managing the official reserves of gold and foreign exchange. When necessary, it intervenes in the foreign exchange market to smooth out sudden excessive movements in the external value of sterling.

8. *Acting as government banker*   The Bank of England acts as the banker for the government. Among its functions is the management of the National Debt which includes redeeming, or repaying the capital on, gilts and Treasury bills as they become due. The Bank also holds the Exchequer account for day-to-day payments from and receipts into government departments. Thus this account will receive the receipts from the Inland Revenue and HM Customs and Excise. It will also handle the payments made by government departments. Other central banks fulfil this function for their governments. It is sometimes forgotten that modern governments, even with the privatization programme which has swept Europe, are major employers, contractors for public works, spenders on armaments and providers of infrastructure.

9. *Normal banking*   Originally the Bank of England also undertook normal banking but this gradually diminished and now it only operates normal accounts for its employees.

The function which the Bank has of being the government's access to the City markets and control of the economy is very important, and will be mentioned again in Chapters 14 and 15.

Other central banks

In many respects the functions of the Bank of England are very similar to those of other central banks. Most countries have a bank, whether state-owned or not, which controls the banking system, influences interest rates and perhaps prints notes. In the USA it is known as the Federal Reserve Bank or, more popularly, as 'the Fed'. All EU countries have central banks and in recent years they have been active in upholding the exchange rates of their currencies and controlling inflation, with interest rates being a key tool in meeting those objectives.

One central bank which is different is the German Bundesbank. It is different because it is not under state control. The German constitution has given the Bundesbank clear objectives, especially control of inflation, without reference to the policy objectives of the government. As a result, Germany has had enviably low inflation for many years and many people see this as a major contribution to its economic success. During the near-collapse of the ERM following a run on the French franc in August 1993, the Bundesbank was criticized by many for not cutting interest rates, since it was excessive purchases of deutschmarks which were causing trouble to other ERM currencies. The Bundesbank, however, maintained its constitutional objectives of putting the German economy first, to the embarrassment of the German government.

Despite this criticism, many economists and political leaders see the Bundesbank as a model for other countries. The idea of a central bank which is not subject to the whim of politicians and their theories yet is responsible for controlling the key elements in an economy has an appeal. In time the European Union will need a central bank and it remains to be seen whether the German model will prevail.

Advanced Study Topic 12.1 concerns the question of central bank indendence.

Advanced Study Topic 12.1   Central banks: the big question

One major issue in economics in the 1990s is the degree of independence which should be accorded the central banks. Most countries have a central bank which is responsible for oversight of the banking system and probably acting as the government's banker. The Bank of England is the institution which we concentrate on in this book but the Federal Reserve Bank in the USA has a vital role in that country's economy.

In Europe, the central banks are increasingly seen as providing an interlinking framework following the Basle Accord of 1988 and the onset of the Single Market. The dominant bank in Europe has undoubtedly been the Bundesbank, and this has roused a considerable amount of controversy because of its unique position in the German constitution. The Bundesbank is independent of the German government and has a constitutional responsibility to safeguard inflation as a priority. The lack of power which the German government has over the Bundesbank was seen in 1993 while there was pressure on the French franc and there was a demand for the Bundesbank to reduce interest rates.

Many economists argue that central banks should imitate the Bundesbank and that the independence of central banks should be the norm rather than the exception. While there is no denying the success of the Bundesbank in controlling inflation and strengthening the German economy, there is some doubt as to whether it is good for economic policy to have a central bank pursuing independent action. There are other objectives to inflation control, including supervision of financial markets and control of money supply which should be subject to democratic oversight.

Essay questions

1. (a) Why are there a number of different interest rates in the economy?
   (b) Critically examine the role of interest rates in a government's management of the economy. (*Source*: The Associated Examining Board, June 1991)
2. (a) Explain the role of the Bank of England in the UK economy.
   (b) Discuss how the Bank of England might attempt to control total bank lending in the UK. (*Source*: The Associated Examining Board, November 1992)
3. (a) Explain the role of the commercial banks in a modern economy.
   (b) Evaluate the arguments for and against the commercial banks in the UK being more closely controlled. (*Source*: The Associated Examining Board, June 1993)
4. 'If continuing reductions in the burden of direct taxation are pursued, then a more positive monetary policy is essential to control the economy.' Discuss. (*Source*: Oxford and Cambridge Schools Examination Board, June 1992)
5. What might be the effects of increased interest rates on the UK economy? (*Source*: University of Oxford, June 1990)
6. 'Only a continuing fall in the UK's inflation rate will lead to a marked improvement in the balance of payments on current account'. Discuss. (*Source*: University of Oxford, June 1991)

13

The value of money

Topic 13.1 The equation of exchange

We have so far in this book used money as a measure of the value of goods and services but, as we have seen, money itself has some of the characteristics of a product. Its 'price' (interest) is determined by supply and demand, although there is some debate as to what the supply and demand consist of, and we have seen that as a product money comes in many forms. We need now to consider not so much the price of borrowing money but its value.

How is money valued? Just as we use money to value products so we use products to value money. Money in itself—coins and notes—is worth very little but its purchasing power is considerable and it is an everyday experience to think of the money in our pockets as being able to buy certain commodities. We may have £6 left for the week and think 'will this do me until Saturday or do I need to go to the hole in the wall before then?' Economists, inevitably, have a more sophisticated approach to the problem.

Our more scientific approach to money values begins with a simple logical formula. Irving Fisher, an American economist (1867–1947), formulated what is known as the *equation of exchange* or the Fisher equation. This expressed in mathematical terms the relationship between four features of money. The equation which Fisher put forward can be expressed as:

$$MV = PT$$

where

$M =$ money (the total amount of money in existence)
$V =$ the *velocity of circulation* (the average number of times that a unit of currency changes hands in a given period, e.g. the number of times a pound coin circulates in one year)
$P =$ prices (the general price level)
$T =$ transactions (the volume of transactions that have taken place in a given period, e.g. one year)

Sometimes the equation is re-phrased as:

$$MV = Y$$

where y = national income or output.

In many ways the Fisher equation is a truism since the value of sales in the economy must, of necessity, equal the receipts. Rather than call it an 'equation' in the mathematical sense we should perhaps refer to it as an 'identity' since both sides are equal by definition. It is, however, more than this as it draws attention to the part played by the four elements in influencing the value of money.

If the formula is rewritten following algebraic principles, we can see that the value of money (i.e. the general price level) can be related to the other three as follows:

$$P = \frac{MV}{T}$$

It is usually held by monetarists that V and T are constant, or at least predictable, and so the main influence on P is M, the money supply. So it can be seen that an increase in M will lead to a higher price level, which means that money is worth less in real terms.

Suppose that on a small island in Scotland there are, within a given time period, 100 transactions made; the amount of money in circulation is £1000; and the money circulates, on average, five times. The price level would be:

$$P = \frac{1000 \times 5}{100} = \frac{5000}{100} = £50$$

since all the money which has changed hands in the time period (£5000) has been spent on 100 items.

This means that the average price per transaction is £50. If the money supply is increased to 1500 then the figure changes to:

$$P = \frac{1500 \times 5}{100} = \frac{7500}{100} = 75$$

An increase in money supply by 50 per cent has produced a similar increase in the price level and a reduction in the purchasing power of each pound.

It is this influence of money supply on price levels which has encouraged economists to use the equation as the basis of a theory of inflation, known as the quantity theory of money. In this form we will be shortly returning to the theme below.

There are some other criticisms of the equation as it stands. Keynesian economists argue that V and T are not necessarily constant but vary over time. Others, of a practical turn of mind, maintain that V and T are impossible to measure in any case. The number of transactions, especially, is difficult to measure since there is no such thing as a 'standard transaction'! Is it realistic to equate the sale of a tin of beans with that of a Rolls-Royce car?

Many economists are unhappy that in Fisher's original formulation, T included second-hand sales and the equation is sometimes rewritten as:

$$MV = PY$$

where Y = the sales of current output, i.e. national output or income in real terms. This is sometimes known as the Cambridge equation, although that term is perhaps best applied to the version which isolates the *demand* for money, and is usually presented as:

$$M_d = k_Y$$

where k = the proportion of national income which is required in money (M_d) balances. What this is saying is that the demand for money is the same as that proportion of national income which is required as money—again very much a truism but still helpful as a guide to quantifying the money demand.

Topic 13.2   Measuring changes in money value

Following on from the end of the previous section we next need to examine how we actually set about measuring money values. As we have already noticed, while we measure the values of goods and services in terms of money we can logically measure money in terms of goods and services. There is a problem here, however—what goods and services can we use? Money is a convenient common measure of value for goods but what common goods can be used to measure money values?

It is normal for older people to recall former days when 'a pound was a pound' and students are told by parents and teachers that when *they* were at college they lived on £5 a week! We have this consensus that the value of money has fallen but being precise about it is difficult. As a result, figures on changes in money values tend to be *index numbers* which offer a comparison as accurately as possible. For details of how index numbers are formed, the reader should refer to the discussion of statistics in Chapter 1.

The figures used in the UK to measure changes in money value are known as the Retail Prices Index (RPI). This index acts as the official guide to changes in price values and is quoted as evidence for the level of *inflation*, which is the term we use to describe persistent price rises. There are other indices used to measure wholesale prices, earnings, interest rates and share prices but the RPI is the predominant index used.

Who is interested?

A number of groups of people have an interest in what is happening to the value of money, including:

- Workers who want increased wages because of an apparent rise in the cost of living
- Employers who wish to resist wage claims and who will need to be conversant with other indices such as the Tax and Price Index and the Producer Price Index
- Some employees will have wages that are based on movements in the cost of living
- Some forms of savings are also 'index linked', including pensions under certain circumstances
- Firms will want to judge their profit potential and plan future production in the light of recent price changes
- The government will wish to know how well its policies are succeeding. One of the main objectives of government policy is a stable and low rate of inflation (see Chapter 15) and this is considered vital to a stable economy.

How do we measure price changes?

Different countries have statistical techniques for measuring inflation and there is rarely an identity between the methods of any two countries. However, the UK system is broadly parallel to that in most industrialized nations.

The UK has a number of indices of prices, but the main ones are:

1. *The general index of retail prices or RPI*   This measures changes in the prices of typical household goods by using an imaginary 'basket' of goods and services. The composition of this basket is liable to change as consumer tastes change and as government decisions are made on the inclusion of items like mortgage interest. This is not a problem since the changes are not usually significant but it does enable us to keep the index up to date.

    More of a problem is deciding the relative importance of the items in this 'basket'. It is little use listing butter, bread and salmon as if they are equal. Bread, for a family with three hungry children, may be a daily purchase but salmon will be an infrequent treat for all except the more wealthy. To get round this problem the goods and services are weighted. This means that some items are regarded as more significant and the price changes are multiplied by a weighting figure to reflect this. The weights in 1992 are shown in Table 13.1.

Table 13.1   Weighting of RPI 1993

Item	Weight/1000
Food and catering	189
Alcohol and tobacco	113
Housing and house expenditure	336
Personal expenditure	97
Travel and leisure	265
Seasonal food	21
Non–seasonal food	123
Consumer durables	127

The RPI is the most commonly used standard of inflation and is the one normally used in wage or savings agreements. The index is currently based on 1987 (13 January) equated with 100. Each year's bundle of goods and services is priced and the weights applied. An index figure is compiled which indicates the general change in prices since 1987. For example in May 1992, the index stood at 139.3 indicating a 39.3 per cent price increase since base date.

2. *The Tax and Price Index (TPI)*   This index takes into account changes in direct taxation and National Insurance contributions. It includes prices of goods and services as with the RPI as well as the changes in tax, so it measures the degree to which total or gross income has become more or less valuable.

3. *The Producer Price Index* used to be known as the Wholesale Price Index and measures price changes in producer goods and, as a result, is of particular value to firms rather than to individuals.

How have money values changed?

One of the key problems of recent years has been the phenomenon of regular and significant increases in RPI, in other words, *inflation*. However, inflation has not necessarily been typical of economic life but historically there have been periods when prices have fallen, i.e. money has increased in value. Other times have seen considerable stability. Figure 13.1 shows the main changes for the last few years and persistent inflation has tended to be a feature of the last century.

If we look closer at more recent years and at a number of countries (Fig. 13.2) we can see that inflation tends to be a feature which transcends national boundaries. It may affect some countries more than others, with Germany between the wars and Israel in more recent years being well known, and it is a persistent problem in Russia at present.

Topic 13.3   Types of inflation

Inflation is used to describe the situation when prices rise persistently and significantly over a period of time. The governments of the European states have declared that a primary target is to keep inflation down to a low level (under 4 per cent in the case of the UK) and the German Bundesbank also has a statutory obligation to keep inflation low. It is a very important economic feature (see Case Study 13.1) and in the next section we will be looking at its causes in some detail. First, however, we need to consider the main types of inflation:

1. *Long-term upward price movements*   Figure 13.1 indicates a long-term general trend for prices to rise and in the UK the average price level in almost every century (except the nineteenth) has been higher than in the preceding century. The exception for the nineteenth century would seem to stem from the increase in the number of transactions (T in the Fisher equation) and this exceeded the growth in M and V.

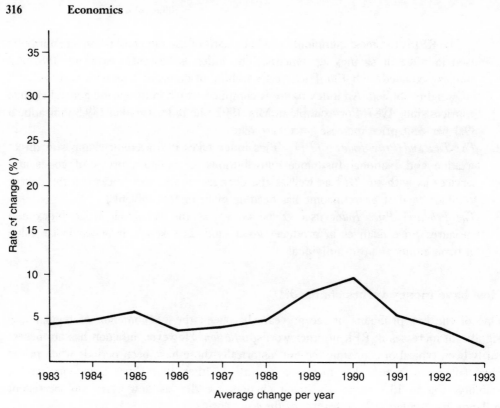

Figure 13.1   Inflation 1983–93. (*Source*: CSO, *Key Data*, HMSO, various years.)

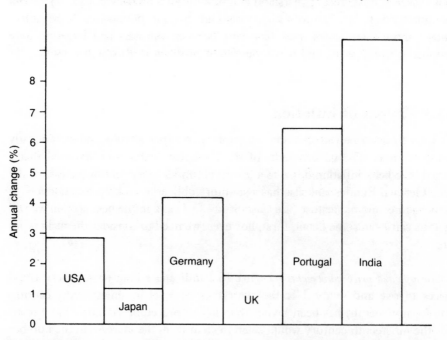

Figure 13.2   Comparative inflation 1993 (estimates). (*Source*: *Barclays Bank Review* (3rd Quarter) 1993.)

Apart from this, there has tended to be a 'creeping' inflation over the long term so that economic historians deal in wage levels and prices for former centuries which seem ridiculously small to us today.

2. *The 25-year cycle of price movements*   This is also well illustrated by the nineteenth-century experience. Given the long-term upward movement of prices, it would be expected that in most cases each upward cycle would be at a higher level than the previous one. 'Twenty-five years' is only an arbitrary period but there are generally accepted periods of price movement which approximate to that. In the nineteenth century these can be seen as:
   (a)   1821–49 falling prices
   (b)   1850–73 rising prices
   (c)   1874–95 falling prices
   (d)   1896–1914 rising prices
   These cycles are general trends and the concept must not be interpreted too literally.

3. *The short-term sharp price cycle*   The typical or classical trade cycle lasted about nine years—for example, the steep rise in prices in 1929 falling to the trough of the depression in 1931–3. The 1980s saw a sharp rise in inflation which fell in the recession of 1990–93, partly as a result of determined action by Western governments, and a rise in unemployment (see below).

4. *Hyperinflation*   Extreme and very rapid inflation can dominate an economy and produce severe problems for the citizens of any country suffering from it. The classic case is Germany in 1922–3. Following reparations after the First World War, the German government had considerable financial difficulties which it tried to solve by increasing the money supply. The result was a worthless mark and stories of people carrying their wages home in wheelbarrows. In more recent times we have seen high inflation for a short time in some countries such as Israel, Chile and Bolivia. In the last case it reached over 11 000 per cent at one point.

Topic 13.4   The causes of inflation

There is far from complete agreement about the causes of inflation. For monetarists, they are identified simply as a direct consequence of previous expansions of the money supply. Suggested alternative causes, such as increasing costs of production or *cost-push inflation* are totally denied by many monetarists. However, it is noticeable that many governments which have adopted monetarist policies (for example, the USA and the UK in the 1980s) have nevertheless attempted to keep wage settlements low and even blamed trade unions for increased wage costs!

There are a number of theories of the causes of inflation, and there are strong views by monetarists and Keynesians over the role played by the money supply. Most of the theories do not claim to be exclusive reasons but at any particular point of time inflation can be the result of more than one cause. The main theories which should be examined are as follows.

The quantity theory of money

'Inflation over any substantial period is always and everywhere a monetary phenomenon arising from a more rapid growth in the quantity of money than output.' So asserted Professor Milton Friedman in a memorandum submitted to the UK Treasury and Civil Service Committee in the summer of 1980. Indeed, so convinced is Professor Friedman of this truth that he feels able to continue: 'Few economic propositions are more firmly grounded in experience . . . experience extended over thousands of years.'

Monetarists see the emergence of an apparently irreversible inflationary trend in Western economies as a result of excessive increases in money supply. Policy makers, it is said, developed a general acceptance of Keynesian economics and relegated money supply to a very minor role. Ironically, by failing to take account of the monetary implication of expansionary fiscal policies, the authorities were fuelling the very inflation that was to lead to the re-emergence of monetary policies. The basis of it all is the quantity theory of money.

> *Monetarism* holds that the root cause of inflation is an increase in the supply of money. It is based on the *quantity theory of money*.

The quantity theory of money is really a statement of the Fisher equation with specific assumptions. We noted above that Fisher's equation of exchange expressed relationships between the supply and value of money, the number of transactions in the economy over a specific period of time and the velocity of circulation of currency. It was not a theory of inflation but monetarist economists have adopted it and applied it to the inflation problem.

Thus, as we have seen, the basic equation $MV = PT$ can be turned round to:

$$P = \frac{MV}{T}$$

The monetarist argument is that the number of transactions and the velocity of circulation are both constant. If these assumptions are correct—and Keynes disputed them—then the price level is dependent on the amount of money in the economy. If the supply of money increases then the price level will also rise. If we use the Cambridge formula (see above) which takes final output (national income) instead of using T and the level of money income as the main factor influencing demand for money, we still come to the same conclusion—that price level is largely determined by money supply. Further, if money supply is increased then there will be surplus spending power in the economy and people will wish to spend this surplus. In other words, aggregate demand will rise.

Monetarism and the quantity theory have been at the forefront of economic policy in the UK, in many other West European countries and in the USA for most of the last ten years or more with 'tight' money supply as the key to containing rates of price increases.

For most of the 1980s the policy did not seem to work in the UK although Germany under the watchful eye of the Bundesbank has achieved commendably low inflation rates. By 1993 the UK had achieved inflation below the official 4 per cent target but whether it was entirely due to tight money supply is a matter of debate. Since there was a recession on, unemployment was over 3 million and there was a drastic reduction in demand for goods and services, Keynes' approach might be just as good a claimant for the prize! To this theory we must now turn.

Keynes and demand-pull inflation

Keynes agreed that increasing demand was one of the main causes of inflation but his emphasis was rather different from that of the classical economists and Keynesian theory has a separate approach from that of the monetarists. In particular, Keynes did not agree that money supply has a direct influence on price levels and saw the transmission mechanism as far more complex—so complex, in fact, that increasing money supply need not influence price levels at all.

Figure 13.3 illustrates the process in the form of a diagram and we need to look at the six steps in the process and how they fit logically together. Keynes argued that an increase in money supply (stage 1) would lead to certain consequences:

- *Stage 1*   an increase in money supply, leading to:
- *Stage 2*   a reduction in interest rates. Simple supply and demand analysis suggests that if supply increases then the price of any commodity (in this case, loanable money) will fall. (See Fig. 13.4.)
- *Stage 3*   the lower interest rates will persuade firms to borrow money for investment and, as a result, productivity will increase.
- *Stage 4*   this will produce a higher level of national output (= income). The multiplier will be at work producing the effect shown in Fig. 13.5:
- *Stage 5*   The increased income level will result in a higher level of aggregate demand as the workers find themselves better off.
- *Stage 6*   This is the link which Keynesians regard as more problematical—an increase in the total demand in the economy *may* lead to a general price rise in certain circumstances. What are these circumstances?

The reader should refer back to Chapter 9, when we discussed aggregate demand and supply. It will be recalled that Keynes' concept of aggregate supply was of an inverted L-shaped curve. Supply could be increased without any effect on prices as long as output was below the equilibrium level for full employment. Once this was reached, however, the supply curve bent quite sharply upwards. In other words, once full employment was reached, any attempt to increase output would only result in higher prices. The graph representing this can usefully be repeated here (Fig. 13.6).

In other words, the Keynesian approach to money supply and price levels is that the mechanism is rather long-winded and operates via the effect of lower interest rates on

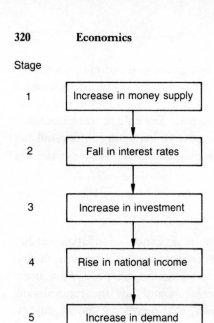

Figure 13.3   Keynes and money supply.

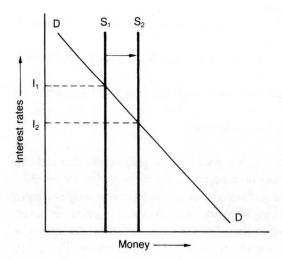

Figure 13.4   Increase in money supply.

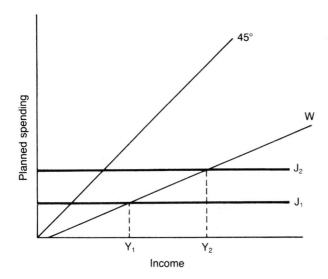

Figure 13.5 Multiplier effect. W = withdrawals, J = injection (investment).

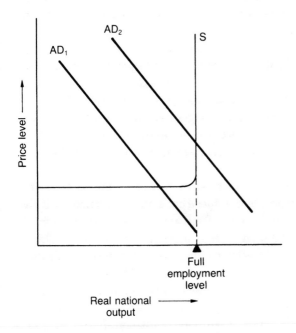

Figure 13.6 Full employment and inflation (Keynes).

consumption and investment. It also varies according to whether the economy is in full employment (however that is defined) or not. If the level of output is below equilibrium level then money supply can be increased without inflation resulting, but if that full employment point has been reached then inflation will result. It can be seen why many economists contested in the early 1990s that tight money supply would not necessarily be the answer to inflation with 3 million unemployed!

The reader should refer back to the analysis of national income using the 45° line. It was demonstrated in Chapter 9 that an inflationary gap is produced if the equilibrium level of output (= income) is more than the full employment equilibrium. It might be asked how output can rise above full employment level if the economy is in equilibrium. The explanation is that much of the impetus for inflationary increases in output comes from increased investment, either private or government. This explains some of the official policy of trying to keep government expenditure low.

Cost-push inflation

This type of inflation results from an increase in costs of production and especially labour costs, because wages are the most volatile of productive costs. Increases in the price of raw materials and power are just as much part of cost-push inflation, however. Many people, especially some politicians, consider that trade unions are major instigators of inflation as they force employers to concede wage claims which can only be met by raising the prices of consumer goods.

The cost-push theory is a favourite with the popular press, especially those newspapers which have a right-wing political stance. The theme is that greedy workers and their unions demand more and more in wages and this pushes up prices. This may happen, of course, but it is equally possible for higher wages to be the result of increased productivity and more often now wage increases are tied to improvements in output. In such cases the wage rises are simply a case of the workers gaining their share of the extra profits from productivity.

A type of cost-push inflation is the result of an increase in the cost of raw materials and this is in fact probably more common than wage-induced inflation. In particular, if the cost of imported raw materials increases as a result of inflation overseas or a rise in oil prices (which are always set in US dollars) then there is little that can be done. This is often known as 'imported inflation'. After the effective devaluation of sterling following withdrawal from the ERM, imports became more expensive and added to costs.

Finally, shortages of raw material can result in cost-push inflation. The supply curve for a commodity will contract leftwards and if enough products are involved a general price rise can result. This was a common cause of temporary inflation in ancient times and the Middle Ages, when poor weather or warfare resulted in shortages of a whole range of foodstuffs. It was a feature after the Black Death in the fourteenth century, when the number of agricultural workers was decimated, producing a rise in the prices of bread and other farm commodities.

Topic 13.5   Inflation and employment

We have seen that inflation is related to unemployment and that there is a concept of the natural level of unemployment in the economy. To Keynes, the question of whether inflation was likely following increased activity in the economy would depend on the level of unemployment and how close the economy was to that equilibrium level. The relationship between inflation and unemployment was studied especially, in the late 1950s, by A.W. Phillips at the London School of Economics, and the resulting model was quickly adopted as a key idea and tool for inflation analysis.

The formulation of the *Phillips curve* dates from 1958, yet the statistical relationships given expression in it had been observed and researched over thirty years earlier by Irving Fisher. According to Phillips' findings there existed a remarkably accurate inverse relationship between the rate of wage inflation and the unemployment rate (see Fig. 13.7). What is more, Phillips suggested that the relationship could be shown to have existed in the UK for as long as ninety years.

The slope of the Phillips curve was important for two main reasons:

- It suggested that as unemployment fell this would produce an accelerated rate of wage inflation.
- The curve becomes progressively wage inelastic as it moves below the horizontal axis, so that, beyond a certain point, increasing unemployment will not exert a proportional effect on wage inflation.

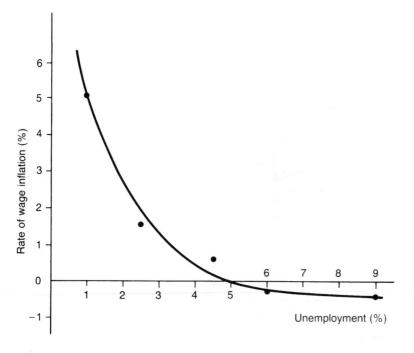

Figure 13.7   The Phillips curve (based on data for 1861–1913).

The *Phillips curve* expresses an inverse relationship between the rate of wage inflation and the rate of unemployment.

Although Phillips used *wage* inflation as the indicator, the long-term relationship between wages and prices is such that the vertical axis on the Phillips graph can be seen as an indicator of inflation in general.

The policy implications of the Phillips curve were quickly assimilated. Keynes had provided the tools to manage aggregate demand and hence unemployment; controlling employment now meant, effectively, also controlling inflation. Unfortunately, it was not possible to enjoy the best of both worlds, but careful tuning of the economy could ensure an acceptable level of both unemployment and inflation.

The Phillips curve seemed so ideal for policy makers because it gave the opportunity cost of reducing unemployment in terms of inflation, so that a trade-off between the two could be used. It was intended as a means of measuring the variations in inflation rate with excess demand but was not seen by Phillips as a theory of inflation or necessarily as a support for Keynesian demand-pull theories.

However, while the Phillips curve seemed to fit the situation in the early decades of the century very well it increasingly looked unrealistic in the 1970s and 1980s. The 1970s especially, saw a considerable cost-push inflation from rises in the prices of all and other raw materials. Consider Fig. 13.8 for example. The relationship appears to work for some

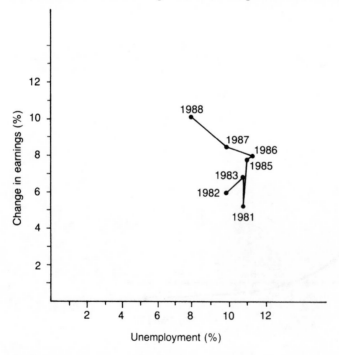

Figure 13.8   Earnings inflation/employment 1982–8.

years but not for more recent ones. Why is this? Has the Phillips curve been a spurious tool or have economic conditions changed?

Monetarist economists have an explanation, resting on their theory that inflation is the result of excess demand which in turn results from increases in the money supply. In order to examine the monetarist explanation for the combining of high unemployment and high inflation in the 1970s and 1980s we need to look at the 'natural' rate of unemployment. Phillips noted two significant rates for unemployment from his analysis. One was the rate that coincided with stable prices which was $2\frac{1}{2}$ per cent, assuming a 2 per cent per year productivity growth. The second figure was at $5\frac{1}{2}$ per cent, which marked the level when wages would be stable—in other words, the zero position on the vertical axis in Fig. 13.8.

To monetarists the natural rate of unemployment is that which exists when there is stable inflation. It uses the assumption that both employers and employees, through collective bargaining, use their estimates of future price levels as the key to the current wage agreements. This produces an important role for expectations and the result is sometimes called the *expectations augmented Phillips curve*, developed by Milton Friedman. If workers and employers believe that inflation will rise at a specific level they will negotiate wage increases accordingly.

However, increased wages will result in higher prices as firms seek to pass on wage rises while, at the same time, reducing the demand for labour. They may continue with the same demand for labour but only if they anticipate revenues rising faster than costs. Meanwhile, the supply of labour is increasing (Fig. 13.9) as workers are encouraged to enter the workforce by rising wages.

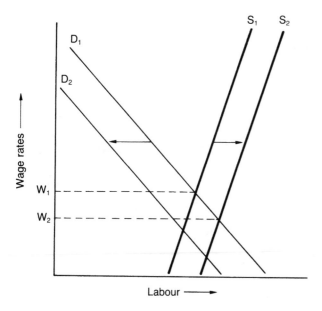

Figure 13.9 Changes in supply and demand for labour—expectations theory.

There is a further development. While nominal wages may rise, real wages in these circumstances will not, or at least not by the amount expected. Workers, and probably employers, are suffering what is called *money illusion.*

> *Expectations* play a major part in wage increases but rising prices as a result leads to workers and employers suffering from *money illusion.*

Monetarist economists, in any case, see the Philips curve as a short-term feature. They maintain that there is a long-run 'Phillips curve' which is vertical at the natural rate of unemployment. We can now see how the argument used above will produce inflation without reducing unemployment in the long run. (Fig. 13.10).

We can see what happens if we follow carefully a sequence of events which summarize the process. Let us assume that unemployment has settled at its natural rate (UN in Fig. 13.11). The actual rate of inflation is therefore zero. Assume now that the authorities have decided to employ an inflation/unemployment trade-off of 5 per cent and 3 per cent, respectively.

This is achieved primarily through monetary expansion of 5 per cent. Initially, money illusion is created, an illusion that fools both workers and employers. Demand for goods and services rise with employers' increasing demand for labour resulting in a rise in wages. Previously unemployed workers interpret these rising money wages to be rising real wages and so offer themselves for employment. Unemployment in this way falls to U1 or 3 per cent in Fig. 13.11.

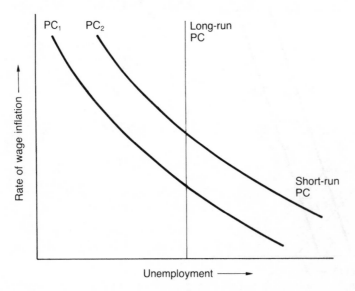

Figure 13.10   Monetarist model—long- and short-run Phillips curves.

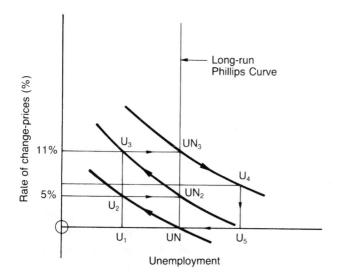

Figure 13.11   The monetarist model of inflation and unemployment.

Unfortunately, rising money wages have increased costs and consequently prices, so real wages remain constant. Before long the illusion becomes all too transparent and workers begin to remove themselves from the labour market, so unemployment rises to its natural rate. However, the departure from the stable money supply situation has created 5 per cent inflation and inflationary expectations have risen by 5 per cent. If the government ignores the existence of a natural level of unemployment then it may once again mistakenly attempt to reduce the level of unemployment below UN (Fig. 13.11). Now, of course, the ground has shifted upwards so that the 'cost' of reducing unemployment has risen in sympathy with the newly created inflation rate. Only wage increases in excess of 5 per cent will reduce unemployment for only 5 per cent plus increases will raise real wages.

This means, in policy terms, an additional boost in the money supply of, perhaps, 6 per cent which again artificially raises both labour demand and labour supply. The accompanying inflation rate—the cost of reducing unemployment below its natural level—has, as predicted, risen to 11 per cent. The inflationary spiral will only stop when the authorities accept:

- The inevitability of a natural unemployment level and
- The inflationary consequences of an accelerating money supply growth.

This may seem a complicated process and it may well need more than one read-through to comprehend! It does emphasize, however, the importance of inflation and the unemployment relationship as a key area of economic policy, and we will meet it again in Chapter 15.

Case Study 13.1—Keeping inflation down

Inflation has been a persistent problem in many parts of the world. In Brazil it has been in recent years about 1000 per cent and even some growing and fairly successful economies like Turkey have seen inflation approaching 100 per cent. Yet inflation can be extremely varied among neighbouring countries. In 1992 Kenya's inflation rate was 32 per cent while to the north-east, Saudi Arabia experienced 1.1 per cent. In Europe, Germany experienced 4 per cent, France 2.4 per cent and the UK 3.7 per cent. At the other end of Europe, Greece suffered an inflation in that year of 15.9 per cent.

Inflation is a problem felt more by some countries than others. In many cases countries accept a measure of inflation as a trade-off for economic growth and high levels of employment while others, like the UK under the Thatcher and Major administrations and Germany under the control of the Bundesbank, aimed at low inflation with high unemployment as the price worth paying. So the UK in 1990 suffered a negative growth (−0.5 per cent GDP) as the price for its 3.7 per cent inflation. Turkey's inflation rate of over 70 per cent did, however, accompany a growth of 5 per cent GDP which was the highest of all developed countries.

Source of statistics: Barclays Economic Review (2nd Quarter) 1993.

1. Why is low growth or high unemployment often a trade-off for low inflation?
2. Is low inflation worth while?

Advanced Study Topic 13.1   The IS/LM model

Some examinations may require that the student examines the relationships between the money and the goods markets using a graph with interest rates and national income as the two variables. This is known as IS/LM analysis. The IS schedule is derived from the aggregate demand curve and indicates the combinations of interest rates and national income at which equilibrium prevails in the goods market. The LM schedule is obtained from the money market schedules and indicates the equilibrium positions of the money market in terms, again, of interest rates and income.

The result is a graph which shows both IS and LM schedules together and is very useful for examining the effect of policy decisions on the economy, especially where interest rates are concerned (Fig. AST 13.1). The student who wishes to pursue this further is advised to read Begg *et al.*, Chapter 25, and Dornbusch and Fischer, Chapter 4.

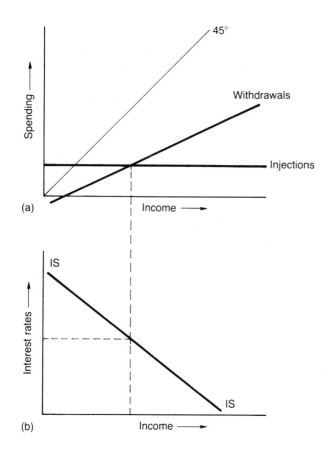

Figure AST 13.1   Deriving the IS line. (a) Spending. (b) Interest rates.

Essay questions

1. 'In the fight against inflation, it is more important to control inflationary expectations than to control the money supply.' Discuss. (*Source*: The Associated Examining Board, June 1991)
2. Discuss whether it is possible to have low unemployment at the same time as a low rate of inflation. (*Source*: The Associated Examining Board, June 1990)
3. 'Inflation is triggered by excess demand but sustained by rising costs.'
   (a) Explain this statement.
   (b) Discuss its implications for the successful control of inflation.
   (*Source*: The Associated Examining Board, November 1992)
4. (a) What do you understand by monetary policy?
   (b) How does membership of the exchange rate mechanism of the European Monetary System affect a government's ability to pursue an independent monetary policy?
   (*Source*: The Associated Examining Board, June 1992)

5. Compare the relative costs of unemployment and inflation to the economy. Discuss whether or not it is possible to reduce unemployment without increasing inflation. (*Source*: Northern Examinations and Assessment Board, June 1992)

6. What is inflation and why is it commonly regarded as a problem? In what ways have anti-inflationary policies changed in Britain over the last two decades? (*Source*: Northern Examinations and Assessment Board, June 1991)

7. Are the benefits that are said to arise from the control of inflation worth the costs involved in achieving that control? (*Source*: University of Oxford, June 1992)

8. Compare and contrast the use of:
   (a)   Variations in income tax;
   (b)   Variations in interest rates;
   (c)   Methods of controlling the inflation rate in the UK.
        (*Source*: University of Oxford, June 1993)

9. Explain why inflation is regarded as a major problem for macro-economic management. Discuss whether or not, in your view, zero inflation is a feasible or desirable objective for economic policy. (*Source*: Northern Examinations and Assessment Board, June 1993)

Chapter 14

Public finance

Topic 14.1   Government and EU expenditure

What is public expenditure?

Public expenditure is equal in size to about 20 per cent of national output in the case of the UK and this includes all spending by government departments and local authorities. It comprises spending of many kinds, including investment in the construction of roads, the cost of the armed forces, police, teachers and other public servants, fixed investment in the few remaining state-owned enterprises and interest on money borrowed. About 60 per cent of all public spending is undertaken directly by central government and about 40 per cent by local authorities. The general trend since 1980 has been to reduce the amount of public spending in real terms and to encourage the private sector, even in the area of road building, power production and the railways.

We also need to see increasingly public finance from all aspects as a European phenomenon and not just limit our attentions to the UK. It is impossible in the years after 1992 to consider the UK in isolation and EU spending and taxation are important in painting the total economic picture.

Should the government be involved?

It is a matter of debate as to what goods or services should be provided by the individual and what should be provided by the community as a whole. In common speech, one often hears such expression as 'They should provide . . .' or 'Such things ought to be free'. 'They' presumably refers to the government, either central or local, and by 'free' the speaker means that the things under consideration should be provided from government expenditure. Economic goods are not free, but have a monetary value and as we saw earlier in this book, even the supply of water has to be paid for. There are those who would argue that housing and public transport should be free in the sense of being provided by the community.

It is a matter of allocation and choice whether housing should be paid for by public or private spending. Very often the choice is made by a political party putting forward a programme to reduce public spending, increase it or keep it the same. Voters have to choose where to place their cross on the ballot paper according to their own preferences on these and many other issues. In the UK we have adopted a middle course and between 1945 and 1979 there was a fair degree of agreement among the political parties. The argument over the role of the public sector in the economy has been heightened since the general consensus which used to exist between the main political parties in the UK was broken by the adoption of strong monetarist policies by the Conservative government of the 1980s under Margaret Thatcher. This will be examined in more detail later.

The dispute is not confined to the UK. There have been similar changes in most of the EU countries including Sweden, which has for many years had a considerable government input into the economy. In Eastern Europe the break-up of Communism has brought about further easing of the economic situation with former publicly owned industries being sold to individuals or even foreign companies. An example of the latter is the take-over of the Skoda car works in the Czech Republic by the German firm Volkswagen.

Public expenditure in the UK

At the beginning of the twentieth century it was generally thought that the UK government should be responsible for the defence of the realm, the administration of justice and very basic social services. The majority of items for economic and social welfare were considered to be the responsibility of private individuals who were expected to provide for their families and their education, health care, housing, etc. from their own resources. After 1945 a Labour government influenced by the Beveridge Report and the community spirit which had been experienced during the war years introduced a far greater input of government spending which lasted until Margaret Thatcher's premiership from 1979 to 1991.

It is interesting, though, that despite the privatization programme and encouragement given to private pensions and health care, not to mention the reduction in spending on the armed forces, the proportion of national expenditure which is by the government, including local authorities, remained at about 21 per cent between 1980 and 1992.

Table 14.1 shows the main items in central government public expenditure and Fig. 14.1 illustrates each item as a percentage of total state spending. It can be seen that social security is the largest single area of spending, and it is this which has probably kept total public expenditure high over the years. Health and defence are also major areas of spending. The phrase 'public expenditure' covers a number of organizations, and it must not be assumed that it is all personally authorized by the Cabinet.

The main bodies we are concerned with are:

1. The central government departments such as the Home Office, Department of Trade & Industry, and the Department of the Environment.
2. The local authorities in the UK—this includes county councils, district councils and (in a very small way) parish councils.

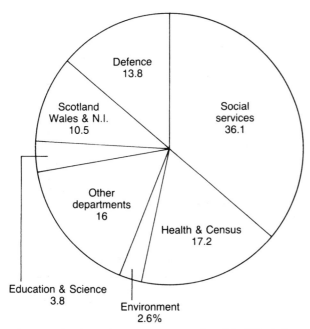

Figure 14.1 Central government spending (%) 1993–4 (Consolidated fund). (*Source: Annual Abstract of Statistics*, HMSO, 1993.)

3. The European Union.
4. Miscellaneous government bodies including the public corporations, various 'Quangos' and other councils and public bodies.

The question of which bodies are responsible for what expenditure is becoming extremely complex with government changes in which, for example, money formerly spent by the National Health Service (and so part of the Department of Health) is now in many cases managed by health trusts which are supposed to be independent bodies. It is probably best if we discuss the matter of public expenditure by type of spending rather than by who is responsible and the reader is advised to keep up to date on the changes in public administration by reading the press.

Table 14.1 gives an outline of public expenditure which is the responsibility of central government and Table 14.2 deals with UK local authorities. The complication is that central government funds are important sources of income for local authorities especially for certain key services such as education. So some of the expenditure in Table 14.1 will be routed via local authorities or various government councils and other bodies.

Local authority spending, as seen in Table 14.2, indicates the importance of education as clearly far and away the largest absorber of local government moneys but social services and police also figure prominently (see Fig. 14.2).

Table 14.3 looks at the spending by the European Union. The UK will receive a proportion of this expenditure as a member of the Union. It can be seen that the dominant sector of the economy for expenditure is agriculture through the Common

Table 14.1 Public expenditure: Central government Estimate 1993–1994

Department	£m	Department	£m
Defence	23 440	Lord Chancellor's Dept	2 188
Agric., Fishery and Food	3 207	Education	6 543
Overseas Development	2 276	Health and census	29 328
Employment	3 398	Social services	61 288
Transport	2 735	Scotland	7 390
Environment	4 400	Wales	3 441
Home Office	2 477	N Ireland	7 044
Chancellor of Exchequer	3 438	Others	7 260
		Total	169 853

Source: HM Treasury—Public Expenditure, Feb 1994 (HMSO)

Table 14.2 Public expenditure: Local authorities Projected Revenue Account 1994–1995

England		Scotland	
Department	£m	Department	£m
Education	17 087	Education, libraries and Museums	2 629
Social services	6 403	Health and social services	866
Police	5 795	Law, order and protection	731
Fire	1 168	Roads and transport	391
Highway maintenance	1 759	Environmental services	580
Other services	8 533	Miscellaneous	12
Capital financing	1 909	Other services	51
Restructuring	10	Loans and lease charges	753

Source: HM Treasury—Public Expenditure, Feb 1994, HMSO.

Table 14.3 The European Community Budget 1991

Expenditure		Revenue	
Spending Area	% of Total Spending	Source	Proportion (%)
Agriculture	63.5	VAT	54.9
Regional and Fisheries	13.2	Customs duties	21.5
Social Fund	8.0	GNP based resources	15.2
Development co-operation	3.9	Agricultural levies	2.1
Research, energy and technology	3.5	Sugar and isoglucose	2.0
Administrative costs	3.4	Miscellaneous	4.2
Miscellaneous	3.4		

Source: Eurostat: *Europe in Figures*, 3rd edn., 1992.

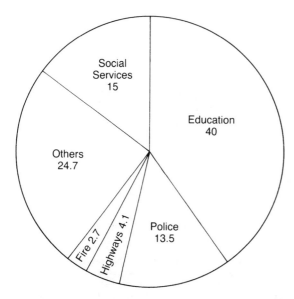

Figure 14.2 Local authority spending (%) 1994–5 (projection). (*Source*: *Annual Abstract of Statistics*, HMSO, 1993.)

Agricultural Policy. This received 62 per cent of the total EC budget in 1989 although this was a distinct fall from 1980, when it was as high as 72 per cent.

Why is public expenditure necessary?

There are a number of different answers to this question, because the different categories of public spending have their roots in different needs. It might be useful to examine Case Study 14.1 below, which is an extract from a newsletter issued by Broadland District Council in Norfolk. We can use the activities shown as examples of some types of public spending.

Public goods have been already described in Chapter 3 when we saw that they are goods/services which, even when consumed by one person, are still fully available to others. Everyone benefits—or has the opportunity to benefit—fully and usually without individual cost. The example given in the case study is the historic tours programme ('Off the Beaten Track'). This is provided as a general service to local residents and if Mr and Mrs Smith of Aylsham use the route it in no way reduces the facilities for Mr and Mrs Jones of Catton. On a national level, we noted in Chapter 4 that public goods include such items as defence and, on a local level, parks. Both local and the national parks are a good example.

Merit goods were also introduced in Chapter 4 where we saw that they are goods or services which can be provided by private enterprise and can be individually purchased. However, it is thought by most people, especially by governments, that they should be provided for all on a free, subsidized or full-cost basis.

Case Study 14.1—Extract from newsletter of Broadland District Council

CHRISTMAS CHECK-UP

ONCE again, Broadland's environmental health officers will be visiting local food premises during December. The Christmas Campaign is designed to ensure that potential food poisoning in the area is kept to an absolute minimum. 'High risk' premises are targeted where, for example, the sheer increase in trade might create hygiene problems.

We would ask anyone involved in providing food for public consumption to remember the following:

★ keep food at or below the required legal temperatures
★ avoid preparing or cooking food too far in advance of consumption
★ basic cleanliness must not be overlooked during the busy period
★ frozen foods, especially turkeys, must be thoroughly defrosted and cooked as directed

★ raw and cooked foods must be kept well apart

★ don't forget health and safety at work – this will also be checked

★ officers have a legal right of entry to check premises, and obstruction is an offence

★ all food premises in the District should be registered with the Council

We are pleased to report that previous campaigns have been very successful, with fewer unsatisfactory premises each year. This is due to no small part to the co-operation of local businesses. Food poisoning, especially at Christmas, can be very distressing. It causes pain and misery, and, at its worst, can even be fatal. With everyone's help, we should all be able to avoid such problems.

RECYCLING PLAN APPROVED

THE Recycling Plan was approved by the members of the Full Council on 20th October. The Plan was sent to the Department of the Environment (DoE) in the last week of July, in time for the August 1st deadline. The DoE has suggested one minor amendment in the wording of the plan, and is happy that the Plan complies with the requirements of the Environmental Protection Act 1990.

Now that the formalities are completed, and the Plan is Council policy, the next stage will be to implement it. In the next issue of Broadland News we will give you a clear picture of exactly what the strategy will be.

In the meantime, copies can be inspected at the council's offices in Thorpe St. Andrew, local libraries, and Norwich Central Library.

OFF THE BEATEN TRACK

DID you know that Woodbastwick Old Hall was machine-gunned in 1940? Or that, in 1770, Ranworth's wild Colonel Sidley was summoned from a party by the devil? If the answer is no, then you need to go "Off the Beaten Track" with Broadland's new series of historic tours.

The Council's Leisure and Tourism Department has put together the new tours, which should prove popular with both visitors and local people. The first three have been designed for motorists and cover Horsham St Faith to Aylsham, Plumstead to Acle, and Blickling to Cawston. The next three are for cyclists, and will be ready by the end of this year.

The routes can be followed with the aid of a free leaflet, giving clear directions and information on many places of interest. These can be obtained from the Council by contacting Kirstin Hilliard on Norwich 31133, ext 5005.

This case study is referred to in the text and so questions have not been set on it.

In Case Study 14.1 the refuse collection details are an example. Refuse collection is a responsibility of the district council and is provided free to domestic households although firms have to pay for it. It is possible to leave refuse collection to the private market sector, but whereas business managers see the disadvantage of having a lot of rubbish about and so will pay for collection and disposal, some domestic households will not. The result is flies, smells and health problems which justify public and free provision.

A merit good over which there has been some discussion recently is transport, with the privatization of British Rail and the suggestion in some quarters of increased provision of private toll roads.

Regulation of businesses is an important function of local government, central government and the European Union. Increasingly, much of industry and commerce is subject to regulation as in the 'Christmas Check-Up' over food hygiene in the case study. The Department of Trade & Industry has an overall responsibility for a number of industries including the massive insurance sector. The cost of this regulation in personnel and technical equipment is quite significant. One important area of regulation is in the control of externalities, discussed in Chapter 3 at some length. Inevitably, due to the local nature of much pollution and noise, the state 'watchdog' for any locality will be the district or county council, but central government also has a role, especially the Department of the Environment.

Transfer expenditure is a category of public spending which is different in kind from all the above. Spending on roads, schools, parks and wheely-bins increases the total of national output because goods or services are made and value put into the community. However, a large volume of government spending is on pensions, social welfare benefits and other payments where money is taken from some people via the tax system and given to others. No new output is achieved and there is nothing added to national income.

Subsidies and grants are available from both central and local government and from the EU. Of considerable importance are farm subsidies and regional development grants, in both cases increasingly funded by the EU. Many local authorities set up trading estates and give subsidized or free facilities to encourage new industry into their area.

The objectives of transfer payments are usually to achieve some aim which may or may not be economic. Subsidies to farms or manufacturing are intended to support specific industries or regions. Most transfer payments, however, are intended to equalize incomes and/or wealth by giving financial assistance to those who are retired, widowed, long-term ill or unemployed or who otherwise lack a decent income. In the UK such benefits are paid for from a combination of income tax and National Insurance contributions. Sweden is famous for its very extensive social welfare provision.

Purpose of spending

We can also look at a simple division of public expenditure by the purpose to which it is directed. The official statistics classify public spending as *capital expenditure* and *current expenditure*. As the name suggests, capital expenditure includes the financing of major capital projects including construction of schools, hospitals, new roads, etc. On the other hand, current expenditure will pay for teachers' and nurses' salaries and for normal road maintenance. Care should be taken when using official statistics to distinguish between the two types of spending.

The role of the EU

We have mentioned the place of the European Union in public spending and, in view of its increasing importance, it would be useful to review how Union expenditure works. For details of the EU the reader should turn to Chapter 10.

The European Union has a budget in the region of £30–40 billion and Table 14.3 gives an indication of the distribution of this vast amount of spending. The bulk of the expenditure is in the area of the Common Agricultural Policy, mainly in the form of price guarantee payments. Regional subsidies are also significant but over 16 per cent of the total budget is spent on administration and reimbursements to member countries in connection with the collection of tariffs (Fig. 14.3).

The agricultural policy spending is mainly in the form of purchases of foodstuffs at the guaranteed prices, hence accumulating the famous 'mountains' and 'lakes' of various foods. The regional aid is usually routed through the national governments of member states. This has resulted in some governments reducing their own aid packages knowing that the EU funds will enable the total spent in such subsidies to stay much the same.

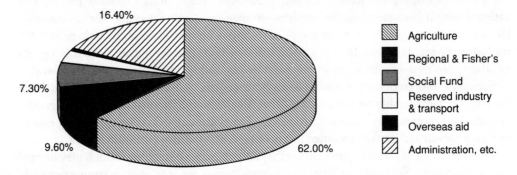

Figure 14.3   EC budget 1989.

Topic 14.2   Principles and aims of taxation

What is a good tax?

Many people would have no hesitation in saying that no tax is a good tax, but it is important to consider that some taxes are worse than others. It must be accepted that taxes are inevitable because some government expenditure is necessary if anarchy and chaos are to be avoided.

Adam Smith enumerated four principles or 'canons' of taxation to which today we would probably add another four. Sometimes the principles conflict with each other but they are intended as a framework for a taxation system which is generally acceptable:

1. *Equity* was the first principle of Adam Smith. This does not mean that each taxpayer contributes the same amount but rather that the state should have no favourites. Each person in the same situation should pay the same tax. A single person earning £12 000 a year should pay the same income tax as another single person earning £12 000 a year.
2. *Economy* is another of Smith's canons. It is in no-one's interests if the cost of collecting the tax is unnecessarily high. Some small taxes have proved to be costly to collect and have been abandoned. For example, at one time there was a radio licence separate from that for a TV but eventually so few people owned a radio without also having a TV that it was dispensed with as being too expensive to collect.
3. *Certainty* is the canon which stipulates that both the government and the taxpayer should know how much is to be paid. This includes the timing of payment and the accepted method as well as the amount.
4. *Convenience*   Adam Smith wrote 'A tax will be easier to administer if its object and time of payment are related to the habits of the community'. One of the features of the Pay-As-You-Earn system of collecting income tax (to be explained later) is its convenience. Most people get used to having a salary or wage paid net of tax and National Insurance and can forget about tax considerations.

There are another four principles that are not included in Smith's four canons but which are normally accepted as important:

5. *Efficiency*   Where possible, taxes should help to promote the economic efficiency of a country. Taxation helps to control the level of demand and may thus be used to control inflation. The amount of government revenue extracted in various spheres must be kept below taxable capacity. High rates of tax may dissuade a person from working overtime—therefore the economy suffers from excessive taxation.
6. *Ability to pay*   Taxes should be geared to a person's ability to pay, i.e. the burden of taxation should fall upon these who are able to bear it, upon the rich more than upon the poor.
7. *Social considerations*   Governments today use the tax structure to level out the inequalities of income. The National Health Service, although moving into independent trust status, is still maintained mainly from taxation. Social security benefits are also paid for from taxes. Many politicians aim at using taxation to redistribute income and wealth in a society, and there is some evidence from economics that a more even spread of wealth increases aggregate demand and so stimulates the economy.
8. *Flexibility*   In the light of the varied uses of taxation and the growing need for each of the EU member countries to make sure that their taxes are compatible with those

in the EU a degree of flexibility is important. For example, all EU countries have moved into using VAT as the main indirect tax and part of its proceeds go towards EU funds. It is easier for the UK government, for example, to adjust the VAT rate to fall into line with other EU countries than if it has to use the old purchase tax.

The aims of taxation

The *principles* of taxation must not be confused with its *aims*. The principles are guidelines as to the characteristics we expect from a tax; the aims are the objectives we have in setting the tax in the first place.

In general, taxation can be seen as having three main aims:

1. *To raise revenue* for the public authorities. This is a fundamental aim and was the sole aim in the Middle Ages when taxes were largely raised to support the king in his warfare and perhaps to provide for his regular revenue. The objective in public finance under the system prevailing before Keynes was to balance the budget. This is now popular again and financing expenditure is once more seen as the prime aim of taxation.
2. *To manage the economy*   Keynes saw fiscal policy (i.e. using taxation and public spending) as of vital importance to economic management and under this approach taxation might be used as a means of increasing or reducing consumer demand. The importance of *discretionary fiscal policy* and the arguments surrounding it will be discussed in the next chapter.
3. *To deal with inequality* of income, *moral* problems and certain *market failures*. For example, progressive income tax will have the effect of reducing the net incomes of the better-paid more than those less well off and transfer payments will positively boost the incomes of those in special need. Taxes on tobacco and spirits may be set to discourage consumption although one suspects that the Treasury appreciates the benefits of the inelastic demand for some of these products. Taxation is one possible way of dealing with such negative externalities as industrial pollution or with excessive monopoly profit.

Types of tax system

Before looking at the actual taxes which are levied in the UK and EU we need to consider a way of classifying taxes which economists and politicians find very useful. Consider the situation in Figs. 14.4 and 14.5. These graphs show how the proportion of a taxpayer's income is taken in tax as income grows. In fact, in Fig. 14.4 we have a horizontal line indicating that whatever the income level the same proportion of that income is taken as tax.

This may seem to be fair but many people hold that this is not the case. A person earning £6000 a year and paying 30 per cent of this as tax is actually suffering more from

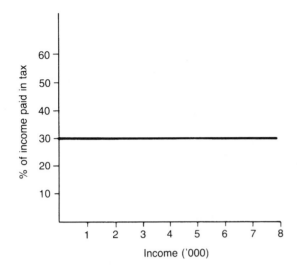

Figure 14.4 Proportional tax.

the tax system than someone who earns, say, £20 000. The latter may pay more tax but it is more affordable.

The result has been that modern taxation tends to favour taxes which produce a higher proportion of tax contribution at higher income levels. This is known as a *progressive* tax as opposed to the *proportional* tax outlined above. A tax which results in higher earners paying a lower proportion of their income as tax is called a *regressive* tax. Figure 14.5 shows the effects of progressive and regressive taxes, starting at 23 per cent, as incomes rise to £8000. In the analysis of the common types of tax which follows, frequent reference will be made to the degree to which any tax fits into the above categories.

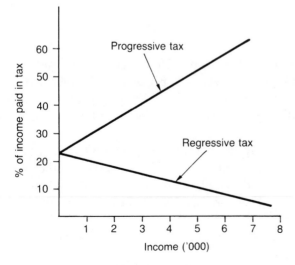

Figure 14.5 Progressive and regressive taxes.

Topic 14.3   Types of tax

There is a wide variety of taxes that can be levied by central and local government and the choice of which to adopt in order to secure revenue depends on a number of factors. These include the potential tax that can be obtained, the possible use of the tax to achieve political aims such as more equal distribution of wealth, the likely incidence of the tax and possible political consequences of any taxation decision.

It is normal to divide taxes into two broad categories: direct and indirect (see Fig. 14.6). Direct taxes raise money directly from the person or body who will be paying them whereas indirect taxes are levied on goods or services. While the responsibility for paying the tax rests with manufacturers, agents or retailers, in most cases the ultimate cost is borne by the consumer.

We will consider these and other issues when we have reviewed the taxes currently in use.

Direct taxes

Most countries have a system of direct taxation although its importance varies. The UK generally raises just under 40 per cent of its revenue from direct personal taxes, which is comparatively low by the standards of other developed nations. For example, the figure for the USA is about 50 per cent and for Italy it is 67 per cent.

The most important direct taxes are the following.

Income tax

This is perhaps the best-known tax in the UK and is raised by a body known as the Inland Revenue. For some years there has been a basic rate of tax which is designed to apply to most people with earned income, but there are higher bands for those who are considered to be earning distinctly more than the typical employee. Since the Conservative Party came to power in 1979 the higher rate bands have been reduced to one (40 per cent in 1992–3) and the basic rate has fallen to 25 per cent. It is the declared aim of the Conservative Party to reduce the basic rate to 20 per cent. In the 1992 budget the Chancellor instituted a lower rate band at 20 per cent, which was intended to help with the problems of lower earners who gain pay rises or promotion and begin to come into the tax bracket.

It is quite useful to look at the details of how income tax is levied and Advanced Study Topic 14.1 takes on this task. Most readers will find it helpful. Tax payers for the most part fall into two categories—Schedule E for the employed person or Schedule D for the self-employed. There are other categories but they are less important. For employed workers tax is deducted at source by the employer under a system called Pay-As-You-Earn (PAYE) but the self-employed have to declare their income at the end of each tax year (6 April) and then tax is assessed on their gross earnings less allowable expenses. The difference in operation is quite important for the government because tax is paid

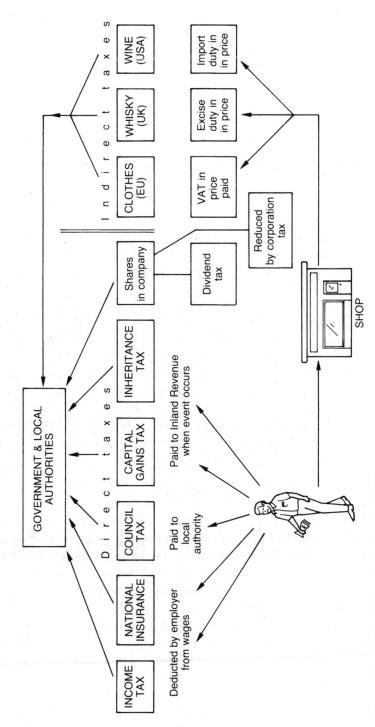

Figure 14.6 Direct and indirect taxes in the UK.

within 3 weeks (in theory!) under PAYE but there may be a delay of 6 to 12 months for Schedule D payers.

The tax is regarded as progressive although it is less so than it was in the 1970s when the 'top slice' was as high as 83 per cent for a time. It is considered to be normally fair, as those who earn most, pay most, and there are a number of allowances which contribute to individual tax codes. The higher the code, the higher the 'free pay' and the lower the threshold at which tax is paid (see Advanced Study Topic 14.1 for detail). For those paying under PAYE it is also efficient and cost effective. In fact, the cost of collection is borne by employers but the self-employed usually have the cost of using an accountant.

National Insurance

These contributions are regarded by some textbooks as a separate issue from taxation but in reality they are a special type of tax since payment is compulsory. Each employee has a National Insurance contribution deducted from earnings along with income tax. The deduction is made for earnings between two levels known as the lower and higher earnings levels. Not only do employers have the job of deducting National Insurance but they also have to pay a contribution themselves, which is usually a little higher than that paid by the employee. This can be seen as an example of a payroll tax which exists in some countries as a tax on the number of employees.

National Insurance is different from other taxes in that it is designated to pay for certain benefits under the social welfare system prevailing in the UK. Some benefits such as old-age pensions and unemployment pay ('dole') are only paid in full if a set minimum number of contributions have been paid. Self-employed people also pay National Insurance at a different rate from the employed. Some employers and employees try to get a job classified as self-employed to avoid the need for immediate payment of contributions.

Local government taxes

Students who read older textbooks will find that one of the contentious issues in taxation was the local authority tax known as the rates. For many years the rates were the main means by which local authorities raised income. The rate was collected by the district councils but they included in the sum demanded amounts known as 'precepts' requested by the county and, in rural areas, parish councils.

Rates were considered to be unfair as they were based on the value of property and not on income, and many people living in rented property did not pay them while some pensioners and widows living in large houses paid a disproportionately large sum. Rates were replaced by the controversial community charge or 'poll tax', which had as its basis a per capita levy with relief for the low-paid and people with special circumstances. This proved equally unpopular, especially as it was clearly a regressive tax, hitting the poorer members of society much harder than the better off.

The current council tax, introduced from 1993, reverts to a property basis but instead of the individual assessment of a rateable value which caused so much dispute with the rates, property is placed in value bands and tax levied accordingly. There are some discounts and exemptions to alleviate the worst problems but it is still making the assumption that the larger and more imposing the property, the better the owner is equipped to pay a higher tax. This may be a generally correct assumption, but there can be no certainty that this scheme will have more success than its predecessors.

Proposals for a local income tax or VAT have been made and some have suggested that as local authorities already depend on central government subsidies for many things and come under 'rate capping' restrictions by Whitehall, then it might be easier to fund local expenditure by increasing national income tax.

Corporation tax

So far, we have looked at taxes paid by individuals but a large source of revenue is the taxation of companies. A limited company, whether private or public, has to file an annual return with the Inland Revenue and annual accounts with Companies House. In principle, tax is levied in much the same way as for the self-employed as outlined in the extract from leaflet IR105 shown in Case Study 14.2.

Basically, a company and the Inland Revenue agree on its profit for a tax year and then during the following year corporation tax is levied on turnover less allowable expenses such as wages. The rate for small companies is based on the basic rate of income tax but there is a higher rate for companies with greater profits. Some of the profit of a limited company is distributed to shareholders, and while this is paid gross, tax is paid by the company on this and a tax credit sent to the shareholder. The tax collected in this way is known as advanced corporation tax (ACT) and is offset against mainstream corporation tax.

It is argued that corporation tax is fair because in law a limited company is a separate body from the individuals (shareholders) who own it and so its profits should be taxed. However, there is the question of whether or not this tax discourages firms from investing for the future. It certainly tends to favour capital projects which use tax-deductible methods such as borrowing from a bank, the interest on which is set against tax, than funding by the reinvestment of profit.

Capital taxes

A further type of direct tax is that which is based not on income but on the amount of wealth or capital which a person has. In the UK we do not have a wealth tax as such, although some in the Labour Party have suggested it, but we do have taxes that are triggered by movements of capital. The two main ones are:

- *Capital gains tax*   this is paid if an asset is sold and it is assessed on the difference between the sale price and the original cost of acquisition. There is an exemption of

Case Study 14.2—Advice to the self-employed (Inland Revenue Booklet IR105)

Starting in business

What happens when I start in business?
The first thing you should do is tell the Tax Office you have started in business. If you have not done this already, ask the Tax Office for a form 41G to complete. This form gives us the information we need about you and your business. You may find it useful to read our leaflet IR28 'Starting in Business', and this leaflet contains a form 41G which you can use. You can get this leaflet from any Tax Office or Tax Enquiry Centre.

Most self-employed people prepare accounts at least once a year so they know what profits their business is making. To do this, you need to keep your records of business earnings and expenses accurate and up-to-date.

It is up to you to decide the date to which you prepare your first accounts, or summary if your business turnover is below £15,000 for a full year. (Our leaflet IR104 'Simple Tax Accounts' will tell you whether you can send in a summary instead of detailed accounts.)

You can prepare your accounts or summary from the date your business started to
• the following 5 April (the end of the tax year) or
• the date which is 12 months after the date on which you started.
Whatever date you choose, it is easier to stick to it in future years.

Example 1 shows how your tax assessments are worked out by the Tax Office for the first three years in the life of your business. You do not need to work this out for yourself.

Example 1
Suppose you start your business on 6 October 1990 and you decide to work out your profits after you have been in business for a full year. Your business results for the year from 6 October 1990 to 5 October 1991 are as follows.

Turnover	£6,122
less purchases and expenses	£998
First year's profits	£5,125

First tax year 1990–91
You are taxed on the profits for the period from the date you started to the following 5 April. That is from 6 October 1990 to 5 April 1991. The figure of profit is worked out by taking your profit for the first 12 months of your business and multiplying it by 6/12. (The top figure of the fraction is the number of months you are in business during the first tax year and the bottom figure is 12 because your profits were earned over a 12 month period.)

First year's profits $£5,125 \times 6/12 = £2,562$.

Your 1990–91 assessment will show profits of £2,562.

Second tax year 1991–92
You are taxed on the profits made in your first full year of business. So in this example it is the profit to 5 October 1991.

Your assessment would show £5,124.

Third tax year 1992–93
The usual rule (see page 1) applies for this year. This means you are taxed on the profits for your accounting year which ended in the previous tax year 1991–92. So in this example it is the profits of the year ended 5 October 1991, £5,124.

Consider the above text which is from an Inland Revenue booklet for those starting a self-employed business.

1. Using the figures provided (i.e. first year's profits of £5124), calculate the tax due if the individual is given a personal allowance of £3445.
2. How do the rules for taxing the self-employed lead to a delay in payments being made to the Inland Revenue?

£5800 (1992–3). The reason for this tax is to prevent people avoiding tax altogether by dealing in assets rather than earning an income. For example, some people earn a lot of money by buying and selling shares, property or works of art and it would seem unfair if they could escape tax simply because they were making capital profit instead of receiving a regular salary.

- *Inheritance tax*   this tax has undergone a number of changes in name as well as nature over the years. Originally conceived as a tax on the transfer of assets following the death of the owner it was changed to include any transfers of capital and then back to dealing with transfers mainly on death. A transfer within 7 years of death is embraced by the tax which includes the value of a domestic house. It is not applicable between husbands and wives and there is a generous threshold (see Table 14.4).

Table 14.4   Tax data table

	1994–5	1995–6	1996–7	1997–8	1998–9
Income Tax					
Personal Allowance	3445				
P.A. aged 65–74	4200				
P.A. aged 75 & over	2705				
Rates of Tax:					
Basic rate	25				
Lower rate	20				
Higher rate(s)	40				
Inheritance Tax					
Limit of gift to one person	250				
Small gift upper limit	3000				
Threshold for tax	150 000				
Rate of tax	40				
Capital Gains Tax					
Annual exemption	5800				
Rate of Tax	Income T				
National Insurance					
Lower earnings level	57/week				
Upper earnings level	430/week				
Corporation Tax					
Rate (small firms)	25%				
Rate (other firms)	33%				
Value Added Tax:					
Standard Rate	17.50%				
Minimum turnover	45 000				
New taxes or changes					
VAT on insurance & fuel					

Note: The figures for 1994–5 are given above but as rates change every year further columns are provided and the reader is invited to complete them following the budget each year.

A number of accountants and financial advisers make a living advising those with assets in excess of this figure on the best ways of adjusting their affairs to reduce liability to this tax by their heirs or beneficiaries.

The argument in favour of inheritance tax is that wealth can be acquired without cost by some individuals simply because they have wealthy relatives or friends. This may seem unfair and many politicians see advantages in the breaking up of estates and wealth by this tax. Many art treasures and stately homes have been given to the state in lieu of inheritance tax.

Licences and fees

Just as National Insurance pays for certain benefits, so there are some specific levies which people may pay. These include licences for TV sets (which funds the BBC), the road fund licence for cars, and licences for owning guns, for obtaining a consumer credit licence or a licence under the Data Protection Act.

One small tax that causes much annoyance is stamp duty, which is payable on many contracts including that to buy a house, and the government has recently given periods of exemption from this tax for house purchase to try to encourage the housing market.

Advantages of direct taxes

Some of the main advantages of direct taxes may be briefly summarized:

1. *Progressive*   Direct taxes are usually administered in accordance with a graded scale and so are both progressive and equitable, especially as allowances are made for dependants.
2. *Non-inflationary*   Direct taxes do not increase prices and therefore are not inflationary. They take money from consumers thus reducing purchasing power and helping to keep prices in check.
3. *Exemption of very poor*   Several million workers pay no direct taxation at all. Yet in spite of the exemptions for lower income groups which are found in most countries' tax systems, rising wage rates tend to bring increasing numbers of people into the tax bracket.
4. *Inequalities can be reduced*   Governments usually tax the richer members of the community and use the money to give assistance to widows, schoolchildren, students, expectant mothers, etc.
5. *Easier estimation of revenue*   The Chancellor is able to estimate more precisely the likely revenue from direct taxation. If taxes on commodities are increased, people may buy fewer items.
6. *Tax liability known*   Taxpayers will know exactly what they have to pay. Moreover, PAYE is deducted at an appropriate moment in accordance with the principles of certainty and convenience.

UK indirect taxes

Direct taxes are more socially just than indirect taxes as the burden of these falls on those who are not able to bear them. A damning attack on the excess of indirect taxes was made in 1820, by Sydney Smith in the *Edinburgh Review*, when he wrote:

> The dying Englishman pouring his medicine, which has paid seven per cent, into a spoon that has paid fifteen per cent—flings himself back upon his chintz bed which has paid twenty-two per cent—makes his will on an eight pound stamp, and expires in the arms of an apothecary who has paid a licence of £100 for the privilege of putting him to death. His whole property is then immediately taxed from two to ten per cent. Besides the probate, large fees are demanded for burying him in the chancel; his virtues are handed down to posterity on taxed marble; and he is then gathered to his fathers—to be taxed no more.

Indirect taxes can be defined as those which are not levied directly on those who will ultimately pay them. Usually this means taxes on goods and services. The main indirect taxes are as follows.

Value Added Tax (VAT)

This tax is the most significant indirect tax in the EU and had its origins in Europe. It was brought into the UK in 1973 to replace purchase tax and as one of the changes necessary for the UK's joining the EC.

VAT is a sales tax collected, not in a single stage like the old purchase tax, but in instalments at each stage of the production and distribution process. Each manufacturer, wholesaler or retailer is accountable for tax on the full value of what is sold but is allowed to take credit for the tax already paid on purchases. The tax paid by the manufacturer must be invoiced separately to the wholesaler; the tax the wholesaler pays must be invoiced separately to the retailer, and so on (see Fig. 14.7).

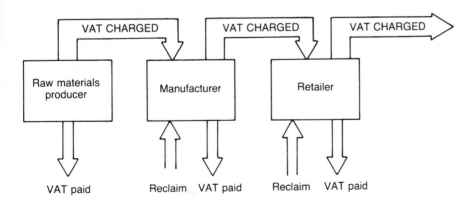

Figure 14.7 The VAT process.

VAT thus provides for the main principle of indirect taxation because it taxes the final good or service and not producer goods. The problem is the enormous cost of administration by the Customs & Excise who collect VAT and the cost of ensuring that rules are kept. This latter cost has been estimated at about 10 per cent of the revenue earned.

There is also need for European harmonization. While the European Commission has not been able to ensure uniform rates of VAT across the EU it is attempting to reduce the amount of zero rating. The use of the system across the EU enables exports to EU members to be dealt with in the normal way as far as VAT is concerned.

Customs & Excise duties

Import duties (tariffs) are dealt with in Chapter 10 as part of our treatment of international trade. From the beginning of 1993 there have been no duties between countries in the EU but there are import duties imposed on goods coming in from other countries. The purpose of these taxes is not just that of obtaining income for the government but also has the objective of protecting European industry.

Excise duties must not be confused with customs duties although they are levied by the same body. They are fixed levies and, unlike VAT, which is proportional to value, excise duties tend to be fixed amounts for a specific volume of the commodity taxed.

Tobacco, alcohol and petrol are the goods on which European nations tend to levy excise duties. Countries in southern Europe tend to tax alcohol, especially wine, very lightly compared with the UK and states in northern Europe. With the absence of tariffs between EU members, this means a considerable discrepancy in retail prices between whisky and wine.

Proposed and unusual taxes

We have described the main taxes that are met in the UK and Europe but there are a few others of less importance which are or have been imposed and others that have their advocates as useful for one or another reason:

1. *Wealth tax* This is a tax on wealth as opposed to income or capital movements. It is found in a number of countries including Germany and India, and was used by the kings of England centuries ago when wealth was easier to estimate than income. The famous window tax of the seventeenth century was an example. It is based on total taxable capacity instead of income as a basis for making contributions to the public purse.

   In 1974 a government Green Paper on a wealth tax was proposed by the Labour government under Harold Wilson but agreement could not be reached on how it was to be administered and it is unlikely to be introduced in the near future. The objective of the tax was more rapid redistribution of wealth rather than more efficient raising of revenue.

2. *Payroll tax*   It has been argued that income taxes provide disincentives, especially to those who pay a high marginal rate of tax. One alternative suggested has been a payroll tax which is used in some countries. This is a tax on jobs, and while it may relieve the pressure on the taxation of incomes it is liable to make employers reluctant to give pay rises and to take on new staff. In the UK we have a payroll tax in the form of employers' National Insurance contribution and between 1966 and 1974 the UK had a Selective Employment Tax (SET) which was a tax on the number of employees. In a number of our European neighbours, however, this type of tax is more common.

3. *Investment surcharge*   Until 1984 in the UK individuals could face an investment income surcharge of 15 per cent. This was based on the idea that income from capital investment should be subject to higher rates of tax than earned income. While tax rules and laws are still careful to define 'earned' income there is no separate treatment of interest, dividends, or other forms of investment income.

Table 14.4 gives the major tax rates at the time this edition was published with space for purchasers of copies to add later changes—this way, you can keep up-to-date figures to hand when reading this chapter. Attention is also drawn to Case Study 14.3 which concerns advice given to the Chancellor of the Exchequer regarding taxation.

Case Study 14.3—Advice to a Chancellor

In 1993 there were two budgets. The last March budget was presented by Norman Lamont and this article from the *Observer* discusses some of the advice which the Chancellor was given from different sources. In November that year the Autumn Statement and Budget were combined and delivered by a new Chancellor, Kenneth Clarke.

BANK URGES LAMONT TO RAISE TAXES
William Keegan
Economics Editor

The Bank of England is believed to be pressing for tax increases in the Budget to help finance a soaring public sector borrowing requirement that could reach £50 billion in 1993–94.

The Bank is supported by certain Treasury officials on the finance side, who are also concerned by the PSBR problem. But the pre-Budget strategy meeting at Chevening in Kent yesterday is understood to have come to no firm conclusions.

Chancellor Norman Lamont's options range from raising VAT, broadening the scope of indirect taxation, and even attacking the Conservatives' sacred cow of mortgage tax relief. But the prevailing view was that it is too early to make a final Budget judgement, because economic indicators are ambiguous.

The two day Chevening meeting of Treasury Ministers and officials was chaired by Lamont. Some of his key officials have some sympathy with the Prime Minister's view that with economic recovery far from established and unemployment still mounting fast, it would be dangerous—both politically and economically—to risk a further blow to industry and consumer confidence with tax increases.

But officials from the Bank as well as some from the Treasury, are concerned about market reaction to the growing PSBR. They argue that a determined assault on the PSBR should be mounted soon, with the aim of securing lower long-term interest rates and a sound basis for economic recovery in the medium term.

According to such officials, institutional cash flow cannot support a PSBR of much more than £40 billion, and the financing of the PSBR would be dangerously dependent on inflows from overseas, with worrying implications for future reductions in interest rates. But leading monetarist economists who have shown concern for the PSBR in the past are so worried about the poor prospects for recovery that they would rather abandon the present 'full funding' rule and 'print money' to establish a firm economic recovery.

Given the uncertainty about the state of the economy, and the strong differences on opinion about policy, senior Whitehall sources indicate that the key measures may effectively be delayed until December, which sees the beginning of the new Budget timetable. The Chancellor announced last spring that the Budget and Autumn statement would in future be presented together, with two budgets this year.

Officials also emphasise that much of this March's Budget was contained in the November Autumn Statement. The Chancellor then announced a temporary increase in capital allowances, ruled out increases in National Insurance contributions 'given the current weakness of the economy', and signalled other tax rises this spring to offset the budgetary cost of the removal of car tax.

Any tax increases this year are almost certain to involve contradiction of the spirit (and possibly the letter) of pledges made by the Conservatives during the election campaign. Given the Government's general unpopularity, this is another reason why John Major would prefer to delay fiscal action until later this year.

One particularly sensitive area is the form any tax increases would take. While urging action to contain the deficit, the Bank is not keen on any VAT actions which would affect the retail prices index. This is regarded as a sensitive time in the battle to convince the markets that the conquest of inflation is still a top priority and VAT-induced increases in the RPI would be seen as 'own goals'.

Source: *Observer*, 10 January 1993, reproduced with permission.

With the help of this article by a leading economic journalist, you might like to consider the following questions:

1. What methods of satisfying the PSBR are mentioned here? Why would some economists like to abandon 'full funding'?
2. If the aim of raising taxes is to generate revenue and so cut the PSBR, what taxes would be most suitable and why? What are the particular problems with VAT mentioned here?

Advantages of indirect taxation

The main advantages of indirect taxes are usually seen as being the following:

1. They are *less detrimental to production*. Indirect taxes, or 'outlay' taxes, do not deter overtime work as may do high direct taxes.
2. They give *greater freedom of choice*. Indirect taxation leaves an individual with more disposable income than would be the case if the revenue were gained by direct taxation. More may be paid for goods and services but there is more freedom of choice.
3. They are *avoidable*. As an extension of the previous point, we can see that it is possible actually to avoid paying indirect tax, i.e. to avoid buying goods that are taxed, assuming that there are any untaxed commodities available! Life would be rather dull, however, and since there is an increasing spread of VAT across the range of goods and services, it would be very difficult to avoid tax altogether.
4. They are *hidden taxes* An indirect tax is usually hidden. Apart from the week when the annual review of taxes takes place (the 'Budget' in the UK), people are not so aware of paying taxes when they are a component of prices.
5. They are *difficult to evade*. Whereas income tax is dodged at every level, VAT and excise duties are levied through businesses and it is very difficult for a firm of any size and reputation to hide an attempt at evasion.
6. They can be a *corrective tax*. Taxes may be placed on goods that the government does not want people to buy in excess such as tobacco products and alcohol. Import duties can be used to control the level of imports, although powers to do this are diminishing with increased free trade.

Disadvantages of indirect taxation

Although we have compiled an impressive list of advantages of indirect taxation and it is the favoured tax in France and a number of other countries, there are some serious disadvantages. Two in particular are sufficiently serious to cause many people to view indirect taxation with suspicion:

1. *They are inflationary.* By imposing a tax on a good the price will increase, and this has an inflationary effect. This is especially the case if the tax is on a vital product such as petrol or food. In the UK food has been generally free of tax but in some European countries this is not the case, and there have been suggestions that it be extended to food in the UK.

   Experience with taxing petrol does not give encouragement to extend taxation to food in view of the effect on the cost of living. Petrol and diesel fuel are especially suspect as the targets for heavy tax, although they are usually among the regular sufferers in the Budget. Demand is inelastic, which makes them good earners for the Treasury, but the effect makes itself felt throughout most of the economy in view of the importance of transport for industry and retailing.

2. *They are regressive.* Again, this is the case particularly with essentials such as food, alcohol, petrol and clothes. If the tax is paid, at least to some extent, by the final consumer then the amount paid in tax will only indirectly be related to income. A family on low income, perhaps below the income tax threshold, will still be liable for VAT or excise duties because they are incorporated into the price of the products they buy. This tax element in purchases is likely to be a far higher proportion of income than the tax element for a richer person, even though the latter may spend a lot more in total.

Some taxes are better than others

We have just seen that there are many types of tax and as we have described them we have also mentioned some advantages and disadvantages. How, then, can we, as economists, make an analysis of taxes to see if one is better than another?

There is probably no such thing as the perfect tax and which of the many types is preferred by a government will depend very much on the objectives in imposing the tax. However, there are certain concepts and tools which we can use to make the decision a little more precise.

Is the tax progressive?

We have already demonstrated that there is a difference between proportional, progressive and regressive taxes. There is some argument among politicians as to whether a progressive tax is fairer or not than a proportional tax. Few people would support the idea of a tax being deliberately regressive, but unfortunately many common taxes are. We have seen that excise duties and the now–defunct 'poll tax' are regressive. In fact, any tax which involves people paying the same amount whatever their income is going to be regressive, even if there is a measure of proportional measurement in it, like VAT. There is an unfortunate tendency for governments to levy such taxes on goods which are especially favoured by the less well off, such as tobacco and alcohol.

Progressive taxes are used if re-distribution of wealth is desired either as a prime or a secondary use of a tax. It can involve using higher rates of, say, income tax for people with higher incomes. In the UK there have been higher rate tax bands to achieve that. It is, however, achieved to some extent by any system which allows non-taxable allowances to be claimed before tax is levied. Again, this is a characteristic of the UK income tax, capital gains and inheritance taxes. To see how this works in practice for UK income tax the reader is advised to refer to Advanced Study Topic 14.1 and for further theoretical treatment to Begg, Chapter 16.

We can perhaps best explore the idea further by examining two further concepts, i.e. average and marginal tax rates.

What is the rate of tax paid?

If we assume that income tax has 'free pay' of £3000 for all taxpayers then someone earning £4000 will only pay tax on £1000. If the rate is 25 per cent then £250 will be paid. This amounts to an average rate of 6.25 per cent on total earnings (i.e. £250 is 6.25 per cent of £4000). A neighbour earning £10 000, on the other hand, will pay tax on £7000, i.e. £1750. This represents an average tax rate of 17.5 per cent. Not only is the person with the higher income paying more in total but they also have a higher *average* rate of tax. This key figure is found simply by calculating the total tax paid and expressing it as a proportion of the total income.

We can use this simple figure to show that a tax with an allowance or lower threshold will be progressive because the free allowance becomes an increasingly smaller proportion of total income as earnings rise and so the average tax rate will increase.

However, an equally important statistic is the *marginal* tax rate which is the proportion of the last pound, lira or franc earned which disappears to the government as tax. In the case of income tax it will be the tax rate as a percentage applying to the final unit of earnings. For UK income tax a person on a normal tax code will have a nil marginal rate of tax if their total earnings are, say, £3000 a year. On the other hand, if earnings are £10 000 a year then the marginal rate will be the standard rate of tax. Someone earning £50 000 a year will have a marginal tax rate which will be at the higher level. Both our £10 000 earner and our £50 000 big-timer will have personal and other allowances and so do not pay tax on all of their earnings—but the marginal rate is that which applies to the highest £1.

The marginal tax rate helps us to understand one major problem with progressive taxes. They may help to equalize earnings and wealth but they do create a disincentive to work. Higher band rates went up to as much as 83 per cent in 1978–9 although it fell considerably during the following decade. This does explain why some 'top people' get large pay rises, and while this may seem unfair when others have only limited increases, a large amount of the increase may well be going to the Inland Revenue.

If people work harder or get a better job and then end up paying more tax because they get into a higher marginal rate, then they may not be inclined to make the effort. This can apply at both the higher earnings level, which will produce newspaper articles on the 'brain drain' of talent overseas, and also at the lower end, where we get the problem of people who have earned very little, perhaps being unemployed or on benefit, getting a job which pays slightly above the upper limit for benefits and the lower limit for income tax and National Insurance. Many unemployed people refuse low-paid jobs because they will be little better off and perhaps even worse off. Their marginal tax rate has moved from nil to the initial rate.

Steps have been taken to deal with the problem at both ends in the UK system. At the higher earnings end, the bands for higher rates have been cut in number as well as in rate on the grounds that the highest disincentives occur if people get a rise which takes them into a new band. For the tax year 1992–3 there was only one higher rate band (40 per cent) but back in 1978–9 there were ten bands above the basic rate. Some of the bands were only £1000 wide so a sizeable pay rise for higher earners could easily move them into a higher band and eliminate a fair proportion of the rise. In Fig. 14.8 we can see a simplified banding as applied in 1987–8 with five bands above the basic.

At the other end of the income scale various possible solutions have been put forward to solve the problem, including the concept of a negative income tax. This means that there would be more of a sliding scale and below a certain level of income, benefits would gradually become available but above this level, the income would be taxable, at gradually

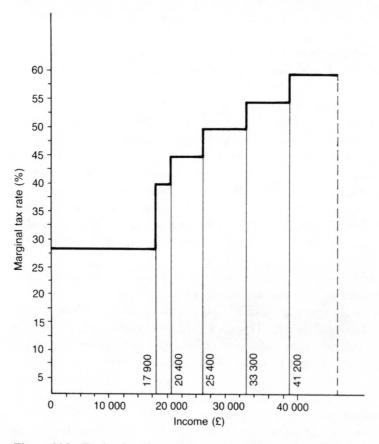

Figure 14.8 Tax bands and marginal tax rate—UK income tax 1987–8.

increasing rates. The 20 per cent lower rate band in the UK income tax system was inserted especially to remove some of the disincentives for lower-paid workers and those on benefit in getting a job.

Who pays indirect taxes?

If we want to analyse indirect taxes we come up against another problem—does the tax get paid by the person whom it was originally intended should pay it? This question involves looking at a concept called the *incidence* of a tax.

In Chapter 5 we looked at the movement of a supply curve as a result of the imposition of a tax and saw that this had an effect on price and that this effect varied with the elasticities of supply and demand. We need to consider this again and ask what this means in terms of who pays the tax.

Consider Fig. 14.9 which gives possible demand and supply curves for bottles of cider. If we assume that the market demand and supply curves are D–D and S_1, respectively then the equilibrium price is at P_1 and the quantity purchased at this price is Q_1. Now the government decides to impose an excise duty of 20p a litre bottle. As we saw in Chapter 5, the producer will now revise the supply schedule to make allowance for this tax for which the producer will be made responsible for paying to Customs & Excise. A new supply curve will now appear, S_2 and new equilibrium price level will be found at P_2.

Now the question is, *who* pays the tax? The producer pays the 20p per bottle to the tax collectors but the question is whether or not it can be passed on to the customer. If it is

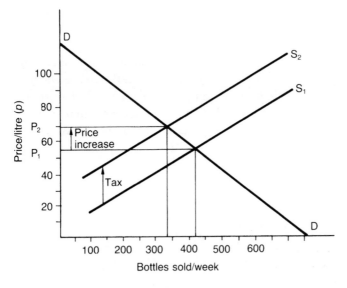

Figure 14.9   Excise duty on cider.

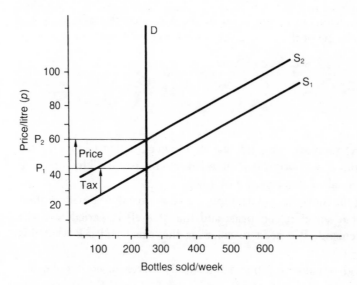

Figure 14.10   Excise duty: inelastic demand.

all passed on, then the incidence of the tax is said to fall on the final consumer, but if it is not all passed on then the producer will bear some of the incidence in reduced profit.

In the example above, not all of the tax is passed on to the consumer but in Fig. 14.10 it is. What is the difference?

In Fig. 14.10 the demand is totally inelastic and the demand curve is a straight line. In general, we can say that for a product with inelastic demand, where the customers cannot go anywhere else and must buy, then the incidence of the tax is completely passed on. If demand is totally elastic then the incidence will rest on the producer. At elasticities between, the degree to which incidence of a tax can be passed on will depend on the shape of the demand curve.

We have used the example here of a flat duty of a specific amount per unit which causes the supply curve to move upwards parallel to the original one. But in the UK most goods have VAT imposed on them which is a proportional tax, i.e. instead of a flat level tax per unit we have a tax of a set percentage of each £1 value. These are often known as *ad valorem* taxes (i.e. tax is according to value). In such a case the supply curve will still move upwards but not parallel to the original position. This is shown in Fig. 14.11 and was also discussed and illustrated in Chapter 5 and Fig. 5.37.

Is the tax efficient?

One of the principles of taxation is that it should be efficient, in terms of both collecting as much revenue with minimum cost as possible and also least interference with the efficiency of the economy as a whole. Any tax is likely to interfere with market forces and so disturb equilibrium positions and create artificial price rises.

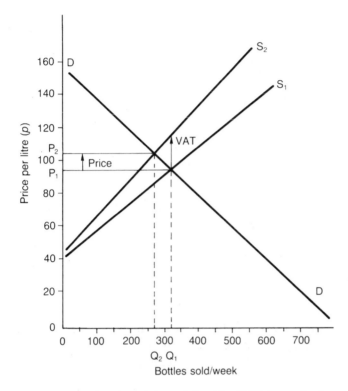

Figure 14.11   Supply and demand for cider: VAT-imposed price per litre (*p*).

One of the tools of analysis to help us here is known as the *Laffer curve*. Developed by the American economist Arthur Laffer, this relates tax rates to tax revenue and demonstrates the relative efficiency or inefficiency of a particular rate of tax in producing revenue and indicates, at the same time, the effect of tax rates on incentives to work.

The Laffer curve as it has been applied to the UK is seen in Fig. 14.12. This shows that as tax rates rise so revenue rises until a peak is reached, after which revenue falls. The fall is due to lack of incentive for work by those being taxed. M. Beenstock of the London Business School considered that a rate of 60 per cent of GDP for both direct and indirect taxes was the UK limit. In the USA, where the concept was developed, a rate of more like 75–80 per cent with an almost vertical slope thereafter was about right.

One use of the Laffer curve might be to suggest to the Exchequer that a reduction in overall rates could increase revenues. For example, if rates were at 65 per cent in the UK it would be more efficient for them to be reduced to 55 per cent, as more revenue would result.

The further use of the curve to indicate motivation problems with high tax rates has had some support, by now legendary, from former US president Ronald Reagan. On learning of this relationship he commented that he had experienced the situation in his days as a young film actor at a time when income tax rates were very high. It was

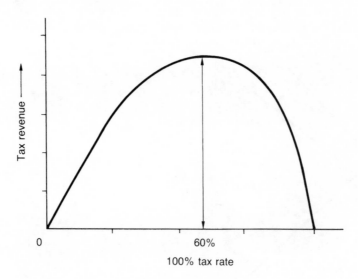

Figure 14.12   The Laffer curve (UK).

accepted in the industry that if an actor made four films a year that was the maximum it made sense to make, since the fifth film's earnings mainly went to the tax inspector! This is sometimes called a *supply side* problem in that output is held back by the disincentive.

Tax yield

In relation to this question we might find it useful to look at the *yield* of a tax. The government must consider not only the best tax rate with the Laffer curve in mind but also whether a tax increase will bring in more revenue in any case. There is much expense in administering the tax system, and any amendments to rates or procedure involves a lot of printing and distribution costs as well as the problems caused by those who do not receive the new rates.

In Fig. 14.10 we looked at the situation when an excise tax was imposed on a good. If the Exchequer wishes to increase a rate even further it has to take into account the simple question 'Will it bring in more money?' The answer usually depends on the elasticity of demand for that product. Consider Fig. 14.13. If the shaded areas represent tax yields for the two tax levels, the reader might like to compare the result of the increase in the light of the difference in the gradients of the two demand curves.

Taxable capacity

It has been suggested that there is an upper limit to the amount that a government can take in the form of taxation. When the economy is harmed by excessive taxation we can say that it has reached its *taxable capacity*. The results of taxing in excess of this limit can include encouraging a 'brain drain' of top managers and scientists, reduction in overtime

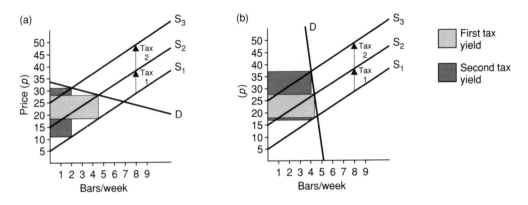

Figure 14.13   Tax yield on chocolate bars assuming two types of demand curve.

and incentives to work, reduction on private investment and either wage or price inflation.

The taxable capacity of a nation depends to some extent on the level of services which are being provided. If the state provides universal pensions, a health service and education then taxes can be higher than they would be in a country without these benefits. Basically, people are simply paying for the benefits through the tax system instead of privately.

Topic 14.4   The budget and borrowing

What is the 'budget'?

One of the most important tasks which any government has to do is to ensure that its income balances its expenditure. Some people have likened this role to that of the household, which also has to ensure that spending does not exceed the income received. In fact, as we will see later, it is more complex than just balancing the books, but it is of fundamental importance that each year the government decides what it will spend and how it is to receive the money.

All governments have a member who is responsible for ensuring this is done and they usually have the title of Finance Minister or something similar. In the UK the job title is 'Chancellor of the Exchequer' and in many respects this job is second in importance only to that of Prime Minister. The Chancellor's department of state is called the Treasury and it is responsible for coordinating all government spending and for allocating revenue, although the detailed collection of taxes is undertaken by the Inland Revenue and other agencies.

The estimates of expenditure are prepared for each government department annually and are made within a broad long-term framework. Each year the Chancellor presents to Parliament the Finance Act for that year in the form of a document which is known as the

Budget. Each November this document will give details of proposed spending, a general review of the economy and its prospects and the Chancellor's proposals for taxation and government borrowing. It is usually a matter of some publicity and debate and receives wide press coverage because it has an immediate input into all our lives. Before 1993, the Budget was introduced in March and there was a separate 'Autumn Statement' which outlined proposed spending but these are now combined in the autumn.

The main task of the Chancellor is to ensure that the government can meet its bills and that whatever it decides to spend will be matched by taxation revenue, the small amount of trading revenue, or government borrowing. The amount which the government intends to borrow is known as the *public sector borrowing requirement*. It has much more significance than just being a means of bridging the gap between spending levels and tax revenue.

Years ago, budgetary measures (or *fiscal policies*, as they are normally called) were looked upon merely as a means of raising revenue. It is now realized that the Budget may be used as an instrument of economic policy. When assessing his or her proposals the Chancellor needs to consider the country's economic prospects as well as simply balancing the books.

Taxation and the budget

As we have seen, the Chancellor has a wide range of taxes available. As Case Study 14.3 shows, there is no shortage of advice on which ones are the best. The tax system has evolved gradually over the years and, despite the annual changes, there is a high degree of consistency over the relative importance of each tax. Figure 14.14 indicates the main sources of tax revenue in recent years. National Insurance funds are not included in that figure.

The trends over the last ten years have been in the direction of an increase in total revenue from taxes on income (for the most part, collected by the Inland Revenue) and on expenditure (collected by Customs & Excise). There has, however, been a decrease in revenue from the petroleum revenue tax and from alcohol and tobacco. The largest increase has been in revenue from corporation tax.

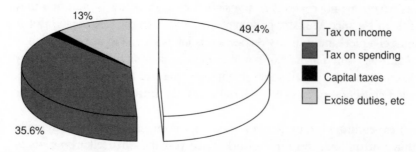

Figure 14.14 UK tax revenue 1990–91 (%). (*Source: Annual Abstract of Statistics.*)

Government borrowing

Although in an ideal world the spending of the government departments would be funded from taxation, in reality this is rarely the case. For one thing, it takes time to assess people for tax and to collect the money in. Companies and the self-employed pay tax on income acquired during the previous tax year, and only with direct taxes and income tax is there any immediate levy. Even then, it can take time for employers to pass on the tax and National Insurance collected and for shops and manufacturers to pass on VAT and excise duties.

Some borrowing is likely to be required, then, to finance public spending while waiting for tax receipts to arrive. However, at times many governments prefer to borrow rather than to tax. If interest rates are low this may be cost-effective. More usually, borrowing is seen as a way of manipulating the economy. For example, if it is felt that not enough of private savings is being used for investment in industry or infrastructure then by systematic borrowing of these savings the government can ensure that they are diverted to a use which will benefit the economy of the country.

In many cases the government will wish to spend more than it can collect from taxes and not wish to increase taxation appreciably. This may be with the object of increasing demand in the economy and so stimulating growth, since public spending can be directed to industries, regions and projects where it can have most effect.

A planned shortfall of tax receipts over spending is known as a *budget deficit* and if this is to be met entirely by borrowing then it becomes the PSBR. This figure includes local government and public corporations as well as central government needs. Figure 14.15 indicates recent changes in the PSBR, especially in the period from 1988 to 1992. In fact, in recent years, far from borrowing money, the UK government has sought to provide a net repayment of the total debt. This has largely been achieved by strict control and restriction of public spending. The government has also gained from the sale of former state-owned industries in its privatization campaign.

If the government borrows money it will do this in one of three ways:

1. To increase the money supply through the Bank of England. Through this method the government sells securities to the Bank in return for newly printed cash which it can spend.
2. To borrow from the UK private sector, again by selling securities. In this case they are sold on by the Bank of England to banking institutions or the public at large. Gilts, for example, can be bought through post offices.
3. The government can borrow from overseas investors.

Which option is chosen may well depend on the other objectives of government policy such as inflation control and this will be examined in the next chapter.

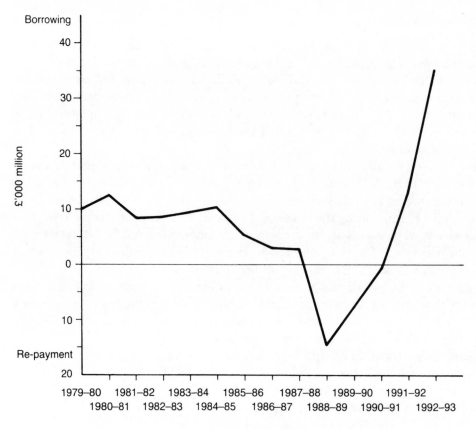

Figure 14.15   Public sector borrowing requirements 1979–93.

Topic 14.5   What is the National Debt?

The National Debt is the accumulated borrowing of the government and represents a *stock* of debt as opposed to the *flow* deficiency represented by the PSBR. It is money owed by a country to its citizens and, to some extent, also overseas citizens and governments. It represents central government debt and not that of local authorities. Some countries are notorious for the size of their national debt, especially the less-developed countries which may have borrowed heavily from banks and international agencies.

The National Debt may be divided broadly into two types of liability:

1. *Marketable securities*   These can be bought and sold in the open market, usually the Stock Exchange in the UK or the equivalent institution in other countries. The money markets in general also deal in many of these securities and they provide valuable 'oil' to the machinery of the financial markets. The securities include gilts (gilt-edged securities) and Treasury bills (see Chapter 12).

2. *Non-marketable securities*   These must be held and redeemed by the original buyer and cannot be sold on. It is mainly in the form of National Savings and especially appeals to the ordinary citizen looking for a very safe form of saving.

The largest section of the National Debt is classified as UK *official holdings*. These include:

- Holdings of the National Debt Commissioners—for example, investment in government securities, National Insurance funds and money deposited in the ordinary accounts of the National savings Bank
- Holdings of the Bank of England's Issue Department as backing for the issue of banknotes
- Holdings of the Banking Department of the Bank of England.

How much of a burden is the National Debt?

Although we have seen that the National Debt has increased enormously and now stands at about £200 000 million, it is not much more of a burden than it was before the Second World War. In real terms per head of population there is little difference between 1939 and 1993. In terms of interest it costs the UK about £11 000 million per year or about £200 per person.

As the National Debt is shared between a larger number of people because of population growth, and as the value of money has fallen with inflation, the National Debt is not the overwhelming burden it might be thought to be. Some of the old debt is very cheap—War Loan, for example, pays an interest rate ($3\frac{1}{2}$ per cent) which would be far too low to gain any 'takers' if it were issued at that rate today. Most of the National Debt is internal to the UK and so interest payments are little more than transfer payments within the UK. The same can be observed for most European countries and the USA, although not necessarily for less-developed nations with a large burden of overseas debt.

Effectively, then, the UK economy is no worse off for the National Debt. Interest paid by the government provides income for UK residents which in turn is spent, generating further income and further taxation revenues. As long as the National Debt continues to rise at a lower rate than GDP in the long term, there will be a net benefit rather than problems. In recent years, as we have seen, there has even been some repayment of the National Debt.

One problem of the National Debt however, is that interest payments go to those who hold government securities and the money spent in this way can be seen to deprive other sections of the community of schools, hospitals, roads and other possible spending projects. On the other hand, securities, and especially gilts, lie behind many of the long-term assets of all sections of the population, including life assurance and pension funds, so few people gain nothing from its existence.

Topic 14.6   Public enterprise

We have already seen in Chapter 7 that alongside the limited companies, partnerships and sole traders there are large corporate bodies which are state owned and that these are called public corporations. There are also some firms that are public limited companies (i.e. normal companies owned by shareholders) in which the government has a shareholding, and there have been bodies known as 'statutory boards' which have been usually responsible for administering key public utilities.

In recent years the number of bodies in all three categories which are state owned has been considerably reduced by the policy of *privatization* introduced by the Conservative government. Students of economics fifteen years ago studied the public sector with great interest and it was indeed very important because of its size. Today it is much smaller and is likely to reduce further as the railways and coal industry, the last two major areas of state ownership, move into private hands. The same process has also been carried out in most EU countries, including France, Germany, Spain and Italy. As a result, this section now looks at privatization rather than nationalization.

It is useful, however, to consider why much of UK industry was brought into state hands. Apart from a few industries and public utilities (the largest being the Post Office, originally part of the Civil Service), the nationalization of key industries took place mainly under the Labour administration of Clement Attlee which came to power in 1945. Prime targets were the Bank of England, the coal industry, the railways, public utilities such as gas and electricity, the airlines (originally BOAC and BEA) and, controversially, the iron and steel industry. As it happens, the Conservative Party was generally happy to accept these changes with the exception of iron and steel, which suffered successive acts of nationalization and denationalization as power changed between the parties.

In the 1970s the National Enterprise Board was established to aid industries in difficulties, holding shares in return for financial input. A number of 'lame ducks' were helped, some through the NEB with the government holding either a majority or a minority stake—Rolls-Royce, British Leyland and Alfred Herbert, to name just three. A stake was also obtained in the North Sea oil industry through the British National Oil Corporation.

The reasons for nationalization included:

1.   The desire to control key sectors of the economy, sometimes called the 'commanding heights of the economy', such as the Bank of England and the coal industry.
2.   Some public utilities and services, such as gas and electricity supply, the railways and the Port of London, can only effectively be operated by one body. These 'natural monopolies' were thought to be safer under state control.
3.   In the case of some industries economies of scale will only operate if the scale of ownership and operation is large enough and state ownership also facilitates this type of natural monopoly.

4. There was a desire to establish uniform standards of public service throughout the country. Reduction of negative externalities was also a factor of importance.
5. National security was a reason for state ownership of nuclear power.

Marginal cost pricing

In perfect competition products are priced by the interaction of supply and demand and the supply curve is also the industry's marginal cost curve. In 1967 the government introduced the idea that state-owned industries should adopt marginal cost pricing as a principle. The concept of marginal cost pricing was introduced in Chapter 5, and at this point the reader might wish to refer to the graph and text which describes it. Governments found, however, that this proved difficult because there was also a view held, especially by those of socialist persuasion, that these industries should provide a public service. What, for example, should be done about small railway branch lines which were uneconomic but provided an essential service to local communities? In the late 1950s Dr Richard Beeching, as Minister of Transport, solved this problem by axing most of the branch network. The result was that a number of isolated villages lost a vital service and more pressure was placed on roads in rural areas.

Consequently, the government adopted what has been called a 'second-best' option of insisting on marginal cost pricing as a basis but being willing to subsidize public services where this was necessary. However, by the end of the 1970s many state-owned enterprises were absorbing a lot of state funding, running at a loss because marginal costs were below average costs, and inefficient. The result was the privatization programme.

The list of privatized industries in Table 14.5 is still being added to and the amount of industrial output and essential services in state hands is becoming very small. It is

Table 14.5   UK privatization in outline

Year	Major corporations/industries
1979	British Petroleum (stage 1)
1981	British Aerospace (stage 1); British Petroleum (stage 2)
1982	Britoil; National Freight
1983	British Petroleum (stage 3)
1984	British Telecom; Jaguar Cars
1985	British Aerospace (stage 2); Britoil (stage 2)
1986	British Gas; National Bus Co.
1987	British Airways; British Petroleum (stage 4); Rolls-Royce
1988	British Steel; Rover Group
1989	Water Boards
1990	Electricity Boards (power distribution)
1991	National Power (generation)
1993	British Telecom (stage 2)
1994	British Rail (services)

unlikely that the Bank of England will be returned to private hands, but most other enterprises are likely to be, even if a state monopoly is replaced by a private one.

The roots of privatization actually go back to the Heath administration in the early 1970s when a programme of 'hiving off' of profitable parts of state enterprise was carried on, but during the Thatcher era a widespread plan to privatize whole industries was carried out. British Petroleum, a public company in which the government had a substantial shareholding, was the first to be sold off, in stages. Some of the public developed a taste, deliberately fostered by the government, for buying shares, and when British Telecom was privatized in 1984 there was considerable public enthusiasm. To follow was British Gas, British Airways and the water boards, with smaller sell-offs *en route*.

The public enthusiasm was in large part the result of the government's decision to sell off the enterprises at a price below the likely market price. Only Britoil showed a loss on share prices. The result was that a nation of 'stags' was produced, and the early success of the privatization was one contributing factor producing the stock market crash of 1987.

One of the reasons for privatization is said to be the encouragement of competition, but in most cases the natural monopoly conditions effectively shut out competitors. Even the competition of Mercury to British Telecom has not been effective enough to make much difference to the telecommunications giant. Arguments over privatization tend to be of a political nature and in economic terms the change of ownership may be of little significance. A private monopoly, unless closely regulated by state 'watchdogs', is not likely to provide a better service without considerably raising prices. One advantage to the government is the 'windfall' income from the sale of privatized shares.

The reader wishing to explore this topic further is advised to consult Begg, Chapter 18.

Advanced Study Topic 14.1   The pay slip

Most people work in order to earn and the best time in the month is pay day! However, many workers have great difficulty in interpreting the entries on a pay slip because in the UK employers have the responsibility for deducting income tax and National Insurance through the PAYE system.

Each person in employment has a tax code which is the basis for their tax calculation. This code determines the level of pay which is not subject to tax—known as 'free pay'. After free pay has been deducted the rest is subject to tax and is known therefore as 'taxable pay'. The employer will deduct tax at basic rate and then reduce the tax bill to account for the lower rate element. If the employer is subject to higher band tax this is also deducted.

National Insurance is deducted at the same time. Earnings are banded and total or gross earnings give a level of National Insurance which is due. The employer pays part of the total, usually rather more than half, and the employee the rest.

The whole system is designed to make tax and National Insurance collection easy and economical. The employer has the responsibility to pay the Inland Revenue, which receives both tax and National Insurance contributions, so that the collection costs are kept to a minimum. For a person with an employed job and no other source of income, tax and National Insurance are taken care of very neatly.

Students wishing to investigate the PAYE system are recommended to visit one of the local Inland Revenue offices which normally have a wide range of leaflets available.

Essay questions

1. (a) Outline the principles which ought to be considered when deciding to introduce a new tax.
   (b) Evaluate the relative merits of local income taxes and property taxes as methods of raising revenue to finance local government expenditure.
   (*Source*: The Associated Examining Board, June 1993)
2. What have been the main trends in the competition of public expenditure over the last decade? Should the continuing growth of public expenditure be a source of concern? (*Source*: Oxford and Cambridge Schools Examination Board, June 1991)
3. 'The riches of North Sea Oil—over £100 billion in tax revenue alone—could have been used to transform Britain's economy. Instead they have been squandered.' Do you agree? (*Source*: Oxford and Cambridge Schools Examination Board, June 1992)
4. Most of the recently privatized companies are regularly reporting large profits. Is this a cause for concern? (*Source*: Oxford and Cambridge Schools Examination Board, June 1992)
5. Consider the relative merits of a local value added tax and a poll tax. (*Source*: Oxford and Cambridge Schools Examination Board, June 1991)
6. 'When the revenue from indirect taxes equals expenditure on subsidies, economic welfare is unchanged.' Discuss. (*Source*: Oxford and Cambridge Schools Examination Board, June 1992)
7. Explain the relationship between the PSBR and the National Debt. Would there be any advantage to the UK in repaying the National Debt? (*Source*: Northern Examinations and Assessment Board, June 1992)
8. 'The Public Sector Borrowing Requirement will always rise in a recession and it is desirable that it does so.'
   'The Public Sector Borrowing Requirement contributes to the rate of growth of the money supply and it is essential that it is strictly controlled at all times.' Discuss. (*Source*: University of Oxford, June 1993)
9. Explain why we need taxes and outline the requirements of a good tax. Compare the community charge, the council tax, and a local income tax as means of raising revenue to finance local government. (*Source*: Northern Examination and Assessment Board, June 1993)

Chapter 15

Principles of government economic policy

This chapter applies much of the theory we have examined in previous chapters to political reality and explores how governments use economic theory in order to achieve specific policy objectives. In many ways the chapter looks at the major issues found in the newspapers when economic matters are prominent. It also has the benefit of bringing together much of the subject matter of economics and provides a fitting finale to our studies.

Topic 15.1 Macro-economic objectives of government

Governments use economic theory in order to achieve certain objectives or goals which are desirable for reasons of either social welfare or politics. We need here to be clear in the distinction between the *objectives* of policy and the means by which these objectives are attained. The latter are usually known as *policy instruments*. There can be some overlap between them, as with interest rates, which can be both objective and instrument, but, on the whole, they are distinct.

Policy objectives

Objectives will vary from country to country and between political groups. For example, the Labour Party in Britain had a long-standing objective of bringing under public ownership 'the means of production, distribution and exchange', but few members of the party would now want to take that objective to its logical conclusion. Similarly, there are wide differences both between and within parties on attitudes to social welfare and benefits. Environmental objectives come to the political fore with some parties such as the Greens in Germany while nationalistic objectives are prominent, with tragic consequences in some cases, in many East European countries.

The common objectives which most governments hold fundamental are the following:

1. Maintaining a high level of *employment* so that most people in the working population who desire a job do in fact have one. The former USSR refused to recognize

unemployment and everyone had a job, but the result was a lot of underemployment and deliberate job creation. The UK under Margaret Thatcher in the 1980s tended to adopt a more *laissez-faire* attitude to employment.

Unemployment is often a spin-off of other objectives and cannot be pursued in isolation.

There can be a trade-off between unemployment and inflation, and whatever the accuracy of the Phillips curve relationship, the two objectives are certainly connected. The policy of John Major's administration in the UK in the early 1990s recognized the likelihood of relatively high unemployment as part of the cost of lower inflation.

One of the problems with the objective of 'full employment', as it is usually phrased, is in practical definition. We have already seen that the term cannot reasonably mean that every able-bodied person has a job, since there are always some voluntary and temporary unemployed plus those who are ill or retired or workshy. The concept of a 'natural' level of unemployment, considered by many economists to be about 6 per cent, is useful and has been adopted by many governments, but those of more left-wing persuasion may wish to reduce the figures further. In the UK, the significance of different levels of unemployment to politicians has been almost psychological, with the 1 million and 3 million marks being seen as especially important. In economics, specific numbers are not significant, but percentages are.

There are many reasons why people can be out of a job. Not surprisingly, therefore, there are many ways of reducing unemployment and when we look at policy instruments later we will explore this variety further.

2. Control of *inflation* is a second important objective and is, as we have seen, related to the question of unemployment. The causes and problems of inflation were fully discussed in Chapter 13. For a government there are two decisions which have to be made in relation to inflation.

The first of these is what level to accept. It is usually considered that business benefits from inflation at a low level in that firms can gain small 'windfall' profits from gradually increasing prices. There is no reason, however, why there should be inflation at all, and 0 per cent growth in price levels has been suggested as a long-term objective in the UK, although the official aim is a growth of less than 4 per cent. The Bundesbank has had the responsibility of keeping Germany's inflation rate low and taking whatever steps are necessary to do this, but the bank is independent of the federal government, and so this is long-term national strategy rather than a government objective. In most other countries the central bank is, to a greater or lesser extent, under the control of the government of the day and its actions will thus reflect the policies of that government.

The second problem is which approach to adopt to deal with inflation. There are many policy instruments that can be used, but before deciding on this level of detail a government needs to consider whether it will use a Keynesian or a monetarist approach or perhaps try to get the best of both points of view. The two approaches

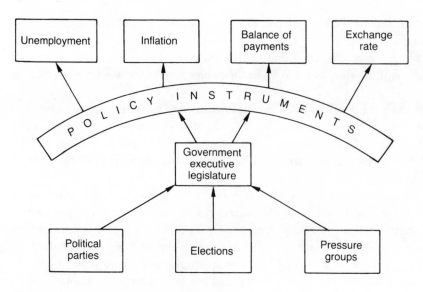

Figure 15.1   Policy objectives and instruments.

are not exclusive, as we will see later, but a government will set its sights on some instruments rather than others from whichever viewpoint it chooses (see Fig. 15.1).

3. The *balance of payments* is another key objective. As with inflation and unemployment, balance of payments figures are quoted regularly—on a monthly basis in the UK—and so there is frequent press comment on the situation. It is important, however, to be sure that the objectives are clear. For example, we can be concerned with the overall balance of payments or with visible trade only; we may restrict our concern to current account or take into account what is happening on capital transactions as well (see Chapter 10). It is also important to define the period of time which we hold as crucial. Any economy will show a deficit or surplus in any one year and a few years of persistent deficit or surplus may not be significant. However, a long-run trend, especially of deficit, will be more serious.

4. A stable *exchange rate* is a policy objective closely linked to any aims concerning balance of payments. However, it is also a policy instrument and objectives for the exchange rate as such are frequently abandoned as it is used as a tool for changing the balance of payments or dealing with inflation. This is the fundamental problem with the European Exchange Rate Mechanism (ERM). A member nation of the ERM will agree to keep its currency within a band in relation to other currencies (see Chapter 10), but in doing this it has to abandon use of the rate as a tool for changing other areas of the economy. Basically, the exchange rate ceases to be an instrument and becomes an objective.

Unfortunately, a high exchange rate is often regarded by politicians as a matter of national pride and they can see devaluation as a disgrace, despite the advantages which a low value for the currency might bring!

5. A fifth objective of governments is *economic growth*. Failure to grow is regarded as a failure of a government's economic policies with a persistent lack of growth in GDP being labelled as *recession*. The recession of the early 1990s was largely a worldwide phenomenon, and certainly not a feature of just one or two countries, but government policies can help or hinder growth out of such problems. Again, the problems are often linked with other objectives such as inflation and employment.

6. *Other objectives* include specifically political ones such as nationalization in the UK in the post-war years or privatization in the 1980s; social objectives such as an equal distribution of income and wealth; or objectives of mixed natures such as the desire to see a balanced growth and prosperity in specific regions of a country. This latter policy has been a key issue for the EU.

Policy instruments

We can look at policy instruments as falling into certain main groups—fiscal policy; monetary policy; exchange rate policy; supply side policies; and the medium-term financial strategy or MTFS. Prices and incomes policy has also been applied in some countries.

These will be examined in more detail in the next few sections. It is important at this stage, however, to recognize that policy instruments are not applied in isolation from each other, but frequently the use of one instrument, such as interest rates, will have a knock-on effect on other areas of the economy and involve counteracting measures with another instrument.

It is also vital not to conclude that governments which carry the label 'monetarist' only use monetary policies or that Keynesians only use fiscal ones. The difference is one of emphasis and priority. For example, the Conservative administration of John Major used high interest rates to reduce demand and help curb inflation, i.e. a monetary policy instrument. However, it also tried to restrict public spending for the same reason, i.e. a fiscal policy.

The next five sections look at the main instruments of economic policy and some aspects of a related issue, welfare economics.

Topic 15.2   Fiscal policy

Fiscal policy can be defined as the approach to economic policy which uses taxation and public expenditure as specific instruments, with the objective of trying to control, or at least influence, total demand in the economy. It has been especially associated with Keynesian economics and was the most common form of economic management in Europe and North America for about thirty years from 1945.

In the earlier post-war years, governments tended to set targets for economic growth; employment or taxation and public spending were adjusted accordingly. For example, if it was desired to expand demand in order to produce economic growth, then taxes could be reduced, especially income tax, which would increase disposable income. An increase in income tax would reduce disposable income and thus demand, while changes in expenditure taxes such as the UK's purchase tax or France's VAT (see Chapter 14) would change prices and thus have an influence on inflation.

The other side of the fiscal coin was public expenditure. After the Second World War, most countries in Western Europe were extensively involved in rebuilding. Germany had been heavily bombed and most of the infrastructure needed reconstruction. France suffered less from physical damage but the German occupation had not helped the economy to develop. In the UK there was bomb damage and also a need to switch factories from war production to that of normal capital and consumer goods.

While aid from the USA was vital in the 1940s the countries of Western Europe gave a high priority to public expenditure using their own funds, much of which was financed by high taxation. In the UK extensive construction took place in the 1960s with motorway and new town projects. Private enterprise took an important part in all of this, of course, with great successes for Volkswagen, Renault and Fiat in the motor industry, computer technology and financial services in the UK and, by the later 1960s, the North Sea oil industry providing a bonanza for some large multinational companies. However, there was considerable public investment in infrastructure, and by the 1970s some private companies in the UK also were asking for government finance to keep afloat.

Throughout much of the first thirty years after the war, there was little attempt to target or actively use the public sector borrowing requirement. The PSBR was regarded as the result of tax and spending decisions as a sort of automatic balancing mechanism. If more money was spent on roads, hospitals and schools, for example, than accrued from taxation, then the PSBR would be positive. The government would borrow the difference. The ultimate aim of fiscal policy was demand management using Keynes' model of macro-economics and this instrument either stimulated the economy by increasing employment or dampened down inflation.

The concept of the National Debt was introduced in Chapter 14 when we saw that this was the accumulated amount of indebtedness acquired by successive governments over the years. In any one year the National Debt can either be increased if there is a positive PSBR (i.e. money is borrowed from the money markets) or it can be reduced if tax and other revenues exceed public spending—in which case we have a PSDR (public sector debt repayment). Until 1987 a PSDR was rare but the government of Margaret Thatcher made it a minor objective of policy.

In general, the size of the National Debt is not a problem although the larger it becomes, the more tax revenues have to be diverted to paying the interest on it (known as 'servicing the debt'). The key feature is the changes taking place in the PSBR/PSDR. An increasing PSBR would normally indicate a policy of economic growth and expansion, although other factors such as business confidence in the private sector will also play a part in such growth. A falling PSBR could indicate restrictions on public spending and a tightening in the economy.

It is also important to appreciate that some of the debt is the result of factors outside the government's immediate control. For example, just as many businesses have overdraft facilities to cover a temporary shortfall of cash, even though on an annual basis they make a good profit, so the government may need to spend money before tax revenues have begun to arrive.

The process of managing the economy through fiscal means is known as *discretionary fiscal policy*. In the case of the UK the Chancellor of the Exchequer will adjust taxation or spending in the annual budget in late autumn to respond to any disequilibrium in the economy. The Budget (see Chapter 14), or financial statement in other European countries, sets the scene for the next 12 months but is usually prepared in response to a situation. It can be used to steer the public away from certain goods considered harmful (such as cigarettes), to stimulate supply or to redistribute wealth or income. (See Chapter 14 for details of types of tax.) The multiplier (Chapter 9) has a vital part to play here because if there is input of government funds then income will be created and the multiplier effect will produce an income ultimately some way in excess of the investment.

In addition to discretionary fiscal policy the government can rely on the operation of certain features known as *automatic stabilizers*. Figure 15.2 illustrates the operation of these. The stabilizers have the effect of moving changes in the level of national income towards a stable equilibrium. For example, with a progressive income tax system a rise in incomes will produce a more than proportional increase in tax revenues and perhaps marginal tax rates. In the end the better-off individuals will pay more to the tax office and disposable income will be reduced.

In theory, fiscal policy uses its two main instruments of taxation and public spending, with or without a PSBR, to 'fine-tune' the economy. A need for economic growth will

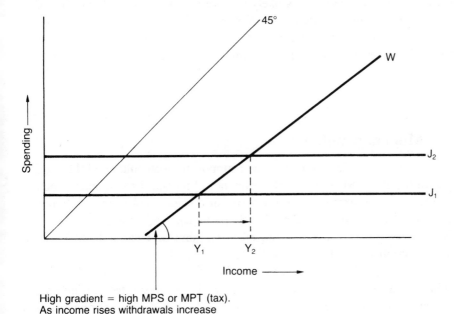

High gradient = high MPS or MPT (tax).
As income rises withdrawals increase

Figure 15.2   Automatic stabilizers.

result in a *reflationary* budget with a reduction in income tax and/or an increase in public spending. If, however, the result is inflation at too high a rate then the government will take *deflationary* measures such as increasing personal taxes or reducing public spending. The level of PSBR relates this to the money supply with monetary policy being used as a 'back-up' to the main fiscal stance.

Is fiscal policy effective? The answer will depend on a number of circumstances. The automatic stabilizers can be very useful. Suppose that the economy is in recession as in 1990–93. We do not want to have stability at that level of growth but if policies are taken to encourage expansion then the stabilizer effect may dampen down growth. This especially occurs where there is *fiscal drag* because increasing income results in higher tax deductions. There are also problems such as:

1. The time lag between implementing fine-tuning and obtaining the result. A long delay can reduce the effectiveness of the government's action.
2. If the time lag is long then external influences can begin to take effect such as a sudden deterioration or improvement in the exchange rate.
3. There are problems of knowledge and information—can future effects be accurately forecast and can we be certain of the value of the multiplier?
4. There may also be questions over the government's correct understanding of future effects of the fiscal policies in any case. This especially applies to possible adverse effects—for example, an increase in taxation may reduce spending and check inflation but it may also discourage extra effort at work and act as a disincentive.
5. An increase in public expenditure is likely to have the effect of producing a rise in interest rates through an increase in government borrowing and a rise in aggregate demand. One result of this is that private investment is faced with a higher cost of borrowing and some private sector projects might not be carried out. This feature is usually known as *crowding out* and is described in Advanced Study Topic 15.1.

Topic 15.3   Monetary policy

As we have seen, monetary policy can be used as a support to fiscal policy and this tended to be its role until the 1970s when, under the influence of monetarist economists such as Milton Friedman, the governments in the Western world began to place monetary policy at the forefront of economic management. It was particularly associated with the presidency of Ronald Reagan in the USA, the chancellorship of Helmut Kohl in West Germany and the premiership of Margaret Thatcher in the UK.

Monetary policy is the use of a range of instruments designed to control the supply of money, including the availability of credit, and its price, i.e. interest rates. It is important to remember that when governments use monetary policy they do not entirely abandon fiscal policy but simply elevate monetary instruments to a more predominant position. In view of the problems attached to using fiscal policy for fine-tuning the economy, monetary policy instruments were often used for this purpose, but in the past fifteen years they have increasingly attained a major role.

The main monetary policy instruments are:

1. Changes in the banks' liquidity ratio can be used to control the growth of credit in the economy, an instrument known as *monetary base control*. There is reluctance to use this as a method in recent years as it conflicts with the idea of a free market which monetarism, now very much dominant in Western government thinking, holds very dear. The Swiss Central Bank, however, uses this approach as its main instrument.

2. The government can use *direct controls* in the form of directives on lending ceilings. Such direct controls can be immediately effective and enable the government to exercise tighter and more precise control. However, problems can arise if borrowers circumvent the system by finding sources of funds elsewhere where controls are absent—a process known as *disintermediation*. Again, this approach conflicts with a free market philosophy.

   Changes in methods of financing the PSBR can be used. The selling of gilts (bonds) or Treasury bills has the advantage of not increasing the money supply, although it may necessitate increasing interest rates and so result in the crowding out of the private sector. On the other hand, borrowing from the Bank of England would avoid this but would increase the money supply as the Bank would pay for bills by printing banknotes.

3. Fluctuations in interest rates are a third important instrument of monetary policy. It assumes that interest rates, as the price of loanable funds, influence the amount of borrowing required in the economy. The main problem with using interest rates is the time lag between the decision to change rates and the change becoming effective, especially if firms, individuals and institutions believe that such a change is short term only. It will also raise costs for industry, including public corporations which borrow on the open market.

   Interest rates in the market are closely tied to the use of the Bank of England as a lender of last resort. As long as the commercial banks need to borrow from the Bank, it can control interest rates in the system. The Bank's official rate used to be known simply as the bank rate until 1972, when it was changed to the minimum lending rate (MLR). This in turn was abolished in 1981 but the need for financial institutions to borrow from the Bank of England remained. If the banking system was sufficiently healthy not to need the central bank, a need could be created by the Bank selling securities. People pay for these by drawing on their bank deposits, e.g. by signing a cheque, and thus through use of the market mechanism funds move from the commercial banks to the Bank of England.

   The central banks in other countries follow similar procedures except that they do not have that unique British institution, the discount house. The main exception is the Bundesbank which, as we have seen, is outside state control and pursues long-term objectives set by the German constitution.

Manipulation of interest rates is a useful instrument for controlling money supply. In fact in recent years it has been the main form of short-term monetary control. High interest rates have been seen as a means of curbing demand and thus controlling inflation, which has been the main policy objective under monetarist influences. The operation of this can be seen by recalling our liquidity preference curve and interest rates. In Fig. 15.13 an equilibrium stock of money in the economy is indicated by MS_1. Now traditionally, it has been accepted monetary policy to use money stock control as an instrument with an agreed rate of interest as the objective. However, a change in recent years has seen a reverse of this position with interest rates changed quite frequently and the money supply following.

For example, in Fig. 15.3 we can reduce money supply from MS_1 to MS_2 and expect interest rates to rise, but we can also fix interest rates at R_2 and expect the money supply to reduce accordingly as more firms and individuals find the new rates too high to make borrowing worth while.

4. Exchange rate policy can be regarded as a separate area of control but it is more usually used as an instrument within the broad area of monetary policy. At least, this was the case as long as a country's currency was allowed to float. In the case of most EU countries, the exchange rate is tied within the bands of the ERM (see Chapter 10) and, as noted earlier, it becomes an objective of policy rather than an instrument. For those countries outside the ERM (including, at the time of writing, the UK) the exchange rate can be used as an instrument for influencing balance of payments and perhaps inflation. One of the reasons given by the then Chancellor, Norman Lamont, for the UK's withdrawal from the ERM was that the country needed freedom to use control of exchange rates to produce policy objectives and targets elsewhere rather than being an objective itself.

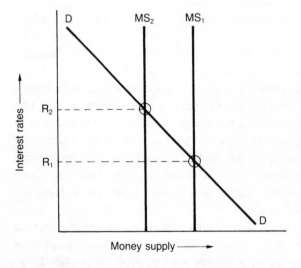

Figure 15.3 Money supply and interest rates.

5. Finally, we can look at the development in recent years of the medium-term financial strategy (MTFS). Used by the Conservative government of the UK in the 1980s, the MTFS became a tool for control of inflation by limiting money supply. Targets were set and expected to be adhered to with the intention of creating an atmosphere of financial stability. While there had been a tentative effort during the 1970s to set a money supply target (in 1976 using M3) it was only when the MTFS was created in 1980 that there was a permanent system in operation to create money supply stability.

It is perhaps a little ironic that a right-wing Conservative government should use a policy which, superficially at least, resembled the plans produced by the Kremlin to control the economy of the former USSR. In the end it was just as ineffective. The M3 target was rarely hit and by 1987 the government abandoned any set target for money supply.

One of the ideas behind the MTFS was, however, more than just to limit money supply to a set figure but also to create an atmosphere of stability and business confidence. It was to be a cornerstone around which interest rates and prices were to be stabilized. Expectations of people are important, and any policy changes which produce a feeling of suspicion or uncertainty may well influence the economy in inhibiting business investment, consumer borrowing and demand.

There are two problems with fixing a level for money supply. One is deciding which definition to adopt and the second is ensuring that the economy keeps on target. The wide monetary base (M0) has a lot of attraction but can be unrealistically narrow and M3 was the original favourite. Currently, M0 and M4 are widely used but they differ very much in the degree of change, with M0 being much more stable as shown in Table 15.1.

The second problem is in keeping to target. Interest rates have been a favourite instrument to work with MTFS, maintaining a short-term target by intervention from the Bank of England in the money markets. This explains some of the concern with interest rates during the chancellorship of Norman Lamont, who reduced them from the previous high level after considerable public pressure, especially from the business world.

The MTFS and other attempts to control money supply are good illustrations of Goodhart's law—that if in economics the symptoms are treated rather than the cause

Table 15.1 Monetary aggregates in the 1990s

	% change over previous year				
	1990	1991	1992	1993	1994 (forecast)
M0	2.6	2.9	2.8	5.9	5.5
M4	12.1	6.2	3.7	5.4	7.0

Source: Barclays Bank Review (2nd Quarter 1993 and 2nd Quarter 1994)

of the problem, then the symptoms fail to indicate accurately the nature of the economic illness. By targeting money supply, which, after all, is really simply a measure of the strength of aggregate demand in money terms, the government simply produces a faster circulation of the money stock. Demand is the result of other factors such as income levels and is not determined by the money supply.

Topic 15.4   Supply side policies

The term 'supply side economics' is often used as if identical to 'monetarism'. This is not strictly correct since, as we will see, Keynesian economists have supply side policies, but nevertheless there is a fundamental difference between the two approaches to the supply side. To examine this difference we need to recall the analysis of aggregate demand and supply (Chapter 9).

Figure 15.4 indicates the aggregate demand and supply situation from the Keynesian point of view. The initial supply is indicated by AS with its typical inverse L-shape. There is an initial aggregate demand curve AD_1. This produces an equilibrium level of national output in real terms at $N0_1$. However, if we make the assumption that the horizontal sector of the AS curve is below the full employment level, there will be a desire by the government to increase output.

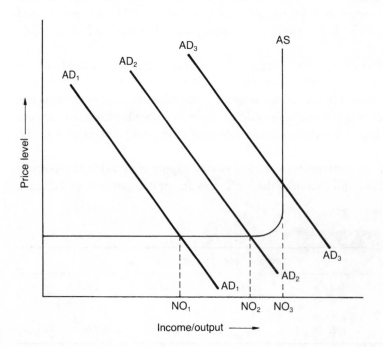

Figure 15.4   Aggregate demand and supply (Keynes).

If demand side policies such as tax reductions are applied then the AD curve will move to the right, with an increase in output and only a small increase in price levels. On the other hand, if the economy is at or near full employment level then a move of the demand curve to the right will produce price increases but little or no increase in output. At this point the Keynesian economist will wish to do something to increase the level of supply and so move the AS curve to the right. This would produce a new equilibrium level.

Another way of looking at the situation is to see the effect on the Phillips curve of an increase in output. If all other factors remain the same, then an increase in output without any corresponding inflation would move the Phillips curve to the left as in Fig. 15.5.

Keynesian thinkers will advocate supply side policies as a supplement to demand management and with the intention of shifting the inflation/unemployment trade-off of the Phillips curve to the left and the full employment output level to the right. Such policy instruments might include training schemes to improve labour productivity or tax concessions to encourage firms to produce more. For example, agricultural output has been maintained for many years by subsidies, even before the UK joined the EC and the Common Agricultural Policy.

Monetarists have, however, approached a supply side stance differently, in two distinct ways:

1. In the first place, monetarist economics views the AS and long-term Phillips curves as both being vertical at the full employment level in a more rigid way than Keynesian economists. It is contended that any attempt to increase output at full employment levels will result in price rises. As prices rise, firms wish to increase output since wages are falling in real terms but before long workers will want to negotiate wage increases which reflect these changes—in other words, the wage bill

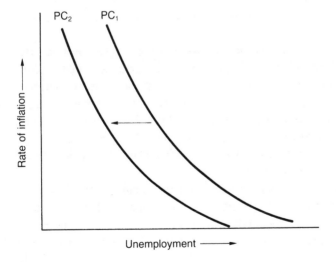

Figure 15.5   Shift of Phillips curve.

in real terms as a proportion of revenue will be back at its original level. The firm will reduce labour to cut costs and so output will be back where it was—but with prices and wages higher.

As a result, monetarist economics sees a rightward move of the AS curve as the only way forward, with firms wishing to produce more at the existing price levels. If demand is likely to increase then it will be essential to increase supply, preferably ahead of the demand, to avoid inflation.

2.   The second significant approach of the monetarist is to see supply side policies as essentially helping a free market economy. The government's application of supply side policies is seen as essentially being support for a market economy with a reduction to a minimum of state intervention. This market philosophy is essentially tied to the privatization and deregulation which has swept the UK since 1979 and is also rampant in most European countries. We have already seen that Spain and Italy have current privatization programmes and the former Communist countries are rapidly seeking to release productive units into a market structure.

The main instruments of supply side policies

What are supply side policies? In many cases economists of all persuasions agree that certain types of supply side policy are beneficial and worth pursuing. Other instruments have a less than unanimous following. The main supply side policies being followed in the 1990s are:

1.   *Improved quality of labour*   There is general agreement that the skill level in the labour force is a vital factor in increasing national output. Various training schemes have been in existence for some time funded by private industry, and in most European countries there is state funding of a basic educational system from schools to universities.

Under the Conservatives in the 1980s the most significant development was the Youth Training Scheme (YTS, now simply known as YT) and its twin for older people in the Employee Training Scheme (ET). YT has been much derided, especially by left-wing politicians, as being a scheme to supply cheap labour to firms and where training has been inadequate there is little doubt that it has been just that. However, in many other cases training has been excellent and young people have two years of guaranteed employment with a training place. For a time (until 1993) there was a similar scheme in France.

Other developments supporting skill acquisition have included the introduction of standardized qualifications   (National   Vocational   Qualifications— NVQs) taught in colleges of further education and sixth forms. These are replacing the BTEC (Business & Technological Council) qualifications which have provided a more practical alternative to 'A' levels. Further policies in the UK are aimed at increasing university-level provision although cut-backs in government funding for universities and student grants are threatening this development.

2. *Reduction in trade union power*   This has been a much more controversial development in the UK, the USA and a number of other Western countries. Many right-wing politicians see union power as fundamental in producing wage rates which are 'sticky' downwards and that strong unions make for a labour force which is unresponsive to economic conditions.

Along with wage restraints there have been laws passed to restrict trade union rights to take industrial action, removal of legal immunities for some union activities such as picketing and the necessity for a ballot of members prior to industrial action. It is this policy which was at the heart of the opposition by John Major to the Social Chapter of the Maastricht Treaty, with its safeguards for employees.

3. *Taxation measures*   Although we might associate tax changes with fiscal policy attempting to manage demand, they can also be used as incentives for increasing output. In the UK corporation tax takes a large slice of profits and employers' National Insurance acts in effect like a payroll tax. Tax incentives have been used in regional location policies for some years with local authorities sometimes rivalling each other to offer periods of occupancy free of business rates. Reductions of stamp duty requirements on house purchase in 1992 and 1993 were similar moves, in this case designed to encourage house building by increasing demand for housing.

One effect of income tax is, of course, to encourage or discourage the labour force. A reduction in income tax, especially of the higher bands, is seen as removing a substantial disincentive to work. Many professional employees hover dangerously around the base of the higher rate band for income tax, and additional earnings for overtime, or a bonus, or royalties from a book(!) can place the recipient in the higher band, and so net earnings from the extra effort are proportionately less.

4. *Privatization and deregulation*   These have been mentioned above as common in many Western countries. The idea behind privatizing state-owned industries and deregulating markets is to create freer markets and so raise productivity. In the UK, the financial markets were 'deregulated' in 1986 but the consequences have not been entirely a success. One of the early results was the stock market crash of autumn 1987, coinciding with some of the most destructive gales of the century. Freedom for banks and building societies has resulted in over-lending, in competition to sell investment products through high-pressure sales techniques and in a confusion in the sources of supply. In addition, while institutions were given freedom to deal in products, they have been subjected to a rather draconian regulatory system which has increased the costs of the products (see below).

There is still considerable debate over the effect of privatization in the UK. The intention was to remove state monopolies to create contestable markets, but in most cases the government simply created a privately owned monopoly with a 'watchdog' committee overlooking it—OFTEL for the telecommunications market (basically BT plus Mercury); OFGAS for the gas industry, etc. Whether productivity has increased in these industries is still open to debate. The idea is that private enterprise can provide a more efficient service with lower prices than a state-owned corporation.

One feature of these policies is the glorification of the small firm, The large multinational or home-grown monopoly is less in favour and in many countries of Europe and in the USA anti-monopolistic measures extend deeply into oligopoly situations to support the smaller firm (recall Chapter 6). A problem is that the small firm is very vulnerable to cash flow crises and the recession of the early 1990s saw many small firms in Europe go into liquidation as demand fell away, the banks withdrew financial support, and governments did little to help.

5. *Miscellaneous support instruments*   In addition, most countries of Europe provide a range of support for firms alongside that provided by the EU itself. For example, Ireland is very strong on instruments involving training but not as strong as tax policy. In contrast, Germany is stronger in terms of tax incentives but weak on training support.

Topic 15.5   Welfare economics

Many textbooks include a whole chapter with the title 'Welfare Economics' while others do not mention it at all. A popular topic at the universities, it has been absent from most 'A' level and Business Studies syllabuses but it nevertheless is becoming increasingly important. In fact, most of the issues which form part of welfare economics have already been mentioned in various parts of this book, which is why we do not have a chapter devoted to it. However, it is worth a brief summary discussion in which we can draw out the main themes of this area of economics, and relate it to official economic policy.

The distinctive characteristic of welfare economics is that it looks at the problem of resource distribution deliberately from a *normative* rather than a positive attitude (see Chapter 1). In other words, value judgements come into play as we seek to examine how the economic system functions in relation to some predetermined aims. Usually we are concerned with a 'battle' between the quest for efficiency and that for *equity* or fair dealing.

The concept of *Pareto efficiency* has been dealt with earlier in Chapter 3 and we saw the importance of this concept in attempting to assess how close an economy is to optimum resource use. The reader will recall that Pareto efficiency is reached when, in allocating resources, an economy can only increase benefits for one person or group if benefits are reduced for another person or group. Figure 15.6 gives the usual illustration of this, in this case assuming that in an economy there are two groups of people, landowners and workers.

We assume that the curve in Fig. 15.6 represents the frontier for efficiency for the level of technology and know-how available. If technology or skills improve then we could move from point A to point B with an increase in goods for both landowners and farmworkers. This is objective and can be recognized as a recordable and indisputable fact. However, if we move from point A to point C we are moving along the curve. We

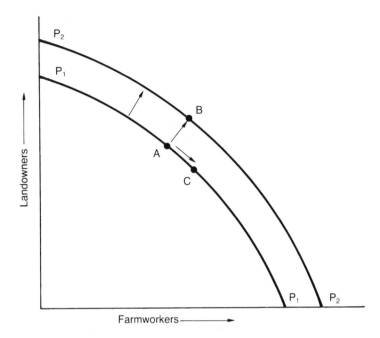

Figure 15.6 Pareto efficiency and technological changes.

are still producing at the efficiency frontier but have made the decision that farmworkers will receive more benefits from production at the expense of landowners.

> *Reminder: Pareto efficiency* for a given level of technology and resources exists at the point where we can only increase benefits for one person or group at the expense of another.

Now the point is that the decision to move benefits from landowners to farmworkers is not one which economists can recommend or suggest as economists—the decision is a *normative* one, involving value judgements. Welfare economics looks at normative judgements and their effects and tries to assess how well the economy is functioning in terms of norms and preconceived ideas on what type of society we should be living in.

Even when we are considering how to achieve Pareto efficiency, we find ourselves facing normative decisions on the route forward. The political parties present alternative agendas towards economic success. In Western Europe most major political parties would believe in the advantages of the market economy, but an important point of disagreement is the extent to which the state needs to intervene in an attempt to achieve the efficiency of the free market and Adam Smith's 'invisible hand'. To a large extent, the differences rest only partly on Keynesian, Marxist or monetarist views of how economic systems work but perhaps more on assumptions about *equity*.

The word 'equity' can be misleading and needs to be used with care. We have already come across its use as an alternative word for ordinary shares, and it can mean unallocated value in an asset being considered as security for a loan. In this context, however, it refers to how people are treated in society in relation to each other. For example, it might be argued that all people should be treated alike whereas others may say that some groups should be given privileged treatment because they are at a disadvantage and this disadvantage is seen as wrong.

The reader wishing to explore these issues further is recommended to consult Begg, Chapter 15. It would be useful here, however, to look at a few issues in welfare economics which are significant and prominent. These are the questions of redistribution of wealth; externalities; and imperfect competition.

Redistribution of wealth is an important issue in modern politics. If we look at the history of the world we find that societies have been divided into groups which sociologists refer to as *classes*. In extreme cases they form very rigid divisions known as *castes*. Frequently the owners of land and firms have formed a relatively wealthy group possessing wealth and earning relatively high incomes, in contrast to those who are employed by them, who earn a lot less and have little wealth. Since the end of the Middle Ages in Europe an increasingly large middle class has developed.

It is not an economist's task to study the structure of classes but the existence of wide differences of wealth is a matter that has concerned practitioners of the subject since the days of Adam Smith. In Chapter 2 we looked at some of the goods which can be regarded as 'wealth' by individuals or companies, but only in the case study did we deal with the question of the distribution of wealth. Both wealth (a stock) and income (a flow) vary in size over time, geographically and between individuals and groups. Variations include differences by sex, marital status, region, urban or rural areas, and class.

We have already come across inequality of wealth in Chapter 2 and especially in Advanced Study Topic 2.1, which looked at ways of measuring the degree of inequality. The question before us here is not, however, just to demonstrate inequality but to consider what action might be taken by a government to combat it. Some governments have not wished to do so because the ministers of state come from a privileged class or race within society. Most modern governments, though, recognize that inequality is not only unfair by most ethical considerations but it is also a drain on resources in that state benefits paid for by taxation and borrowing need to be paid out and increasing income and wealth to the less well off will tend to increase consumption more than allowing it to remain with the wealthy groups. Governments can deal with the problem in several ways:

1. They can raise taxes. Income tax is particularly useful as an instrument of income redistribution, especially if it is progressive with higher bands attracting higher rates.
2. Money benefits paid for from taxes or borrowing can be given to those with lower incomes. These range in the UK from income support and child benefit which are

non-contributory (i.e. not consequent on making certain payments) to unemployment and maternity pay which depend on having contributed to National Insurance.
3. Non-monetary benefits can also be important such as the provision of a health service, education and, in some cases, subsidized food or other benefits.

Policies on externalities

In Chapter 3 we looked at externalities as an example of market failure and saw how firms can, in their commercial activities, produce effects outside the market that can be positive or negative. So farmers keeping sheep on many highland moors help to keep the moors accessible to walkers but other farmers using nitrates on arable land can produce an excess of nitrates in the drinking water of a town lower down the valley.

Policies on externalities form a large part of a new area of study known as *environmental economics*. The issue which is addressed here is whether firms and governments can be environmentally 'friendly' without their action involving such large costs as to render the firm unprofitable or force the governments to raise taxes alarmingly. In many cases we are dealing with cost-benefit situations, whether it is a question of building a dam in West Africa, dealing with sewage in England or tackling the hole in the ozone layer which threatens us all.

Both national governments and the United Nations are concerned with environmental issues and the main means of dealing with them were discussed in Chapter 3.

Unfair competition

The details of possible approaches to lack of competition in markets, especially in the UK, are dealt with in the following section. There is no need to anticipate the details here, but it may be useful to consider the ethical issues involved.

The basis of government action against firms is the idea that the body-politic, whether Parliament, National Assembly or the EU Council of Ministers, can perceive what is good for society better than can individual firms. Yet in many ways this runs counter to the 'invisible hand' ethic of Adam Smith and the general move of Western governments towards the classical economics of the free market. If a market tends to produce monopoly, is it logical that government should intervene to prevent it? It may be that a monopoly or collusive oligopoly provides the most effective form of supply of some goods. On the other hand there can be serious loss of consumer surplus: see Advanced Study Topic 15.2

The same argument may be applied to many consumer protection laws. Again, in terms of classical theory, if firms overprice goods, demand will fall as customers look for substitutes. If firms put additives in food which people do not like then the customers will go elsewhere and if a market is contestable then some firm somewhere will produce the products required. Problems can occur where customers may need information to be available if accurate decisions are to be made and the lists of 'E' numbers on many packet foods are an attempt to do this. (See the following section on these issues.)

One area in which governments are often involved is in provision of services which are classed as merit goods—education and health, for example. If left to market forces provision is usually inadequate and obtained largely by those with higher incomes. Yet the existence of a large proportion of the population which is unwell and uneducated is not good for any country. Currently, there is a certain amount of international competition to provide a well-educated workforce but state financial input into schools, colleges and universities varies enormously.

Similarly, we can look at health provision where currently the UK government is tending to cut back on state input and push health authorities into becoming privatized trusts, while in the USA the emphasis is on greater state provision. As with education, health provision is not just a case of equity or ethics—a sick workforce does not make good economic sense any more than does a poorly educated one. National wealth must be increased by greater provision of medicines and health care but the issue is at what point in terms of income or wealth does the state provide as opposed to individuals. There is a healthy private market for health insurance but not everyone can obtain cover at an affordable premium. Therefore the state becomes involved in the interests of a fair distribution of medical resources—which is perhaps typical of the type of decision considered in welfare economics.

Topic 15.6   Regulating the market

One of the oldest forms of government involvement in economic affairs concerns the enacting of laws, rules and regulations. These can vary from laws prohibiting the debasing of currency or the forging of bank notes to complex rules on the levels of ingredients in packaged food or the procedures necessary in selling life assurance. All governments have enacted laws and rules with varying degrees of enthusiasm, but the last few decades have seen a proliferation of this activity in most countries and, above all, in the bureaucracy of the EU.

Regulation of business activity tends to take three forms.

1. The legislative body of a country can pass laws which regulate certain aspects of an industry. The European Commission performs the function of issuing similar rules which apply throughout the EU and, increasingly, it is the European Commission rules which take prominence.

    Examples of such rules and regulations include standards of hygiene and cleanliness in food preparation for restaurants and food-processing firms; rules emanating from the EU on the names that can legitimately be used for products and the shape and size of vegetables and other foods, and rules on additives which can be used in food. These are aimed at consumer protection as distinct from laws on, for example, exhaust emissions or spillage of waste, which are enacted to protect society as a whole. Mention has been made of these above.

One general measure of protection was the Trades Description Act (1968) which dealt with widespread abuses using the legal dictum 'let the buyer beware'. This principle had meant that it was up to the customer to establish that a product was adequate and as described by the retailer, but the Act made it an offence to describe any product wrongly or to use misleading pricing.

2. Regulation can take the form of the setting up of regulatory bodies, often as *quangos*, and these in turn make most of the rules. One such body is the Office of Fair Trading which is actually a government department. The OFT, for example, regulates consumer credit, issues licence for those who give or negotiate credit and controls the standards of advertisements.

   One of the best examples of such regulation by quango lies in the financial services industry. The phrase 'deregulation' when applied to banks, building societies and similar institutions should not be misunderstood. The legislation in the UK which deregulated these institutions simply removed restriction on *what* they could sell. A whole new regulatory edifice was set up controlling *how* they sold the now-increasingly bewildering range of products.

   The Financial Services Act 1986 set up a body known as the Securities & Investment Board (SIB) to regulate the whole industry concerned with selling 'investments' which includes unit trusts and other collective investments, life assurance, shares and futures. Any firm or individual selling investment products has to be authorized to do so and has to follow strict rules in advising the public. The SIB authorizes firms and individuals but has also encouraged the setting up of 'self-regulatory organizations' with the aim of getting the industry itself to undertake the policing.

   The regulatory framework has proved to be unfortunate. Some of the regulatory bodies have been so overwhelmed by the costs of the operation that they have been on the verge of bankruptcy, and many small brokers and agents have found the costs of authorization and compliance with the rules far too expensive and have gone out of business or merged. The EU is also legislating for the industry and the overall result is a considerable reduction in the number of small brokers and other outlets advising the public and a strengthening of the banks and larger building societies. This follows the pattern elsewhere in industry where the cost of regulations are more easily absorbed by larger companies while the small firm struggles to survive. Thus rules which set out to protect market conditions may end up in producing an oligopolistic market instead.

3. A third approach, which follows on naturally from the last statement, is the existence of rules to control monopoly and oligopoly power. These were mentioned in general terms in Chapter 7. The collection of such laws and rules is known as *competition policy*. The aim of competition policy in the UK has been officially declared by the OFT as 'to encourage and enhance the competitive process' (OFT, *An Outline of United Kingdom Competition Policy*, 1990).

   The focus of competition policy in the UK is the Monopolies and Mergers Commission (MMC) which, along with the Director-General of Fair Trading, keeps a watching brief on large companies with significant market shares. The OFT has the power to refer to the MMC any situation which it considers to be anti-competitive, with the Restrictive Practices Court and the Secretary of State for Trade & Industry as ultimate authorities. Typical situations where competition policy is involved are:

(a) The existence or creation of 'monopolies'—these are defined by the Fair Trading Act 1973 as a situation where one company provides, or is likely to provide, 25 per cent of the market for a commodity or service. In the EU context, the European Merger Control Regulation 1990 has a brief to control mergers which threaten the pan-European market in a commodity or service.

(b) Anti-competitive practices such as price fixing or restricting the supply of goods to certain retailers only can also be dealt with under both UK and EU legislation. Under UK law (the Competition Act 1980), smaller firms, defined as those with a turnover of less than £5 million, can gain exemption from control as long as their market share is less than 25 per cent.

(c) The creation of mergers is watched carefully. Again, the significant market share benchmark is 25 per cent but firms that are likely to be specially large after merger, i.e. with gross assets in excess of £30 million, are liable for investigation.

(d) Resale Price Maintenance (RPM) was a major case for controversy in the 1960s and early 1970s until dealt with by the Resale Prices Act 1976. Apart from pharmaceuticals and books, it is illegal for a manufacturer to insist on products being sold at a minimum price.

On the face of it, the activities of the government and the various agencies it has set up may be very beneficial. However, they can create more problems than they solve and a number of exceptions to the rules have had to be created. The case against monopoly (however defined by market share) is that it represents inefficiency as a result of the abnormal profits gained, especially if the market is not really contestable (see Chapter 6). However, in many cases the larger unit obtains economies of scale not obtained if the market is divided into smaller firms. For example, local electricity and gas supply benefits from a sole supplier who can instal plant of adequate size, unlike the small local gas suppliers of the nineteenth century, as well as economies from bulk purchase—perhaps with monopsony buyer advantages.

The intense regulation of financial services and farming, the latter especially by the EU, has produced high costs for small producers leading to financial advantages for larger players in the market. There is particularly a mushrooming of paperwork and red tape as anyone who has recently entered into a life assurance contract will be able to recognize. While consumer protection in many areas is important it has to be paid for, and the cost, in terms of higher prices and increasing delays in the purchasing procedure, can be high. Some of the customer information which legislation insists on is not really meaningful to the average person, for example, the use of annual percentage rates of interest (APR) for loans under the Consumer Credit Act (1974).

One of the major problems with competition policy and consumer protection legislation, whether in the UK or other countries or the EU is that it is increasingly being effectively introduced by bureaucratic processes (for example, the civil servants in Whitehall or the EU Commission) without the legislators or perhaps even ministers really understanding the technicalities or consequences. In the long term the ultimate question is whether the benefits are really there and if so, whether they are worth the inevitable increases in prices and perhaps inconvenience.

Topic 15.7   Policies on Third World aid

There is considerable difference from one economics syllabus to another at this level in attitude to economic aid or, as it is often called, *development economics*. For some readers of this book there may be a need to delve deeper into the issues below and if so they are recommended to read Begg, Chapter 35, for further information. For others this topic may be surplus to requirements, but any study of economics is inadequate if there are not at least a few pages on the issues raised.

First of all, some definitions. What is 'aid', who is to receive it and who is to deliver it? *Aid* is usually in three forms:

1. *Money*, usually in the form of a loan either at a low interest rate or nil interest. In many cases the finance is intended for a specific project such as a dam or drainage scheme but some financial aid is more general in nature. Sometimes 'strings' have been attached to these grants in that they are given on condition that the money is spent on purchases from firms in the donor country.
2. *Goods and equipment*, especially capital equipment. This is often also on a 'strings attached' basis. For example, a government may arrange for a recipient country to receive machines but on condition that they are surplus government stock or from a specific supplier. This has been common with aid from the former Communist countries in the days before *perestroika*.
3. *Technical assistance and expertise* is usually cheaper than the other two methods of aid and has the advantage of not involving possible long-term investment of money in unstable or uncertain regions of the world. Very often the assistance has been under the auspices of the United Nations or the World Bank.
4. Governments have increasingly encouraged private firms in their countries to invest in the Third World. Banks especially have been encouraged to grant loans although the experience of repayment has not been good. Firms have built factories in poorer countries using cheaper labour but, at the same time, providing jobs and industrial output. Union Carbide (USA) in India is an example.

The recipients of aid have so far been referred to as 'Third World countries'. This title has lost popularity lately, especially as the 'second' world (the Soviet bloc) has disappeared as a distinct political entity. The term 'underdeveloped countries' was favoured many years ago but when this was considered rather demeaning it was changed to 'developing countries'. The term 'less-developed countries' (LDCs) is currently gaining in popularity as it identifies the recipient countries but it is still rather patronizing.

The donors of aid are normally the developed countries of North America and Europe, the now much-reduced Communist bloc (mainly China) and the United Nations and its agencies In particular, here we will consider the European and UN contributions, but this does not deny the substantial assistance given by the USA and Canada and, in the past at least, by the former USSR.

What are the problems of the Third World?

Most LDCs can be identified as having low levels of per capita GDP (see Table 15.2) which distinguish them from the more developed countries. However, there is no clear distinction between the two groups and, as might be expected, there are many examples of countries which are not clearly in one camp or another. What is more, some countries have problems in one region but prosperity in another, as in the cases of India and Zimbabwe; others have problems for specific and, hopefully, temporary reasons such as immigration and a large defence budget for Israel, war and famine for Ethiopia or civil and ethnic fighting in the case of Lebanon.

However, we can identify certain problems which tend to be common to most LDCs:

1. *Population* problems, especially rapid growth. There are a few examples of under-population, especially in the world's deserts or mountains (Chad and Afghanistan), but the major problem is too many people. The introduction of modern medical facilities into these countries has reduced the death rate, especially the infant mortality rate, without a corresponding reduction in household ideas on family

Table 15.2   GDP per capita in Third World countries (1991) (in US$)

Country	GDP/capita	Country	GDP/capita
Egypt	620	China (PR)	310
Ghana	430	India	320
Tunisia	1 570	Malaysia	2 580
Zambia	370	Philippines	720
Brazil	2 650	Thailand	1 730
Ecuador	1 200	Poland	1 680
Comparisons:			
Hong Kong	14 230	Singapore	14 550
USA	21 790	Germany	22 360

Sources: *Barclays Bank Economic Review* (3rd Quarter 1993); World Bank, World Tables 1992, Johns Hopkins University Press.

size. The result is that even if GDP does increase, population is increasing faster and so producing a reducing GDP per capita.

2. *Limited resources* can be a problem. Many countries are founded on the basis of racial groups or old imperial divisions (for example, in West Africa), but not around natural resources. As a result, while some LDCs, such as India, have rich resources, others have very few. In some cases an economy is, in terms of statistics, successful, but is based on one major commodity. Many of the oil states such as Kuwait or Bahrain are in this category.

3. *Limited labour skills* is also a problem. Again, some LDCs have long-established universities or colleges, especially in the Moslem world, but the average citizen has very limited education or training. If this is combined with a high level of ill health, civil war or general reluctance to move from traditional attitudes then a country can be stuck in a pit from which it is difficult to rise. The successes of Taiwan, South Korea and Hong Kong have been largely on the basis of exceptionally hard-working and intelligent people who have made the best of limited resources.

4. *Capital limitations* are also important. Lack of finance for development is serious in many LDCs and can be self-perpetuating since low incomes allow little surplus for saving. If we add to the problem the debt to developed countries as a result of past loans we have a serious matter. In many cases multinational companies operating in LDCs have failed to use local labour other than for the most menial jobs and have transferred all profits outside the LDC. Developing a strong financial base for the economy is a major problem and these countries have often only a poorly developed banking and insurance sector. Again, significant exceptions are countries such as Taiwan and Hong Kong.

5. *Inadequate infrastructure* limits development and often one of the first things needed before a country can adequately develop is the building of modern roads, bridges, airports and rail links. Some of the more spectacular schemes have been the building of major routes or the damming of rivers.

6. *Low productivity* has dogged many countries. Agricultural methods may be very traditional and give low output per capita. In many cases the system is designed to keep a large family nominally 'employed' but, in practice, it provides very low incomes. Industrial output can suffer from inefficient equipment. It has been regrettable that in some cases developed countries have sold off their own outdated equipment to LDCs, and traditional societies without many trained industrial workers often cannot operate industrial plant efficiently.

Who is giving aid?

Aid is being provided by many countries and organizations but, as mentioned above, we will concentrate on European and UN sources. The EU attitude to development aid centres on two types of recipient:

1. *Associated countries* are those countries which formerly had special relationships with
    EU member states. The French were the only members of the original 'six' with
    large overseas territories that were colonies or former colonies, but when the UK
    joined the EU the Commonwealth countries were also involved. Such countries were
    covered by the 'Part Four Association' provisions in the Treaty of Rome allowing
    special trade relationships, and in 1964 the Yaounde Convention recognized the
    independence of most of these territories and formalized relations with the EU. In
    1975 the Lomé Convention replaced the previous accord.

    The nations covered by Lomé are known as the ACP countries (African,
    Caribbean and Pacific states) and they gain tariff preferences for their exports to
    the EU states. In addition, an aid package was drawn up which for the 1990–95
    period is scheduled at 12 000 million ECU. This includes moneys under the
    European Development Fund (EDF) and the STABEX scheme for stabilizing
    earnings from agricultural products exported to the EU which may suffer from
    wide fluctuations in price.

    One interesting insight into this policy of special treatment for associated coun-
    tries is the great banana dispute which came to a head in 1993 with an appeal to
    GATT.

2. The second approach to aid from Europe lies in assistance for countries which are
    not associates. As a result of complaints from such countries in the 1960s and
    discussions at the United Nations Conference on Trade and Development
    (UNCTAD) in 1968 it was agreed that there would be a more generalized prefer-
    ence to all LDCs, but while the agreement was to equalize tariffs there was still the
    option to impose quotas. Agreements on cooperation with various countries have
    been made and food aid is a common enough feature of the EU approach to world
    emergencies. In recent years this has included aid to Russia and emergency supplies
    to the war zones in the former Yugoslavia.

    European countries have also taken part in general aid programmes. Apart from
    the UNCTAD conferences there has been participation in the IBRD and the IMF
    (see Chapter 10 for details) and specific financial assistance by governments and by
    banks. In the UK, banks such as National Westminster and Midland have made
    loans to LDCs although not without problems, as debt repayment has produced
    financial problems not only for the debtors but also for the creditor banks. Another
    European initiative was the Brandt Report (1980) which took the theme of a world
    divided into a prosperous North and a poor South and made specific proposals to
    remedy the inequalities. The report has not really been implemented as a result of
    economic problems in the developed countries, but it successfully underlined a
    number of the problems.

Is aid working?

One of the major questions which must be asked is whether aid is working or not.
Success in producing growth and higher benefits for LDCs has been patchy. It has

not proved easy to 'kick-start' some economies and funds lent have too often been used to pay interest on older loans or to build prestige projects rather than essential infrastructure. In addition, civil war or persistent local military action has hindered development and has even produced widespread poverty. Ethiopia, the Sudan, Angola, Iraq, Afghanistan and Cambodia come to mind as just some of the countries which have been held back by civil or international wars.

One of the problems is in building up the skills of the labour force as well as constructing factories, roads and ports. It takes a long time to develop a large bank of workers who are capable of producing manufactured goods, and while some countries such as India have been involved in manufacturing for a century or more, others are still largely agricultural. Rural development projects have also, however, met problems. Often the methods used in cooler and damper countries of Europe or North America have proved unsuitable for tropical countries. Western experts have sometimes assumed that methods such as 'slash and burn' are inefficient and have tried to replace them with more settled farming, only to find that soil erosion or leaching have produced a lower output than before. Nevertheless, even if aid is not always used effectively a good deal of it has proved invaluable. Yet it is certainly still very inadequate to produce proper development in many LDCs (see Advanced Study Topic 15.3).

Advanced Study Topic 15.1   Crowding out

One of the features of economic expansion by fiscal policies is the side-effect known as *crowding out*. It arises when a government increases public spending, perhaps financed by borrowing. The result is an increase not only in aggregate demand but also in government demand for funds and, as a result, interest rates rise. Private sector investment is 'crowded out' of the market in the sense that many private firms can no longer afford to borrow funds for investment.

The mechanism for this is simple enough. The government spends on public works such as building a motorway. Through operation of the multiplier there is an increase in national income perhaps three or four times the original investment and, as a result, the demand for money for transaction purposes rises. This will shift the liquidity preference curve to the right and interest rates will increase. The same process will follow if taxes are reduced since more money will be available for spending by households and/or firms.

Although crowding out is often seen as a problem there are those who feel that increased government spending can have the reverse effect—that, in fact, the rise in incomes can produce an increased motivation to firms to invest in order to purchase additional plant.

Students wishing to investigate this feature and the arguments surrounding it are advised to consult Begg *et al.*, Chapter 25, Section 4, or Samuelson and Nordhaus, Chapter 34.

Advanced Study Topic 15.2   Welfare triangles

One of the arguments in favour of state intervention in the economy, especially as far as monopoly and oligopoly power is concerned, rests on some basic microeconomic analysis. The reader is advised to turn again to Fig. 6.4. Here we saw how the monopolist fixes an equilibrium level of output and the price which follows from that. The price (P_y on the vertical axis) is not at the point where MC = MR or even where MC = AC but where the AR or demand curve lies for that level of output. The result was seen as providing a surplus profit for the monopolist.

Now in a competitive market, price and quantity are found at the point where the demand and supply curve meet, which is the same as the point where the AR curve and MC curves meet. If we assume that AR is equal to the marginal social benefit of an operation and MC is the marginal social cost (i.e. takes all costs into consideration, not just private corporate ones), then the point where AR = MC represents the Pareto-efficient output and price levels. If the industry were perfectly competitive, then MC would equal AC and would be a horizontal line—a perfectly elastic supply curve.

If this is the case, then there is a loss of consumer surplus as a result of the existence of the monopoly. Consumer surplus is the whole of the triangular area between the price under perfect competition and the demand (AR) curve above it. The loss of this surplus, or *deadweight loss*, is a smaller triangle occupying the bottom-left corner of our consumer surplus area, but bounded to the left by the line linking the monopolist's equilibrium output (Q_e in Fig. 6.4).

For further reading see Begg *et al.*, Chapter 17, Units 1 and 2, and Chapter 15.

Advanced Study Topic 15.3   Less-developed countries

The previous section has introduced some of the problems associated with those countries known as 'Third World' or less-developed countries (LDCs). While this treatment will be adequate for many syllabuses and perhaps too much for some, there will be examinations which require a more detailed treatment not possible in a book of this size.

There are many issues in connection with LDCs, including the problems of population growth, difficulties in 'kick-starting' an economy, overdependence on a few raw material products and the problems of aid. The student wishing to pursue further studies in this area will be faced with an enormous range of materials on these and any other topics. Indeed, Development Studies is a separate discipline in many universities, combining economics with demography, sociology and anthropology, political science and other related areas. The literature is vast and can be confusing.

It is recommended that initially studies continue with Begg *et al.*, Chapter 35, and Samuelson and Nordhaus, Chapter 38. The latter is especially good on the demographic perspective and both deal with the processes involved in economic development.

Essay questions

1. (a) Explain, giving examples, the difference between a direct tax and an indirect tax.
    (b) Discuss the case for and against a policy of shifting the structure of taxation away from direct taxation and towards indirect taxation.
         (*Source*: The Associated Examining Board, November 1990)

2. Either
    (a) What are the implications for the British economy of the single European market?

    Or
    (b) What exactly is meant by 'European Economic and Monetary Union'? Is such a goal either attainable or desirable? (*Source*: Oxford and Cambridge Schools Examination Board, June 1992)

3. Explain what is meant by the 'single European market'. Discuss how the standard of living in Europe in general, and that of Britain in particular, is likely to be affected by the single European market. (*Source*: Northern Examinations and Assessment Board, June 1991)

4. Compare the effects of government purchases of aircraft which are (a) home produced and (b) imported on
     (i) The national income,
    (ii) The budget balance,
    (iii) The balance of trade. (*Source* University of Oxford, June 1991)

5. Why does the government wish to measure the following, and how is that measurement achieved?
    (a) Public sector borrowing requirement.
    (b) Retail prices.
    (c) Gross Domestic Product. (*Source*: University of Oxford, June 1992)

6. Briefly outline the determinants of the level of economic activity in an economy such as the UK. Is it possible for the government to do anything to avoid economic fluctuations or to reduce their effects? (*Source*: Northern Examinations and Assessment Board, June 1993)

Index

Numbers in bold indicate location of a definition